the essential

dessert

cookbook

the essential
dessert
cookbook

MURDOCH BOOKS

Published by Murdoch Books Pty Limited.

Murdoch Books Australia
Pier 8/9, 23 Hickson Road
Millers Point NSW 2000
Telephone: +61 (0) 2 8220 2000
Fax: +61 (0) 2 8220 2558

Murdoch Books UK Ltd
Erico House, 6th Floor North
93/99 Upper Richmond Road
Putney, London SW15 2TG
Telephone: +44 (0) 20 8785 5995
Fax: +44 (0) 20 8785 5985

Series Editor: Wendy Stephen
Managing Editor: Jane Price
Designer: Vivien Valk
Design Concept: Marylouise Brammer
Food Editor: Lulu Grimes
Food Director: Jody Vassallo
Editorial Assistant: Faith McKinnon
Photographer (special features): Chris Jones Photographer (cover): Ian Hofstetter
Stylist (special features): Mary Harris Stylist (cover): Katy Holder
Stylist's Assistants (special features): Kathy Knudsen, Michelle Lawton,
Kerrie Mullins, Kerrie Ray
Background painter (special features): Sandra Anderson from Painted Vision, Mudgee NSW
Additional text: Lulu Grimes, Tracy Rutherford, Jody Vassallo
Picture Librarian: Denise Martin

CEO: Juliet Rogers
Publisher: Kay Scarlett

ISBN 1 74045 411 1

PRINTED IN CHINA
Printed by 1010 Printing International Limited
First printed 1998. This edition published 2004. Reprinted 2004 (twice), 2005 (three times).

OUR STAR RATING: When we test recipes, we rate them for ease of preparation.
The following cookery ratings are used in this book:
✭ A single star indicates a recipe that is simple and generally quick to make—perfect for beginners.
✭✭ Two stars indicate the need for just a little more care, or perhaps a little more time.
✭✭✭ Three stars indicate special dishes that need more investment in time,
care and patience   ginners can make these
di   refully.

IMPORTANT: Those   of salmonella food poisoning
(the elderly, pregnant w   ing from immune deficiency
diseases) should   out eating raw eggs.

DESSERT

Sweet food is one of life's primeval joys. We all know that dessert isn't strictly necessary, life isn't going to end without it, but then who among us would choose to live on bread and water? Dessert gives us something to look forward to as a child while we plough through our worthy meat and vegetables. It brings a lovingly prepared meal to a close with a fanfare, not a whimper. While salty food sparks the appetite, sweet food soothes and caresses it, leaving us warm and contented. It is a luxury, an exquisite indulgence, something that gives us true pleasure but in a duller, greyer world is completely expendable. The names of older desserts reflect this... the unimportant trifle, the silly syllabub, the flummery and the fool. Yet these charming concoctions of sugar, cream, eggs and fruit live on through the ages to defy their names and prove their worth. Desserts are not mere trifles, they are truly essentially life-enhancing... as you are about to find out.

CONTENTS

SPECIAL FEATURES

JUST DESSERTS

It could be said that dessert is the mark of a truly civilized society. As our ancestors gathered round the fire at the end of a hard day's hunting, there is one thought we can be certain did not cross their minds: 'now, are we having cheesecake or pavlova for dessert?' Desserts are rarely eaten to satisfy hunger, but to provide a sweet finish, a closing fanfare to a meal. They are meant for pleasure, not sustenance.

Antonin Carême, the artistic French chef who served for princes, kings and emperors, including the future King George IV and Tsar Alexander I, is said to have remarked that there were five fine arts, one of which was architecture, and that the main branch of architecture was confectionery. Many of his creations were based on ideas he copied from architectural drawings.

Man has been eating luxurious sweet food for a long time. In Asia thousands of years ago, cane syrup was being used as a sweetener and in Europe, fruit and honey were used. Sugar is the backbone of desserts and its increasing availability as a more refined sugar and a less expensive product has given rise to the invention of a million recipes.

Sugar, like spices, reached the Western world via the Arab trade routes and, when it first appeared, was available only in tiny quantities and used medicinally. Known as white gold, it was prohibitively expensive. During the next few centuries, the rich used sugar, like spices, indiscriminately as a sign of wealth, sprinkled on everything they ate. It wasn't until the 15th century that the Italians went back to Arabic traditions of using sugar in a select few dishes.

The rich may have been enjoying sweet food for hundreds of years but, in the Western world, the idea of dessert as a separate course is relatively modern. Sweet dishes were originally served on the banqueting table with the savoury: a typical example of one 'course' might be veal, tongue, chicken, blancmange, vol-au-vent, a cake and a fish. Many desserts actually evolved from savoury dishes to sweet. For example, one of the oldest known desserts is blancmange, which started life as a dish of pounded chicken breasts and almonds. Pies often included both sweet (fruit) and savoury (meat) fillings together.

Jelly began as a savoury decorative dish at banquets—gelatine boiled from animal bones and moulded creatively would be the centrepiece of the table, displaying the chef's great talents and control of his raw ingredients. This gelatine then began to be sweetened. When the Victorians invented the copper jelly mould the idea took off with a vengeance, leading to a frenzy of moulded blancmanges, creams and cakes (often named simply 'shapes'). Powdered gelatine was created in the 1840s but did not really become popular until much later with the advent of ice boxes and home refrigeration.

The sweet pudding has only existed for the last couple of centuries—before that the pudding was a savoury mixture of grain and dried fruit stuffed into animal guts and boiled in the same broth as the meat and vegetables. (Fortunately for our squeamish modern palates, today's only reminder of this is the beef suet in a traditional Christmas plum pudding.) This manner of cooking, using nothing but an open hearth, was available to all, while cakes and other desserts requiring ovens were still only enjoyed by the rich. The invention of the pudding cloth in the 17th century coincided with an increased importation of dried fruit to England and a drop in the price of sugar, making it available to the

not-so-rich. Hence the sweet pudding was born.

A well-stocked table, with a multitude of dishes set out, had always been a graphic way of displaying wealth, but in the 16th century the banqueting tables began to be cleared for dessert. The word itself derives from the French 'desservie', the cleared or de-served table. Plates were removed and the table swept clear of crumbs. Sometimes the guests would retire to another room (or another building!) for dessert. In Victorian England the tradition arose of removing the tablecloth before serving dessert.

Although there are obviously many old and traditional desserts, the last couple of centuries has seen a plethora of newer recipes. The development of transportation, the invention of refrigeration, and the exploration of the world which transplanted hundreds of different types of fruit from one place to the next and introduced new ingredients such as chocolate, spices and sugar to the Western world has created a myriad of wonderful recipes.

Ice cream, now taken entirely for granted, was, as a commercially available product, the direct result of the invention of refrigeration techniques. Cold food was originally thought to be poisonous or dangerous to eat and was a novelty served at special occasions and eaten with some bravado. Food and drinks were usually taken tepid (hot drinks such as tea and coffee were equally frowned upon when they first arrived on the scene). Ice, until the first ice-making machines appeared in the 1860s, was a natural commodity that had to be gathered, transported and stored in insulated ice houses. The advent of ice boxes changed the face of what could be stored at home. It was also now possible to set jelly and freeze ice cream at home.

All over the world different cultures have their own versions of desserts and it is surprising how similar they can be. Rice puddings come in many forms, from hot creamy and oven baked

in the West to sticky black varieties in the East. Puddings made with bread and noodles are common in many cuisines and ice creams are fairly universal, from the gelati of Italy to the kulfi of India. Migrants from Europe who settled in America and Australia took with them the desserts from their own cultures as well as inventing new ones with ingredients now available. Many countries took on their own national desserts: Pavlova is as Australian as Ned Kelly, and ice cream became a national symbol in America—it was deemed an essential foodstuff and indispensable to the morale of the army. (Ironically, in 1942 ice cream was banned as part of the war effort in Britain where it was named as a 'luxury' item.) The British themselves are associated with steamed and baked puddings.

As well as the favouritism of nationality, desserts fall in and out of fashion: Jell-o made its all-encompassing appearance in the 40s and 50s, baked alaska and black forest gateaux wowed the 70s, tiramisu was the dessert of the 80s, and the 90s gave us sticky date pudding and the ubiquitous crème brûlée. Who knows what the new millennium holds...

BEFORE YOU START

BASICS

- Read the recipe through and take note of any soaking, standing and overnight refrigeration times, and necessary equipment.

- Cooking times will vary, so if your pudding is sloppy or your soufflé not puffed, and the specified time is up, leave it a little longer.

- Many recipes can be varied by substituting or adding your favourite flavours.

MEASUREMENTS

- Always follow one set of measurements—metric or imperial, or cups. We have included cup measurements for ingredients such as flour, sugar and liquids, and weights for everything else.

- For accuracy, cups and spoons should be levelled with the back of a knife if possible.

- For liquid measures, plastic and glass jugs with the calibrations visible both inside and outside are easiest to use.

- Balance scales can be used with most metric and imperial weights. The scale pans hold the weights on one side and the ingredients on the other and weights are measured by evenly balancing both sides.

- Electronic scales have a digital display and can be programmed for metric and imperial weights. They tend to be slightly less accurate for weights under 30 g (1 oz).

- Spring weights have a scale pan on top of a calibrated scale. Choose one with an adjustable tension screw as they will need to be adjusted to keep them true.

INGREDIENTS

- The sweetness of recipes can be varied where sugar is not an integral part of the recipe. Sugar in pies, jellies and fruit desserts is generally variable, whereas if it is part of a liquid:dry ratio in a pudding, it cannot be changed without altering the texture of the dish.

- Butter should be fresh and unsalted but if you only have salted butter, the flavour of the dish will only be slightly different. Keep butter well wrapped in the fridge and away from anything strong smelling. Grate butter into a bowl to soften it more quickly.

- Eggs are taken to be 60 g (2 oz) in weight. Eggs should be refrigerated and used as soon as possible after purchase.

- Eggs should be brought to room temperature before use in cooking.

- Very fresh egg whites and old egg whites do not beat as well as those a few days old. Fresh eggs are easier to separate as the white is stronger and more viscous and the yolk holds its shape better.

- When beating egg whites, the bowls and beaters must be completely clean and there must be no trace of yolk in the whites.

- Cream for whipping should have a minimum of 35% fat. Thick (double) cream is not thickened with gelatine.

- Whip cream slowly at first, then speed up. Start with cold cream and a chilled bowl in hot weather. Whipped cream should be white and form a stiff peak which droops slightly at the top. Cream is overwhipped if it starts to turn grainy and yellowish.

- Cream for piping from a piping bag should be slightly under-whipped as the heat from your hand and the continued working of the cream will cause it to thicken further.

- Flour may be dry or slightly damp according to the humidity in the air and will absorb more or less liquid accordingly.

- Doughs and pastries may need a little more flour on a sticky day, but avoid adding too much as it will make them tougher.

- Nuts keep best if frozen in airtight bags. Toasting nuts gives them a fresh flavour.

- Grind cold nuts in a food processor, with a tablespoon of sugar or flour from the recipe to help absorb any excess oil.

- Vanilla extract or essence should be pure as it gives a much better flavour.

- A humid day will not be kind to caramel or meringues, so choose something else.

- Lemon and lime juice should be freshly squeezed for the best flavour.

EQUIPMENT

- A few pieces of good equipment will go a long way towards successful results. Choose carefully to get something which really lasts.

- If you don't have exactly the right size tin, it may not matter. A 1 cm (½ inch) difference will not ruin a pie or tart— you may just have a little too much, or not quite enough filling and the pastry will be a bit thinner or thicker. Any more than 2 cm (1 inch) may change things too much, so use your judgement.

- Ovens do not all behave in the same way. Fan-forced ovens will cook more quickly and can be used to cook more than one thing at a time as they have a more even overall heat.

- Not all ovens are accurate so use an oven thermometer placed in the centre of the oven.

- Pastry which needs a quick exposure to heat to set it is best cooked near the oven element, whereas dishes cooked in a water bath should not be cooked too near the element.

- Bakeware should respond quickly and evenly to the oven temperature. Shiny metal bakeware will deflect heat and prevent scorching, whereas dark non-stick bakeware will absorb and hold heat and may need a lower cooking temperature. Baking trays should be very solid so they don't buckle.

- Good-quality pans work best. Stainless steel pans with a heavy base are best for even heat distribution. Non-reactive pans will not react with food acids and cause discolouration. Choose pans with comfortable handles, rounded edges and lids with a tight seal.

- Non-stick pans are good for custards but caramelizing sugar should be done in a stainless steel pan where you can see the colour changes. Do not use metal utensils with non-stick pans.

- Glass heatproof bowls are useful for whisking egg whites and melting chocolate. Stainless steel bowls also work well for these functions, as well as heating up and cooling down quickly when required. A large ceramic bowl is invaluable for mixing large quantities.

- Buy a good-quality food processor with a bowl large enough to cope with large quantities. A spice grinder attachment or separate spice grinder will take care of any small quantities.

- Blenders should have a good motor and blades which sit both up and down in the goblet, otherwise small amounts will simply go round and round.

- Beating to aerate and combine ingredients can be done with a balloon whisk or electric beaters. Run a spatula down the bowl occasionally. Don't use a food processor for beating as it will not aerate the ingredients.

- If your heat source does not turn down very low, use a heat diffuser. These are small mats which spread the heat over the base of saucepans to prevent them getting too hot.

- Freezer thermometers are used for accurate freezer temperature readings. Food that is stored at -18°C (0°F) will be free from bacterial and enzyme activity. A few degrees higher at -10°C (14°F), enzymes take effect. Ice cream should be frozen at -18°C (0°F).

- Deep-fat thermometers are essential for accurate oil measurements. Oil at the correct temperature will cook the food and seal in the flavours with a minimum of absorption.

- Sugar thermometers are essential for accurate sugar solution measurements. Sugar syrup also has a series of critical temperatures for soft and hard-ball stages until it begins to caramelize.

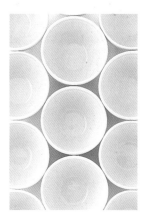

- Kitchen timers are essential for accurate timing and to prevent burning food.

- Baking paper or parchment should be non-stick to be most effective. Greaseproof paper is not non-stick but is useful for making piping bags.

IN THE KITCHEN

A few basic utensils will simplify the creation of superb, enticing desserts. The better quality ones will last longer.

RUBBER SPATULAS
These can scrape a bowl completely clean and are useful for getting residue out of food processors. Tiny versions are available for scraping jars clean. Hand wash to make them last longer. They tend to absorb colour and flavour, so keep separate ones for sweet and savoury use.

CANELLE KNIFE OR CITRUS ZESTER
Zesters have a row of holes with sharpened edges running across the top. When they are drawn firmly across a citrus fruit, they peel off the zest in long thin shreds. Many zesters have a canelle knife on one side which removes a larger v-shaped piece of zest. Both leave the bitter pith behind.

CUTTERS
Cutters come in various shapes and sizes. Graded sets of plain and fluted round cutters have a sharp cutting edge and a blunter, rolled-top edge for pressing down on. Metal cutters have a better edge. Fancy cutters should be kept carefully as they can easily get squashed.

SPOONS
Wooden spoons are useful for stirring, mixing and beating as they do not conduct heat or scratch non-stick surfaces. Some spoons have a flat edge and corner to help you get into the sides of saucepans. Choose spoons made of hard, close-grained wood for durability.

MEASURING CUPS AND SPOONS
All spoon and cup measures in this book are level, not heaped. Dry ingredients should be levelled off with a knife.

CREAM HORN MOULDS
Useful for shaping biscuits and moulding ice creams. Available in different sizes.

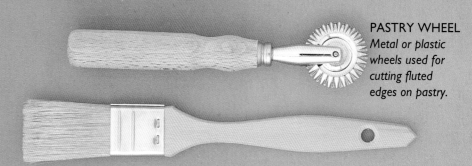

PASTRY WHEEL
Metal or plastic wheels used for cutting fluted edges on pastry.

PASTRY BRUSH
Made with nylon or natural bristles, these can be flat or round. Also used for glazing and oiling. Be careful when using nylon bristles with hot liquids as they may melt. Dry brushes thoroughly before storage. A separate brush should be used for oil.

FLOUR SIFTER/DREDGER
Useful for dusting work surfaces with flour, or for filling with icing sugar/cocoa and dusting for decoration.

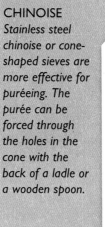

CHINOISE
Stainless steel chinoise or cone-shaped sieves are more effective for puréeing. The purée can be forced through the holes in the cone with the back of a ladle or a wooden spoon.

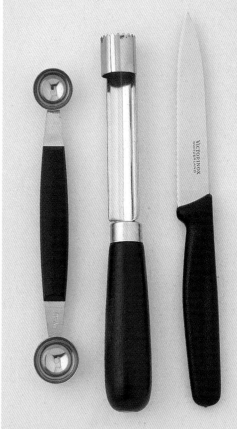

BAKING BEADS
Small reusable ceramic or metal beads used for blind baking pastry. Rice or dried beans can be substituted.

MELON BALLER, CORER, FRUIT KNIFE
Used for coring and cutting fruit. The sharp serrated edges of the corer cut the fruit without squashing. Melon ballers can be used for coring, as can the sharp tip of fruit knives.

WHISKS
Whisks beat air into ingredients and lumps out. Balloon whisks consist of loops of stainless steel joined by a handle. They range from large ones for egg white through to small ones for sauces and dressings. Flat whisks, which consist of a wire coiled around a loop, are useful for whisking in saucepans or containers without rounded bottoms and can also be used on flat plates.

PALETTE KNIFE

These have long flexible blades for spreading. Available in different sizes, smaller ones are useful for more fiddly jobs and larger ones for cake fillings etc. as they can slide across the whole surface in one smooth motion. They can also be used for turning food (flipping pancakes in frying pans etc.).

TART/FLAN TINS

These can be fluted or plain. Loose-bottomed ones enable you to remove the tart easily. Metal is better for pastry. Tart rings are used on a baking tray and give a straight edge. To prevent rust, dry well (in the warm oven) before storing.

SPOONS

Large metal spoons are best for folding in dry ingredients or combining one mixture with another without losing too much air.

LATTICE CUTTER

For topping pies and tarts, this will cut a lattice pattern into rolled out pastry with a minimum of fuss. Usually made from plastic so it will not mark work surfaces.

JELLY MOULDS

Moulds are used for shaping jellies and other set desserts. They are available in different shapes and sizes. Metal moulds are the most commonly available. These are good conductors of cold which helps set the jelly and are easier to heat when unmoulding. Moulds are also available in glass and ceramic. All moulds should be filled right to the top to give the full effect of the pattern. Some moulds can be used for baked desserts but may be difficult to unmould if the pattern is too detailed.

ROLLING PIN

This should be large enough to roll out a full sheet of pastry, ensuring a smooth surface. Good-quality rolling pins are made of hard wood with a close grain and very smooth finish. Wood is preferable to ceramic and marble as its surface collects and holds a fine layer of flour. Available in various shapes and sizes, different cultures use different thicknesses of pin. Those used for large sheets of pastry such as strudel can be as long and thin as curtain rods.

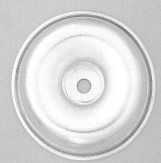

CERAMIC HEATPROOF MOULDS

Heart-shaped mould with draining holes for coeur à la crème, petit pots and a ramekin for baked and set desserts and soufflés.

METAL MOULDS

Dariole, baba and mini pudding basin, used for baked and steamed puddings or moulding set puddings and jellies.

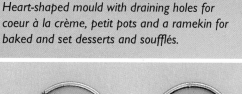

DECORATING EQUIPMENT

These nozzles, made from plastic or metal, vary in size from large for cream and pastry, to small for intricate decoration. You can buy special patterned nozzles for stars, shells etc.

LEMON SQUEEZER

Available in glass, ceramic, plastic and wood, the squeezers that have a container underneath to catch the juice are the most useful.

CUSTARDS AND OTHER CREAMY THINGS

The starting point for any comprehensive book of desserts has to be the custard. The basis for so many favourite desserts is this gentle and nourishing mixture of eggs and cream, sweetened with sugar. And from the custard it is but a magical flick of the whisk to soufflés and mousses, syllabubs and flummeries—creamy creations that tantalize on the spoon and literally melt in the mouth.

PERFECT CUSTARD Streaming

smoothly over a pudding, baked in the oven or chilled in ramekins, custard comes in

a myriad of different guises—all of them a perfect spoonful of creaminess.

Custard forms the basis of many desserts, either in its purest form as crème anglaise, with a wine base as zabaglione or sabayon, or thickened with flour and cornflour as crème patisserie. Pouring custard (home-made or even out of a packet) is a deliciously traditional accompaniment to pies, tarts and steamed puddings. Custard can create a base for ice creams, soufflés, baked puddings, and desserts set with gelatine, like bavarois.

As the name crème anglaise suggests, custard is of English origin.

There are two types of custard, pouring (made on the stovetop) and baked. The main ingredients of both are eggs, which are better if brought to room temperature first, and milk. To make a perfect smooth velvety custard, of whichever type, the golden rule is to keep the heat low. Never let custard overcook or you will end up with a pan

full of scrambled eggs. Custards made with whole eggs will set more quickly, as the egg white sets at a lower temperature.

POURING CUSTARD

To make a perfect pouring custard, separate 3 eggs, put the yolks in a bowl with 2 tablespoons caster sugar and beat with a balloon whisk until light and fluffy. When properly beaten, the mixture will fall in a ribbon which will

hold its shape for a few seconds. Pour 1½ cups (375 ml/12 fl oz) milk into a saucepan and bring to scalding point—small bubbles will appear around the edge. Stir if a skin appears to be forming. Pour into the egg mixture, stirring with the balloon whisk until well combined. If there is any milk protein on the base of the saucepan, rinse it out as this may cause the custard to catch on the bottom. Return the custard to the pan and stir over low heat.

If you have a double boiler, you can use it for custard making. Alternatively, use a metal bowl set over a pan of simmering water (don't let the bowl touch the water) for a more gentle heat. However, a pan over gentle heat is quite adequate. Keep the custard below simmering point as the egg yolks will thicken evenly if heated slowly. To prevent lumps forming, stir continuously.

There is even a technique for efficient stirring Make sure the wooden spoon passes through the middle of the pan and around the edge, where the custard is hottest and so will thicken quickest. Keep stirring to ensure the custard thickens evenly. (If the custard curdles a little, try removing it from the heat, adding a teaspoon of iced water and beating well. This will prevent further curdling but will not make a smooth custard.) The custard is ready when it forms a coating on the back of a spoon that you can draw a line through which will hold its shape. When ready, either pour it quickly through a sieve into a bowl or plunge the base of the saucepan into iced water to stop the cooking process. If chilling the custard, lay a piece of baking paper or plastic wrap directly over the surface to prevent a skin forming. If keeping the custard warm, put it in a bowl over a pan of hot water. For a

vanilla custard, add a split vanilla bean to the milk when you scald it and leave to infuse for 5–30 minutes, depending on the strength of flavour required. Remove the bean before adding the milk to the eggs. Alternatively, add 2 teaspoons of vanilla essence to the finished custard. If you add it earlier, it will evaporate.

BAKED CUSTARD
Baked custard should be cooked in a *bain-marie* or water bath to ensure a gentle heat, so the mixture does not curdle. The ramekins or moulds should be placed in a baking dish with enough water to come halfway up their sides. To prevent water bubbling around the edges, you can sit the moulds on a tea towel inside the dish. The custard is cooked when the centre is set but still wobbles when the mould is shaken. The custard will stiffen as it cools. The texture should be smooth and creamy.

VANILLA BAVAROIS

Whisk the egg yolks and sugar together until thick and pale.

When the bavarois has set, use your index finger to gently pull it away from the edge of the mould.

ABOVE: Vanilla bavarois

VANILLA BAVAROIS

Preparation time: 40 minutes + standing + chilling
Total cooking time: 10–15 minutes
Serves 4

★ ★

2³/4 cups (685 ml/22 fl oz) milk

1 vanilla bean

1 cinnamon stick

6 egg yolks

²/3 cup (160 g/5¹/2 oz) caster sugar

3 teaspoons gelatine

³/4 cup (185 ml/6 fl oz) cream

1 Gently heat the milk, vanilla bean and cinnamon stick in a pan until almost boiling. Remove from the heat and set aside to infuse for 5 minutes. Remove the cinnamon stick and vanilla bean.

2 Whisk together the egg yolks and sugar until thick and pale. Gradually whisk in the milk. Pour into a large clean pan and stir continuously over low heat until the mixture thickens. Do not boil. Remove from the heat. Cover the surface with plastic wrap to prevent a skin forming.

3 Place 2 tablespoons water in a small heatproof bowl, sprinkle the gelatine in an even layer over the surface and leave to go spongy. Bring a large pan filled with about 4 cm (1¹/2 inches) water to the boil, remove from the heat, carefully lower the gelatine bowl into the water (it should come halfway up the side of the bowl) and stir until dissolved. Whisk into the custard. Cover as before and leave to cool.

4 Beat the cream until soft peaks form and fold into the cold custard. Spoon into four 250 ml (8 fl oz) ramekins or moulds, tap the bases gently on a worktop to remove air bubbles, then refrigerate overnight.

5 To unmould, tilt each ramekin slightly on its side. Use your finger to gently pull the bavarois away from the edge, allowing air to enter and break the suction. Turn the bavarois out onto a plate. If it does not come out straight away, wipe a cloth dipped in hot water over the outside of the mould. If you wish, you can garnish with pieces of fresh fruit.

CREME BRULEE

Preparation time: 30 minutes + standing + chilling
Total cooking time: 30 minutes
Serves 6

★★

3 cups (750 ml/24 fl oz) cream
2 vanilla beans
8 egg yolks
¹/₂ cup (125 g/4 oz) sugar
3 teaspoons sugar

1 Gently heat the cream and vanilla beans in a large, heavy-based pan until almost boiling. Remove from the heat and set aside to infuse for 30 minutes. Remove the vanilla beans.
2 Beat or whisk the egg yolks and sugar in a large bowl until thick and pale. Add the cream, then pour into a clean pan over low heat and stir until the mixture thickens slightly and coats the back of a wooden spoon. Do not boil or you will curdle the mixture. Remove from the heat and divide among six 170 ml (5½ fl oz)

ramekins. Cover with plastic wrap and refrigerate for at least 3 hours, or overnight.
3 Just before serving, preheat the grill to very hot. Sprinkle a layer of sugar about 3 mm (⅛ inch) thick over the surface of the brûlées. To do this, put the ramekins on a sheet of baking paper and sift the sugar over—you can pour the dry sugar off the baking paper back into your container.
4 Place the ramekins in a large baking dish and pack ice around the sides to prevent the custards being heated. Place under the grill until the sugar caramelizes into an even sheet. Keep watching or you may burn the caramel. The sugar needs to caramelize quickly so that the custard doesn't have time to melt. If your grill does not get particularly hot (restaurants use special hot grills called salamanders) you might want to invest in a mini blowtorch which also does the job well. Play the flame evenly over the surface. Do not put too much sugar on or the crust will be too thick to break with a spoon.
5 Chill the crème brûlées until you serve them but not for longer than an hour or the crust will soften. This dessert can be garnished with fresh fruit such as blueberries.

CREME BRULEE
Crème brûlée is taken from the original English dish 'burnt cream', said to have been invented at Trinity College, Cambridge. It is traditionally made in a large shallow dish, thus giving as much surface area for the toffee as possible. You can use any type of sugar for a brûlée topping, but the results will be different. Granulated sugar melts well and brown sugar gives a stronger caramel flavour.

ABOVE: Crème brûlée

and chill for 2 hours, or until set. Unmould by wiping a cloth dipped in hot water over the mould and upending it onto a plate.

3 To make the ruby sauce, stir the sugar with 1 cup (250 ml/8 fl oz) water in a pan over medium heat until the sugar has completely dissolved (do not allow to boil). Add the cinnamon stick and simmer for 5 minutes. Add the raspberries and wine and boil rapidly for 5 minutes. Remove the cinnamon stick and push the sauce through a sieve; discard the seeds. Cool, then chill before serving with the panna cotta. Can be garnished with fruit.

NOTE: Translated from the Italian 'cooked cream', panna cotta takes its name from the cream being cooked over heat before being set with gelatine as a thick creamy custard. If you wish, you can split the vanilla bean and add the seeds to the custard.

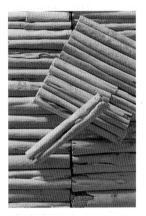

PANNA COTTA WITH RUBY SAUCE

Preparation time: 20 minutes + chilling
Total cooking time: 20 minutes
Serves 6

☆ ☆

3 cups (750 ml/24 fl oz) cream
3 teaspoons gelatine
1 vanilla bean
1/3 cup (90 g/3 oz) caster sugar

Ruby sauce

1 cup (250 g/8 oz) caster sugar
1 cinnamon stick
125 g (4 oz) fresh or frozen raspberries
1/2 cup (125 ml/4 fl oz) good-quality red wine

1 Lightly grease the inside of six 150 ml (5 fl oz) ramekins or moulds with flavourless oil. Place 3 tablespoons of the cream in a small bowl, sprinkle the gelatine in an even layer over the surface and leave to go spongy.

2 Put the remaining cream in a pan with the vanilla bean and sugar and heat gently while stirring, until almost boiling. Remove from the heat and whisk the gelatine into the cream mixture until dissolved. Pour into the moulds

ABOVE: Panna cotta with ruby sauce

BAKED CUSTARD

Preparation time: 5 minutes
Total cooking time: 35 minutes
Serves 4

☆

3 eggs
1/2 cup (95 g/3 oz) soft brown sugar
1 1/2 cups (375 ml/12 fl oz) milk
1/2 cup (125 ml/4 fl oz) cream
1 teaspoon vanilla essence
ground nutmeg, to dust

1 Preheat the oven to moderate 180°C (350°F/ Gas 4). Brush a 1 litre ovenproof dish with melted butter.

2 Whisk the eggs, sugar, milk, cream and vanilla essence in a bowl for 1 minute. Pour into the dish and place the dish in a shallow baking dish. Pour enough boiling water into the baking dish to come halfway up the side of the ovenproof dish. Place on the oven shelf, sprinkle the top of the custard with nutmeg and bake for 15 minutes.

3 Reduce the heat to warm 160°C (315°F/ Gas 2–3) and bake for another 20 minutes, or until the custard is set. It should no longer be liquid but should wobble slightly when the dish is shaken lightly. Remove the dish from the water bath immediately. Serve warm or cold.

VANILLA BEAN CREAM POTS WITH TAMARILLOS

Preparation time: 1 hour + standing + chilling
Total cooking time: 1 hour
Serves 6

✷ ✷

700 ml (23 fl oz) cream
1 vanilla bean
2 eggs
2 egg yolks
2 tablespoons caster sugar

Poached tamarillos

6 tamarillos with stalks
1 1/2 cups (375 g/12 oz) caster sugar
5 cm (2 inch) piece of orange rind
2–3 tablespoons Kirsch or cherry liqueur, optional

1 Put six 125 ml (4 fl oz) ramekins in a large baking dish. Put the cream and vanilla bean in a pan, bring slowly to the boil then reduce the heat and simmer for 5 minutes. Remove from the heat, split the bean, scrape out the seeds and return the bean and seeds to the cream. Cover and set aside for 30 minutes. Strain.

2 Preheat the oven to warm 160°C (315°F/ Gas 2–3). Whisk the eggs, yolks and sugar in a jug. Whisk in the cream, pour into the ramekins and cover each securely with foil. Pour hot water into the baking dish to come halfway up the ramekins. Bake for 30 minutes, or until just set. Refrigerate, covered, for 4 hours, or overnight.

3 Plunge the tamarillos into boiling water for 10 seconds, then put in iced water and peel away the skins, leaving the stalks attached. Put the sugar in a pan with 3 cups (750 ml/24 fl oz) water and the orange rind. Stir to dissolve the sugar. Bring to the boil and boil for 3 minutes. Reduce the heat to a simmer and add the tamarillos. Poach for 6–8 minutes, depending on their ripeness. Turn off the heat, add the liqueur and leave the fruit in the syrup to cool. When ready to serve, remove the fruit from the pan, then bring the syrup to the boil and boil for 5–10 minutes, until reduced and thickened. Pour into a jug, cover and cool. Cut each tamarillo in half, leaving the stalk end intact, and serve with the sauce and vanilla bean cream.

NOTE: You can use 1 teaspoon of vanilla essence instead of the bean if you wish. Add it to the finished custard.

EGGS

Eggs are not only nutritious, but they are also extremely versatile when it comes to cooking. Egg yolks enrich and thicken custards and creamy desserts and beaten egg whites are the foundation of meringues, soufflés and mousses. Eggs are used in cheesecakes, pastries and steamed puddings and make wonderful shiny glazes for puff pastry. Fresh eggs have a bright whole yolk surrounded by a thick viscous white. As they become stale, the white breaks down and becomes runny. Stale egg whites do not beat to a foam as successfully, though neither will eggs only one or two days old. To test an egg for freshness, place it in a glass of water. A fresh egg will stay horizontal at the bottom of the glass because it has very little air in the air cell at the round end of the egg. As eggs age, the air cell becomes larger and the eggs will float.

LEFT: Vanilla bean cream pots with tamarillos

CHOCOLATE

Chocolate was originally taken as a drink or used in recipes. It was sold as a paste or in solid bars and was very expensive. Milk was added to chocolate in England, but it was the Swiss who made the first commercial milk chocolate. Cocoa beans were known to Europeans from the time of Colombus, but it wasn't until 1519 when Hernando Cortes tasted chocolate drink, given to him by the Aztecs, that the Europeans knew how to use them. Chocolate drink was thought to be energy-giving and was used as a restorative. It was also taken up with enthusiasm by temperance societies in the 19th century, as an alternative to alcohol.

ABOVE: Petits pots au chocolat

PETITS POTS AU CHOCOLAT

Preparation time: 20 minutes + chilling
Total cooking time: 1 hour
Serves 8

★★

^{2}/3 cup (170 ml/5^1/2 fl oz) thick (double) cream
^{1}/2 vanilla bean, split lengthways
150 g (5 oz) good-quality dark bittersweet
   chocolate, chopped
^{1}/3 cup (80 ml/2^3/4 fl oz) milk
2 egg yolks
^{1}/4 cup (60 g/2 oz) caster sugar
whipped cream and cocoa powder, for serving

1 Lightly brush eight 80 ml (2^3/4 fl oz) moulds or ramekins with melted butter and put them in a deep baking dish. Preheat the oven to very slow 140°C (275°F/Gas 1). Heat the cream in a small pan with the vanilla bean until the cream is warm, then leave to infuse.

2 Combine the chocolate and milk in a small pan. Stir constantly over low heat until the chocolate has just melted.

3 Place the egg yolks in a small bowl, and slowly whisk in the sugar. Continue whisking until the sugar has dissolved and the mixture is light and creamy. Scrape the seeds out of the vanilla bean into the cream, and discard the empty bean. Add the vanilla cream and the melted chocolate mixture to the beaten egg yolks, and mix until well combined.

4 Pour the mixture into the ramekins, filling approximately two-thirds of the way. Fill the baking dish with enough boiling water to come halfway up the pots. Bake for 45 minutes, or until the chocolate pots have puffed up slightly and feel spongy. Remove from the baking dish and cool completely. Cover with plastic wrap and refrigerate for 6 hours before serving. Serve with a dollop of cream and a sprinkle of sifted cocoa powder.

NOTE: The pots will have a slight crust on the top when they first come out of the oven.

CHOCOLATE BAVAROIS

Preparation time: 30 minutes + chilling
Total cooking time: 5 minutes
Serves 6

★ ★

200 g (6¹/₂ oz) good-quality dark
   chocolate, chopped
1¹/₂ cups (375 ml/12 fl oz) milk
4 egg yolks
¹/₃ cup (90 g/3 oz) caster sugar
1 tablespoon gelatine
1¹/₄ cups (315 ml/10 fl oz) cream

1 Combine the chocolate and milk in a small pan. Stir over low heat until the chocolate has melted and the milk just comes to the boil. Remove from the heat.
2 Beat the egg yolks and sugar until combined. Gradually add the hot chocolate milk, whisking until combined. Return to a clean pan and cook over low heat until the mixture thickens enough to coat the back of a wooden spoon. Do not allow to boil. Remove from the heat.
3 Put 2 tablespoons water in a small heatproof bowl, sprinkle the gelatine in an even layer over the surface and leave to go spongy. Stir into the hot chocolate mixture until dissolved.
4 Refrigerate until the mixture is cold but not set, stirring occasionally. Beat the cream until soft peaks form, then fold into the chocolate mixture in two batches. Pour into six 250 ml (8 fl oz) glasses and refrigerate for several hours or overnight, or until set.

BLANCMANGE

Preparation time: 40 minutes + chilling
Total cooking time: 10 minutes
Serves 6

★ ★

100 g (3¹/₂ oz) blanched almonds
1 cup (250 ml/8 fl oz) milk
¹/₂ cup (125 g/4 oz) caster sugar
3 teaspoons gelatine
1¹/₄ cups (315 ml/10 fl oz) cream

1 Grease six 125 ml (4 fl oz) fluted moulds or ramekins. Process the almonds and 3 tablespoons water in a small food processor until finely chopped and paste-like. With the motor running, gradually add the milk. Pour into a small

pan, add the sugar and stir over low heat until the sugar has completely dissolved. Allow to cool.
2 Strain the milk through a strainer lined with muslin. Twist the muslin tightly to extract as much milk as possible—you should have 1¹/₄ cups (315 ml/10 fl oz) of almond milk.
3 Place 3 tablespoons cold water in a small heatproof bowl, sprinkle the gelatine in an even layer over the surface and leave to go spongy. Do not stir. Bring a small pan filled with about 4 cm (1¹/₂ inches) water to the boil, remove from the heat and place the bowl into the pan. The water should come halfway up the side of the bowl. Stir the gelatine until clear and dissolved, then stir it through the almond milk. Allow to cool completely.
4 Whip the cream into firm peaks, then fold the almond mixture through. Pour into the moulds and refrigerate for 6–8 hours, or until set. To unmould, loosen the edge with your fingertip and turn out onto a plate. If the blancmange do not unmould easily, wipe the outside of the moulds with a cloth dipped in hot water.

BLANCMANGE
Blancmange is a moulded jellied pudding, originally set using finely ground bitter and sweet almonds, but now made with gelatine or cornflour. It started life as a French savoury dish called *blanc manger,* made with chicken and almonds.

ABOVE: Chocolate bavarois

CREME CARAMEL

Pour a little of the hot caramel mixture into each ramekin, covering the base.

BELOW: Crème caramel

CRÈME CARAMEL

Preparation time: 25 minutes + chilling
Total cooking time: 35 minutes
Serves 8

✷ ✷

3/4 cup (185 g/6 oz) sugar

Custard

3 cups (750 ml/24 fl oz) milk

1/3 cup (90 g/3 oz) caster sugar

4 eggs

1 teaspoon vanilla essence

1 Preheat the oven to warm 160°C (315°F/ Gas 2–3). Brush eight 125 ml (4 fl oz) ramekins or moulds with melted butter.
2 Place the sugar and 1/4 cup (60 ml/2 fl oz) water in a pan. Stir over low heat until the sugar dissolves. Bring to the boil, reduce the heat and simmer until the mixture turns golden and starts to caramelize. Remove from the heat immediately and pour enough hot caramel into each ramekin to cover the base. The caramel will continue cooking in the pan so work quickly and be careful not to burn yourself.
3 To make the custard, heat the milk in a pan over low heat until almost boiling. Remove from the heat. Whisk together the sugar, eggs and vanilla essence for 2 minutes, then stir in the warm milk. Strain the mixture into a jug and pour into the ramekins.
4 Place the ramekins in a baking dish and pour in enough boiling water to come halfway up the sides of the ramekins. Bake for 30 minutes, or until the custard is set. The custards should be no longer liquid and should wobble slightly when the dish is shaken lightly. Allow to cool, then refrigerate for at least 2 hours, or until set. To unmould, run a knife carefully around the edge of each custard and gently upturn onto serving plates. Shake gently to assist removal, if necessary. Crème caramel can be served by itself or with fresh berries, whipped cream and wafers.
NOTE: This recipe can be varied by flavouring the custard with spices such as cardamom, cinnamon and nutmeg, lemon or orange rind, or with a little of your favourite spirit or liqueur. Crème caramel appears in France as *crème renversée*, in Italy as *crema caramella* and in Spain, South America and Mexico as a flan.

BANANA CUSTARD

Preparation time: 15 minutes
Total cooking time: 5 minutes
Serves 4

✷

1 egg, lightly beaten

2 tablespoons custard powder

2 tablespoons sugar

1 cup (250 ml/8 fl oz) milk

1/2 cup (125 ml/4 fl oz) thick (double) cream

2 bananas, sliced diagonally

1 Combine the beaten egg, custard powder, sugar, milk and cream in a heatproof bowl and whisk until smooth.
2 Pour into a pan and stir constantly over low heat for 5 minutes, or until the custard thickens slightly and coats the back of a wooden spoon.
3 Remove the bowl from the heat and gently stir in the banana. Serve hot or cold.

SPICY COCONUT CUSTARD

Preparation time: 20 minutes
Total cooking time: 1 hour
Serves 8

☆

2 cinnamon sticks
1 teaspoon ground nutmeg
2 teaspoons whole cloves
1 1/4 cups (315 ml/10 fl oz) cream
90 g (3 oz) palm sugar, chopped, or
    soft brown sugar
280 ml (9 fl oz) coconut milk
3 eggs, lightly beaten
2 egg yolks, lightly beaten

1 Preheat the oven to warm 160°C (315°F/ Gas 2–3). Combine the spices, cream and 1 cup (250 ml/8 fl oz) water in a pan, bring to simmering point, reduce the heat to very low and leave for 5 minutes to allow the spices to flavour the liquid. Add the sugar and coconut milk, return to low heat and stir until the sugar has dissolved.
2 Whisk the eggs and egg yolks in a bowl until combined. Stir in the spiced mixture, strain into a jug, then discard the whole spices. Pour into eight 125 ml (4 fl oz) ramekins. Place in a baking dish and pour in hot water to come halfway up the sides of the ramekins. Bake for 40–45 minutes, until set. The custards should be no longer liquid and should wobble slightly when the dish is shaken lightly. Remove the custards from the baking dish. Serve hot or chilled. Can be served with whipped cream and toasted coconut shreds.

RICE CUSTARD

Preheat the oven to slow 150°C (300°F/ Gas 2). Lightly grease a 1 litre ovenproof dish, then add 1 cup (185 g/6 oz) cooked rice and 3 tablespoons sultanas and put the dish inside a baking dish half filled with water. Combine 3 lightly beaten eggs, 2 1/2 cups (600 ml/20 fl oz) milk, 1 teaspoon vanilla essence and 3 tablespoons caster sugar. When thoroughly mixed, pour it over the rice and sultanas. Bake for 30 minutes, stir gently with a fork and cook for another 30 minutes. Stir again and, if you like, sprinkle the surface with freshly ground nutmeg. Bake for another 20 minutes, or until the custard is just set. Serve warm or cold.

COCONUT

Indigenous to India, coastal Southeast Asia and the Caribbean, the coconut is a versatile fruit. It has a fibrous husk, a hard brown shell and soft white flesh which changes from a jelly-like consistency when young to a harder and oilier texture when mature. The coconut milk contained within the nut is not the one used in cooking—this is derived from pressing the flesh of the coconut to extract first the cream and then the milk. Coconut milk is sold in cans, as a powder and in solid blocks. In its desiccated form, it appears on lamingtons and in coconut ice. It marries especially well with lime.

ABOVE: Spicy coconut custard

27

ORANGE SPANISH CREAM

Preparation time: 20 minutes + chilling
Total cooking time: 10 minutes
Serves 6

★ ★

3 eggs, separated
2/3 cup (160 g/5 1/2 oz) caster sugar
2 teaspoons finely grated orange rind
1/2 cup (125 ml/4 fl oz) fresh orange juice
1 1/2 tablespoons gelatine
3 cups (750 ml/24 fl oz) milk

1 Beat the egg yolks, sugar and orange rind in a small bowl with electric beaters or a balloon whisk for about 5 minutes, or until thick and creamy.
2 Pour the orange juice into a small heatproof bowl, sprinkle the gelatine in an even layer over the surface and leave to go spongy. Do not stir. Bring a large pan filled with about 4 cm (1 1/2 inches) water to the boil, remove from the heat, carefully lower the gelatine bowl into the water (it should come halfway up the side of the bowl), then stir the gelatine until it has dissolved.
3 Combine the gelatine mixture with the milk in a saucepan and bring almost to the boil—do not boil or the gelatine will lose its setting properties. Remove from the heat and gradually pour onto the egg yolk mixture, mixing continually as you pour.
4 Beat the egg whites in a metal or glass bowl until stiff peaks form, then gently fold them into the milk mixture with a large metal spoon. Pour carefully into a 1.5 litre glass serving dish or six 250 ml (8 fl oz) dishes and cover with plastic wrap. Refrigerate for several hours, or overnight, until set.
NOTE: Spanish cream is also known as Honeycomb mould, Snow cream and New England quaking custard. This recipe appears in old English and American recipe books including Shaker recipes. It is a custard which separates into two or three layers—a bubbly layer on top and smooth layers underneath, created by folding the egg whites into a warm mixture rather than a cold one. If the custard mixture is cold when the egg whites are folded in, they will stay suspended by the gelatine and not separate out.

MONT BLANC

Preparation time: 10 minutes
Total cooking time: 25 minutes
Serves 4

★

1 cup (250 ml/8 fl oz) cream
1 teaspoon vanilla essence
1/3 cup (90 g/3 oz) caster sugar
435 g (14 oz) plain chestnut purée
2 teaspoons icing sugar

1 Combine half of the cream with the vanilla, sugar and chestnut purée in a pan. Stir over low heat until well combined. Increase the heat to medium and stir for 15–20 minutes, or until the mixture has thickened. Cover with plastic wrap and cool completely.
2 Divide the mixture into four, then push each portion through a ricer (or a metal strainer) held over a serving plate. Leave the mounds untouched as the threads are fragile and will crumble easily.
3 Whip the remaining cream and icing sugar together, using electric beaters, until firm peaks form. Spoon decoratively over the mounds of chestnut.

LEMON POSSET

Preparation time: 5 minutes + chilling
Total cooking time: 5 minutes
Serves 4

★

110 g (3 1/2 oz) caster sugar
1 1/4 cups (315 ml/10 fl oz) thick (double) cream
juice of 2 lemons (about 100 ml/3 1/2 fl oz)

1 Place the sugar and cream in a saucepan over low heat and bring to the boil slowly, stirring so the sugar dissolves and the cream does not boil over. Boil for 2–3 minutes, then add the lemon juice and mix well.
2 Pour the mixture into four 100 ml (3 1/2 fl oz) ramekins, cover with plastic wrap and chill well for at least 2 hours or overnight. Serve with biscuits such as tuiles.

MONT BLANC
The dessert Mont Blanc is supposed to resemble the snow-capped peak of the French mountain Mont Blanc. It is flavoured with chestnuts, sweetened and puréed before being pressed through a ricer to form strands. The cap is made from sweetened whipped cream. Italians call it Monte Bianco and they add chocolate to the recipe.

OPPOSITE PAGE: Orange Spanish cream (top); Lemon posset

SOUFFLE SECRETS Soufflés

are held up by beaten egg whites and hot air. As the soufflé cooks, the air within it

expands and pushes it upwards, sometimes as much as doubling its height.

Soufflés are, technically, always hot. Although iced or cold soufflés are actually mousses, they are sometimes called soufflés—they are held up by gelatine and beaten egg whites and will not collapse like hot soufflés. The lightness in a cold soufflé comes from the egg whites themselves, rather than the expansion of hot air. Soufflés can be made on a custard-type base, a roux base, or, for a really light result, a fruit purée.

MAKING A PERFECT SOUFFLE

To get the best rise out of a soufflé, you will need a straight-sided ovenproof glass or ceramic soufflé dish (a metal dish will give a quicker cooking time, but be careful as some fruits react with metal and turn the soufflé grey around the edge). If the mixture comes more than two-thirds of the way up the dish, you will need to make a collar. The following instructions are for a soufflé based on a fruit purée.

You will need about 250 g (8 oz) of fruit (we've used 2 mangoes and the pulp from 4 passionfruit), 4 egg whites and 3 tablespoons caster sugar. Separate the eggs one by one into a smaller bowl, just in case one of them breaks.

I To make a collar, wrap a double layer of non-stick baking paper around a 1.5 litre soufflé dish so that it extends 5 cm (2 inches) above the rim. Fix it firmly in place with a piece of string.

2 Lightly grease the inside of the dish and collar with melted butter or flavourless oil and sprinkle with a little caster sugar. Turn the dish so the sugar coats the entire surface of the dish and collar, then turn the dish upside down and tap to loosen any excess sugar. The sugar will help the soufflé grip and climb up the side of the dish as it cooks. Preheat the oven to hot 220°C (425°F/Gas 7) and put a baking tray on the middle shelf.

3 Purée the mango in a food processor and then add the passionfruit (leave the seeds in if you wish but do not process).

4 Place the egg whites in a large, very clean, dry stainless steel or glass bowl—any hint of grease will prevent them foaming. (Traditionally, egg whites are beaten in copper bowls as the copper and whites react to form a more stable foam. If you use a copper bowl, you must clean it with 2 tablespoons salt mixed with

2 tablespoons lemon juice or vinegar, and rinse and dry it thoroughly JUST before you use it.) Leave the whites for a few minutes to reach room temperature, then beat with a balloon whisk or electric beaters. A balloon whisk gives better volume than electric beaters as each sweep of the whisk passes through the whole amount of whites, but make sure you use a large enough whisk—a small one will not give you enough volume. Beat slowly until the whites start to become a frothy foam, then increase your speed until the bubbles in the foam have become small and evenly-sized. When the foam forms stiff peaks, add the sugar little by little. Continue beating until the mixture is glossy—don't overbeat or it will become grainy and not rise well.

5 Fold two spoonfuls of the whites into the fruit purée and mix well to loosen and lighten the mixture. Fold in the

remaining whites with a large metal spoon, being careful not to lose any volume. Pour into the dish and run your finger around the edge to loosen the mixture from the side of the dish. Place on the baking tray in the oven—unless it's an emergency, don't open the oven door until the cooking time is up. It should take 20–25 minutes to cook. If the soufflé is rising more on one side than the other, carefully rotate the dish. Some fruit may have a higher sugar content and cause the top of the soufflé to brown too quickly. If so, rest a piece of foil on top of the soufflé to prevent over-browning. When the soufflé is ready, it should have a pale gold crust and not wobble too much. It should be served immediately, as soufflés wait for no-one. Traditionally, you would make a hole in the centre and pour in a contrasting fruit sauce or cream.

2 Melt the butter in a pan, add the flour and stir over low heat for 2 minutes, or until lightly golden. Add the milk gradually, stirring until smooth. Stir over medium heat until the mixture boils and thickens; boil for another minute, then remove from the heat. Transfer to a large bowl.
3 Dissolve the coffee in 1 tablespoon hot water, add to the milk with the remaining sugar, melted chocolate and egg yolks, then beat until smooth.
4 Beat the egg whites in a clean dry bowl until stiff peaks form and then fold a little into the chocolate mixture to loosen it slightly. Gently fold in the remaining egg white, then spoon the mixture into the soufflé dish and bake for 40 minutes, or until well risen and just firm. Remove the collar, dust the soufflé with icing sugar and serve immediately.

HOT CHOCOLATE SOUFFLE

Preparation time: 30 minutes
Total cooking time: 20 minutes
Serves 6

★ ★

175 g (6 oz) good-quality dark chocolate, chopped
5 egg yolks, lightly beaten
$^{1}/_{4}$ cup (60 g/2 oz) caster sugar
7 egg whites
icing sugar, to dust

1 Preheat the oven to moderately hot 200°C (400°F/Gas 6). Wrap a double layer of baking paper around six 250 ml (8 fl oz) ramekins, to come 3 cm (1¼ inches) above the rim. Secure with string. Brush the insides with melted butter, sprinkle with caster sugar, shake to coat evenly, then tip out excess. Place on a baking tray.
2 Put the chocolate in a heatproof bowl. Half fill a saucepan with water and bring to the boil. Remove from the heat and place the bowl over the pan—don't let it touch the water. Stir occasionally until the chocolate has melted. Stir in the egg yolks and sugar. Transfer the mixture to a large bowl. Beat the egg whites in a large bowl until firm peaks form.
3 Fold a third of the beaten egg white through the chocolate mixture to loosen it. Using a metal spoon, fold through the remaining egg white until just combined. Spoon the mixture into the ramekins and bake for 12–15 minutes, or until well risen and just set. Cut the string and remove the collars. Serve immediately, dusted lightly with the sifted icing sugar.

HOT MOCHA SOUFFLE

Preparation time: 25 minutes
Total cooking time: 45 minutes
Serves 20

★ ★

3 tablespoons caster sugar
40 g (1¼ oz) unsalted butter
2 tablespoons plain flour
$^{3}/_{4}$ cup (185 ml/6 fl oz) milk
1 tablespoon instant espresso-style coffee powder
100 g (3½ oz) good-quality dark chocolate, melted
4 eggs, separated
icing sugar, to dust

1 Preheat the oven to moderate 180°C (350°F/ Gas 4). Wrap a double thickness of baking paper around a 1.25 litre soufflé dish extending 3 cm (1¼ inches) above the rim, then tie securely with string. Brush with oil or melted butter, sprinkle 1 tablespoon of the sugar into the dish, shake the dish to coat the base and side evenly, then shake out the excess.

ABOVE: Hot mocha soufflé

HOT FRUIT SOUFFLE

Preparation time: 15 minutes
Total cooking time: 25–30 minutes
Serves 4

✳ ✳

60 g (2 oz) unsalted butter
¹/₂ cup (60 g/2 oz) plain flour
1¹/₂ cups (375 ml/12 fl oz) puréed fruit
¹/₄ cup (60 g/2 oz) caster sugar
4 egg whites
icing sugar, to dust

1 Brush a 1.25 litre soufflé dish with melted butter, sprinkle with caster sugar, shake to coat evenly, then tip out any excess. Preheat the oven to moderately hot 200°C (400°F/Gas 6) and put a baking tray on the top shelf to heat.
2 Melt the butter in a saucepan, add the flour and mix well. Remove from the heat, stir until smooth, then stir in the fruit purée. Return to the heat, bring to the boil and simmer for 2 minutes. Add the sugar and stir until dissolved (taste in case it is too tart). Leave to cool.
3 Whisk the egg whites in a large clean bowl until soft peaks form, add 1 tablespoon to the fruit mixture and mix well. Fold in the remaining whites, being careful not to lose too much volume. Fill the soufflé dish to three-quarters full and run your thumb or a knife around the inside edge to create a small gap between the soufflé and the dish—this will help the soufflé rise evenly.
4 Put the soufflé on the hot baking tray and bake for 20–25 minutes. Serve immediately, dusted with icing sugar. Can be served with cream.
NOTE: Suitable fruit to use are those that make a good purée, such as raspberries, strawberries, mango, peaches, apricots and passionfruit. Bananas are a little too heavy. You could use apples or plums, or dried fruit, but you'd have to cook them into a purée first.

HOT FRUIT SOUFFLE

Sprinkle the greased soufflé dish with caster sugar, then shake to coat evenly and tip out any excess.

To help the soufflé rise evenly, run your thumb or a knife around the inside edge to make a small gap between the soufflé and the dish. This gives a 'hat' effect when the soufflé is cooked.

LEFT: Hot fruit soufflé

CHILLED BERRY SOUFFLE

Preparation time: 35 minutes + chilling
Total cooking time: Nil
Serves 6

✷ ✷

3 teaspoons gelatine
300 g (10 oz) raspberries
1¼ cups (315 ml/10 fl oz) cream
4 egg whites
2–3 tablespoons caster sugar

1 Prepare six 125 ml (4 fl oz) soufflé dishes by wrapping a double strip of baking paper around the outside of each, extending 2 cm (¾ inch) above the rim, then tying with string. Brush the collar and dish with oil or butter, sprinkle with sugar, shake to coat evenly, then tip out any excess.
2 Place 3 tablespoons water in a small heatproof bowl. Sprinkle evenly with the gelatine and leave to go spongy. Bring a large pan filled with about 4 cm (1½ inches) water to the boil, remove from the heat and carefully lower the gelatine bowl into the water. Stir until dissolved; cool slightly.
3 Purée half the raspberries and push through a sieve. Mash the other half and mix both lots together. Fold in the cooled gelatine mixture.

Beat the cream into soft peaks. In a separate bowl, beat the egg whites into stiff peaks. Gradually beat in 2 tablespoons of the sugar until dissolved—if the raspberries are tart, add the remaining sugar. Fold the cream into the raspberries, followed by the egg white, using a large metal spoon. Spoon into the dishes and chill for several hours, until set. Remove the collars to serve. Can be served with cream and raspberries.

ORANGE AND LEMON SOUFFLE

Preparation time: 50 minutes + chilling
Total cooking time: 10 minutes
Serves 6

✷ ✷

3 eggs, separated
1 cup (250 g/8 oz) caster sugar
2 teaspoons grated orange rind
2 teaspoons grated lemon rind
⅓ cup (80 ml/2¾ fl oz) lemon juice, strained
⅓ cup (80 ml/2¾ fl oz) orange juice, strained
3 teaspoons gelatine
2½ cups (600 ml/20 fl oz) cream

BELOW: Chilled berry soufflé

1 Cut a strip of baking paper long enough to fit around a 1 litre soufflé dish. Fold in half lengthways and wrap around the dish, extending 4 cm (1½ inches) above the rim, then secure with string. Brush the inside of the collar with melted butter or oil. Sprinkle with caster sugar, shake to coat evenly, then tip out any excess.

2 Combine the egg yolks, sugar, grated orange and lemon rind and lemon juice in a metal or heatproof bowl. Stir with a wooden spoon over a simmering pan of water, making sure the base of the bowl doesn't touch the water, until the mixture becomes thick and syrupy.

3 Remove from the heat and stir until the mixture is cold. Pour the orange juice into a small heatproof bowl, sprinkle the gelatine in an even layer over the surface and leave to go spongy. Bring a large pan filled with about 4 cm (1½ inches) water to the boil, remove from the heat, carefully lower the gelatine bowl into the water (it should come halfway up the side of the bowl), then stir until dissolved. Cool slightly, then gradually stir into the lemon mixture. Cover with plastic wrap and refrigerate for 15 minutes, or until thickened but not set. Beat the cream until thick and fold gently into the mixture. Beat the egg whites and fold into the mixture using a large metal spoon. Chill. When the soufflé is starting to set, pour or spoon it into the soufflé dish or glass serving bowl. When completely set, remove the collar carefully and serve immediately.

CHILLED LIME SOUFFLE

Preparation time: 35 minutes + chilling
Total cooking time: Nil
Serves 4

✳ ✳

5 eggs, separated
1 cup (250 g/8 oz) caster sugar
2 teaspoons finely grated lime rind
¾ cup (185 ml/6 fl oz) lime juice, strained
1 tablespoon gelatine
1¼ cups (315 ml/10 fl oz) cream, lightly whipped

1 Cut four strips of baking paper or foil long enough to fit around 250 ml (8 fl oz) soufflé dishes. Fold each in half lengthways, wrap one around each dish, extending 4 cm (1½ inches) above the rim, then secure with string. Brush the inside of the collar with melted butter, sprinkle with caster sugar, shake to coat, then tip out excess.

2 Using electric beaters, beat the egg yolks, sugar and lime rind in a small bowl for 3 minutes, until the sugar has dissolved and the mixture is thick and pale. Heat the lime juice in a small pan, then gradually add to the yolk mixture while beating, until well mixed.

3 Pour ¼ cup (60 ml/2 fl oz) water into a small heatproof bowl, sprinkle the gelatine in an even layer over the surface and leave to go spongy. Bring a large pan filled with about 4 cm (1½ inches) water to the boil, remove from the heat, carefully lower the gelatine bowl into the water (it should come halfway up the side of the bowl), then stir until dissolved. Cool slightly, then add gradually to the lime mixture, beating on low speed until combined. Transfer to a large bowl, cover with plastic wrap and refrigerate for 15 minutes, or until thickened but not set. Using a metal spoon, fold the cream into the lime mixture until almost combined.

4 Using electric beaters, beat the egg whites in a clean, dry bowl until soft peaks form. Fold the egg white quickly and lightly into the lime mixture, using a large metal spoon, until just combined with no lumps of egg white remaining. Spoon gently into the soufflé dishes and chill until set. Remove the collars when ready to serve. Can be served with whipped cream.

CHILLED LIME SOUFFLE

Wrap the foil or baking paper around the soufflé dishes, extending above the rims. Secure with string.

Fold the beaten egg white quickly and lightly into the lime mixture, using a large metal spoon.

ABOVE: Chilled lime soufflé

ZABAGLIONE

Combine the egg yolks, caster sugar and Marsala in a heatproof bowl set over a pan of simmering water.

Whisk the ingredients together until the mixture is smooth and foamy and has tripled in volume.

OPPOSITE PAGE:
*Zabaglione (top);
Lemon passionfruit
syllabub with berries*

ZABAGLIONE

Preparation time: 5 minutes + chilling
Total cooking time: 10 minutes
Serves 4

★★

4 egg yolks
1/3 cup (90 g/3 oz) caster sugar
1/3 cup (80 ml/2¾ fl oz) Marsala

1 Combine all the ingredients in a large heatproof bowl set over a pan of barely simmering water. Make sure the base of the bowl does not touch the water. Whisk with a balloon whisk or electric beaters until the mixture is smooth and foamy and has tripled in volume. Do not stop whisking and do not allow the bowl to become too hot or the eggs will scramble. The final result will be creamy, pale and mousse-like.
2 Pour the zabaglione into four glasses and serve immediately with biscuits such as langue de chat.
3 For chilled zabaglione, place the glasses, covered with plastic wrap, in the refrigerator and chill for at least 1 hour. You must make sure the zabaglione is properly cooked if you are going to chill it or it may separate when left to stand.
NOTES: Zabaglione is known as sabayon in France. It is a custard traditionally made in a copper bowl. Zabaglione is usually served as soon as it is made although sometimes it is chilled for several hours and served iced. It is also delicious poured over fruit in a gratin dish and browned under the grill. It can also be made using sweet Madeira or dessert wine.

Marsala is a fortified wine made in Sicily. It is available both dry and sweet, the sweet being more common. It is drunk as a dessert wine and used in desserts such as Zabaglione and Tiramisu. Marsala all'uovo is a blend which contains eggs.

FRUIT GRATIN

Slice some fresh peaches and strawberries and layer them evenly in four small gratin dishes. Sprinkle with a few raspberries, making the surface of the fruit reasonably flat. Coat the fruit with an even thick layer of zabaglione and place the dishes under a preheated grill. Grill under low heat until the surface turns golden brown, then serve immediately. You can also spoon up to a tablespoon of brandy or liqueur over the fruit if you wish. Serves 4.

LEMON PASSIONFRUIT SYLLABUB WITH BERRIES

Preparation time: 40 minutes + standing
  + chilling
Total cooking time: Nil
Serves 8–10

★★

2 teaspoons grated lemon rind
1/3 cup (80 ml/2¾ fl oz) lemon juice
1/2 cup (125 g/4 oz) caster sugar
1/2 cup (125 ml/4 fl oz) dry white wine
8 passionfruit
2 cups (500 ml/16 fl oz) thick (double) cream
500 g (1 lb) blueberries
500 g (1 lb) raspberries
2 tablespoons icing sugar
500 g (1 lb) strawberries, halved
icing sugar, extra, to dust

1 Stir the rind, juice, sugar and white wine together in a jug and set aside for 10 minutes. Cut the passionfruit in half and push the pulp through a sieve to remove the seeds. Add half the passionfruit pulp to the lemon, sugar and wine mixture.
2 Beat the cream with electric beaters until soft peaks form. Gradually beat in the lemon and passionfruit syrup until all the syrup is added (mixture will have the consistency of softly whipped cream). Stir in the remaining passionfruit, cover and refrigerate for 1 hour.
3 Combine the blueberries, raspberries and icing sugar and place in a 2.5–3 litre serving bowl. Spoon the cream mixture over the top, decorate with strawberries, dust with icing sugar and serve immediately.
NOTE: This thick, custardy dessert was originally made by beating milk or cream with wine, sugar, lemon juice and possibly spices, the acid curdling and thickening the mixture. Some versions were based on cider while others were further fortified with brandy. Syllabub was sometimes used in place of cream on desserts such as trifle, and instead of meringue for floating islands. A thinner version was made as a drink and served at festive occasions in special syllabub glasses.

2 Using electric beaters, beat the eggs and sugar in a small bowl for 5 minutes, or until thick, pale and increased in volume.

3 Transfer the mixture to a large bowl. Using a metal spoon, fold in the melted chocolate with the rum, leave the mixture to cool, then fold in the whipped cream until just combined.

4 Spoon into four 250 ml (8 fl oz) ramekins or dessert glasses. Refrigerate for 2 hours, or until set. This dessert can be decorated with chocolate leaves (see page 239).

CARAMEL MOUSSE

Preparation time: 20 minutes + chilling
Total cooking time: 10 minutes
Serves 6

★★★

2 tablespoons lemon juice
1 tablespoon gelatine
1 cup (250 g/8 oz) sugar
5 eggs
1/4 cup (60 g/2 oz) caster sugar
220 ml (7 fl oz) cream

1 Put the lemon juice in a small bowl, sprinkle the gelatine in an even layer over the surface and leave it to go spongy. Bring a pan filled with about 4 cm (1½ inches) water to the boil, then remove from the heat. Stand the gelatine bowl in the pan and stir until the gelatine has completely dissolved.

2 Put the sugar in a heavy-based pan and place over low heat. Melt the sugar, swirling the pan as it melts and then turn up the heat and cook the sugar until it turns to caramel. As soon as it turns a dark golden brown, plunge the base of the pan into a sink of cold water to stop the caramel colouring any further. Place the pan back on the heat, add 6 tablespoons of water, then melt the caramel gently until it is a smooth liquid. Leave to cool a little.

3 Beat the eggs with the caster sugar until they are fluffy and lighter in colour, add the caramel and gelatine and continue beating until everything is mixed. Cool the mixture in the refrigerator, stirring every few minutes. When it begins to thicken, whisk the cream until it reaches soft peaks and fold it into the mixture. If the caramel has settled at the bottom, make sure you fold it through well.

CHOCOLATE RUM MOUSSE

Preparation time: 20 minutes + chilling
Total cooking time: 5 minutes
Serves 4

★★

250 g (8 oz) good-quality dark chocolate, chopped
3 eggs
1/4 cup (60 g/2 oz) caster sugar
2 teaspoons dark rum
1 cup (250 ml/8 fl oz) cream, softly whipped

1 Put the chocolate in a heatproof bowl. Half fill a saucepan with water and bring to the boil. Remove from the heat and place the bowl over the pan, making sure it is not touching the water. Stir occasionally until the chocolate has melted. Set aside to cool.

ABOVE: Chocolate rum mousse

DECADENT WHITE CHOCOLATE MOUSSE

Preparation time: 40 minutes + chilling
Total cooking time: 5 minutes
Serves 6

★ ★

60 g (2 oz) good-quality dark chocolate, melted
4 egg yolks
1/2 cup (125 g/4 oz) caster sugar
1 tablespoon honey
1 teaspoon instant coffee powder, optional
200 g (61/2 oz) white chocolate, melted
125 g (4 oz) unsalted butter
2/3 cup (170 ml/51/2 fl oz) thick (double) cream

Praline

80 g (23/4 oz) blanched almonds, lightly toasted
1/2 cup (125 g/4 oz) sugar

1 Place the chocolate in a small paper piping bag and pipe in a swirling pattern over the inside surface of six dessert glasses. Refrigerate until set.
2 To make the praline, line a baking tray with baking paper and spread the almonds over it. Combine the sugar with 1/3 cup (80 ml/23/4 fl oz) water in a small pan and stir over low heat, without boiling, until the sugar has dissolved. Brush the edges of the pan with water. Bring to the boil, reduce the heat and simmer, without stirring, until golden brown. Remove from the heat immediately and pour carefully over the almonds. Allow to set until hard. Break half into pieces for topping. Chop or process the remainder into fine crumbs.
3 Using electric beaters, beat the egg yolks, sugar, honey and the coffee blended with 1 teaspoon of hot water in a small bowl until very thick. Beat in the white chocolate until smooth. In a medium bowl, beat the butter with electric beaters until light and creamy. Add the egg yolk mixture and beat until smooth.
4 Beat the cream until soft peaks form. Using a metal spoon, gently fold the cream into the chocolate mixture. Fold in the finely chopped or processed praline. Spoon the mixture into dessert glasses. Refrigerate for 2–3 hours. Serve decorated with large praline pieces and perhaps whipped cream.

QUICK CHOCOLATE MOUSSE

This recipe is handy to use when you don't have much time. Break 175 g (6 oz) dark chocolate into pieces, place it in a heatproof bowl over a pan of steaming water and stir until the chocolate melts. Separate 5 eggs and put the whites in a large clean glass bowl. Cool the chocolate a little and gently stir in the egg yolks. Whisk the egg whites with a balloon whisk or electric beaters until they are stiff, add one tablespoon of the egg whites to the chocolate mixture and mix it in well. Add the chocolate mixture to the remaining egg whites and fold the whites into the chocolate, making sure you do not lose too much volume. Divide the mixture among six 150 ml (5 oz) ramekins. Chill in the refrigerator for 4 hours, or until set. Serve with cream. Serves 6.

BELOW: Decadent white chocolate mousse

CHOCOLATE CUPS

Spread circles of melted white chocolate onto freezer wrap.

When the chocolate cup is set, gently peel away the freezer wrap.

DOUBLE CHOCOLATE MOUSSE

Preparation time: 45 minutes + chilling
Total cooking time: 5 minutes
Serves 6

★ ★

250 g (8 oz) white chocolate, melted
90 g (3 oz) good-quality dark chocolate, chopped
15 g (¹/₂ oz) unsalted butter
2 eggs, separated
1 cup (250 ml/8 fl oz) cream, whipped to
    soft peaks

1 Cut some freezer wrap into six 16 cm (6¹/₂ inch) squares. Place the white chocolate in a heatproof bowl. Half fill a saucepan with water and bring to the boil. Remove from the heat and place the bowl over the pan, making sure the base of the bowl does not touch the water. Stir until the chocolate is melted, then keep it warm by leaving the bowl over the pan. Working with one sheet at a time, spread 6 circles of white chocolate onto the freezer wrap. Drape each piece over the rim of a glass or mould, chocolate-side-up. When set, carefully peel away the freezer wrap, then refrigerate.

2 To make the mousse, melt the dark chocolate with the butter in a double saucepan. (Alternatively, bring a small pan of water to a simmer, remove from the heat and place a heatproof bowl over the pan, making sure you don't let the bottom of the bowl touch the water. Add the chocolate and butter to the bowl.) Stir the mixture over the hot water until melted. Alternatively, melt in the microwave for 1 minute on High (100%), stirring after 30 seconds. Whisk in the egg yolks and allow to cool. Fold in half the cream. Beat the egg whites until soft peaks form and fold lightly into the mousse until well combined. Fold in the remaining cream to make a swirled pattern. Spoon the mousse into the chocolate cups and chill for several hours before serving.

ABOVE: Double chocolate mousse

ORANGE-CHOCOLATE CUPS

Preparation time: 25 minutes
Total cooking time: 10 minutes
Serves 6

★★

125 g (4 oz) good-quality dark chocolate,
    finely chopped
1½ cups (375 ml/12 fl oz) milk
5 egg yolks
2 teaspoons finely grated orange rind
⅓ cup (90 g/3 oz) caster sugar
1 tablespoon gelatine
¾ cup (185 ml/6 fl oz) cream, softly whipped

1 Warm the chocolate and milk in a pan over low heat until the chocolate melts. Whisk the yolks with the rind and sugar until the mixture is light and creamy. Pour the chocolate milk mixture into the egg while stirring, then return the mixture to the pan. Stir over low heat until the custard thickens slightly and coats the back of a wooden spoon—do not boil. Remove from the heat, transfer to a bowl, then allow to cool.
2 Place 3 tablespoons water in a small heatproof bowl. Sprinkle evenly with the gelatine and leave to go spongy. Bring a large pan filled with about 4 cm (1½ inches) water to the boil, remove from the heat and lower the gelatine bowl into the water. Stir until dissolved. Stir into the warm custard and mix well.
3 Allow the mixture to cool completely and thicken slightly. Using a metal spoon, fold in the whipped cream. Pour into six dessert dishes and refrigerate until firm. Can be decorated with whipped cream, chocolate and candied peel.
NOTE: Whip the cream lightly—if it is too stiff, it will not fold evenly through the mixture.

CAPPUCCINO MOUSSE

Preparation time: 1 hour + chilling
Total cooking time: 5 minutes
Serves 6

★★

250 g (8 oz) white chocolate, melted
125 g (4 oz) unsalted butter, softened
2 eggs, lightly beaten
3 teaspoons gelatine
1¼ cups (315 ml/10 fl oz) cream
3 teaspoons instant coffee powder

1 Stir the chocolate, butter and eggs together in a bowl until smooth. Place 2 tablespoons water in a small heatproof bowl. Sprinkle evenly with the gelatine and leave to go spongy. Bring a large pan filled with about 4 cm (1½ inches) water to the boil, remove from the heat and carefully lower the gelatine bowl into the water. Stir until dissolved, then cool slightly before stirring into the chocolate mixture. Mix well, then cover and chill for 30 minutes, or until just starting to set.
2 Beat the cream into soft peaks and gently fold into the mousse. Spoon about a third of the mousse into a separate bowl and set aside. Mix the coffee powder with 3 teaspoons hot water. Allow to cool, then fold into the remaining mousse.
3 Spoon the coffee mousse evenly into six small glasses or dessert dishes and smooth the surface. Spoon or pipe the white mousse over the top, cover and refrigerate for several hours or overnight, before serving. If you wish, you can decorate the top with ground nutmeg.

ABOVE: Orange-chocolate cups

41

JUNKET

Junket, also known as Devonshire junket, comes from the French *jonquet,* the name for a small basket made of rushes (jonques) used for draining cheese. It is a sweet slippery dessert made by coagulating milk with rennet, which separates into curds and whey. In France, the curds are broken up, rather than left as a whole. Junket is traditionally served chilled with a layer of cream and a sprinkle of nutmeg. Rennet is available in bottles.

ABOVE: Chilled orange creams

CHILLED ORANGE CREAMS

Preparation time: 30 minutes + chilling
Total cooking time: 5 minutes
Serves 6

★ ★

1/2 cup (125 ml/4 fl oz) juice of blood oranges
3 teaspoons gelatine
4 egg yolks
1/2 cup (125 g/4 oz) caster sugar
1 1/4 cups (315 ml/10 fl oz) milk
1 teaspoon finely grated rind of blood oranges
1 cup (250 ml/8 fl oz) cream

1 Chill a large bowl in the freezer. Lightly grease six 125 ml (4 fl oz) ramekins or dariole moulds with flavourless oil. Pour the orange juice into a small heatproof bowl, sprinkle the gelatine in an even layer over the surface and leave until spongy. Bring a large pan filled with about 4 cm (1½ inches) water to the boil, remove from the heat, carefully lower the gelatine bowl into the water (it should come halfway up the side of the bowl), then stir until dissolved. Cool slightly.

2 Whisk the egg yolks and sugar in a small bowl until thick. Heat the milk and grated orange rind in a pan and gradually pour onto the egg mixture while whisking. Return to the pan and stir until the custard coats the back of the spoon. Do not allow to boil. Add the gelatine mixture and stir.

3 Pour the mixture immediately through a strainer into the chilled bowl. Cool, stirring occasionally, until beginning to thicken.

4 Whip the cream into soft peaks and fold gently into the custard. Spoon into the greased ramekins and chill to set. Can be served with wedges of blood orange or thin strips of rind.

COEUR A LA CREME

Preparation time: 20 minutes + draining
Total cooking time: Nil
Serves 6

✫

225 g (7 oz) cottage cheese, drained
1/2 cup (60 g/2 oz) icing sugar
1 1/4 cups (315 ml/10 fl oz) cream, whipped

1 Process the drained cottage cheese until smooth in a food processor or push it through a fine sieve. Mix in the icing sugar, then fold in the cream.

2 Line six coeur à la crème moulds with muslin and fill with the prepared mixture. Cover and leave to drain overnight. Unmould the ramekins and serve with fruit sauce or berries.

NOTE: If you do not have any coeur à la crème moulds, line ramekins with muslin and fill with the mixture. Put another piece of muslin over each ramekin and attach it with an elastic band or a tie it with a piece of string. Invert each ramekin on a wire rack and allow to drain overnight before unmoulding.

PASSIONFRUIT FLUMMERY

Preparation time: 15 minutes + chilling
Total cooking time: Nil
Serves 6

✫

85 g (3 oz) passionfruit jelly crystals
375 g (12 oz) can well-chilled evaporated milk
3 passionfruit

1 Stir the jelly crystals into 1 cup (250 ml/ 8 fl oz) boiling water until dissolved. Pour into a shallow metal tray and refrigerate until the consistency of unbeaten egg white.

2 Transfer the jelly to a bowl, add the evaporated milk and beat with electric beaters, on high, for 5–8 minutes, or until doubled in volume. Using a large metal spoon, fold in the pulp from 2 passionfruit.

3 Spoon into six 1 cup (250 ml/8 fl oz) capacity glasses, or a serving bowl, cover loosely with plastic wrap and chill for 1 hour, or until set. Top with pulp from the remaining passionfruit.

NOTE: Different fruit jellies can be used and decorated with the appropriate fruit.

FLUMMERY

Flummery is a generic term for puddings that are thickened with starch or gelatine. Flummeries date back to medieval times. Later varieties of flummery were usually fruit puddings thickened with starch, a sort of fruit porridge. Modern flummeries also include cream and milk and use gelatine as a thickener. They are also known as Dutch flummery.

BELOW: Coeur à la crème (left); Passionfruit flummery

CHEESECAKES

Astonishingly, for such a modern bistro favourite, cheesecake actually hails from days of old. In fact, it is one of the earliest of all baked desserts. The moment we learnt to transform milk into curd cheese was the moment the cheesecake came into creation. The ancient Romans were baking cheese into tiny cakes on the hearth and there are a multitude of early written recipes for cheesecakes from the middle ages. The modern day version—a pastry or biscuity crumb base with a creamy topping—was perfected by the Americans, who ushered this culinary creation into their gleaming kitchens and made the New York cheesecake a world-beater.

FLAVOURING WITH VANILLA

Vanilla extract and essence are produced by steeping vanilla beans in alcohol and water and ageing the product for several months. Pure vanilla extract is very strong, requiring only a few drops per recipe. Vanilla essence tends to have a large proportion of water. Look for products marked 'natural vanilla' or 'pure vanilla extract'. Extract should be added after the cooking process, to prevent evaporation and loss of flavour.

Vanilla powder is ground dried beans. It holds flavour well and does not evaporate on heating.

Cheaper synthetic vanilla flavouring is made entirely with chemicals which are a by-product of the paper-making industry. It has a harsher taste. To add to the confusion, the chemical is called 'artificial vanillin'.

ABOVE: Baked cheesecake with sour cream

BAKED CHEESECAKE WITH SOUR CREAM

Preparation time: 30 minutes + chilling
Total cooking time: 50 minutes
Serves 8–10

★

250 g (8 oz) plain sweet biscuits
1 teaspoon mixed spice
100 g (3^1/$_2$ oz) unsalted butter, melted

Filling

500 g (1 lb) cream cheese, softened
^{2}/$_3$ cup (160 g/5^1/$_2$ oz) caster sugar
1 teaspoon vanilla essence
1 tablespoon lemon juice
4 eggs

Topping

1 cup (250 g/8 oz) sour cream
^{1}/$_2$ teaspoon vanilla essence
3 teaspoons lemon juice
1 tablespoon caster sugar
nutmeg, for sprinkling

1 Lightly grease a 20 cm (8 inch) diameter springform tin and line the base with baking paper. Finely crush the biscuits in a food processor or place them in a sealed plastic bag and crush them with a rolling pin. Transfer to a bowl, add the spice and butter and stir until the crumbs are all moistened. Press firmly over the base and up the side of the tin to create an even shell. Refrigerate for 20 minutes, or until firm. Preheat the oven to moderate 180°C (350°F/Gas 4).
2 To make the filling, beat the cream cheese with electric beaters, until smooth. Add the sugar, vanilla essence and lemon juice, then beat until smooth. Add the eggs, one at a time, beating well after each addition. Pour carefully over the crumbs and bake for 45 minutes, or until just firm to touch.
3 To make the topping, combine the sour cream, vanilla essence, lemon juice and sugar in a bowl. Spread over the hot cheesecake. Sprinkle with nutmeg and return to the oven for another 7 minutes. Turn off the oven and leave to cool with the door ajar. When cool, refrigerate until firm. Can be decorated with strawberries.
NOTE: Cheesecake tends to be quite heavy and will be easier to cut using a knife dipped in hot water and dried between each slice.

CHOCOLATE COLLAR CHEESECAKE

Preparation time: 1 hour 30 minutes + chilling
Total cooking time: 50 minutes
Serves 8–10

☆ ☆ ☆

200 g (6½ oz) plain chocolate biscuits, crushed
70 g (2¼ oz) unsalted butter, melted

Filling

500 g (1 lb) cream cheese, softened
⅓ cup (90 g/3 oz) sugar
2 eggs
1 tablespoon cocoa powder
300 g (10 oz) sour cream
250 g (8 oz) good-quality dark chocolate, melted
⅓ cup (80 ml/2¾ fl oz) Bailey's Irish Cream

Collar

50 g (1¾ oz) white chocolate, melted
150 g (5 oz) good-quality dark chocolate, melted

1¼ cups (315 ml/10 fl oz) cream, whipped
cocoa powder and icing sugar, to dust

1 Brush a 23 cm (9 inch) round springform tin with melted butter or oil and line the base and side with baking paper. Mix together the biscuit crumbs and butter, press firmly into the base of the tin and refrigerate for 10 minutes. Preheat the oven to moderate 180°C (350°F/Gas 4).

2 Beat the cream cheese and sugar with electric beaters until smooth and creamy. Add the eggs, one at a time, beating well after each addition. Beat in the cocoa and sour cream until smooth. Beat in the cooled melted dark chocolate. Beat in the liqueur and pour over the base. Smooth the surface and bake for 45 minutes. The cheesecake may not be fully set, but will firm up. Refrigerate, overnight if possible, until cold.

3 Remove the cheesecake from the tin and put it on a board. Measure the height and add 5 mm (¼ inch). Cut a strip of baking paper this wide and 75 cm (30 inches) long. Pipe or drizzle the melted white chocolate in a figure eight pattern along the paper. When just set, spread the dark chocolate over the entire strip of paper. Allow the chocolate to set a little, but you need to be able to bend the paper without it cracking.

4 Wrap the paper around the cheesecake with the chocolate inside. Seal the ends and hold the paper in place until the chocolate is completely set. Peel away the paper. Spread the top with cream. Dust with cocoa powder and icing sugar.

CHOCOLATE COLLAR

Pipe or drizzle the cooled, melted white chocolate in a pattern along the strip of baking paper.

When the white chocolate is just set, use a spatula to spread the melted dark chocolate over all the baking paper.

When slightly set, but still pliable, wrap the paper around the cake with the chocolate inside. Seal the ends and hold until set.

When set, carefully peel away the paper to leave the chocolate collar around the outside of the cheesecake.

LEFT: Chocolate collar cheesecake

TROPICAL CHEESECAKE

When the biscuits are finely crushed, add the coconut.

BELOW: Tropical cheesecake

TROPICAL CHEESECAKE

Preparation time: 50 minutes + chilling
Total cooking time: Nil
Serves 8

★

145 g (5 oz) plain sweet biscuits
1/4 cup (25 g/3/4 oz) desiccated coconut
90 g (3 oz) unsalted butter, melted

Filling

1/2 cup (125 ml/4 fl oz) fresh orange juice
6 teaspoons gelatine
350 g (11 oz) cream cheese, softened
1/3 cup (90 g/3 oz) caster sugar
2 tablespoons lemon juice
425 g (14 oz) can mangoes, drained and
   chopped, or 2 fresh mangoes, chopped
450 g (14 oz) can unsweetened crushed
   pineapple, drained
11/4 cups (315 ml/10 fl oz) cream
extra whipped cream, kiwi fruit and mango
   wedges, to decorate

1 Lightly grease a 20 cm (8 inch) diameter springform tin and line the base with baking paper. Put the biscuits in a food processor and chop until they are finely crushed. Add the coconut and butter and process until well combined. Spoon into the tin, press firmly over the base, then refrigerate.
2 Put the fresh orange juice in a small heatproof bowl, sprinkle the gelatine in an even layer over the surface and leave to go spongy. Bring a large pan filled with about 4 cm (1 1/2 inches) water to the boil, then remove from the heat. Carefully lower the gelatine bowl into the water (it should come halfway up the side of the bowl), then stir until the gelatine has dissolved. Allow to cool.
3 Beat the softened cream cheese and caster sugar in a bowl for 3 minutes, or until smooth. Beat in the lemon juice and gently fold in the mango and crushed pineapple. Fold in the dissolved gelatine.
4 Whip the cream into firm peaks. Fold into the mixture with a metal spoon. Pour into the tin, smooth and chill overnight. Decorate with extra cream and slices of fruit.
NOTE: If you are using fresh mangoes, increase the caster sugar to 1/2 cup (125 g/4 oz).

NEW YORK CHEESECAKE

Preparation time: I hour + chilling
Total cooking time: I hour 50 minutes
Serves 10–12

★

1/2 cup (60 g/2 oz) self-raising flour
I cup (125 g/4 oz) plain flour
1/4 cup (60 g/2 oz) caster sugar
I teaspoon grated lemon rind
80 g (23/4 oz) unsalted butter, chopped
I egg
1 1/2 cups (375 ml/12 fl oz) cream, for serving

Filling

750 g (1 1/2 lb) cream cheese, softened
I cup (250 g/8 oz) caster sugar
1/4 cup (30 g/1 oz) plain flour
2 teaspoons grated orange rind
2 teaspoons grated lemon rind
4 eggs
2/3 cup (170 ml/5 1/2 fl oz) cream

Candied rind

finely shredded rind of 3 limes, 3 lemons
    and 3 oranges
I cup (250 g/8 oz) caster sugar

1 Combine the flours, sugar, lemon rind and unsalted butter for about 30 seconds in a food processor, until crumbly. Add the egg and process briefly until the mixture just comes together. Turn out onto a lightly floured surface and gather together into a ball. Refrigerate in plastic wrap for about 20 minutes, or until the mixture is firm.
2 Preheat the oven to hot 210°C (415°F/ Gas 6–7). Lightly grease a 23 cm (9 inch) diameter springform tin. Roll the pastry between 2 sheets of baking paper until large enough to fit the base and side of the tin. Ease into the tin and trim the edges. Cover the pastry with baking paper, then rice or dried beans. Bake for 10 minutes, then remove the baking paper and rice. Flatten the pastry lightly with the back of a spoon and bake for another 5 minutes. Set aside to cool.
3 To make the filling, reduce the oven to slow 150°C (300°F/Gas 2). Beat the cream cheese, sugar, flour and rinds until smooth. Add the eggs, one at a time, beating after each addition. Beat in the cream, pour over the pastry and bake

for 1 hour 25–35 minutes, or until almost set. Turn off the oven and leave to cool with the door ajar. When cool, refrigerate.
4 To make the candied rind, place a little water in a pan with the rind, bring to the boil and simmer for 1 minute. Drain the rind and repeat with fresh water. This will get rid of any bitterness in the rind and syrup. Put the sugar in a pan with 1/4 cup (60 ml/2 fl oz) water and stir over low heat until dissolved. Add the rind, bring to the boil, reduce the heat and simmer for 5–6 minutes, or until the rind looks translucent. Allow to cool, drain the rind and place on baking paper to dry (you can save the syrup to serve with the cheesecake). Whip the cream, spoon over the cold cheesecake and top with candied rind.
NOTE: To make the cheesecake easier to cut, heap the rind in mounds, then cut between the mounds of rind.

CANDIED RIND

Add the rind to the sugar syrup and bring to the boil.

Transfer the rind to a sheet of non-stick baking paper.

ABOVE: New York cheesecake

PEAR AND GINGER CHEESECAKE

Preparation time: 50 minutes + chilling
Total cooking time: 1 hour 10 minutes
Serves 10

★

250 g (8 oz) plain sweet biscuits
2 tablespoons ground ginger
100 g (3½ oz) unsalted butter, melted

Filling

3–4 firm ripe pears
1 cup (250 g/8 oz) caster sugar
2 tablespoons lemon juice
500 g (1 lb) cream cheese, softened
2 eggs
2 tablespoons ground ginger
300 g (10 oz) sour cream

ABOVE: Pear and ginger cheesecake

1 Lightly grease a 23 cm (9 inch) diameter springform tin and line the base with baking paper. Sprinkle with flour and shake off excess.
2 Finely crush the biscuits with the ginger in a food processor. Add the butter and mix well. Spoon into the tin and press firmly onto the base and up the side. Refrigerate for 10 minutes. Preheat the oven to slow 150°C (300°F/Gas 2).
3 To make the filling, peel, core and thinly slice the pears and put them with half the sugar, the lemon juice and 1½ cups (375 ml/12 fl oz) water in a pan. Bring to the boil, lower the heat and simmer until the pears are tender but not breaking up. Strain and set aside to cool.
4 Process the cream cheese and remaining sugar in a food processor until light and smooth. Mix in the eggs and ginger. Add the sour cream and process to combine. Arrange the pears over the crust, pour the filling over the top and bake for 1 hour, or until set. Cool in the tin, then refrigerate overnight. Can be served with cream.
NOTE: For a stronger ginger flavour, use gingernuts instead of plain biscuits for the base.

RASPBERRY SWIRL CHEESECAKE

Preparation time: 40 minutes + chilling
Total cooking time: Nil
Serves 8–10

★

250 g (8 oz) plain sweet biscuits
90 g (3 oz) unsalted butter, melted

Filling

2 tablespoons gelatine
500 g (1 lb) light cream cheese, softened
1/3 cup (80 ml/2¾ fl oz) lemon juice
1/2 cup (125 g/4 oz) caster sugar
1¼ cups (315 ml/10 fl oz) cream, whipped
250 g (8 oz) frozen raspberries
2 tablespoons caster sugar, extra

1 Lightly grease a 23 cm (9 inch) diameter springform tin and line the base with baking paper. Finely crush the biscuits in a food processor, then mix in the butter. Spoon into the tin, press firmly over the base and up the side and refrigerate for 20 minutes, or until firm.
2 Put 1/4 cup (60 ml/2 fl oz) water in a small heatproof bowl, sprinkle evenly with the gelatine and leave to go spongy. Bring a large pan filled with about 4 cm (1½ inches) water to the boil, remove from the heat, carefully lower the gelatine bowl into the water (it should come halfway up the side of the bowl), then stir until dissolved. Allow to cool.
3 Using electric beaters, beat the cream cheese until creamy, add the juice and sugar and beat until smooth. Gently fold in the whipped cream and half the gelatine.
4 Process the raspberries and extra sugar in a food processor until smooth. Push the purée through a fine-meshed nylon sieve to remove any pips. Fold the remaining gelatine into the raspberry mixture. Place blobs of cheesecake mixture into the tin and fill the gaps with the raspberry. Swirl the two mixtures together, using a skewer or the point of a knife. Refrigerate for 4 hours, or until set. Can be decorated with whipped cream and raspberries.

HINTS AND TIPS

CHEESE
Different types of soft cheese used in cheesecake recipes have different moisture and fat contents and are not inter-changeable. Using the wrong type of cheese may result in a cheesecake that separates or sinks.

COOLING
Cheesecakes should be cooled slowly, preferably in the oven with the heat switched off and the door ajar, before refrigeration. A cheesecake that is cooked too quickly may crack across the top.

TINS
Non-stick tins with a very dark coating conduct heat quickly and may cause the outside of a cheesecake to cook and darken, or burn, before the centre is cooked.

ABOVE: Raspberry swirl cheesecake

ALL ABOUT CREAM

Milk is amazing—it contains nourishing proteins, sugars, fats, vitamins and minerals and it can be transformed into a host of other dairy products.

CREAM

If fresh milk is left to stand, a layer of cream will form on top as the butterfat rises. So cream is simply a form of milk in which the butterfat is more concentrated. It is either skimmed off the top after rising naturally or removed by the use of centrifugal force. Cream varies in thickness and richness, according to how much butterfat it contains—the thicker the cream, the higher the percentage of butterfat. But cream labelled 'thickened cream' has had thickening agents such as gelatine added to help it hold its shape. Cream for whipping must have at least 35% butterfat to trap the air bubbles and hold them in place. Reduced fat cream has a maximum of 25% fat and light cream around 18%. Pouring cream has a butterfat content higher than both English single cream and American light cream, neither of which can be whipped—it varies between 35% and 48%. Thick cream ('double' in England and 'heavy' in America) has a minimum butterfat content of 48%. Clotted, scalded or Devonshire cream is the thickest and yellowest of all. All cream should be well chilled before whipping and should be refrigerated when not in use.

SOUR CREAM

Originally made by leaving cream at room temperature to sour, today it is made by adding a culture to cream. It is thickened and slightly acidic because the milk sugar (lactose) converts to lactic acid. Low-fat varieties are now available.

CREME FRAICHE

This French version of cultured sour cream is smooth, rich and slightly acidic, with a higher fat content than thick cream. Its mild acidity complements the sweetness of chocolate and fruit.

RICOTTA

This was originally made from the whey of milk but nowadays is often made from milk. It is low in fat, has a slight sweetness and short shelf life. It should look moist and white, not dry and discoloured.

QUARK/FROMAGE FRAIS/ FROMAGE BLANC/CREAM CHEESE

These are soft curd cheeses made from both full-fat and non full-fat milk. Fromage frais and fromage blanc have been homogenized to give a smoother texture and have a slightly acidic edge. Cream cheese is also sold as Neufchatel.

BUTTERMILK

Butter is produced by churning cream until the fat comes together and, traditionally, buttermilk was the liquid remaining after this process. However, cultured buttermilk is made from skim milk which has a bacterial culture added to ripen and thicken it slightly. It becomes slightly acidic as the lactose turns to lactic acid. It activates bicarbonate of soda, so is often used in baking to give a light texture.

YOGHURT

This is made by adding a culture of Lactobacillus bulgaricus, Lactobacillus acidophilus or Streptococcus thermophilus to warm milk. The bacilli create acidity which ferments and thickens the milk and destroys some of the intrinsic bacteria, giving it a longer 'edible' life and making it an easily digested food.

MASCARPONE

This rich creamy cheese originated in Italy. Traditional in tiramisu, it also works well in cheesecakes and ice cream.

CLOCKWISE, FROM TOP LEFT: Double (thick) cream, cream, buttermilk, milk, mascarpone, ricotta, yoghurt, (on plate: fromage blanc, quark, cream cheese), crème fraîche, sour cream, clotted cream

RICOTTA

Ricotta literally means 'recooked'. This reflects its method of manufacture, in which whey and skim cows' milk are heated, thus causing the albumin or protein to collect in flakes, a process known as flocculating. As it is made from whey, ricotta is not strictly a cheese, but a by-product of cheesemaking.

Ricotta is relatively low in fat, with a sweetish edge due to the presence of lactose or milk sugar. It is high in calcium and makes a good alternative to cream cheese. Ricotta can be whipped, eaten fresh or cooked in baked goods. It is also available in lower fat varieties. If ricotta seems a little wet, drain overnight in a muslin-lined sieve. Ricotta is traditionally used in Italian cooking, especially cassata and cheesecakes.

ABOVE: Chocolate ricotta tart

CHOCOLATE RICOTTA TART

Preparation time: 20 minutes + chilling
Total cooking time: 1 hour
Serves 8–10

★

1 1/2 cups (185 g/6 oz) plain flour
100 g (3 1/2 oz) unsalted butter, chopped
2 tablespoons caster sugar

Filling

1.25 kg (2 1/2 lb) ricotta
1/2 cup (125 g/4 oz) caster sugar
2 tablespoons plain flour
1 teaspoon instant coffee
125 g (4 oz) chocolate, finely chopped
4 egg yolks
40 g (1 1/4 oz) chocolate, extra
1/2 teaspoon vegetable oil

1 Make sweet shortcrust pastry by sifting the flour into a large bowl and adding the butter. Rub the butter into the flour with your fingertips, until fine and crumbly. Stir in the sugar. Add 3 tablespoons cold water and cut with a knife to form a dough, adding a little more water if necessary. Turn out onto a lightly floured surface and gather together into a ball. Lightly grease a 25 cm (10 inch) diameter springform tin. Roll out the dough, then line the tin so that the pastry comes about two-thirds of the way up the side. Cover and refrigerate while making the filling.

2 To make the filling, mix together the ricotta, sugar, flour and a pinch of salt until smooth. Dissolve the coffee in 2 teaspoons hot water. Stir into the ricotta mixture, with the chocolate and egg yolks, until well mixed. Spoon into the chilled pastry shell and smooth. Chill for 30 minutes, or until firm. Preheat the oven to moderate 180°C (350°F/Gas 4).

3 Put the springform tin on a baking tray. Bake for 1 hour, or until firm. Turn off the oven and leave to cool with the door ajar—the tart may crack slightly but this will not be noticeable when it cools and has been decorated. To decorate, melt the extra chocolate and stir in the oil. With a fork, flick thin drizzles of melted chocolate over the tart, or pipe over for a neater finish. Cool completely before cutting into wedges for serving.

FROZEN HONEY CHEESECAKE WITH PRALINE CRUST

Preparation time: 1 hour + freezing
Total cooking time: 25 minutes
Serves 8–10

★ ★

100 g (3¹/₂ oz) flaked almonds
³/₄ cup (185 g/6 oz) sugar
225 g (7 oz) plain sweet biscuits
100 g (3¹/₂ oz) unsalted butter, melted

Filling

250 g (8 oz) mascarpone cheese
250 g (8 oz) cream cheese, softened to room temperature
400 g (13 oz) can condensed milk
¹/₄ cup (60 ml/2 fl oz) honey
1¹/₄ cups (315 ml/10 fl oz) cream
2 teaspoons ground cinnamon

1 Preheat the oven to slow 150°C (300°F/ Gas 2). To make the praline, spread the almonds on a foil-lined, greased baking tray. Put the sugar in a pan with ¹/₂ cup (125 ml/4 fl oz) water and stir over low heat until the sugar has dissolved. Bring to the boil, then simmer without stirring until the toffee is golden brown. Pour over the almonds, then set aside to cool and harden before breaking into pieces.

2 Lightly grease a 23 cm (9 inch) diameter springform tin and line the base with baking paper. Reserve about half the praline and finely chop the rest with the biscuits in a food processor. Stir in the butter, spoon into the base and press firmly on the side of the tin. Bake for 15 minutes and then leave to cool.

3 To make the filling, process the mascarpone and cream cheese together until soft and creamy. Add the condensed milk and honey. Whip the cream until soft peaks form and then fold in. Pour into the tin, sprinkle with cinnamon and swirl gently with a skewer. Do not overmix. Freeze for several hours, or until firm, and decorate with the remaining praline.

CHEESECAKE WITH PRALINE CRUST

Pour the toffee over the flaked almonds on the foil-lined greased baking tray.

Use a skewer to swirl the cinnamon through the cheesecake filling.

LEFT: Frozen honey cheesecake with praline crust

HAZELNUTS

Hazelnuts, also known as cobnuts and filberts, are smallish, round, smooth nuts with brown skin and a hard brown shell. They are native to North America, southeast Europe and Asia and are grown extensively in Turkey, Italy and Spain. Lightly toasting the nuts will bring out their flavour as will slow roasting them in the oven. Hazelnuts are delicious with chocolate, cinnamon and orange. To remove the skins, roast the hazelnuts in a 180°C (350°F/Gas 4) oven for about 8 minutes and then rub them in a tea towel to loosen the skins.

ABOVE: Liqueur coffee cheesecake

LIQUEUR COFFEE CHEESECAKE

Preparation time: 50 minutes + chilling
Total cooking time: 1 hour
Serves 6–8

★ ★

150 g (5 oz) speculaas or ginger biscuits, finely crushed
3/4 cup (80 g/2 3/4 oz) ground hazelnuts
100 g (3 1/2 oz) unsalted butter, melted
400 g (13 oz) cream cheese, softened
1/4 cup (60 g/2 oz) sugar
3 eggs
6 teaspoons plain flour
1/2 cup (125 ml/4 fl oz) cream
1/3 cup (80 ml/2 3/4 fl oz) Kahlua, Tia Maria or Bailey's Irish Cream

Topping

1 1/2 cups (375 g/12 oz) sugar
1 teaspoon instant coffee powder
100 g (3 1/2 oz) whole roasted hazelnuts
1 1/4 cups (315 ml/10 fl oz) cream

1 Lightly grease a 20 cm (8 inch) diameter springform tin and line the base with baking paper. Mix the biscuits, hazelnuts and butter and press half firmly into the base of the tin. Gradually press the remainder around the side, using a glass to firm it into place. Refrigerate for 10–15 minutes.

2 Preheat the oven to moderate 180°C (350°F/ Gas 4). Beat the cream cheese and sugar with electric beaters until smooth. Add the eggs one at a time, beating well after each addition. Blend together the flour and cream, beat into the cream cheese mixture, then add the liqueur. Pour into the tin and put on a baking tray to catch any drips. Bake for 40–50 minutes, or until almost set. Set aside until set completely. Refrigerate for several hours.

3 To make the topping, combine the sugar in a pan with 3/4 cup (185 ml/6 fl oz) water. Stir over low heat without boiling until the sugar has dissolved. Simmer for 10–12 minutes, until golden. Remove from the heat and gently stir in the coffee. Using two spoons, dip the nuts one at a time into the toffee and put on a lightly oiled foil-lined tray. Allow to set. Whip the cream to firm peaks. Ease the cheesecake out of the tin and top with whipped cream, toffee hazelnuts and perhaps some spun toffee.

MINI ORANGE CHEESECAKES

Preparation time: 40 minutes + chilling
Total cooking time: Nil
Makes 8

☆

250 g (8 oz) plain sweet biscuits
125 g (4 oz) unsalted butter, melted

Filling

4 oranges
250 g (8 oz) cream cheese, softened
1 teaspoon grated orange rind
3/4 cup (185 ml/6 fl oz) condensed milk
2 tablespoons lemon juice
1 tablespoon orange juice

1/2 cup (125 ml/4 fl oz) cream, whipped,
   to decorate
slivers of orange rind, to decorate

1 Lightly grease eight 8 cm (3 inch) fluted flan tins. To make the crust, finely crush the biscuits in a food processor. Add the melted butter and process for another 15 seconds. Divide the mixture evenly among the tins and press firmly into the base and side of the tins. Place on a tray and refrigerate while preparing the filling.
2 To make the filling, place the oranges on a board and cut a 2 cm (3/4 inch) slice off each end of orange to where the flesh starts. Cut the skin away in a circular motion, cutting only deep enough to remove all the white membrane. Separate the segments by cutting between the membrane and the flesh. Do this over a bowl to catch any juice. Reserve two or three segments for each cheesecake, to decorate. Cut the remainder in small pieces.
3 Using electric beaters, beat the cream cheese and rind in a small bowl until light and creamy. Gradually add the condensed milk, lemon and orange juice. Beat on medium speed for 5 minutes, or until smooth and increased in volume. Fold in the chopped orange.
4 Pour the mixture evenly into the prepared tins and smooth the surface. Refrigerate overnight. Decorate with whipped cream, slivers of orange rind and the reserved orange segments.

ABOVE: Mini orange cheesecakes

BUTTERMILK CHEESECAKE WITH RASPBERRY SAUCE

Preparation time: 35 minutes + chilling
Total cooking time: 1 hour 20 minutes
Serves 8

★

250 g (8 oz) plain sweet biscuits
125 g (4 oz) unsalted butter, melted
3 teaspoons grated lemon rind

Filling

750 g (1 1/2 lb) ricotta
4 eggs, lightly beaten
1 cup (250 ml/8 fl oz) buttermilk
2 tablespoons cornflour
1/2 cup (125 ml/4 fl oz) honey
1 tablespoon lemon juice
icing sugar, to dust

Raspberry sauce

300 g (10 oz) fresh or frozen raspberries
1/4 cup (30 g/1 oz) icing sugar
1 teaspoon lemon juice

*BELOW: Buttermilk
cheesecake with
raspberry sauce*

1 Grease a 23 cm (9 inch) diameter springform tin and line the base with baking paper. Preheat the oven to warm 160°C (315°F/Gas 2–3). Finely crush the biscuits in a processor and stir in the butter and 2 teaspoons of rind, until combined. Spoon into the tin and press firmly over the base. Refrigerate while preparing the filling.
2 Beat the ricotta with electric beaters for 2 minutes, or until smooth. Add the beaten egg gradually, beating well after each addition. Whisk together the buttermilk and cornflour until smooth and add gradually to the ricotta mixture. Beat in the honey, remaining lemon rind and the lemon juice. Pour into the tin and bake for 1 hour 20 minutes, or until set. Cool, then refrigerate for at least 6 hours.
3 To make the raspberry sauce, defrost the raspberries, reserve a few as garnish, and process the rest with the icing sugar for 20 seconds, or until smooth. Add lemon juice, to taste. Bring the cheesecake to room temperature and serve with raspberries and sauce. Lightly dust with icing sugar.

SICILIAN CHEESECAKE

Preparation time: 45 minutes + chilling
Total cooking time: 1 hour 25 minutes
Serves 8

★

2 cups (250 g/8 oz) plain flour
160 g (5 1/2 oz) unsalted butter, chopped
1/4 cup (60 g/2 oz) caster sugar
1 teaspoon grated lemon rind
1 egg, lightly beaten

Filling

60 g (2 oz) raisins, chopped
1/3 cup (80 ml/2 3/4 fl oz) Marsala
500 g (1 lb) ricotta
1/2 cup (125 g/4 oz) caster sugar
1 tablespoon plain flour
4 eggs, separated
1/2 cup (125 ml/4 fl oz) cream

1 Lightly grease a 26 cm (10 1/2 inch) diameter springform tin. Sift the flour and a pinch of salt into a large bowl and rub in the butter, using just your fingertips. Add the sugar, rind, egg and a little water, if necessary and, using a knife, cut through until a rough dough forms. Gather the dough together into a ball.

2 Roll out the dough between two sheets of baking paper to fit the base and side of the tin, then chill for 30 minutes. Preheat the oven to moderately hot 190°C (375°F/Gas 5). Prick the pastry base, line with baking paper and fill with dried beans or rice. Bake for 15 minutes, remove the beans and paper and bake for 8 minutes, or until the pastry is dry. If the base puffs up, gently press down with the back of a spoon. Allow to cool. Reduce the oven temperature to warm 160°C (315°F/Gas 2–3).

3 To make the filling, put the raisins and Marsala in a small bowl, cover and leave to soak. Push the ricotta through a sieve, then beat with the sugar, using a wooden spoon, until combined. Add the flour and egg yolks, then the cream and undrained raisins and mix well. In a clean, dry bowl, beat the egg whites until soft peaks form, then fold into the ricotta mixture in two batches.

4 Pour the filling into the pastry case and bake for 1 hour, or until just set. Check during cooking and cover with foil if the pastry is overbrowning. Cool a little in the oven with the door ajar to prevent sinking. Serve warm.

NOTE: Marsala is a fortified dark wine made in Sicily with a deep rich flavour. It is available in dry and sweet varieties. Sweet Marsala is used in desserts and as a dessert wine.

BAKED LIME AND PASSIONFRUIT CHEESECAKE

Preparation time: 50 minutes + chilling
Total cooking time: 55 minutes
Serves 6–8

☆

250 g (8 oz) plain sweet biscuits
125 g (4 oz) unsalted butter, melted

Filling

500 g (1 lb) cream cheese, softened to room temperature
1/3 cup (90 g/3 oz) caster sugar
3 teaspoons grated lime rind
2 tablespoons fresh lime juice
2 eggs, lightly beaten
1/2 cup (125 ml/4 fl oz) passionfruit pulp

Passionfruit topping

1 tablespoon caster sugar
3 teaspoons cornflour
1/2 cup (125 ml/4 fl oz) passionfruit pulp

1 Lightly grease a 20 cm (8 inch) diameter springform tin and line the base with baking paper. Preheat the oven to warm 160°C (315°F/Gas 2–3). Finely crush the biscuits in a food processor and mix in the butter. Spoon into the tin and press firmly into the base and side of the tin. Chill for 30 minutes.

2 Using electric beaters, beat the cream cheese, sugar, lime rind and juice until creamy. Gradually beat in the eggs and passionfruit pulp. Pour into the tin, put on a baking tray to catch any drips, and bake for 45–50 minutes, or until just set. Cool completely.

3 To make the topping, combine the sugar, cornflour and 2 tablespoons water in a small pan over low heat. Stir until smooth, add 2 more tablespoons water and the passionfruit pulp and stir until the mixture boils and thickens. Pour the hot topping over the cooled cheesecake, spread evenly and cool completely. Refrigerate overnight. Can be served with piped cream.

NOTE: You will need to use the pulp from about eight fresh passionfruit for this recipe.

ABOVE: Baked lime and passionfruit cheesecake

MERINGUE

Meringue is a quite miraculous mixture of egg whites and sugar whipped together until firm, then baked into delicate peaks and swirls. Australia's most popular and renowned culinary creation is the timeless pavlova, named in honour of the Russian ballerina, Anna Pavlova. Meringue connoisseurs will debate over the relative merits of the crunchy brittle variety that explodes into a thousand crumbs of sweetness when bitten into; and 'grandmother's pavlova', with its crisp outer shell and gooey chewy centre.

GRANDMOTHER'S PAVLOVA

Preparation time: 30 minutes
Total cooking time: 1 hour
Serves 6–8

★

4 egg whites

1 cup (250 g/8 oz) caster sugar

2 teaspoons cornflour

1 teaspoon white vinegar

1 cup (250 ml/8 fl oz) cream

pulp from 3 passionfruit, to decorate

strawberries and kiwi fruit, to decorate

1 Preheat the oven to warm 160°C (315°F/ Gas 2–3). Line a 32 x 28 cm (13 x 11 inch) baking tray with baking paper.
2 Place the egg whites and a pinch of salt in a large, very clean, dry stainless steel or glass bowl— any hint of grease will prevent the egg whites foaming. Leave the whites for a few minutes to reach room temperature, then, using electric beaters, beat slowly until the whites start to become a frothy foam, then increase the speed until the bubbles in the foam have become small and evenly-sized. When the foam forms stiff peaks, add the sugar gradually, beating constantly after each addition, until the mixture is thick and glossy and all the sugar has dissolved. Don't overbeat or the mixture will become grainy.
3 Using a metal spoon, fold in the sifted cornflour and the vinegar. Spoon the mixture into a mound on the prepared tray. Lightly flatten the top of the pavlova and smooth the sides. (This pavlova should have a cake shape and be about 2.5 cm/1 inch high.) Bake for 1 hour, or until pale cream and crisp on the outside. Remove from the oven while warm and carefully turn upside down onto a plate.
4 Lightly whip the cream until soft peaks form and spread over the soft centre. Decorate with passionfruit pulp, halved strawberries and sliced kiwi fruit. Cut into wedges to serve.
NOTE: The addition of cornflour and vinegar gives the meringue a marshmallow centre.

BELOW: Grandmother's pavlova

Beat the egg whites until stiff peaks form, then add the sugar gradually and beat until the mixture is thick and glossy.

Spread the mixture evenly into a circle. Draw a 20 cm (8 inch) circle on the paper first if you find it easier to have a guide.

PAVLOVA WITH FRESH FRUIT

Preparation time: 15 minutes
Total cooking time: 40 minutes
Serves 6–8

★

4 egg whites
1 cup (250 g/8 oz) caster sugar
1¹/₂ cups (375 ml/12 fl oz) cream, whipped
1 banana, sliced
125 g (4 oz) raspberries
125 g (4 oz) blueberries

1 Preheat the oven to slow 150°C (300°F/Gas 2). Line a baking tray with baking paper. Mark a 20 cm (8 inch) circle on the paper as a guide if you find it easier.
2 Place the egg whites in a large, very clean, dry stainless steel or glass bowl—any hint of grease will prevent the egg whites foaming. Leave the whites for a few minutes to reach room temperature, then, using electric beaters, beat slowly until the whites start to become a frothy foam, then increase the speed until the bubbles in the foam have become small and evenly-sized. When the foam forms stiff peaks, add the sugar gradually, beating constantly after each addition, until the mixture is thick and glossy and all the sugar has dissolved. Don't overbeat or the mixture will become grainy.
3 Spread the mixture on the paper and shape it evenly into a circle, running a flat-bladed knife or spatula around the edge and over the top. Run a knife or spatula up the edge of the mixture, all the way around, to make furrows. This will strengthen the pavlova and give it a decorative finish.
4 Bake for 40 minutes, or until pale and crisp. Turn off the oven and cool the pavlova in the oven with the door ajar. When cold, decorate with cream, banana, raspberries and blueberries.
NOTE: The meringue can be cooked in advance and kept overnight in an airtight container. Serve within 1 hour of decorating.

ABOVE: Pavlova with fresh fruit

MERINGUE

There are several types of meringue—ordinary, Italian, and meringue *cuite*. Each egg white needs at least 45 g sugar—lesser amounts give a very soft meringue suitable for pie toppings.

To beat well, egg whites need to be fresh and at room temperature, as well as free from any oil or egg yolk. For ordinary meringue, the sugar is added in at least two batches and beaten until the sugar dissolves and stabilises the whites. Meringue should be thick and shiny and hold its shape when piped. It might not work on a humid day, when it may break down.

Italian meringue is made by adding boiling sugar syrup to beaten egg white. Meringue *cuite* is made by beating egg white and icing sugar over heat. Both these methods give a solid meringue which holds up well.

OPPOSITE PAGE, FILLED MERINGUE NESTS, FROM TOP: Gingered custard and rhubarb; Rich chocolate mousse; Grilled fig and ricotta

MERINGUE NESTS

Preparation time: 20 minutes
Total cooking time: 35 minutes + cooling
Makes 4

✫

2 egg whites
1/2 cup (125 g/4 oz) caster sugar

1 Preheat the oven to slow 150° (300°F/Gas 2). Line a baking tray with greaseproof paper. Mark out four 9 cm (3 1/2 inch) circles. Put the egg whites in a large clean, dry bowl and leave for a few minutes to reach room temperature. Using electric beaters, whisk the egg whites until soft peaks form. Gradually add the sugar, beating well after each addition, until the mixture is thick and glossy. Do not overbeat.
2 Spread 1 tablespoon of the mixture evenly over each of the circles to a thickness of 5 mm (1/4 inch). Put the remaining mixture in a piping bag fitted with a 1 cm (1/2 inch) star nozzle. Pipe the mixture on the edge of the meringue circles to make a nest 1–2 cm (1/2–3/4 inch) high.
3 Bake for 30–35 minutes, or until lightly golden, then turn the oven off and leave the meringues to cool completely in the oven. Once cooled, carefully remove from the trays. Transfer to an airtight container until required.

GINGERED CUSTARD AND RHUBARB FILLING

In a bowl, whisk 4 egg yolks and 1/2 cup (125 g/4 oz) sugar together until creamy, then stir in 1 tablespoon cornflour. In a small pan, combine 1 cup (250 ml/4 fl oz) milk with 2 teaspoons grated fresh ginger and bring to the boil. Remove from the heat, strain and allow to cool slightly, then gradually whisk into the egg mixture. Return to the pan and stir over low heat for 5 minutes, or until the mixture thickens. Remove from the heat and allow to cool. Cut 2 stalks of rhubarb in half lengthways, then cut into 3 cm (1 1/4 inch) pieces. Combine 1 tablespoon caster sugar and 1/4 cup (60 ml/ 2 fl oz) water in a small pan and stir over low heat until the sugar dissolves. Add the rhubarb and cook gently for 3–5 minutes, or until the rhubarb softens but still holds its shape. Spoon the cooled custard into the nests, arrange the rhubarb over it and serve immediately. Garnish with a dusting of icing sugar or fine strips of preserved ginger. Serves 4.

RASPBERRY MASCARPONE FILLING

Combine 250 g (8 oz) mascarpone with the finely grated rind of 1 lime. Stir in 60 g (2 oz) raspberries, mixing well so that some of the raspberry juices are released into the mascarpone. Divide the mixture evenly among the four nests and garnish, using about 60 g (2 oz) raspberries. Serve garnished with fresh mint leaves or a dusting of icing sugar. Serves 4.

RICH CHOCOLATE MOUSSE FILLING

Bring a pan filled with about 4 cm (1 1/2 inches) water to the boil, then remove it from the heat. Put 60 g (1 oz) roughly chopped dark chocolate in a heatproof bowl and set over the pan, making sure the bowl is not touching the water. Stir until the chocolate has melted. Allow to cool. Using electric beaters, whip 1 cup (250 ml/ 8 fl oz) cream with 1/4 cup (60 g/2 oz) caster sugar until soft peaks form. Mix one-third of the cream into the melted chocolate, stirring until the chocolate and cream are well combined. Fold in the remaining cream mixture, cover and refrigerate for 2 hours. Once firm, spoon into the meringue nests and garnish with chocolate curls (see page 238). Serve immediately, dusted with icing sugar. Serves 4.

GRILLED FIG AND RICOTTA FILLING

Blend 500 g (1 lb) ricotta, 2 tablespoons honey, 2–3 tablespoons orange juice, 2 teaspoons soft brown sugar, 1/2 teaspoon cinnamon and 1/4 teaspoon vanilla essence together in a food processor until smooth. Transfer to a bowl and stir in 50 g (1 3/4 oz) sultanas. Quarter 4 firm, purple figs lengthways, place on a baking tray and sprinkle with 1 tablespoon soft brown sugar. Grill for 5–6 minutes, or until the sugar has begun to caramelize. Spoon the ricotta mixture into the nests, top with the grilled figs, sprinkle with finely chopped pistachios and serve immediately. Any remaining fig can be served separately. Serves 4.

put the halves back together. Stand the peaches in a shallow ovenproof dish.

2 Whisk the egg whites in a large, clean, dry bowl until stiff peaks form, gradually add the sugar and whisk until thick and glossy. Cover the fruit with a layer of meringue, making sure there are no gaps. Using a fork, rough up the surface of the meringue. Sprinkle with demerara sugar and bake for 15–20 minutes, until the meringue is lightly browned. Gently lift out. These can be served with cream or ice cream.

MIXED BERRY MERINGUE STACKS

Preparation time: 50 minutes + chilling
Total cooking time: 35 minutes + cooling
Serves 6

☆

2 egg whites
^{1}/2 cup (125 g/4 oz) caster sugar
250 g (8 oz) strawberries
150 g (5 oz) blueberries
125 g (4 oz) raspberries
1 tablespoon soft brown sugar
1^1/2 cups (375 ml/12 fl oz) cream, whipped
icing sugar, to dust

1 Preheat the oven to slow 150° (300°F/Gas 2). Line baking trays with baking paper and mark out eighteen 9 cm (3^1/2 inch) circles.

2 In a large, clean, dry bowl, using electric beaters, whisk the egg whites until soft peaks form. Gradually add the sugar, beating after each addition, until the mixture is thick and glossy. Spread 1 tablespoon of the mixture evenly over each of the circles to a thickness of 5 mm (1^1/4 inch). Bake for 30–35 minutes, or until lightly golden, then turn the oven off and leave the meringues to cool completely in the oven.

3 Trim the strawberries and combine with the other berries in a large bowl. Sprinkle with the sugar, then cover and refrigerate for 20 minutes.

4 To assemble, using three meringue circles for each, place one on a plate, spread with cream and arrange some of the berry mixture over the cream. Place another circle on top, spread with cream and top with more berry mixture and top with the third circle. Dust liberally with icing sugar. Repeat this with all the circles to make six individual stacks and serve immediately.

ABOVE: Fruit covered with meringue

FRUIT COVERED WITH MERINGUE

Preparation time: 25 minutes
Total cooking time: 20 minutes
Serves 4

☆ ☆

4 ripe peaches or nectarines
40 g (1^1/4 oz) marzipan
3 egg whites
^{2}/3 cup (160 g (5^1/2 oz) caster sugar
demerara sugar, to sprinkle

1 Preheat the oven to moderately hot 200°C (400°F/Gas 6). Cut the peaches in half and remove the stone. To remove the skin, place the peaches cut-side-down on a plate, put the plate in the sink and pour boiling water over, followed by cold water. Drain immediately and peel. Roll the marzipan into 4 small balls, put them in the gaps left by the peach stones, then

NUTS: CHOPPING AND STORING
When chopping nuts in a food processor, make sure they are cold or they will become oily. You can add a tablespoon of sugar or flour to help absorb any excess oil when processing nuts. Nuts keep best frozen or refrigerated in a sealed container.

HAZELNUT MERINGUE STACK

Preparation time: 20 minutes + cooling
Total cooking time: 55 minutes
Serves 8

☆

300 g (10 oz) hazelnuts
8 egg whites
1½ cups (375 g/12 oz) caster sugar
2 teaspoons vanilla essence
2 teaspoons white vinegar
600 g (1¼ lb) sour cream
200 ml (6½ fl oz) cream, whipped
1¼ cups (230 g/7½ oz) soft brown sugar
cream, extra, to decorate
hazelnuts, extra, to decorate

1 Preheat the oven to moderate 180°C (350°F/Gas 4). Roast the hazelnuts on a baking tray for 5–10 minutes, or until golden. Tip the nuts onto a tea towel, rub vigorously in the towel to remove the skins. Transfer to a food processor and chop until finely ground.

2 Reduce the oven temperature to slow 150°C (300°F/Gas 2). Line four baking trays with baking paper and draw a 21 cm (8½ inch) diameter circle on each piece.

3 Bring the egg whites to room temperature in a large, clean, dry bowl, then beat until soft peaks form. Gradually add the caster sugar, beating well after each addition, until stiff and glossy. Fold in the ground hazelnuts, vanilla essence and vinegar.

4 Divide the mixture evenly among the circles and carefully spread it to the edge of each circle. Bake for 45 minutes, or until crisp. Turn off the oven and leave the meringues to cool in the oven, with the door ajar.

5 To make the filling, stir the sour cream, cream and brown sugar in a bowl until combined.

6 Sandwich together the meringue circles with the filling. Decorate with whipped cream and chopped hazelnuts or toffeed hazelnuts.

ABOVE: Hazelnut meringue stack

BERRIES
A tangy summer explosion of glorious colour and bittersweet juices, berries make the perfect partner for crispy sweet meringue, but don't stop there—they have myriad other roles in the dessert world.

BLACKBERRIES
This slightly tart fruit is delicious in pies, crumbles and cobblers and is an essential ingredient in summer pudding. Refrigerate, then wash just before use. Blackberries are delicious with crème fraîche, brandy and apple.

BLUEBERRIES
Blueberries have a blue exterior but are white or pale green inside. Available most of the year, they keep in the refrigerator for up to 7 days. Don't store in a metal container as they react and cause dark stains. Rinse before use. Great in baked desserts, pies and cheesecakes, blueberries taste good with port, cinnamon and cream.

CURRANTS
Available in red, white and black. White currants are a variety of the red and look similar. Leave on the stalk until ready to

use, then remove the stalks by gently loosening the berries between the tines of a fork. Often frosted and used as a cake decoration, moulded in jellies or used in fruit tarts. Redcurrants are often used with almonds, cherries and oranges. Blackcurrants are an excellent source of Vitamin C and are the basic ingredient in the liqueur Cassis. Blackcurrants are good with pears, apples and red wine.

MULBERRIES

The fruit of a tree, mulberries are available in black, red and white, the black having the best flavour. They have a rich, winey flavour and their juice stains very badly. They go well with cream and brandy and can be used in pastries, cakes and crumbles.

PHYSALIS (CAPE GOOSEBERRIES)

A summer fruit that enjoys a relatively short season, this small orange or greeny yellow berry is enclosed in a papery calyx. Peel away the calyx and eat the sharp tasting berry raw, or dipped in caramel or fondant. They make a wonderful garnish for cheesecakes, desserts and fruit platters.

RASPBERRIES

A true summer berry, the red ones are the most common but a golden variety is sometimes available. Store this delicate fruit covered in the refrigerator and get rid of any mouldy ones immediately. Eat them on their own or puréed as part of a cold mousse or hot soufflé.

STRAWBERRIES

Strawberries are available all year round but vary vastly in flavour, size and colour. When they are in season, they have a wonderful aroma and flavour. Store them in the refrigerator and rinse them just before using. They are delicious on their own, with cream or ice cream, or used in traditional recipes such as strawberries romanoff, summer pudding and shortcake.

CLOCKWISE, FROM LEFT: Raspberries, Blackberries, Red, black and white currants, Blueberries, Strawberries, Mulberries, Physalis

BAKED ALASKA

Preparation time: 40 minutes + freezing
Total cooking time: 8 minutes
Serves 6–8

★★

2 litres good-quality vanilla ice cream
250 g (8 oz) mixed glacé fruit,
    finely chopped
1/4 cup (125 ml/4 fl oz) Grand Marnier
    or Cointreau
2 teaspoons grated orange rind
60 g (2 oz) toasted almonds,
    finely chopped
60 g (2 oz) dark chocolate,
    finely chopped
1 sponge or butter cake, cut into
    3 cm (1 1/4 inch) slices
3 egg whites
3/4 cup (185 g/6 oz) caster sugar

BAKED ALASKA
Baking ice cream inside an insulating hot layer is an idea probably invented by the Chinese, who baked ice cream wrapped in pastry. The French used the same idea to make *omelette Norvegienne,* using meringue instead of pastry. The Americans coined the name Baked Alaska.

ABOVE: Baked Alaska

1 Line a 2 litre pudding basin with damp muslin. Soften 1 litre of ice cream enough to enable the glacé fruit to be folded in with 2 tablespoons liqueur and 1 teaspoon orange rind. Spoon into the basin, smooth over the base and up the sides, then put in the freezer until frozen. Soften the remaining ice cream and fold in the almonds, chocolate, remaining liqueur and orange rind. Spoon into the frozen shell and level the surface.
2 Work quickly to evenly cover the ice cream with a 3 cm (1 1/4 inch) thick layer of cake. Cover with foil and freeze for at least 2 hours. Preheat the oven to hot 220°C (425°F/Gas 7). Using electric beaters, beat the egg whites in a dry bowl until soft peaks form. Gradually add the sugar, beating well after each addition. Beat for 4–5 minutes, until thick and glossy.
3 Unmould the ice cream onto an ovenproof dish and remove the muslin. Quickly spread the meringue over the top to cover the ice cream completely. Bake for 5–8 minutes, or until lightly browned. Cut into wedges and serve at once.
NOTE: Partly bury an upturned half egg shell in the top of the meringue before baking. Fill with warmed brandy and set alight to serve.

RASPBERRY AND WHITE CHOCOLATE ROLL

Preparation time: 35 minutes + chilling
Total cooking time: 10 minutes
Serves 6–8

✯ ✯

4 egg whites
3/4 cup (185 g/6 oz) caster sugar
125 g (4 oz) cream cheese, softened
3/4 cup (185 g/6 oz) sour cream
125 g (4 oz) white chocolate, melted
125 g (4 oz) fresh raspberries

1 Preheat the oven to moderate 180°C (350°F/ Gas 4). Line the base and long sides of a 25 x 30 cm (10 x 12 inch) swiss roll tin with baking paper. Beat the egg whites until soft peaks form. Gradually add the sugar, beating constantly. Beat until thick and glossy and the sugar has dissolved.
2 Spread the mixture into the tin and bake for 10 minutes, or until lightly browned and firm to touch. Quickly and carefully turn onto baking paper that has been sprinkled with caster sugar. Leave to cool.
3 Beat the cream cheese and sour cream until smooth and creamy. Add the cooled white chocolate and beat until smooth. Spread over the meringue base, leaving a 1 cm (1/2 inch) border. Top with a layer of raspberries. Carefully roll the meringue, using the paper as a guide, from one short end. Wrap firmly in the sugared paper and plastic wrap and chill until firm. Cut into slices to serve.

FROZEN PRALINE MERINGUE TORTE

Preparation time: 1 hour + freezing
Total cooking time: 1 hour 10 minutes
Serves 8–10

✯ ✯

4 egg whites
1 1/2 cups (375 g/12 oz) caster sugar
100 g (3 1/2 oz) blanched almonds
2 litres good-quality vanilla ice cream, softened

Strawberry sauce

500 g (1 lb) strawberries
2 tablespoons lemon juice
1/4 cup (30 g/1 oz) icing sugar

1 Preheat the oven to slow 150°C (300°F/Gas 2). Line two baking trays with baking paper and mark a 20 cm (8 inch) circle on each. Brush with oil and dust with a little caster sugar. Beat the egg whites to stiff peaks, then gradually add 1 cup (250 g/8 oz) of the sugar, a tablespoon at a time. Beat until thick and glossy and the sugar has dissolved. Pipe in a spiral into the two circles. Bake for 1 hour, turn off the oven and leave the meringues to cool with the oven door ajar.
2 To make the praline, line a baking tray with baking paper and sprinkle with almonds. Combine the remaining sugar with 1/3 cup (80 ml/ 2 3/4 fl oz) water in a pan and stir over low heat until dissolved. Bring to the boil without stirring and, when golden, pour over the almonds. Allow to set and cool before crushing finely in a food processor or with a rolling pin.
3 Process or beat the ice cream until creamy and fold in the praline. Put a meringue circle into a lined 23 cm (9 inch) diameter springform tin, spoon in the ice cream and put the other meringue on top. Freeze until ready to serve.
4 To make the sauce, mix the ingredients in a food processor until smooth. Add a little water if too thick. Serve with the meringue torte.
NOTE: The meringues should be cooked very slowly to be dry and crunchy. The torte will keep up to four days in the freezer.

BELOW: Frozen praline meringue torte

MERINGUE BASKET

Preparation time: 30 minutes
Total cooking time: 2 hours
Serves 6

★ ★

8 egg whites
450 g (14 oz) pure icing sugar, sifted
1½ cups (375 ml/12 fl oz) cream, whipped
450 g (14 oz) fresh fruit

1 Preheat the oven to very slow 140°C (275°/Gas 1). Place 4 egg whites in a large metal or heatproof bowl, leave for a few minutes to come to room temperature, then beat them until stiff peaks form. Set the bowl over a large pan of simmering water and add half the icing sugar while continuing to beat the mixture. Add it carefully or it will fly all over the place. At this stage it is best to use electric beaters as you must now beat the meringue mixture until it is thick and very solid—beyond stiff peak. Set this batch aside and cover with plastic wrap.
2 Line two baking trays with baking paper and draw four 18 cm (7 inch) circles on the paper. If you use pencil, remember to turn the paper over or it will mark the meringue. Stir the meringue a couple of times, fill a piping bag fitted with a 1 cm (½ inch) nozzle with the meringue, and pipe concentric circles into one of the rings, filling it out to the marked line—this will be the base. Pipe a single circle onto the other 3 drawn circles up to the edge of the marked line—these will form the sides of the basket. Bake for 45–50 minutes, until dry and crisp. Cool on wire racks.
3 Make up another batch of meringue as before. Place the base of the basket back on the baking paper and, using a little of the uncooked meringue mixture, 'glue' the circles one on top of the other onto the base. Fit a 1 cm (½ inch) star-shaped nozzle into the piping bag and, with the remaining mixture, pipe the meringue in strips up the edges of the basket all the way around. Finish the basket by tidying up the edges with piped rosettes of meringue. Bake for 50–60 minutes, until dry and crisp and leave to cool before filling with whipped cream and fresh fruit.
NOTE: This meringue is called meringue *cuite* or cooked meringue. It is very stable and does not lose its shape when cooked, so it works very well for piping into shapes. It can also be left in a covered bowl in the fridge overnight.

MERINGUE SWANS

Preparation time: 1 hour 25 minutes
Total cooking time: 1 hour
Serves 6

★ ★

2 egg whites
½ cup (125 g/4 oz) caster sugar
90 g (3 oz) flaked almonds, lightly toasted

Cherry sauce

425 g (14 oz) can pitted black cherries in syrup
1 tablespoon Kirsch
1 teaspoon caster sugar
1 teaspoon lemon juice

Mascarpone filling

250 g (8 oz) mascarpone cheese
2 tablespoons icing sugar
1 teaspoon vanilla essence
½ cup (125 ml/4 fl oz) cream

1 Preheat the oven to slow 150°C (300°F/Gas 2). For the bodies, using two sheets of baking paper, draw six teardrop shapes on each, measuring 5 cm (2 inches) across the widest part and 10 cm (4 inches) long. For the necks, draw six 'S' shapes on baking paper. Draw a few extra 'S' shapes where there is space, to allow for breakages. Put the paper on baking trays. Beat the egg whites in a small, clean, dry bowl with electric beaters until stiff peaks form. Gradually add the sugar, beating well between each addition until the sugar has dissolved. Spread the mixture thickly inside the teardrop shapes, making the widest end slightly thicker. Insert the tips of the flaked almonds at an angle into the teardrop shapes to represent feathers. Spoon some mixture into a piping bag fitted with a 5 mm (¼ inch) plain piping tube and pipe the necks. Use any leftover meringue to pipe extra 'S' shapes. Bake for 1 hour, rotating the trays after 30 minutes. Turn the oven off and cool the meringues in the oven with the door slightly ajar.
2 Drain the cherries, reserving the juice. Purée the cherries with ⅓ cup (80 ml/2¾ fl oz) of the juice, then strain. Stir in the Kirsch, sugar and lemon juice.
3 Mix the mascarpone, icing sugar and vanilla essence. Beat the cream to soft peaks and fold into the mascarpone. Beat to thicken if necessary.
4 To assemble, join two teardrops for the body with the mascarpone and insert an 'S' for the neck. Spoon sauce onto each plate and carefully lift a swan into the centre.

Spread the meringue mixture thickly inside the teardrop shapes.

Insert the tips of the flaked almonds at an angle all over the tops of the teardrops, to represent feathers.

Pipe 'S' shapes for the necks, doing a few extra to allow for breakages.

OPPOSITE PAGE:
Meringue basket (top);
Meringue swans

OEUFS A LA NEIGE

Preparation time: 15 minutes
Total cooking time: 25 minutes
Serves 4–6

★★

4 eggs, separated
1 cup (250 g/8 oz) caster sugar
3 cups (750 ml/24 fl oz) milk
1 vanilla bean, split lengthways
1/2 cup (125 g/4 oz) sugar, extra

1 Put the egg white in a clean, dry bowl, leave for a few minutes to come to room temperature, then beat until soft peaks form. Gradually add 1/3 cup (90 g/3 oz) caster sugar, beating well after each addition, until stiff and glossy.
2 Combine the milk, 1/3 cup (90 g/3 oz) caster sugar and the vanilla bean in a large frying pan and bring to a simmer. Using two dessertspoons, mould the meringue into 16 egg shapes and lower in batches into the simmering milk. Poach for 5 minutes each batch, or until firm to touch, turning once during cooking (being careful as they are delicate and crumble easily). Remove with a slotted spoon and set aside. When they are all done, strain the milk.
3 Whisk the egg yolks with the remaining caster sugar until thick and pale. Gradually pour the milk into the egg yolk mixture, whisking well to combine. Remove and discard the vanilla bean. Pour the custard mixture into a pan and stir over low heat until the custard thickens and coats the back of a wooden spoon. Do not boil the custard. Pour the custard into a shallow serving dish and allow to cool.
4 When the custard is completely cold, arrange the poached meringue on top. Stir the extra sugar with 2 tablespoons water in a small pan over low heat until the sugar has dissolved completely. When the sugar has dissolved, bring to the boil and simmer until the syrup turns golden brown. Working quickly and carefully, drizzle the toffee over the meringues and custard.
NOTE: Oeufs à la neige means 'snow eggs' and is sometimes known as floating islands.

ABOVE: Oeufs à la neige

CHOCOLATE MOUSSE MERINGUE CAKE

Preparation time: 50 minutes
Total cooking time: 45 minutes
Serves 10–12

★ ★

6 eggs, separated
1½ cups (375 g/12 oz) caster sugar
2½ tablespoons cocoa powder
200 g (6½ oz) dark cooking chocolate, melted
1 tablespoon instant coffee powder
2½ cups (600 ml/20 fl oz) cream, whipped

1 Preheat the oven to slow 150°C (300°F/ Gas 2). Line four baking trays with baking paper. Mark 22 cm (8¾ inch) circles on three trays and draw straight lines, 3 cm (1¼ inches) apart, on the remaining tray. Put the egg whites in a large, clean, dry bowl, leave for a few minutes to come to room temperature, then beat until soft peaks form. Gradually add the sugar, beating constantly after each addition. Beat for 5–10 minutes, until thick and glossy and all the sugar has dissolved. Gently fold the sifted cocoa into the meringue.
2 Divide the meringue into four portions. Spread three portions over the marked circles. Put the remaining portion in a piping bag fitted with a 1 cm (½ inch) plain piping nozzle. Pipe long lines over the marked lines. Bake for 45 minutes, or until pale and crisp. Check the meringue strips occasionally to prevent overcooking. Turn off the oven and cool in the oven with the door ajar.
3 Put the melted chocolate in a bowl, whisk in the egg yolks and the coffee dissolved in 1 tablespoon water, and beat until smooth. Fold in the whipped cream and mix until combined. Refrigerate until the mousse is cold and thick.
4 To assemble, place one meringue disc on a plate and spread with one-third of the mousse. Top with another disc and spread with half the remaining mousse. Repeat with the remaining disc and mousse. Run a knife around the edge of the meringue cake to spread the mousse evenly over the edge. Cut or break the strips into short pieces and pile on top of the cake and upright in a row around the outer edge, pressing them into the mousse. Dust with extra cocoa powder and refrigerate until firm.

COCOA
Cocoa powder is made from the seeds of the cacao, a tropical tree. The seeds are roasted and ground into a pure chocolate paste. To make the powder, the vegetable fat, known as cocoa butter, is removed from the paste and the powder ground from the remaining dry solids. Chocolate drink was fashionable in the 17th century and became known as cocoa in the 18th century. Cocoa powder in its present form was invented by the Dutch in 1828. Cocoa available as Dutch, Dutched or dark cocoa, has a mellower flavour than others.

LEFT: Chocolate mousse meringue cake

FRUIT
AND JELLIES

In the world of food, simple certainly doesn't imply 'plain'. A piece of fresh fruit is the simplest dessert we have, and it can also be one of the most stunning. From here, it is but a tiny step to baking, grilling, poaching in a boozy syrup or serving with dollops of thick cream in a fresh fruit salad. Simply perfection... from the tiniest of juicy redcurrants, to the rich extravagance of a ripe fig. And what better way to show off the beauty of fruit than to suspend it in the tangy translucence of a jelly?

COOKING FRUIT

There is no hard and fast rule for cooking fruit except that bad quality under-ripe fruit cannot be disguised by good cooking. Not all fruit holds its shape well during cooking and fruit that collapses after cooking for a long time is still delicious. It can be puréed, or mashed and used as a sauce for ice creams and other fruits. Fresh fruit is beautiful either when left whole or cut to reveal its particular structure.

ABOVE: Grilled oranges with caramel mint butter

GRILLED ORANGES WITH CARAMEL MINT BUTTER

Preparation time: 20 minutes + chilling
Total cooking time: 20 minutes
Serves 4

★ ★

6 oranges
1/3 cup (90 g/3 oz) sugar
1/4 cup (60 ml/2 fl oz) cream
45 g (1 1/2 oz) unsalted butter, chopped
2 teaspoons grated orange rind
2 tablespoons finely chopped fresh mint
cream or mascarpone, for serving
ground nutmeg, for serving

1 Cut the base off each orange to steady it, then cut the skin away in a downward motion, cutting only deep enough to remove all the white membrane. Slice the oranges thinly.
2 Cook the sugar and 3 tablespoons water in a small pan over very low heat, without boiling, until the sugar has dissolved (shake occasionally, but do not stir). Increase the heat, bring to the boil and cook until deep golden or caramel. Remove from the heat and gradually add the cream (the mixture will become lumpy and may spit, so be careful). Return to the heat and stir until the caramel dissolves. Add the butter, orange rind and mint and whisk until blended. Transfer to a bowl and refrigerate.
3 Preheat the grill. Arrange the orange slices slightly overlapping in a 24 cm (9 1/2 inch) diameter shallow ovenproof gratin or pie dish. Dot the top of the oranges with the caramel butter, then grill until the butter has melted and the oranges are hot. Serve with cream or mascarpone. Sprinkle with nutmeg to serve.
NOTE: Caramel mint butter can be prepared ahead and refrigerated for 24 hours.

POACHED PEARS WITH GINGER ZABAGLIONE

Preparation time: 30 minutes
Total cooking time: I hour
Makes 6

★

2 cups (500 ml/16 fl oz) good-quality
   red wine
4 pieces crystallized ginger
1/2 cup (125 g/4 oz) sugar
6 pears, peeled

Ginger zabaglione

8 egg yolks
1/3 cup (90 g/3 oz) caster sugar
I teaspoon ground ginger
I 1/4 cups (315 ml/10 fl oz) Marsala

I Put the wine, ginger and sugar in a large pan with 1 litre water and stir over medium heat until the sugar has dissolved. Add the pears, cover and simmer for 45 minutes, or until tender.
2 To make the zabaglione, put a large pan half filled with water on to boil. When boiling, remove from the heat. Beat the egg yolks, sugar and ginger in a metal or heatproof bowl, using electric beaters, until pale yellow. Set the bowl over the pan of steaming water, making sure the bowl does not touch the water, and beat continuously, adding the Marsala gradually. Beat for 5 minutes, or until very thick and foamy and like a mousse.
3 Remove the pears from the pan with a slotted spoon. Arrange on plates and pour ginger zabaglione over each. Serve immediately.
NOTE: Use as good a quality wine for cooking as you would for drinking.

DATES POACHED IN EARL GREY SYRUP

Infuse 2 Earl Grey tea bags in 1 cup (250 ml/ 8 fl oz) boiling water for 30 minutes. Discard the tea bags and place the liquid in a small pan with 1 cup (250 g/8 oz) sugar. Stir over medium heat until the sugar has dissolved. Bring to the boil and simmer for 10 minutes, without stirring. Add 12 fresh dates and cook for 2–3 minutes, turning once. Serve immediately with thick cream or mascarpone.

PEARS
Pears are a very versatile fruit. As well as being delicious by themselves, they are used in fruit salad, can be poached or baked, and cooked in tarts, puddings and crumbles. They vary in texture, shape and colour. *Beurre Bosc* is an elongated pear with greenish-brown or reddish-brown skin and juicy flesh. It cooks very well for long lengths of time. *Corella* is a smaller pear with a green skin streaked with red. It is equally delicious when hard or soft. *Cornice* has a yellow skin with a red blush. It is sweet and juicy with no grittiness. *Nashi* is an Asian variety with a very crisp and juicy texture. Most varieties are round like apples, with a yellow skin. *Packham's Triumph* is the world's largest selling pear with a light yellow skin when ripe and a white juicy flesh. *Williams*, also known as *Bartlett,* has a yellow skin and sometimes a red blush when ripe. The *Red William* pear is also available as *Red Sensation*.

LEFT: Poached pears with ginger zabaglione

FRUIT KEBABS WITH HONEY CARDAMOM SYRUP

Preparation time: 20 minutes + marinating
Total cooking time: 5 minutes
Makes 8 kebabs

★

1/4 small pineapple or 2 rings canned
    pineapple
I peach
I banana
16 strawberries
cream or yoghurt, for serving, optional

Honey cardamom syrup

2 tablespoons honey
20 g (3/4 oz) unsalted butter, melted
1/2 teaspoon ground cardamom
I tablespoon rum or brandy, optional
I tablespoon soft brown sugar

BELOW: Fruit kebabs with honey cardamom syrup

1 Soak eight wooden skewers in cold water for 20 minutes. Cut the pineapple into 8 bite-sized pieces. Cut the peach into 8 wedges and slice the banana. Thread the fruit alternately on skewers and place in a shallow dish.
2 To make the honey cardamom syrup, combine the honey, butter, cardamom, rum and sugar in a bowl. Pour the mixture over the kebabs and brush to coat. Cover and leave to stand at room temperature for 1 hour. Prepare and heat a barbecue or griller.
3 Cook the kebabs on a hot, lightly greased barbecue flatplate or under the griller, for 5 minutes. Brush with syrup occasionally during cooking. Serve drizzled with the remaining syrup. Can also be served with fresh cream or natural yoghurt.

POACHED NECTARINES IN MIXED SPICE SYRUP

Preparation time: 10 minutes
Total cooking time: 20 minutes
Serves 4

★

4 nectarines
1/2 cup (125 g/4 oz) sugar
4 cardamom pods
2 star anise
I cinnamon stick
2 cloves
cream or mascarpone, for serving, optional

1 Score a cross in the base of each nectarine. Place in a large heatproof bowl and cover with boiling water for 1 minute. Drain, cool for 2–3 minutes and peel.
2 Slowly heat 2 cups (500 ml/16 fl oz) water and the sugar in a pan, stirring until the sugar has dissolved. Lightly bruise the cardamom pods with the back of a knife and add to the pan with the star anise, cinnamon and cloves. Bring to the boil and simmer for 5 minutes.
3 Add the nectarines, cover and simmer for another 8–10 minutes, or until the nectarines are soft. Remove the nectarines with a slotted spoon and transfer to serving bowls.
4 Strain the syrup, pour a little over each nectarine and serve hot or cold, with cream or mascarpone.
NOTE: If preferred, you can stone the nectarines before cooking them by cutting around the circumference and twisting the two halves open.

BAKED APPLES

Preparation time: 20 minutes
Total cooking time: 45 minutes
Serves 6

✫

6 cooking apples
60 g (2 oz) sultanas
3 tablespoons soft brown sugar
1 teaspoon ground mixed spice
40 g (1¼ oz) unsalted butter, chopped
1½ cups (375 ml/12 fl oz) orange juice
cream, whipped, for serving, optional

1 Preheat the oven to moderate 180°C (350°F/ Gas 4). Use an apple corer to core the apples. Using a sharp knife, make a shallow cut through the skin around the middle of the apples to prevent the skin bursting during cooking.
2 Combine the sultanas, sugar and spice and spoon into the apples. Put the apples in a small baking dish with the butter and juice. Bake for 45 minutes, basting occasionally. Cool for 5 minutes, transfer to plates and pour the pan juices over the top. Serve with cream.

POACHED QUINCES

Preparation time: 15 minutes
Total cooking time: 4 hours
Serves 6

✫

6 quinces
2 cups (500 g/1 lb) sugar
2 tablespoons lemon juice
1 vanilla bean
1 cinnamon stick
2 star anise
cream, for serving, optional

1 Peel the quinces and cut them in half.
2 Combine the sugar and 2 litres water in a large pan and stir over low heat until the sugar dissolves.
3 Add the quinces, lemon juice and the spices, then cover and simmer for 4 hours, or until the quinces are pink and tender. Serve warm with cream.

QUINCES
Quinces have a hard, yellow skin which does not soften when ripe. Ripe quinces have a more golden colour. Quinces require long, slow cooking and turn a beautiful deep red colour when cooked.

ABOVE: Baked apples

PAPAYA AND PAWPAW
Papaya and pawpaw, from the same family, are the fruit of a large tropical softwood tree. Their size bears no relation to maturity. Papaya skins range from yellowy-green to pinky-red. The flesh also varies in colour. Some are yellow and some pinky-red or orange. Ripen at room temperature until the skin loses most of its green tinge and the fruit has a pleasant aroma, then store in the refrigerator. Cut in half lengthways and spoon out the seeds. Peel, then slice or chop. Papaya makes good fools and creamy desserts. It does not work well with gelatine as it contains an enzyme, papain, which inhibits setting.

*OPPOSITE PAGE,
CLOCKWISE FROM TOP:
Eastern fruit platter;
Melon medley;
Summer citrus salad*

SUMMER CITRUS SALAD

Preparation time: 15 minutes
Total cooking time: 5 minutes
Serves 4–6

✰

3 ruby grapefruits, peeled and pith removed
3 large oranges, peeled and pith removed
1 tablespoon caster sugar
1 cinnamon stick
3 tablespoons whole mint leaves

1 Cut the grapefruit and orange into segments and mix in a bowl.
2 Put the sugar, cinnamon and mint in a small pan with 3 tablespoons water and stir over low heat until the sugar has dissolved. Remove the cinnamon stick and mint leaves and drizzle the syrup over the fruit.

EASTERN FRUIT PLATTER

Preparation time: 15 minutes
Total cooking time: 5 minutes
Serves 4–6

✰

1 stem lemon grass, white part only, chopped
2 cm (3/4 inch) piece ginger, roughly chopped
1 teaspoon soft brown sugar
1/2 cup (125 ml/4 fl oz) coconut milk
2 mangoes
1 nashi pear, quartered
6 lychees or rambutans, halved and
   stones removed
1/2 pawpaw, seeded and cut into wedges
1/2 red papaya, seeded and cut into wedges
2 star fruit, thickly sliced
1 lime, quartered

1 Simmer the lemon grass, ginger, sugar and coconut milk in a small pan over low heat for 5 minutes. Strain and set aside.
2 Cut down both sides of the mangoes close to the stones. Score a crisscross pattern into each half, without cutting through the skin. Fold the outer edges under, pushing the centre up from underneath. Arrange with the rest of the fruit on a platter. Add the lime, for squeezing on the fruit.
3 Serve the coconut dressing on the side as a dipping sauce or drizzle over just before serving.

MELON MEDLEY

Preparation time: 10 minutes + chilling
Total cooking time: Nil
Serves 4

✰

1/2 rockmelon
1/2 honeydew melon
1/4 watermelon
pulp from 2 passionfruit

1 Cut the melons into bite-sized pieces or use a melon baller to cut them into balls. Chill, covered, for 30 minutes. Drizzle with passionfruit.

RED FRUIT SALAD

Preparation time: 10 minutes + soaking
Total cooking time: 5 minutes
Serves 4

✰

250 g (8 oz) strawberries, halved
125 g (4 oz) raspberries
250 g (8 oz) cherries, pitted
1 tablespoon Cointreau
1 tablespoon soft brown sugar

1 Put the fruit in a bowl, drizzle with Cointreau, cover and set aside for 20 minutes.
2 Stir the sugar with 2 tablespoons water in a small pan over gentle heat for 3 minutes, or until dissolved. Cool, pour over the fruit and serve.

STONE FRUITS

Preparation time: 15 minutes
Total cooking time: Nil
Serves 4

✰

4 apricots, halved and thinly sliced
4 peaches, halved and thinly sliced
4 nectarines, halved and thinly sliced
4 plums, halved and thinly sliced
2 tablespoons apricot juice
125 g (4 oz) mascarpone
1 teaspoon soft brown sugar

1 Mix the fruit together and drizzle with apricot juice. Combine the mascarpone and sugar and serve with the fruit salad.

SOFT FRUIT
The simple perfection of nature is impossible to surpass. When in season, a fresh ripe piece of fruit with tangy flesh and sweet juices is one of life's small joys.

APRICOTS
These soft, sweet fruits are available late spring and summer. To ripen, leave in a paper bag at room temperature. Apricots taste good with honey, almonds, vanilla and Amaretto. Delicious raw, they can also be poached, puréed, used in desserts and ice creams or baked in pies and tarts.

CHERRIES
Available briefly in summer, in both sweet and sour varieties, cherries can be preserved in liqueur before use in cooking, or added fresh to baked dishes such as clafoutis. Cherries are perfect with cream cheese, almonds and chocolate and poached cherries can be used in cheesecakes, trifles and tarts, as well as in fillings for pancakes and pastries.

FIGS
Available in summer and autumn, figs vary from green to black. They have a delicate, sweet flesh and a soft skin which may need to be peeled. Versatile, they

can be eaten raw as part of a dessert or baked, poached and grilled. Figs taste good with vanilla, mascarpone, orange and toffee.

GRAPES

Best known for wine making properties, the grape is one of the first cultivated fruits and the world's largest fruit crop. Refrigerate unwashed and rinse before serving. Grapes go with brown sugar, cream and soft cheeses. Usually eaten raw, grapes can be added to fresh fruit mincemeats and tarts and grilled in gratins.

MANGOES

Available in many shapes and colours, ripe mangoes have a wonderful aroma and a rich, sweet delicious flesh. Ripen at room temperature, then store in the vegetable crisper in the refrigerator. They can be puréed to make ice creams and fools or cooked in crumbles and cobblers, and taste good with lime and coconut.

NECTARINES

A member of the peach family, available in summer, nectarines have a smooth skin and are usually redder than peaches. Press gently along the seam to check that they are ripe. Nectarines can be used in a similar way to peaches in cooking.

PEACHES

Available in summer, there are over 2,000 varieties worldwide. Peaches can be broken into two categories: clingstone or slipstone (freestone). They can be poached, baked and grilled and complement almonds, cinnamon, vanilla and ginger. Peaches can be preserved in alcohol. Peach purée makes delicious ice creams and sorbets.

PLUMS

Available in summer and early autumn, plums vary from white, yellow and green to dark purple. Cooking plums have a drier flesh and sharper taste than the sweet, juicy dessert plums. Plums go well with marzipan and almonds, cinnamon, vanilla, nutmeg and red wine. They are traditional in pies, cobblers and cakes and certain varieties are divine poached in red wine.

FROM TOP LEFT: Apricots, nectarines, mangoes, peaches, plums, nectarines, grapes, cherries.
IN FRONT: Figs (left); peaches (in paper).

to the boil and then taken off the heat—make sure the base of the bowl is not touching the water. Serve from the bowl or fondue with marshmallows and fresh fruit.

NOTE: Fruits which work well in fondues include strawberries, pear, cherries and bananas.

WHITE CHOCOLATE FONDUE WITH FRUIT

Preparation time: 30 minutes
Total cooking time: 20 minutes
Serves 6–8

★

1/2 cup (125 ml/4 fl oz) light corn syrup
2/3 cup (170 ml/5 1/2 fl oz) thick (double) cream
1/4 cup (60 ml/2 fl oz) Cointreau
250 g (8 oz) white chocolate, chopped
marshmallows and chopped fresh fruit,
    for serving

1 Combine the corn syrup and cream in a small pan or fondue. Bring to the boil, then remove from the heat.
2 Add the Cointreau and white chocolate and stir until melted. Serve with marshmallows and fresh fruit.

GRILLED APPLE STACK

Preparation time: 10 minutes
Total cooking time: 5–10 minutes
Serves 4

★

3–4 large apples, cores removed
30 g (1 oz) butter
lime marmalade, or any jam
cream, ice cream or custard, for serving

1 Cut the apples into thin slices across the core and place on a lightly greased grill tray. Top each slice with a small piece of butter and 1/2 teaspoon of marmalade.
2 Cook under a hot grill until the butter has melted and the apple is golden brown. Serve 4–5 slices stacked on top of one another with a spoonful of cream, ice cream or custard.
NOTE: It is best to use apples such as Golden Delicious which will not break up too much when cooked.

DARK CHOCOLATE FONDUE WITH FRUIT

Preparation time: 30 minutes
Total cooking time: 20 minutes
Serves 6–8

★

250 g (8 oz) good-quality dark chocolate,
    chopped
1/2 cup (125 ml/4 fl oz) thick (double) cream
marshmallows and chopped fresh fruit,
    for serving

1 Place the chocolate and cream in a fondue or a heatproof bowl and either heat it gently in the fondue, stirring until it is smooth, or place the bowl over a pan of water which has been brought

ABOVE: White chocolate fondue with fruit (top) and dark chocolate fondue with fruit

PAPAYA LIME FOOL

Preparation time: 15 minutes + chilling
Total cooking time: Nil
Serves 4

★

2 red pawpaw or papaya, about 1 kg
1–2 tablespoons lime juice
3 tablespoons vanilla sugar
1¼ cups (315 ml/10 fl oz) cream

1 Peel the pawpaw, remove the seeds and mash the flesh until smooth. Do not do this in a food processor or the fruit will be too runny.
2 Add the lime juice and vanilla sugar, to taste—the amount will vary according to the sweetness of the fruit.
3 Whisk the cream until soft peaks form, then fold through the mashed pawpaw. Spoon into serving glasses and chill until ready to serve.
NOTE: 500 g (1 lb) stewed rhubarb can be substituted for the pawpaw.

MANGO FOOL

Preparation time: 20 minutes + chilling
Total cooking time: Nil
Serves 6

★

3 large mangoes
1 cup (250 ml/8 fl oz) custard
1²/₃ cups (410 ml/13 fl oz) cream

1 Peel and stone the mangoes and purée the flesh in a food processor. Add the custard and blend to combine.
2 Whip the cream until soft peaks form, then gently fold into the mango mixture until just combined—do not overmix as you want to end up with a decorative marbled effect.
3 Pour the mixture into a serving dish or individual glasses. Gently smooth the top or tops, then refrigerate for at least 1 hour before serving.
NOTE: Fresh fruit can be served with fool.

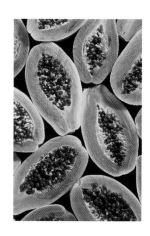

BELOW: Papaya lime fool

SUMMER FRUIT COMPOTE

Preparation time: 40 minutes
Total cooking time: 30 minutes
Serves 8

★

5 apricots, halved

4 nectarines, halved

4 blood plums or other plums, stoned

4 peaches, quartered

200 g (6¹/₂ oz) can pitted cherries

1 cup (250 ml/8 fl oz) good-quality claret

¹/₃ cup (80 ml/2³/₄ fl oz) dry sherry

³/₄ cup (185 g/6 oz) caster sugar

whipped cream, optional, for serving

BELOW: Summer fruit compote

1 Gently plunge the fruit in small batches into boiling water for 30 seconds. Remove with a slotted spoon and place in a bowl of iced water. Peel all the fruit except the cherries.

2 Combine the claret, sherry, sugar and 1 cup (250 ml/8 fl oz) water in a large heavy-based pan. Stir over low heat without boiling until the sugar has dissolved. Bring to the boil, reduce the heat and simmer for 5 minutes.

3 Add the drained fruits to the syrup in small batches and simmer each batch for 5 minutes. Remove with a slotted spoon. Pile the fruit into a bowl. Bring the syrup to the boil, reduce the heat and simmer for another 5 minutes. Remove from the heat and allow to cool slightly—it should be the consistency of a syrup. Pour over the fruit. Serve with a dollop of freshly whipped cream.

NOTE: Blood plum is a generic term covering some Japanese varieties of dark flesh plums such as *satsuma* and *mariposa*. Other plum varieties can be substituted.

This dish can be served hot or cold. It can be stored, covered in the refrigerator, for up to one day. This syrup also works well with a combination of apples, pears and figs, so you can vary the compote, depending on the fruits in season. The fruit will need to be simmered in the syrup until tender.

FIGS WITH ORANGE CREAM AND RAISINS

Preparation time: 20 minutes
  + soaking
Total cooking time: 12 minutes
Serves 8

⭐

250 g (8 oz) raisins

155 ml (5 fl oz) tawny port

1 tablespoon custard powder

1 cup (250 ml/8 fl oz) skim milk

1 tablespoon sugar

100 g (3½ oz) fresh ricotta

200 g (6½ oz) light French vanilla
  frûche or fromage frais

rind and juice of 1 orange

1 teaspoon ground cinnamon

16 fresh figs

1 Soak the raisins in the tawny port for 1 hour or until plumped up.

2 In a small saucepan, blend the custard powder with the milk, add the sugar and stir over low heat until the sugar has dissolved. Increase the heat and stir continuously until the custard boils and thickens. Remove from the heat immediately, pour into a small bowl and cover the surface with plastic wrap. Cool.

3 Transfer the completely cooled custard to the small bowl of an electric mixer, add the fresh ricotta and the frûche and beat until smooth.

4 Just before serving, add the orange rind, juice and cinnamon to the raisin mixture in a small pan and warm over low heat for 2–3 minutes. Cover and keep warm.

5 Starting from the top, cut the figs into quarters, slicing only two-thirds of the way down. Place into ramekins or on a large platter. Place 2 heaped tablespoons of the orange cream into the centre of each fig, top with a tablespoon of the warm raisin mixture and serve at once.

NOTE: Frûche is a type of fromage frais and is set in the cup.

VARIETIES OF FIG
Commercially available figs tend to belong to the common or Adriatic types. They include the *Brown Turkey* which has purple skin and pink flesh and the white *Genoa*, with a greeny-yellow skin and browner flesh.

ABOVE: Figs with orange cream and raisins

STRAWBERRIES ROMANOFF

Preparation time: 20 minutes + chilling
Total cooking time: Nil
Serves 4

☆

750 g (1½ lb) strawberries, quartered
2 tablespoons Cointreau
¼ teaspoon finely grated orange rind
1 tablespoon caster sugar
½ cup (125 ml/4 fl oz) cream
2 tablespoons icing sugar

1 Combine the strawberries, liqueur, rind and the caster sugar in a large bowl, cover and refrigerate for 1 hour. Drain the strawberries, reserving any juices. Purée about one-quarter of the berries with the reserved juices.
2 Divide the remaining berries among four glasses. Beat the cream and icing sugar until soft peaks form, then fold the berry purée through the whipped cream. Spoon the mixture over the top of the strawberries, then cover and refrigerate until required.

COINTREAU GLAZED PEACHES

Preparation time: 10 minutes
Total cooking time: 8 minutes
Serves 6

☆

6 peaches
1–2 tablespoons soft brown sugar
⅓ cup (80 ml/2¾ fl oz) Cointreau
250 g (8 oz) mascarpone
ground nutmeg, to dust

1 Line a grill tray with foil and lightly grease the foil. Preheat the grill to medium. Cut the peaches in half, remove the stones and place the peaches, cut-side-up, on the tray.
2 Sprinkle the peaches with the sugar and Cointreau and grill for 5–8 minutes, or until the peaches are soft and a golden glaze has formed on top.
3 Serve immediately with dollops of mascarpone. Dust lightly with ground nutmeg.

PEACH MELBA

Preparation time: 25 minutes
Total cooking time: 10 minutes
Serves 4

☆

300 g (10 oz) fresh raspberries, or
    frozen, thawed
2 tablespoons icing sugar
1½ cups (375 g/12 oz) sugar
1 vanilla bean, split lengthways
4 firm, ripe peaches
vanilla ice cream, for serving

1 Purée the raspberries and icing sugar together in a food processor. Pass through a strainer and discard the seeds. Stir the sugar, vanilla bean and 2½ cups (600 ml/20 fl oz) water in a pan over low heat until the sugar has completely dissolved.
2 Bring the sugar syrup to the boil and add the peaches, ensuring they are covered with the syrup. Simmer for 5 minutes, or until tender, then remove the peaches with a slotted spoon and carefully remove the skin.
3 Put a scoop of vanilla ice cream on a plate, add a peach, then spoon the purée over the top.

PEARS BELLE HELENE

Preparation time: 15 minutes
Total cooking time: 15 minutes
Serves 6

☆

1½ cups (375 g/12 oz) sugar
2 cinnamon sticks
2 cloves
6 pears, peeled and cored
6 scoops vanilla ice cream
1 cup (250 ml/8 fl oz) dark chocolate sauce
    (see page 204)

1 Combine the sugar, cinnamon and cloves in a large pan with 3 cups (750 ml/24 fl oz) water, stir over low heat until the sugar dissolves, then bring the syrup to the boil. Add the pears and simmer for 10 minutes, or until tender. Remove the pears with a slotted spoon and leave to cool.
2 Put a scoop of ice cream on each plate and make a hollow in each scoop with the back of a spoon. Stand the pears in the hollow and coat with the chocolate sauce.

PEACH MELBA
Created by Escoffier at the Carlton hotel in 1892, Peach Melba consisted of vanilla ice cream with peaches, set between the wings of a swan carved from ice and covered in spun sugar. In 1900, he came up with an easier version of the pudding, in which raspberry sauce is used rather than the swan. Escoffier served the dish to Dame Nellie Melba and asked if he could name his creation after her.

OPPOSITE PAGE:
Strawberries romanoff
(top) and Peach Melba

SUMMER PUDDING

Cut a circle of bread to fit the bottom of the basin and cut the rest of the bread into fingers.

Dip one side of each piece of bread in the fruit juice and fit it, juice-side-down, into the mould, leaving no gaps between each piece.

When filled with fruit, cover the top with a layer of dipped bread and cover with plastic wrap.

SUMMER PUDDING

Preparation time: 30 minutes
  + chilling
Total cooking time: 5 minutes
Serves 4–6

★ ★

150 g (5 oz) blackcurrants
150 g (5 oz) redcurrants
150 g (5 oz) raspberries
150 g (5 oz) blackberries
200 g (6½ oz) strawberries, hulled
  and quartered or halved
caster sugar, to taste
6–8 slices good-quality white bread,
  crusts removed
cream, for serving, optional

1 Put all the berries except the strawberries in a large pan with ½ cup (125 ml/4 fl oz) water and heat gently until the berries begin to collapse.

Add the strawberries and turn off the heat. Add sugar, to taste (how much you need will depend on how ripe the fruit is). Set aside to cool.
2 Line six 150 ml (5 fl oz) moulds or a 1 litre pudding basin with the bread. For the small moulds, use 1 slice of bread for each, cutting a circle to fit the bottom and strips to fit the sides. For the large mould, cut a large circle out of 1 slice for the bottom and cut the rest of the bread into fingers. Drain a little juice off the fruit mixture. Dip one side of each piece of bread in the juice before fitting it, juice-side-down, into the mould, leaving no gaps. Do not squeeze it or flatten it or it will not absorb the juices as well.
3 Fill the centre of the mould with the fruit and add a little juice. Cover the top with a layer of dipped bread, juice-side-up, and cover with plastic wrap. Place a plate which fits inside the dish onto the plastic wrap, then weigh it down. Stack the small ones on top of each other to weigh them down. Refrigerate overnight. Carefully turn out the pudding and serve with any extra mixture and cream.

RIGHT: Summer pudding

STRAWBERRY KISSEL

Preparation time: 15 minutes + chilling
Total cooking time: 10 minutes
Serves 4–6

✷

250 g (8 oz) strawberries, plus extra,
   for serving
1/2 cup (125 g/4 oz) sugar
2 tablespoons arrowroot

1 Wash and clean the strawberries, place in a bowl and pour on the sugar. Refrigerate for a few hours, then process in a food processor or blender and strain through a sieve.
2 Dissolve the arrowroot in 1 1/3 cups (350 ml/ 11 fl oz) water by mixing it with 2 or 3 tablespoons of the water and then adding it to the rest. Place the dissolved arrowroot in a saucepan, bring to the boil, stirring, and add the strawberry purée. Bring to the boil again, stirring constantly, until slightly thickened. Pour into serving dishes to set and serve with extra strawberries.
NOTE: This will not set completely.

MACERATED BERRIES WITH MASCARPONE

Preparation time: 20 minutes + chilling
Total cooking time: 10 minutes
Serves 4–6

✷

125 g (4 oz) blackberries
125 g (4 oz) raspberries
155 g (5 oz) blueberries
125 g (4 oz) loganberries or similar
1–2 tablespoons caster sugar
2 oranges
2 tablespoons sugar
mascarpone, lightly stirred,
   for serving

1 Combine all the berries in a bowl, sprinkle the caster sugar over the top and toss lightly. Cover and refrigerate.
2 Peel the oranges and cut the rind into long, thin strips. Bring a small pan of water to the boil and blanch the orange strips; drain. Repeat this twice more to remove any bitterness from the peel.

3 Combine 1/3 cup (80 ml/2 3/4 fl oz) water with the sugar in a small pan and stir over low heat until the sugar dissolves. Add the orange rind and simmer gently for 1–2 minutes, or until just tender. Cool.
4 Reserve 1 tablespoon of the orange strips and lightly mix the rest with the cooking syrup and berries.
5 To serve, spoon the berry mixture into goblets. Garnish with the mascarpone and reserved orange rind strips.
NOTE: Maceration means to soften fruit and cause it to give out its juice by soaking it in alcohol or sugar.

ABOVE: Strawberry kissel

MAKING JELLY Jellies don't have to be

green and yellow and reminiscent of children's parties. Welcome to grown-up

jellies—sparkling, translucent and tangy with fresh fruit.

Gelatine is best known as a setting agent for jellies, but it is also used in just about any dessert that needs to be moulded or turned out, such as light jellies, creamy bavarois or cheesecakes. Gelatine is available as powder or granules and in clear sheets or leaves. As a rule, 6 sheets of gelatine is equal to 3 teaspoons of powdered gelatine or a 10 g (¼ oz) sachet. This is enough to soft-set 2 cups

(500 ml/16 fl oz) of liquid. Agar-agar, a vegetarian alternative to gelatine, is found in health food shops—use 1 teaspoon agar-agar to set 1 cup (250 ml/8 fl oz) liquid.

Jellies should be firm enough to hold their shape and be turned out without collapsing but, of course, the whole point of a jelly is that it should wobble! If your jelly is too firm to wobble, it may simply be too cold. Jellies become very firm on

chilling and may need to be brought back to room temperature. Gelatine does not freeze well and separates when thawed.

FRUIT JELLIES
Fruit jellies can be made with a variety of fruits. But some fruits just don't work well in jellies—pineapple, papaya, kiwi fruit and figs all contain enzymes which prevent the jelly setting. Fruit juices and

purées can both be set, though juices give clearer, more sparkling jellies.

Cut the fruit into whatever size pieces you think would look best in the jelly. Your spoon should be able to slide through the jelly and cut through the fruit easily, so pieces of fruit which are too big will make it harder to cut and eat if you are making a terrine.

Make up a quantity of jelly using the gelatine as follows. To dissolve powdered gelatine, sprinkle it in an even layer over the surface of a little cold water (about 2 tablespoons) and leave it to become spongy. For it to dissolve properly, it is important that the gelatine lies on top of the water and not underneath. Put a large pan filled with about 4 cm (1¹/₂ inches) water on to boil. When it boils, remove from the heat and carefully lower the gelatine bowl into the water (the water

should come halfway up the side of the bowl). Stir until the gelatine has dissolved, then leave to cool slightly. Leaf gelatine must be soaked in a large bowl of cold water until floppy, then remove it and squeeze out any excess water. It can then be stirred straight into a hot liquid or melted like powdered gelatine. Gelatine sets at 20°C (68°F) so, if you are incorporating melted gelatine into a liquid or purée, make sure it is not too cold or it will form lumps or strings. Leave the jelly to cool.

Rinse out the mould you are using and shake it dry. Make sure the mould is not too big for the jelly or it will be difficult to turn out. Pour a small layer of jelly into the mould and refrigerate until set—this gives a nice shiny surface when the jelly is turned out and ensures the fruit doesn't stick out of the top.

Carefully place the fruit in the mould and pour the rest of the jelly over it. Give the whole thing a sharp tap on the work surface to dislodge any air bubbles, cover and refrigerate until set.

To turn out the jelly, use a wet finger to pull it away from the mould all the way around. Invert onto a plate and give the whole thing a firm shake to break the airlock—you should hear a squelching noise. If this fails, wrap a warm cloth around the mould for a few seconds and try again. If the jelly seems to have melted too much, refrigerate it again until it sets. If you are turning the jelly out onto a plate, remember that unless you wet the plate first, the jelly will stick and you won't be able to move it.

You can, of course, eat jelly out of the dish it is made in. Jellies also look lovely set in wine or champagne glasses.

GELATINE

Before the invention of commercial, unflavoured gelatine in 1889, using gelatine was rather a palaver. Beef or veal bones, or calves' feet, had to be boiled and the resulting liquid strained and clarified before use. Despite its ease of use now, gelatine still holds a certain mystique, unless it comes in the form of a packet of jelly. It is, however, very easy to use. Six sheets of gelatine is the same as 3 teaspoons of powder or a 10 g sachet, all of which will set 500 ml of liquid. If you have a disaster with your jelly and it either sets too solid, has chewy strings through it, or tastes bland, chop it up with a wet knife and fold whipped cream through it— the addition of a liqueur will cover any strong gelatine taste.

OPPOSITE PAGE, FROM TOP: Blackberry jelly; Striped fruit jelly; Orange jellies.

STRIPED FRUIT JELLY

Preparation time: 35 minutes + chilling
Total cooking time: 30 minutes
Serves 6–8

★ ★ ★

200 g (6½ oz) caster sugar
rind and juice of 2 limes
6 teaspoons gelatine
¼ cup (125 ml/4 fl oz) thick (double) cream
1 tablespoon caster sugar, extra
½ cup (125 g/4 oz) natural yoghurt
400 g (13 oz) can pitted cherries, drained and syrup reserved

1 Stir the sugar with 1¼ cups (315 ml/10 fl oz) water in a pan over low heat until the sugar dissolves. Bring slowly to the boil. Simmer for 15 minutes, then remove from the heat. You should have 200 ml (6½ fl oz) liquid—tip half into a jug and reserve. Return the pan to the heat, add the lime rind and juice and cook very gently for 5 minutes. Strain into a bowl. Discard the rind. Put 2 tablespoons water in a small bowl, sprinkle 2 teaspoons gelatine over the surface in an even layer and leave to go spongy. Put a large pan filled with about 4 cm (1½ inches) water on to boil. When it boils, remove from the heat and carefully lower the gelatine bowl into the water (it should come halfway up the side of the bowl), then stir until dissolved. Cool slightly, then add to the lime syrup. Rinse a 3 cup (750 ml/24 fl oz) mould. Pour in the lime syrup and chill until set. Don't leave too long or the next layer won't stick.
2 Place 2 tablespoons water in a small bowl, sprinkle on 2 teaspoons gelatine and leave to go spongy. Put the cream and extra sugar in a small pan and heat slowly, stirring until the sugar is dissolved. Add to the gelatine mixture and stir until dissolved. Whisk in the yoghurt. Cover and cool in the refrigerator (be careful not to leave it too long or it will set). Pour carefully onto the lime layer, then refrigerate until set.
3 Place 2 tablespoons of the cherry liquid in a small bowl, sprinkle on 2 teaspoons gelatine, leave to go spongy, then add to the remaining sugar syrup, which should still be warm. Add to this another 150 ml (5 fl oz) cherry juice, stir to dissolve, cover and cool.
4 When the yoghurt layer has set, spoon in the cherries and pour the cherry juice over them. Chill until set. To unmould, gently pull the jelly away from the sides of the mould with wet fingers and invert onto a plate, shaking to loosen.

BLACKBERRY JELLY

Preparation time: 10 minutes + chilling
Total cooking time: 20 minutes
Serves 6–8

★

300 g (10 oz) fresh blackberries or frozen, thawed
¾ cup (185 g/6 oz) caster sugar
¼ cup (60 ml/2 fl oz) vodka, optional
3 tablespoons gelatine

1 Place the blackberries with any residual juice, caster sugar, vodka and 1 litre water in a pan. Stir over low heat until the sugar has dissolved. Cover and bring to the boil, reduce the heat and simmer gently for 15 minutes. Uncover and cool for 10 minutes.
2 Place the fruit in a muslin-lined sieve and strain into a bowl without pushing any fruit through. Put a little of the juice in a small pan, sprinkle the gelatine in an even layer over the surface, leave to go spongy, then stir over low heat until dissolved. Do not boil. Combine with the remaining juice.
3 Wet a 1.25 litre jelly mould and pour in the jelly mixture. Refrigerate for 4 hours, or until set.

ORANGE JELLIES

Preparation time: 10 minutes + chilling
Total cooking time: 5 minutes
Serves 6

★

3 cups (750 ml/24 fl oz) orange juice
6 teaspoons gelatine
1 tablespoon Grand Marnier, optional

1 Pour ½ cup (125 ml/4 fl oz) of the juice into a small heatproof bowl, sprinkle the gelatine in an even layer over the surface and leave to go spongy. Put a large pan filled with about 4 cm (1½ inches) water on to boil. When it boils, remove from the heat and lower the gelatine bowl into the water (it should come halfway up the side of the bowl), then stir until dissolved. Cool slightly. Stir into the rest of the juice.
2 Strain the liquid and stir in the liqueur. Wet six 125 ml (4 fl oz) moulds and place on a tray. Fill with the jelly mixture and refrigerate for 4 hours, or until set.

BERRY TERRINE

Put the sheets of gelatine in a bowl of cold water and leave until floppy.

Remove the gelatine when floppy and squeeze out any excess water.

Add the gelatine to the hot sugar syrup and stir until thoroughly dissolved.

Spread the fruit across the top of the set layer of jelly, then pour in more jelly, up to the top of the fruit.

ABOVE: Champagne berry terrine

CHAMPAGNE BERRY TERRINE

Preparation time: 15 minutes + cooling + chilling
Total cooking time: 5 minutes
Serves 4–6

★ ★

75 g (2¹/₂ oz) caster sugar
rind of 1 orange
3 teaspoons or 6 sheets gelatine
2¹/₂ cups (600 ml/20 fl oz) pink Champagne
300 g (10 oz) mixed berries, fresh or frozen

1 Put the sugar and orange rind in a pan with 1¹/₃ cups (350 ml/11 fl oz) water. Bring to the boil, stirring over low heat until the sugar dissolves. When dissolved, remove the pan from the heat and leave to cool for 1 hour.
2 Strain the rind out of the syrup. Put about ¹/₄ cup (60 ml/2 fl oz) syrup in a small heatproof bowl, sprinkle the gelatine in an even layer over the top and leave to go spongy. Put a large pan filled with about 4 cm (1¹/₂ inches) water on to boil. When it boils, remove from the heat and carefully lower the gelatine bowl into the water (it should come halfway up the side of the bowl), then stir until dissolved. If you want to use sheets of gelatine, follow the steps shown. Cool slightly, add to the rest of the syrup and mix. Add the Champagne, then pour a little of the jelly into the base of a 1.25 litre loaf tin and refrigerate to set. Do not leave too long or the next layer will not stick.
3 Arrange the fruit in the tin, pour in a little more jelly up to the top of the fruit, set in the refrigerator, then pour the rest of the jelly in and set completely. Setting in layers will ensure a smooth surface on top and stop the fruit floating.
4 When you are ready to serve, unmould by wiping the tin with a cloth dipped in hot water and inverting the terrine onto a plate. Bring the terrine to room temperature before serving. It should not be stiff and should sag very slightly. Can be served with cream or ice cream.

GRAPES

The world's largest fruit crop, grapes are available in many varieties. These include *Muscat*, both white and black, *Flame*, a seedless red grape, *Sultana*, the most widely available variety, and *Waltham Cross*, with large gold-green oval berries. Grapes should be fully ripe before being picked as they do not sweeten with age. They should not be stored damp as they may go mouldy. They are best refrigerated and should be eaten shortly after purchase.

RED WINE JELLY WITH FROSTED FRUITS

Preparation time: 20 minutes + chilling
Total cooking time: 5 minutes
Serves 4

★ ★

2¹/2 cups (600 ml/20 fl oz) good-quality
   red wine
rind of 1 lemon
rind and juice of 1 orange
2 cinnamon sticks
¹/2 cup (125 g/4 oz) caster sugar
5 teaspoons gelatine
1 egg white
caster sugar, for frosting
200 g (6¹/2 oz) blackcurrants and redcurrants
   or mixed seedless grapes

1 Combine the wine, rinds, cinnamon and sugar in a small pan. Heat gently until the sugar has dissolved. Put the orange juice in a small heatproof bowl, sprinkle the gelatine in an even layer over the surface and leave it to go spongy. Put a large pan filled with about 4 cm (1¹/2 inches) water on to boil. When it boils, remove from the heat and carefully lower the gelatine bowl into the water (it should come halfway up the side of the bowl), then stir until dissolved. Cool slightly.
2 Stir the gelatine into the wine mixture. Pour through a muslin-lined strainer into a wetted 1.5 litre mould. Refrigerate until set (about 3 hours).
3 Whisk the egg white lightly in a bowl. Put the caster sugar in another bowl. Dip the fruit first into the egg, then into the caster sugar, shaking off the excess. Leave to dry on non-stick paper. Turn out the jelly and serve with the frosted fruit.

ABOVE: Red wine jelly with frosted fruits

PANCAKES

There is something rather special about pouring the batter into the sizzling pan, tilting and tipping, then flipping it high into the air to reveal the crispy, golden underside. The best thing about pancakes is that they're fun. Fun to make, fun to toss and fun to eat; whether it's just with a squeeze of fresh lemon and sprinkling of sugar, or drizzled with a rich liqueur sauce. Pancakes are a universal treat and we've included all our favourites from the extended family... from delicate lacy crêpes suzette to chunky chocolate waffles; creamy ricotta-filled blintzes and even crunchy golden-fried fruit fritters.

CREPES SUZETTE

Cook the first side of the crepe until the edges just begin to curl.

Add the crepes to the pan one at a time, folding each finished one into quarters and pushing to one side.

ABOVE: Crepes with sugar, lemon and cream

CREPES WITH SUGAR, LEMON AND CREAM

Preparation time: 10 minutes + standing
Total cooking time: 25 minutes
Makes about 14 crepes

★ ★

1 cup (125 g/4 oz) plain flour
1 egg
1¼ cups (315 ml/10 fl oz) milk
30 g (1 oz) unsalted butter, melted
sugar, lemon juice and thick (double) cream,
    for serving

1 Sift the flour and a pinch of salt into a large bowl and make a well in the centre. Gradually whisk in the combined egg and milk until the batter is smooth and free of lumps. Cover and set aside for 30 minutes.
2 Transfer the batter to a jug for easy pouring. Heat a small crepe or non-stick frying pan and brush lightly with melted butter. Pour a little batter into the pan, swirling to thinly cover the base, and pour any excess back into the jug. If the batter is too thick, add 2–3 teaspoons milk. Cook for about 20 seconds, or until the edges just begin to curl, then toss or turn over and lightly brown the other side. Transfer to a plate and cover with a tea towel while cooking the

remaining batter, greasing the pan when necessary. Stack the crepes between greaseproof paper to prevent them sticking together.
3 Sprinkle the crepes with sugar and a little lemon juice and fold into quarters. Put two or three on each plate and top with cream.

CREPES SUZETTE

Preparation time: 10 minutes + standing
Total cooking time: 45 minutes
Serves 4–6

★ ★

Crepes

2 cups (250 g/8 oz) plain flour
3 eggs, lightly beaten
200 ml (6½ fl oz) milk
50 g (1¾ oz) unsalted butter, melted

125 g (4 oz) unsalted butter
½ cup (125 g/4 oz) caster sugar
grated rind of 1 orange
¾ cup (185 ml/6 fl oz) orange juice
3 tablespoons orange liqueur
2 tablespoons brandy
rind of 1 orange, cut into
    thin strips

1 To make the crepes, sift the flour into a large bowl and make a well in the centre. Gradually whisk in the beaten egg, drawing the flour in from the edges. As the mixture becomes thicker, add the milk combined with 1 cup (250 ml/8 fl oz) water and whisk until smooth and free of lumps. Pour in the melted butter and stir to combine. Transfer to a jug for easy pouring, cover and set aside for 30 minutes.

2 Heat a 20 cm (8 inch) crepe pan or non-stick frying pan and brush lightly with melted butter. Pour in a little batter, swirling to thinly cover the base, and pour any excess back into the jug. Cook until the edges just begin to curl, then turn and brown the other side. Transfer to a plate and cover with a tea towel while cooking the remaining batter, greasing the pan when necessary. Stack the crepes between greaseproof paper to prevent them sticking together.

3 Put the butter, sugar, orange rind, juice and liqueur in a large frying pan and simmer for 2 minutes. Add the crepes one at a time to the pan, adding each one flat and then folding into quarters and pushing to one side.

4 Pour the brandy over the crepes and with care, ignite the crepes, either with a gas flame or a match. (Keep a lid large enough to cover the pan beside you in case you need to smother the flame.) Serve on warmed plates with the orange rind scattered over the top.

LEMON SYRUP PEARS WITH PANCAKES

Preparation time: 40 minutes + standing
Total cooking time: 1 hour 10 minutes
Serves 6

★ ★

1 cup (125 g/4 oz) plain flour
2/3 cup (85 g/3 oz) self-raising flour
2 tablespoons caster sugar
3 eggs, lightly beaten
1 1/2 cups (375 ml/12 fl oz) milk
60 g (2 oz) unsalted butter, melted

Lemon syrup pears

5 firm pears such as beurre bosc
1 lemon
3/4 cup (185 g/6 oz) caster sugar
2 tablespoons honey
1/2 cup (125 ml/4 fl oz) lemon juice
1 cup (250 g/8 oz) sour cream

1 Sift the flours into a large bowl, add the sugar, make a well and whisk in the combined eggs, milk and butter. Beat until smooth, then set aside for 30 minutes.

2 To make the lemon syrup pears, peel, halve and core the pears, then cut into wedges. Peel the lemon and cut the rind into thin strips. Combine the sugar, honey and 1 1/2 cups (375 ml/12 fl oz) water in a pan, stirring over low heat until the sugar dissolves. Add the lemon juice, bring to the boil, reduce the heat and simmer for 8 minutes. Skim any froth, add the pears and simmer for another 5 minutes, or until just tender. Remove from the heat, stir in the lemon rind and leave to cool slightly.

3 Pour 1/4 cup (60 ml/2 fl oz) pancake batter into a lightly greased 20 cm (8 inch) non-stick frying pan and cook over medium heat for 2 minutes each side. Continue with the rest of the batter, greasing the pan when necessary. Stack between greaseproof paper to prevent them sticking together. Strain 1/2 cup (125 ml/4 fl oz) of the lemon syrup and mix with the sour cream to make a sauce for the pancakes. Strain the pears to serve. Decorate with strips of rind.
NOTE: Poached pears can be left in the syrup, covered in the refrigerator, for up to two days to allow the flavours to develop. Reheat to serve.

BELOW: Lemon syrup pears with pancakes

COCONUT PANCAKES WITH PALM SUGAR SYRUP

Preparation time: 40 minutes
+ standing
Total cooking time: 45 minutes
Makes about 12 crepes

✶ ✶

Shredded coconut filling

185 g (6 oz) palm sugar, roughly chopped
2 cups (120 g/4 oz) shredded coconut
1/2 cup (125 ml/4 fl oz) coconut cream

1 cup (125 g/4 oz) plain flour
1 egg
1 cup (250 ml/8 fl oz) coconut cream
mango and pineapple slices, for serving

BELOW: Coconut pancakes with palm sugar syrup

1 To make the shredded coconut filling, stir the sugar with 1 1/2 cups (375 ml/12 fl oz) water in a small heavy-based pan over low heat until the sugar has dissolved, then simmer for 15 minutes to make a syrup. Place the coconut in a bowl with 2/3 cup (170 ml/5 1/2 fl oz) of the syrup and the coconut cream and stir to combine. Return the pan with the remaining palm sugar syrup to the heat and simmer for 15 minutes, or until reduced to a thick, sticky syrup.

2 Mix the flour, egg, coconut cream and 1/2 cup (125 ml/4 fl oz) water until smooth and free of lumps. Transfer to a jug for easy pouring, cover and set aside for 30 minutes.

3 Heat a small crepe or non-stick frying pan and brush lightly with melted butter. Pour a little batter into the pan, swirling, to thinly cover the base, then pour off any excess. Cook for about 20 seconds, or until the edges just begin to curl, then turn over and cook the other side. Transfer to a plate and cover with a tea towel while cooking the remaining batter, greasing the pan when necessary. Stack the crepes between greaseproof paper to prevent them sticking together.

4 Place 1 tablespoon of shredded coconut filling in the centre of each crepe. Roll each crepe up firmly, folding in the edges to form a parcel. Serve with sliced fresh mango and pineapple and drizzle with the remaining palm sugar syrup.

HINTS AND TIPS

CREPE PANS

The classic French *pôele* or crepe pan is the best pan for the job. It is available in several sizes and is inexpensive to buy. You will not need to wash it after use—just wipe it clean with a damp cloth. Non-stick pans also work well but tend not to brown the crepes as well. Season your pan by heating vegetable oil and coarse salt until smoking, and then wiping it out.

MAKING CREPES

Whisk the liquid into the flour, rather than beating it in with a spoon. If you do this, the batter will amalgamate more quickly with less lumps. Beating out lumps with a spoon will develop the gluten in the flour and result in a tough batter.

Prepare crepe batter in advance and allow to stand before cooking. This makes the batter lighter by letting the starch in the flour expand and the gluten relax.

The first crepe is often a disaster so don't despair, just throw it away. Adjust the batter if it is too thick by adding a little water until you have right consistency. Be careful as it is much easier to thin batter than thicken it.

RICOTTA CREPES
WITH ORANGE SAUCE

Preparation time: 40 minutes + standing + soaking
Total cooking time: 30 minutes
Serves 4

★ ☆

²/₃ cup (85 g/3 oz) plain flour
pinch of salt
1 egg, lightly beaten
1¹/₃ cups (350 ml/11 fl oz) milk
30 g (1 oz) sultanas
1 cup (250 ml/8 fl oz) orange juice
200 g (6¹/₂ oz) ricotta
1 teaspoon finely grated orange rind
¹/₄ teaspoon vanilla essence

Orange sauce

50 g (1³/₄ oz) unsalted butter
¹/₄ cup (60 g/2 oz) caster sugar

1 Sift the flour and salt into a bowl. Make a well and gradually whisk in the combined egg and milk until the batter is smooth and free of lumps. Cover and set aside for 30 minutes. Transfer the batter to a jug for easy pouring.

2 Heat a small crepe or non-stick frying pan and brush lightly with melted butter. Pour a little batter into the pan, swirling to make a 16 cm (6¹/₂ inch) round. Pour any excess back into the jug. Cook over medium heat for 1–2 minutes, or until the underside is golden. Turn and cook the other side for 30 seconds, or until the edges just begin to curl. Transfer to a plate and repeat with the remaining batter, greasing the pan when necessary. Stack the crepes between greaseproof paper to prevent them sticking together. Preheat the oven to warm 160°C (315°F/Gas 2–3).

3 Put the sultanas in a bowl, cover with orange juice and soak for 15 minutes. Drain, reserving the juice. Mix together the ricotta, rind, essence and sultanas. Place a large tablespoon of mixture at the edge of each crepe, fold in half and then half again. Put the filled crepes in an ovenproof dish and bake for 10 minutes.

4 To make the orange sauce, melt the butter and sugar in a small pan over low heat. Add the reserved juice and stir over low heat until the sugar dissolves. Bring to the boil, reduce the heat and simmer for 10 minutes to thicken. Cool for 3–4 minutes, then pour over the filled crepes. Serve at once. Delicious with poached orange segments.

NOTE: Crepes can be cooked in advance and frozen. Defrost, fill and heat close to serving time.

ABOVE: Ricotta crepes with orange sauce

MACADAMIA NUTS

Macadamia nuts, an Australian indigenous food, are grown commercially. Macadamia trees were also exported to Hawaii as shade trees and the nuts are known in America as Hawaiian nuts. They were part of the Aboriginal diet for thousands of years and have a very high protein content. They are spherical, waxy, creamy-flavoured nuts within a very hard shell which has to be cracked with special equipment. Roasting them brings out the flavour. In Hawaii, macadamia nuts are used in everything from confectionery to biscuits, cakes and jams.

ABOVE: Deep-fried fruit with golden nut sauce

DEEP-FRIED FRUIT WITH GOLDEN NUT SAUCE

Preparation time: 55 minutes + chilling
Total cooking time: 30 minutes
Serves 6

★ ★

1³/4 cups (215 g/7 oz) plain flour, sifted

2¹/2 teaspoons baking powder

2 tablespoons oil

2 tablespoons caster sugar

2 eggs, separated

oil, for deep-frying

800 g (1 lb 10 oz) fresh fruit, such as pitted cherries, pineapple pieces, banana pieces, apple wedges and pear wedges

ice cream or cream, for serving

Golden nut sauce

125 g (4 oz) unsalted butter

1¹/4 cups (230 g/7¹/2 oz) soft brown sugar

¹/2 cup (125 ml/4 fl oz) thick (double) cream

2 teaspoons lemon juice

2 tablespoons chopped roasted macadamias

1 Sift the flour and baking powder into a large bowl and make a well in the centre. Add the oil, sugar, egg yolks and 1 cup (250 ml/8 fl oz) warm water. Whisk until smooth, cover and refrigerate for 2 hours. (You will add the egg white later.)

2 To make the golden nut sauce, melt the butter in a small pan over low heat. Add the sugar and stir until dissolved. Add the cream and lemon juice. Bring to the boil, stirring. Add the nuts and keep warm.

3 Whisk the egg whites until stiff peaks form and fold into the batter. Heat the oil in a large heavy-based pan or deep-fryer to 180°C (350°F), or until a cube of bread will brown in 15 seconds. Turn the heat down. Dip the fruit in the batter, shaking off any excess. Deep-fry in small batches, draining on paper towels. Serve immediately, drizzled with the golden nut sauce. Serve with ice cream or cream.

NOTE: It is very important to deep-fry safely. Keep a saucepan lid nearby to smother any flames, if necessary, and be very careful your oil does not overheat.

DATE PANCAKES WITH CARAMEL SAUCE

Preparation time: 40 minutes
  + standing
Total cooking time: 30 minutes
Makes 10–12 pancakes

✶

185 g (6 oz) pitted dates, chopped
1 teaspoon bicarbonate of soda
2 cups (250 g/8 oz) self-raising flour,
  sifted
1/2 cup (95 g/3 oz) soft brown sugar
1 cup (250 g/8 oz) sour cream
3 eggs, separated
ice cream, for serving

Caramel sauce

1 cup (185 g/6 oz) soft brown sugar
1 cup (250 ml/8 fl oz) cream
200 g (61/2 oz) unsalted butter

1 Put the dates with 1 cup (250 ml/8 fl oz) water in a small pan and bring to the boil. Remove from the heat, stir in the bicarbonate of soda and cool for 5 minutes. Purée in a food processor until smooth. Cool.

2 Mix the flour and sugar in a large bowl. Stir in the date purée and make a well in the centre.

3 Whisk the sour cream and egg yolks together and pour into the well, stirring until the batter is just smooth. Set aside for 15 minutes. Beat the egg whites in a clean, dry bowl until soft peaks form. Stir a heaped tablespoon of egg white into the batter to loosen it, then fold in the remainder until just combined.

4 Heat a frying pan and brush lightly with melted butter or oil. Pour 1/4 cup (60 ml/2 fl oz) batter into the pan. Cook for 2–3 minutes, or until bubbles form on the surface. Turn over and cook the other side. Transfer to a plate and cover with a tea towel while cooking the remaining batter. Grease the pan when necessary. Stack the pancakes between greaseproof paper to prevent them sticking together.

5 To make the sauce, stir all the ingredients in a pan over medium heat, without boiling, until dissolved, then simmer gently for 3–4 minutes. Serve over the pancakes, with ice cream.

DATES

Dates have been an important part of the diet of Arab, Middle Eastern and North African countries for thousands of years. They are always used to break the daily fast during Ramadan. Fresh dates are often frozen when they are imported. Their high sugar content makes them easy to freeze and defrost. They are best eaten at room temperature and do not usually need to be refrigerated. Semi-dried dates have a darker skin than fresh dates, and have a more concentrated sweetness, making them excellent in baked goods and desserts. Choose plump, soft dates when buying. There are many varieties and they are used in desserts such as baked puddings and fruit salads.

ABOVE: Date pancakes with caramel sauce

1 Toast the hazelnuts under a low grill, watching them carefully to ensure they don't burn, then rub off the skins with a tea towel. Roughly chop a third of the nuts, set aside and put the remaining nuts on an oiled baking tray. To make the praline, put 1/3 cup (90 g/3 oz) sugar with 2 tablespoons water in a heavy-based pan. Stir over low heat, without boiling, until the sugar has completely dissolved. Do not boil until the sugar has dissolved or it will crystallize. Bring to the boil and cook without stirring, until golden brown. If the caramel darkens in patches, swirl the pan until you have an even colour. Dip a pastry brush in cold water and brush down the side of the pan if crystals start to form. Be very careful at this stage as the caramel can cause burns. Quickly pour the caramel over the whole nuts and allow to set. (The heat of the caramel will cause the tray to become very hot.) Finely chop the praline in a food processor or crush it with a rolling pin or in a mortar and pestle.

2 Beat the unsalted butter and remaining sugar with electric beaters until creamy. Stir in two-thirds of the praline, cover and keep cool.

3 Sift the flour into a large bowl and make a well in the centre. Gradually whisk in the combined egg, egg yolk and milk until the batter is smooth and free of lumps. Transfer to a jug for easy pouring, cover and set aside for 30 minutes. Heat a medium crepe pan or non-stick frying pan and brush with melted butter. Pour 1/4 cup (60 ml/2 fl oz) batter into the pan, swirling to cover the base. Pour any excess batter back into the jug. Cook for 30 seconds, or until the edges just begin to curl, then turn and cook the other side. Transfer to a plate and cover with a tea towel. Repeat with the remaining batter, greasing the pan when necessary. Stack the crepes between greaseproof paper to prevent them sticking together.

4 Preheat the oven to warm 160°C (315°F/ Gas 2–3). Spread each crepe with a tablespoon of the praline butter. Roll up into cigar shapes and place in a greased ovenproof dish in a single layer. Bake for 10 minutes, or until warm.

5 Meanwhile, heat the chocolate and the remaining butter in a heatproof bowl over a pan of simmering water. When it has melted, add the icing sugar, sour cream and liqueur. Stir the mixture until smooth and glossy.

6 To serve, sprinkle the crepes with the chopped hazelnuts and the remaining praline. Serve with warm chocolate sauce and ice cream.
NOTE: The praline can be made a day in advance and stored in an airtight jar in the refrigerator. It may become sticky but will still have the same flavour.

HAZELNUT PRALINE CREPES WITH CHOCOLATE SAUCE

Preparation time: I hour + standing
Total cooking time: 45 minutes
Makes about 10 crepes

★ ★

100 g (3 1/2 oz) hazelnuts
1/3 cup (90 g/3 oz) caster sugar, plus
   2 tablespoons
90 g (3 oz) unsalted butter, at room
   temperature
I cup (125 g/4 oz) plain flour
I egg, plus I egg yolk
1 1/4 cups (315 ml/10 fl oz) milk
125 g (4 oz) dark chocolate, chopped
50 g (1 3/4 oz) unsalted butter
2 tablespoons sifted icing sugar
1/2 cup (125 g/4 oz) sour cream
2 tablespoons Kahlua or Tia Maria
ice cream, for serving

ABOVE: Hazelnut praline crepes with chocolate sauce

STRAWBERRY RICOTTA CREPES WITH ORANGE LIQUEUR SAUCE

Preparation time: 40 minutes
 + standing
Total cooking time: 30 minutes
Makes about 12 crepes

★★

3/4 cup (90 g/3 oz) plain flour
1 egg, plus 1 egg yolk
3/4 cup (185 ml/6 fl oz) milk
20 g (3/4 oz) unsalted butter, melted
fresh berries, for serving

Ricotta cream filling

350 g (11 oz) ricotta
1/4 cup (60 ml/2 fl oz) cream
1 tablespoon caster sugar
1 teaspoon vanilla essence
300 g (10 oz) strawberries, sliced

Orange liqueur sauce

1/2 teaspoon grated orange rind
3/4 cup (185 ml/6 fl oz) fresh orange juice
2 tablespoons caster sugar
2 tablespoons Grand Marnier or Cointreau
1 tablespoon cornflour
30 g (1 oz) unsalted butter

1 Sift the flour into a large bowl and make a well in the centre. Gradually whisk in the combined egg, egg yolk and milk until the batter is smooth and free of lumps. Mix in the melted butter and transfer the batter to a jug for easy pouring. Cover and set aside for 30 minutes.

2 To make the ricotta cream filling, beat together the ricotta, cream, sugar and vanilla essence until smooth. Fold in the strawberries, cover and refrigerate.

3 To make the orange liqueur sauce, place the orange rind, juice, sugar and liqueur in a small pan. Mix the cornflour with 3 tablespoons water in a small bowl until smooth, add to the pan and stir over low heat for 3–4 minutes, or until the mixture boils and thickens. Add the butter and stir for another minute. Cover and set aside.

4 Heat a small crepe pan or non-stick frying pan and brush lightly with melted butter. Pour a little batter into the pan, swirling, to thinly coat the base. Pour any excess batter back into the jug. If the batter is too thick, add a little more milk. Cook for about 30 seconds, or until the edges just begin to curl, then turn and cook the other side until lightly browned. Transfer to a plate and cover with a tea towel. Repeat with the remaining batter, greasing the pan when necessary. Stack the crepes between greaseproof paper to prevent them sticking together.

5 Place a crepe on a serving plate and spread evenly with filling. Fold the crepe in half, then in half again. Pour the sauce over the top and scatter with berries. Do the same with the remaining crepes.

NOTE: The crepes can be made ahead of time and frozen until needed. Wrap in foil and reheat in a moderate 180°C (350°F/Gas 4) oven before use.

BELOW: Strawberry ricotta crepes with orange liqueur sauce

SUGAR

From the natural soft brown sugars with a lingering taste of sugar cane, to the pure white crystals that give us instant energy, sugar is the sweetest substance known to man.

Worldwide, sugar is produced from sugar cane, sugar beet, palm trees, maple trees and sorghum. Sugar is sucrose, a pure carbohydrate which adds sweetness to dishes, and is either white or brown, refined or unrefined. It is a natural preservative, caramelizes on heating and is used to stabilize egg whites to produce meringue. Sugar cane is harvested and crushed to extract its juice. The juice is purified and any excess water evaporated off to leave a type of molasses. This is 'seeded' with sugar crystals—the crystals are planted in the molasses to grow into bigger crystals. When they reach the required size the crystals are extracted from the molasses. At this stage, they are golden brown and contain some molasses and impurities. Unrefined sugar is only part-purified and contains some molasses.

Refined sugar has all impurities removed and is separated from its molasses.

WHITE SUGAR is bleached in the refining process. It is graded or granulated refined sugar which has no colour or flavour except for sweetness. It is used for caramel, in beverages and in making cakes, puddings, biscuits and jams. It is what to use when a recipe requires 'sugar'.

CASTER SUGAR is white sugar with very small crystals, which dissolves easily and has no colour and flavour other than sweetness. It is used in meringues and baking, and in America is often used instead of granulated sugar.

ICING SUGAR is white sugar crushed to a fine powder. Pure icing sugar has no additives and dissolves easily. Icing sugar mixture contains starch to prevent lumps.

MUSCOVADO SUGAR (dark and light) has small crystals and a rich flavour. Light muscovado is fudge-like, dark is richer. Both contain molasses which coats each crystal, making it a moist soft sugar.

RAW SUGAR is a natural, golden sugar with a distinctive raw flavour. It can be used in the same way as white sugar.

SOFT BROWN SUGAR has a caramel flavour and a light or dark coloured fine grain.

DARK BROWN SUGAR is a richer, moister sugar with a molasses flavour.

SUGAR CUBES are granulated sugar compressed into cubes.

COFFEE SUGAR has large crunchy, golden crystals. Sprinkle on crumble as topping.

GOLDEN DEMERARA has a rich caramel taste, is less refined than white sugars and contains a little molasses.

MOLASSES SUGAR is almost black and has a strong flavour which adds richness.

PALM SUGAR (jaggery) is made from the boiled sap of palm trees. It has a fine

texture and is usually sold in jars or set into solid lumps which must be grated or crushed before use. It has a fudgy flavour and is slightly less sweet than cane sugar.

GOLDEN SYRUP is a golden liquid containing sucrose, glucose and fructose that is manufactured from the syrup left after white sugar is extracted.

TREACLE is produced in the same way as golden syrup but with its original colour and a strong flavour. It adds colour and rich flavour to puddings and cakes.

CLOCKWISE, FROM TOP LEFT: White sugar, caster sugar, icing sugar, light muscovado, dark muscovado, coffee sugar, molasses sugar, golden syrup, treacle, palm sugar, golden demerara, raw sugar, soft brown sugar, white sugar, sugar cubes

BANANA FRITTERS WITH CARAMEL SAUCE

Preparation time: 10 minutes
Total cooking time: 15 minutes
Serves 4

★ ★

Caramel sauce

1¼ cups (230 g/7½ oz) soft brown sugar
½ cup (125 ml/4 fl oz) cream
100 g (3½ oz) unsalted butter, chopped

1 cup (125 g/4 oz) self-raising flour
1 egg, beaten
¾ cup (185 ml/6 fl oz) soda water
oil, for deep-frying
4 bananas, each cut into quarters
ice cream, for serving

BELOW: Banana fritters with caramel sauce

1 To make the caramel sauce, combine all the ingredients in a small pan and stir until the sugar has dissolved and the butter has melted. Bring to the boil, reduce the heat and simmer for 2 minutes.

2 Sift the flour into a bowl. Make a well in the centre and add the egg and soda water all at once. Stir until all the liquid is incorporated and the batter is free of lumps.

3 Heat the oil in a deep heavy-based pan, to 180°C (350°F), or until a cube of bread browns in 15 seconds. Dip the bananas in batter a few pieces at a time, then drain off any excess batter. Gently lower the bananas into the oil and cook for 2 minutes, or until golden, crisp and warmed through. Carefully remove from the oil with a slotted spoon. Drain on paper towels and keep warm. Repeat with the remaining bananas. Serve the fritters immediately with ice cream and caramel sauce.

CREPE RIBBONS WITH ZESTY LEMON SAUCE

Preparation time: 40 minutes
  + standing
Total cooking time: 30–40 minutes
Serves 4–6

★ ★

1¼ cups (155 g/5 oz) plain flour
pinch of salt
3 eggs, beaten
2 cups (500 ml/16 fl oz) milk
20 g (¾ oz) unsalted butter, melted
oil, for shallow-frying
icing sugar, to dust

Zesty lemon sauce

½ cup (125 ml/4 fl oz) lemon juice
1 tablespoon grated lemon rind
80 g (2¾ oz) unsalted butter
½ cup (125 g/4 oz) caster sugar

1 Sift the flour and salt into a large bowl and make a well in the centre. Gradually whisk in the combined egg and milk until smooth and free of lumps. Stir in the melted butter and transfer the batter to a jug for easy pouring, cover and leave to stand for 30 minutes.

2 Heat a small crepe or non-stick frying pan and brush lightly with melted butter. Pour a little batter into the pan, swirling to thinly cover the base, then pour any excess back into the jug. Cook gently for 20 seconds, or until the edges just begin to curl, then turn over and cook the other side. Transfer to a plate and cover with a tea towel. Continue until all the batter is used, greasing the pan when necessary.

3 To make the zesty lemon sauce, combine the lemon juice, rind, butter and sugar in a small pan. Bring to the boil, reduce the heat and simmer until the liquid becomes syrupy. Keep warm until ready to serve.

4 Cut the cold crepes into ribbons about 2 cm (3/4 inch) wide. Heat the oil in a large frying pan and cook the ribbons in batches until crisp. Drain on paper towels. Pile up the ribbons onto individual serving plates, pour the sauce over and dust with icing sugar. Delicious served with fruit and cream.

NOTE: Crepes and sauce can both be made in advance. Fry the ribbons just before serving.

BANANA AND COCONUT PANCAKES

Preparation time: 20 minutes
Total cooking time: 30 minutes
Serves 4–6

✷ ✷

1/3 cup (40 g/1 1/4 oz) plain flour

2 tablespoons rice flour

1/4 cup (60 g/2 oz) caster sugar

1/4 cup (25 g/3/4 oz) desiccated coconut

1 cup (250 ml/8 fl oz) coconut milk

1 egg, lightly beaten

4 large bananas

60 g (2 oz) unsalted butter

1/3 cup (60 g/2 oz) soft brown sugar

1/3 cup (80 ml/2 3/4 fl oz) lime juice

1 tablespoon shredded toasted coconut,
  for serving

strips of lime rind, for serving

1 Sift the flours into a bowl. Add the caster sugar and coconut, mix through and make a well in the centre. Gradually whisk in the combined coconut milk and egg and beat until smooth.

2 Heat a small crepe or non-stick frying pan and brush lightly with melted butter. Pour 3 tablespoons of the pancake mixture into the pan and cook over medium heat until the underside is golden. Turn the pancake over and cook the other side. Transfer to a plate and cover with a tea towel to keep warm. Repeat the process with the remaining batter, buttering the pan when necessary. Stack the pancakes between greaseproof paper to prevent them sticking together. Keep the pancakes warm while preparing the bananas.

3 Cut the bananas diagonally into thick slices. Heat the butter in the pan, add the bananas and toss until coated. Cook over medium heat until the bananas start to soften and brown. Sprinkle with the brown sugar and shake the pan gently until the sugar has melted. Stir in the lime juice. Divide the bananas among the pancakes and fold over to enclose. Sprinkle with toasted coconut and strips of lime rind.

NOTE: These pancakes are quite delicate so it may be easier to turn them over if you slide each one out onto a plate and then invert it back into the frying pan.

ABOVE: Banana and coconut pancakes

ALMOND MASCARPONE CREPES WITH SUMMER FRUIT

Preparation time: 40 minutes + standing
Total cooking time: 35 minutes
Makes about 12 crepes

★ ★

Almond mascarpone

60 g (2 oz) slivered almonds
½ cup (125 g/4 oz) caster sugar
500 g (1 lb) mascarpone

250 g (8 oz) fresh strawberries, sliced
1 tablespoon caster sugar
1 cup (125 g/4 oz) plain flour
2 eggs
½ cup (125 ml/4 fl oz) milk
30 g (1 oz) unsalted butter, melted
4 kiwi fruit, thinly sliced
200 g (6½ oz) raspberries
250 g (8 oz) blueberries

1 To make the almond mascarpone, grill the almonds under a low heat until lightly golden, then place on an oiled baking tray. Put the caster sugar in a small heavy-based pan with ½ cup (125 ml/4 fl oz) water and stir, without boiling, until the sugar has dissolved. Bring to the boil, then reduce the heat and simmer, without stirring, for 15 minutes, or until the liquid turns golden brown. Quickly pour over the almonds and leave to set. Finely grind in a food processor, transfer to a bowl, then stir in the mascarpone, cover and refrigerate.
2 Place the strawberries in a large bowl and sprinkle with the caster sugar. Refrigerate.
3 Mix the flour, eggs and milk in a food processor for 10 seconds. Add ½ cup (125 ml/ 4 fl oz) water and the butter and process until smooth. Pour into a jug and set aside for 30 minutes.
4 Heat a small crepe pan or non-stick frying pan and brush lightly with melted butter. Pour ¼ cup (60 ml/2 fl oz) batter into the pan, swirling to cover the base thinly. Cook for about 30 seconds, or until the edges just begin to curl, turn the crepe over and cook the other side until lightly browned. Transfer to a plate and cover with a tea towel while cooking the remaining batter.
5 Spread each warm crepe with almond mascarpone and fold into quarters. Serve with macerated strawberries and some kiwi fruit, raspberries and blueberries.

FILLINGS FOR CREPES

MIXED BERRY Macerate fresh berries in orange juice with a little icing sugar and grated orange rind for a few hours. They will be ready when they have given off a little syrupy juice.

APPLE Cook slices of peeled, cored apple in melted butter until golden and softened, but still in their shape. Sprinkle with sugar and keep cooking until they caramelize. Sprinkle with lemon juice or cinnamon.

ABOVE: Almond mascarpone crepes with summer fruit

COCONUT CREPES WITH LIQUEUR FIGS

Preparation time: 30 minutes
Total cooking time: 50 minutes
Serves 4

★★

Liqueur figs

375 g (12 oz) dried figs
1 tablespoon soft brown sugar
1 cup (250 ml/8 fl oz) orange juice
1/4 cup (60 ml/2 fl oz) brandy
1 bay leaf
3 cloves
1 cinnamon stick

Mascarpone cream

150 g (5 oz) mascarpone
2 tablespoons soft brown sugar
2 tablespoons thick (double) cream

1/2 cup (60 g/2 oz) plain flour
2 eggs
2 teaspoons oil
3/4 cup (185 ml/6 fl oz) milk
1 cup (60 g/2 oz) shredded coconut, toasted

1 To make the liqueur figs, place the figs, sugar, orange juice, brandy, bay leaf, cloves and cinnamon stick in a pan. Simmer for 20 minutes, or until the figs are plump and the liquid has reduced by two-thirds.

2 To make the mascarpone cream, gently mix together the mascarpone, sugar and cream.

3 Sift the flour and a pinch of salt into a large bowl and make a well in the centre. Gradually whisk in the combined eggs, oil and milk until just smooth and free of lumps. Mix in the coconut.

4 Heat a small crepe or non-stick frying pan and brush lightly with melted butter. Add 1/4 cup (60 ml/2 fl oz) batter to the pan and spread with the back of a spoon. Cook over moderate heat for 1 minute, or until the underside is golden, then turn over and cook the other side. Transfer to a plate and cover with a tea towel while cooking the remaining crepes. Stack the crepes between greaseproof paper to prevent them sticking together.

5 Place a few drained figs in the centre of each crepe. Fold the crepes up and around the figs to form bags and tie with string. Dust lightly with icing sugar and serve with mascarpone cream.

BAY LEAVES

Bay leaves are a dark, glossy green when fresh, with a nutmeg and vanilla type flavour. They respond well to drying which gives them a pepperiness. Bay leaves are an essential part of a bouquet garni for savoury foods but they are also used with desserts— baked custards are often flavoured with bay leaves, with a leaf floated on the top for decoration. Cream can be delicately flavoured with bay and sugar. Fresh bay leaves keep for a few days in a plastic bag in the refrigerator (remember to wash them before use). Dried leaves keep well in an airtight container in a cool dry place, but will lose flavour as they get older. Powdered bay leaf is also available.

ABOVE: Coconut crepes with liqueur figs

115

AMARETTI BISCUITS

Amaretti are small, macaroon-type biscuits from Italy. Amaretti di Saronno, the most well known, are flavoured with bitter almonds and often come as two biscuits wrapped in coloured paper, which is twisted at the ends like a giant sweet. Amaretti are usually eaten with dessert wine or coffee, or crushed and added to desserts.

ABOVE: Amaretti apple stack with caramel sauce

AMARETTI APPLE STACK WITH CARAMEL SAUCE

Preparation time: 40 minutes + standing
Total cooking time: 1 hour
Serves 4–6

★★

1 cup (125 g/4 oz) plain flour

2 eggs

1 cup (250 ml/8 fl oz) milk

30 g (1 oz) unsalted butter, melted

1 tablespoon Amaretto liqueur, optional

125 g (4 oz) Amaretti biscuits

5 cooking apples, peeled and cored

185 g (6 oz) unsalted butter

1 cup (185 g/6 oz) soft brown sugar

1/2 cup (175 g/6 oz) golden syrup

1/2 cup (125 ml/4 fl oz) cream

3/4 cup (185 g/6 oz) light sour cream

1 Sift the flour into a large bowl and make a well. Gradually whisk in the combined eggs and milk until the batter is smooth and free of lumps. Mix in the butter and Amaretto. Transfer to a jug, cover and leave for 30 minutes. Heat a small crepe or non-stick frying pan and brush lightly with melted butter. Pour a little batter into the pan, swirling quickly, to thinly cover the base, pouring any excess back into the jug. Cook for 30 seconds, or until the edges just begin to curl, then turn and cook the other side until lightly browned. Transfer to a plate and cover with a tea towel. Repeat with the remaining batter to make 10 crepes, greasing the pan when necessary. Stack the crepes between greaseproof paper to prevent them sticking together.

2 Preheat the oven to moderate 180°C (350°F/ Gas 4). Roughly chop the biscuits in a food processor. Place on a baking tray and bake for 5–8 minutes, stirring occasionally, until crisp. Cut the apples into very thin slices and mix in a bowl with 60 g (2 oz) of the butter, melted, and half the brown sugar. Spread evenly onto a tray and place under a moderate grill for 5 minutes. Turn and grill until light brown and soft (you may need to do this in batches). Set aside.

3 Put a crepe on a large heatproof plate. Spread evenly with some apple, slightly mounded in the middle, and sprinkle with chopped Amaretti biscuits. Continue to fill and layer until all the crepes are stacked. Cover with foil and heat in the oven for 10 minutes, or until warm.

4 Put the remaining brown sugar with the syrup, cream and remaining butter in a small pan. Stir over low heat until the sugar has dissolved, then simmer for 1 minute. Spread the top crepe with sour cream. Pour a little warm sauce over the pancake stack and cut into wedges to serve.

CHOCOLATE CREPES WITH CHOCOLATE SAUCE

Preparation time: 40 minutes + standing
Total cooking time: 10–15 minutes
Makes 8–10

✷ ✷

1/2 cup (60 g/2 oz) plain flour

1 tablespoon cocoa powder

2 eggs

1 cup (250 ml/8 fl oz) milk

2 tablespoons caster sugar

3 oranges

Sauce

160 g (51/2 oz) good-quality dark
    chocolate, chopped

3/4 cup (185 ml/6 fl oz) cream

1/2 cup (125 g/4 oz) sour cream or
    crème fraîche

75 g (21/2 oz) white chocolate,
    grated

250 g (8 oz) blueberries

1 Sift the flour and cocoa into a large bowl and make a well. Gradually whisk in the combined eggs, milk and sugar until the batter is smooth and free of lumps. Transfer to a jug, cover with plastic wrap and set aside for 30 minutes. Cut a 1 cm (1/2 inch) slice from the ends of each orange. Cut the skin away in a circular motion, cutting only deep enough to remove all the white membrane and skin. Cut the flesh into segments between each membrane. (Do this over a bowl to catch any juice.) Place the segments in a bowl with the juice. Cover with plastic wrap and refrigerate.

2 Heat a 20 cm (8 inch) crepe pan or non-stick frying pan over medium heat and brush lightly with melted butter. Pour 2–3 tablespoons of crepe batter into pan and swirl evenly over the base. Cook over medium heat for 1 minute, or until the underside is cooked. Turn the crepe over and cook the other side. Transfer to a plate and cover with a tea towel. Repeat with the remaining batter, greasing the pan when necessary. Stack the crepes between greaseproof paper to prevent them sticking together.

3 To make the sauce, drain the oranges and reserve the juice. Combine the juice in a pan with the chocolate and cream. Stir over low heat until the chocolate has melted and the mixture is smooth.

4 To assemble the crepes, place a heaped teaspoon of sour cream or crème fraîche on a quarter of each crepe. Sprinkle with grated white chocolate. Fold the crepe in half, and in half again to make a wedge shape. Place two crepes on each serving plate. Spoon warm sauce over the crepes and serve with orange segments and blueberries. If preferred, crepes and sauce can be cooked several hours in advance. Reheat gently, fill and assemble just before serving.

BELOW: Chocolate crepes with chocolate sauce

BLINTZES

Blintzes are filled pancakes which originated in eastern Europe and are part of Jewish cuisine, usually served for breakfast or early supper. They consist of thin pancakes, cooked on one side, then folded in a rectangular shape around a sweet cheese filling before being baked.

RICOTTA BLINTZES

Preparation time: 30 minutes + standing
Total cooking time: 30–40 minutes
Makes about 14

★ ★

1 cup (125 g/4 oz) plain flour
2 eggs
1¼ cups (315 ml/10 fl oz) milk
30 g (1 oz) unsalted butter, melted

Ricotta filling

60 g (2 oz) raisins
1 tablespoon Grand Marnier or
   Cointreau, optional
375 g (12 oz) ricotta
⅓ cup (90 g/3 oz) caster sugar
1 tablespoon grated lemon rind
2 tablespoons lemon juice
20 g (¾ oz) unsalted butter, melted
icing sugar, to dust

1 Sift the flour into a large bowl and make a well. Gradually whisk in the combined eggs and milk until the batter is smooth and free of lumps. Stir in the melted butter, transfer to a jug, cover and set aside for 30 minutes.

2 Heat a crepe pan or non-stick frying pan and brush lightly with melted butter. Pour enough batter into the pan, swirling quickly, to thinly cover the base. Pour any excess back into the jug. Cook for 30 seconds, or until golden brown and completely set on the upper part. Remove and cover with a tea towel while cooking the rest. Stack the crepes between greaseproof paper to prevent them sticking together.

3 To make the ricotta filling, put the raisins in a bowl, mix with the liqueur, if using, then set aside for 30 minutes. Beat the ricotta, sugar, rind and juice for 1–2 minutes, or until smooth. Stir in the raisins and liqueur.

4 Preheat the oven to warm 160°C (315°F/ Gas 2–3). Place a heaped tablespoon of filling on the centre of each crepe, then fold into a flat parcel. Place the filled crepes, fold-side-down, in a greased ovenproof dish in a single layer. Brush each crepe lightly with the melted butter. Cover with foil and bake for about 10–15 minutes, or until hot. Serve with a light dusting of sifted icing sugar.

NOTE: Ricotta blintzes can be assembled several hours in advance and heated just before serving.

BELOW: Ricotta blintzes

CHOCOLATE CHIP PANCAKES WITH HOT FUDGE SAUCE

Preparation time: 35 minutes + standing
Total cooking time: 30 minutes
Makes 16

★

2 cups (250 g/8 oz) self-raising flour
2 tablespoons cocoa powder
1 teaspoon bicarbonate of soda
1/4 cup (60 g/2 oz) caster sugar
3/4 cup (130 g/4 1/2 oz) dark choc bits (drops)
1 cup (250 ml/8 fl oz) milk
1 cup (250 ml/8 fl oz) cream
2 eggs, lightly beaten
30 g (1 oz) unsalted butter, melted
3 egg whites
whipped cream or ice cream, for serving

Hot fudge sauce

150 g (5 oz) good-quality dark chocolate,
   broken into pieces
30 g (1 oz) unsalted butter
2 tablespoons light corn syrup
1/2 cup (95 g/3 oz) soft brown sugar
1/2 cup (125 ml/4 fl oz) cream

1 Sift the flour, cocoa and bicarbonate of soda into a large bowl. Stir in the sugar and choc bits and make a well in the centre. Whisk together the milk, cream, eggs and melted butter in a jug, then gradually pour into the well and stir until just combined. Cover and set aside for 15 minutes.
2 Beat the egg whites in a clean dry bowl until soft peaks form. Using a large metal spoon, stir a heaped tablespoon of the beaten egg white into the batter to loosen it up, then lightly fold in the remaining egg white until just combined.
3 Heat a frying pan and brush lightly with melted butter or oil. Pour 1/4 cup (60 ml/2 fl oz) batter into the pan and cook over moderate heat until the underside is browned. Flip or turn the pancake over with a spatula and cook the other side. Transfer to a plate, and cover with a tea towel while cooking the remaining batter. Stack between greaseproof paper to prevent them sticking together.
4 To make the hot fudge sauce, put all the ingredients in a pan and stir over low heat until melted and smooth. Serve the pancakes warm with whipped cream or ice cream and drizzled with hot fudge sauce.

PANCAKES

Pancakes are thicker and more substantial than delicate crepes. Some are yeasted to help them rise, others have raising agents such as bicarbonate of soda. Pancake batter should be left to rest, like crepe batter, to lighten it. Cook pancakes on a griddle or in a heavy-based pan. They need an even heat or they may burn before they are cooked through. When frying pancakes, wait until a few bubbles break through the top surface before turning them over. If it is still too runny, when you flip it over the inside will leak out and spoil the even shape. Pancakes should be fluffy inside and should be eaten immediately. They do not benefit from keeping, as do crepes.

ABOVE: Chocolate chip pancakes with hot fudge sauce

COFFEE BEANS

Originating in Ethiopia and the Sudan, coffee is made by grinding the seeds or beans of an evergreen shrub. It was considered a gift from God and was adopted by the Sufis—supposedly it helped keep them alert during prayer. The first public coffee house opened in Mecca in about 1511. Coffee drinking then spread via Constantinople to Europe and England. Coffee was very fashionable in the 17th century but in England was eventually ousted by tea, which was cheaper. In America, however, the tax on tea made coffee the cheaper, more popular drink. Varieties of coffee bean include *arabica*, the finest and most robust, and *robusta*, with the highest caffeine content. Coffee is grown in Africa, South America, Arabia, India, the Caribbean, Indonesia, Papua New Guinea and Australia.

ABOVE: Mocha waffles with espresso syrup

MOCHA WAFFLES WITH ESPRESSO SYRUP

Preparation time: 30 minutes
Total cooking time: 45 minutes
Makes 8 waffles

★

Espresso syrup

3/4 cup (185 g/6 oz) caster sugar
1/2 cup (125 ml/4 fl oz) brewed espresso coffee
1/4 cup (60 ml/2 fl oz) cream

2 cups (250 g/8 oz) plain flour
2 tablespoons cocoa powder
2 teaspoons baking powder
1/2 teaspoon salt
1 1/4 cups (315 ml/10 fl oz) milk
2 tablespoons coffee and chicory essence
1/2 cup (125 g/4 oz) caster sugar
3 eggs, separated
60 g (2 oz) unsalted butter, melted

1 To make the espresso syrup, put the sugar, espresso coffee, cream and 3 tablespoons water in a small pan. Bring to the boil, reduce the heat and simmer for 4–5 minutes. Set aside to cool.
2 Preheat the waffle iron. Sift the flour, cocoa, baking powder and salt into a large bowl. Add the milk, essence, sugar, egg yolks and butter and whisk until smooth. In a clean, dry bowl, beat the egg whites until firm peaks form. Using a large metal spoon, stir a tablespoon of egg white into the batter to loosen it up, then gently fold in the remainder.
3 Brush the waffle iron with melted butter. Pour about 1/2 cup (125 ml/4 fl oz) batter (the amount will vary according to your waffle iron) into the centre of the iron and spread almost to the corners of the grid. Cook for about 4–5 minutes, or until crisp and golden. Keep warm while cooking the remaining batter. Spoon espresso syrup over the waffles. Delicious served with freshly whipped cream, chocolate curls (see page 238) and a sifting of cocoa powder.
NOTE: Coffee and chicory essence is also known as camp coffee.

WAFFLES
Waffles are pancakes made from batter, with deep indentations on both sides, formed by baking between hinged irons, which give the waffles a honeycomb effect. Belgian waffles are thicker and fluffier with deeper pockets in their surface. Waffle irons can either be electric or stovetop and, except on older models, usually have non-stick surfaces.

WAFFLES WITH HOT CHOCOLATE SAUCE

Preparation time: 20 minutes
  + standing
Total cooking time: 20–25 minutes
Makes 8 waffles

★

2 cups (250 g/8 oz) self-raising flour
1 teaspoon bicarbonate of soda
2 teaspoons sugar
2 eggs
90 g (3 oz) unsalted butter, melted
1³/₄ cups (440 ml/14 fl oz) buttermilk

Chocolate sauce

50 g (1³/₄ oz) unsalted butter
200 g (6¹/₂ oz) good-quality dark
  chocolate, chopped
¹/₂ cup (125 ml/4 fl oz) cream
1 tablespoon golden syrup

1 Sift the flour, bicarbonate of soda, sugar and a pinch of salt into a large bowl and make a well in the centre. Whisk the eggs, melted butter and the buttermilk in a jug and gradually pour into the well, whisking until the batter is just smooth. Set aside for 10 minutes. Preheat the waffle iron.
2 To make the chocolate sauce, put the butter, chopped chocolate, cream and golden syrup in a pan and stir over low heat until smooth. Remove from the heat and keep warm.
3 Brush the waffle iron with melted butter. Pour about ¹/₂ cup (125 ml/4 fl oz) batter (the amount will vary according to your waffle iron) into the centre and spread almost to the corners of the grid.
4 Cook the waffle for about 2 minutes, or until golden and crisp. Keep the cooked waffles warm while cooking the remaining mixture. Serve with vanilla ice cream and the hot chocolate sauce.

ABOVE: Waffles with hot chocolate sauce

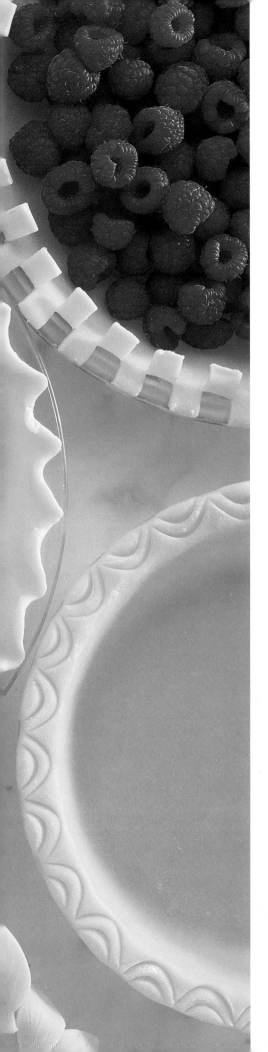

PASTRIES

Perfect pastry is one of the hallmarks of a great cook—it has a reputation as elusive, moody, even downright difficult, but once you've mastered a few commonsense rules you'll probably find it all rather easy. Whether it is puff, shortcrust, choux or filo, beautiful pastry with a light buttery touch can raise any dish to sublime heights, so it is not surprising that almost every country in the world has its own traditional recipe—pecan pie, apple pie, cherry strudel, treacle tart, pithivier... A chapter on pastries really is a mouthwatering journey of culinary exploration.

PUFF PASTRY Made by layering dough

with butter and folding to create hundreds of layers. The butter melts, the dough

produces steam, forcing the layers apart and making the pastry rise to great heights.

For perfect pastry which rises evenly, the edges must be cut cleanly with a sharp knife or cutter, not torn. Egg glazes give a shine but must be applied carefully—any drips down the side may glue the layers together and stop them rising evenly. The pastry should be chilled for at least 30 minutes before baking to relax it.

Always bake puff pastry at a very high temperature—it should rise evenly so, if your oven has areas of uneven heat, turn the pastry around when it has set. If you have an oven with a bottom element, cook your pastry on the bottom shelf. When puff pastry is cooked, the top and base should be browned, with only a small amount of underbaked dough inside, and the layers should be visible. Puff pastry is not always perfect—it may fall over or not rise to quite the heights

you had imagined—but provided you don't burn it and it is well cooked it will still be delicious.

MAKING PUFF PASTRY

We've given a range of fat quantities—if you've never made puff pastry before, you'll find it easier to use the lower amount. This recipe makes about 500 g (1 lb) pastry. You will need 200–250 g

(6½–8 oz) unsalted butter, 2 cups (250 g/ 8 oz) plain flour, ½ teaspoon salt and ⅔ cup (170 ml/5½ fl oz) chilled water.

1 Melt 30 g (1 oz) butter in a pan. Sift the flour and salt onto a work surface and make a well in the centre. Add the butter and water to the centre and blend with your fingertips, gradually drawing in the flour. You should end up with a crumb mixture—if it seems a little dry, add extra drops of water before bringing it all together to form a dough.

2 Cut the dough with a pastry scraper, using a downward cutting action, then turn the dough and repeat in the opposite direction. The dough should now come together to form a soft ball. Score a cross in the top to prevent shrinkage, wrap and refrigerate for 15–20 minutes.

3 Soften the remaining butter by pounding it between 2 sheets of baking paper with a rolling pin. Then, still between the sheets of baking paper, roll it into a 10 cm (4 inch) square. The butter must be the same consistency as the dough or they will not roll out the same amount and the layers will not be even. If the butter is too soft, it will squeeze out of the sides. Too hard and it will break through the dough and disturb the layers.

4 Put the pastry on a well floured surface. Roll it out to form a cross, leaving the centre slightly thicker than the arms. Place the butter in the centre of the cross and fold over each of the arms to make a parcel. Turn the dough so that it looks like a book with the hinge side to the left. Tap and roll out the dough to form a 15 x 45 cm (6 x 18 inch) rectangle. Make this as neat as possible, squaring off the corners—otherwise, every time you fold,

the edges will become less neat and the layers will not be even.

5 Fold the dough like a letter, the top third down and the bottom third up, to form another square, brushing off any excess flour between the layers. Turn the dough 90° to bring the hinge side to your left and press the seam sides down with the rolling pin to seal them. Re-roll and fold as before to complete two turns and mark the dough by gently pressing into the corner with your fingertip for each turn—this will remind you where you're up to. Wrap the dough and chill again.

6 Re-roll and fold twice more and then chill, and then again to complete 6 turns. If it is a very hot day, you may need to chill between each turn. The pastry should now be an even yellow and is ready to use—if it looks a little streaky, roll and fold once more. Refrigerate until required.

PITHIVIER

Pithivier is named after the French town, Pithiviers, in the Loire Valley, where the pastry is traditionally served on Twelfth Night and is known as *Galette des Rois*. It consists of two circles of puff pastry enclosing a frangipan filling. The top is decorated with a rosette pattern and the edges are usually scalloped. The Galette des Rois version usually contains a bean which brings good luck to the person who finds it in their slice.

ABOVE: Lemon brûlée tarts

LEMON BRULEE TARTS

Preparation time: 40 minutes + chilling
Total cooking time: 35 minutes
Serves 4

★★

1¼ cups (315 ml/10 fl oz) cream
2 teaspoons grated lemon rind
4 egg yolks
2 tablespoons caster sugar
2 teaspoons cornflour
2 tablespoons lemon juice
410 g (13 oz) puff pastry or 2 sheets
   ready-rolled
⅓ cup (90 g/3 oz) sugar

1 Heat the cream in a pan with the lemon rind until almost boiling. Allow to cool slightly. Whisk the egg yolks, sugar, cornflour and lemon juice in a bowl until thick and pale.
2 Add the cream gradually, whisking constantly. Strain into a clean pan and stir over low heat until thickened slightly—the mixture should coat the back of a wooden spoon. Pour into a heatproof bowl, cover with plastic wrap and refrigerate for several hours or overnight.
3 Preheat the oven to hot 210°C (415°F/ Gas 6–7). Lightly grease four 12 cm (5 inch) diameter shallow loose-based tart tins. If using block pastry, roll it to 48 x 25 cm (19 x 10 inches), then cut 4 rounds, large enough to fit the base and side of the tart tins. If using sheets, cut 2 rounds of pastry from each sheet to line the tins. Line each tin, trim the edges and prick the bases lightly with a fork. Line with baking paper and spread a layer of dried beans or rice evenly over the paper. Bake for 15 minutes, discard the paper and beans and return to the oven for another 5 minutes, or until lightly golden. Leave to cool.
4 Spoon the lemon custard into each pastry shell, smooth the top, leaving a little room for the sugar layer. Cover the edges of the pastry with foil and sprinkle sugar generously over the surface of the custard in an even layer. Cook under a preheated grill until the sugar just begins to colour. Put the tarts close to the grill so they brown quickly, but watch carefully that they do not burn. Serve immediately.

INDIVIDUAL PITHIVIERS

Preparation time: 40 minutes
Total cooking time: 25 minutes
Serves 8

★★

60 g (2 oz) unsalted butter
1/4 cup (60 g/2 oz) sugar
1 egg
2/3 cup (95 g/3 oz) ground almonds
1 tablespoon plain flour
2 teaspoons grated orange rind
1 tablespoon Cointreau
375 g (12 oz) puff pastry or
   4 sheets ready-rolled
1 egg, lightly beaten
thick (double) cream, for serving

1 Preheat the oven to hot 210°C (415°F/ Gas 6–7). Grease two baking trays and line with baking paper. Using electric beaters, beat the butter and sugar until light and creamy. Add the egg and beat until well combined. Stir in the ground almonds, flour, orange rind and Cointreau. Cover and refrigerate.

2 Cut the block of puff pastry in half. On a lightly floured surface, roll one half out to a large enough rectangle to cut out eight 10 cm (4 inch) rounds. Carefully transfer to baking trays. Using a smaller round cutter, mark a 7 cm (2¾ inch) impression in the middle of each circle. Divide the nut cream among the pastry circles, spreading evenly inside the marked impression. Brush the edges with beaten egg.

3 Roll out the remaining puff pastry. Using a larger cutter, cut out eight 10 cm (4 inch) circles and place over the top of the filling, pressing the edges to seal. Brush the tops with beaten egg, being careful not to let any drip down the side, as this will prevent the pastry rising. Using the tip of a small knife, score a spiral pattern on the top of each pithivier. Bake for 20–25 minutes, or until puffed and golden. Serve with cream.

PITHIVIERS

Use the tip of a small knife to score a spiral pattern on top of each pithivier.

BELOW: Individual pithiviers

JALOUSIE

Preparation time: 40 minutes
Total cooking time: 45 minutes
Serves 4–6

★★

30 g (1 oz) unsalted butter
1/4 cup (45 g/1 1/2 oz) soft brown sugar
500 g (1 lb) apples, peeled, cored and cubed
1 teaspoon grated lemon rind
1 tablespoon lemon juice
1/4 teaspoon nutmeg
1/4 teaspoon cinnamon
30 g (1 oz) sultanas
375 g (12 oz) puff pastry
1 egg, lightly beaten, to glaze

1 Preheat the oven to hot 220°C (425°F/Gas 7). Lightly grease a baking tray and line with baking paper. Melt the butter and sugar in a frying pan.

Add the apple, lemon rind and lemon juice. Cook over medium heat for 10 minutes, stirring occasionally, until the apples are cooked and the mixture is thick and syrupy. Stir in the nutmeg, cinnamon and sultanas. Cool completely.

2 Cut the block of puff pastry in half. On a lightly floured surface roll out one half of the pastry to a 24 x 18 cm (10 x 7 inch) rectangle. Spread the fruit mixture onto the pastry, leaving a 2.5 cm (1 inch) border. Brush the edges lightly with the beaten egg.

3 Roll the second half of the pastry on a lightly floured surface to a 25 x 18 cm (10 x 7 inch) rectangle. Using a sharp knife, cut slashes in the pastry across its width, leaving a 2 cm (3/4 inch) border around the edge. The slashes should open slightly and look like a venetian blind (*jalousie* in French). Place over the fruit and press the edges together. Trim away any extra pastry. Knock up the puff pastry (brush the sides upwards) with a knife to ensure rising during cooking. Glaze the top with egg. Bake for 25–30 minutes, or until puffed and golden.

PUFF PASTRY

Commercially made puff pastry can be bought in different forms. Blocks of puff pastry are available frozen or fresh and sheets are available frozen flat or as a roll, sometimes fresh. You do not need to roll out sheets of puff but they benefit from having their edges trimmed. Commercial puff pastries use vegetable or canola (rapeseed) oil or butter as their fat. If you are using a pastry with vegetable fat as its base, you can add a buttery flavour by brushing the pastry with melted butter and chilling it before glazing.

RIGHT: Jalousie

MILLE FEUILLE

Preparation time: 30 minutes
Total cooking time: 1 hour 30 minutes
Serves 6–8

★

600 g (1¼ lb) puff pastry or 3 sheets
   ready-rolled
2½ cups (600 ml/20 fl oz) thick (double) cream
500 g (1 lb) small strawberries, halved
70 g (2¼ oz) blueberries, optional

1 Preheat the oven to hot 220°C (425°F/Gas 7).
Line a baking tray with baking paper. If using a
block of puff pastry, cut the pastry into three and
roll out to 25 cm (10 inch) squares. Place one
sheet of puff pastry on the tray, prick all over
and top with another piece of baking paper and
another baking tray and bake for 15 minutes.
Turn the trays over and bake on the other side
for 10–15 minutes, or until golden brown. Allow
to cool and repeat with the remaining pastry.
2 Trim the edges of each pastry sheet and cut
each one in half. Pour the cream into a large
bowl and whisk to firm peaks. Place two of the
pastry pieces on a serving dish and spoon some
of the cream on top. Carefully arrange some of
the strawberries and blueberries over the cream,
pressing them well down. Top each one with
another pastry sheet and repeat with the
strawberries and blueberries. Top with a final
layer of pastry and dust with icing sugar.

APPLE GALETTES

Preparation time: 45 minutes + chilling
Total cooking time: 30 minutes
Serves 8

★★

2 cups (250 g/8 oz) plain flour
250 g (8 oz) unsalted butter, chopped
8 apples
¾ cup (185 g/6 oz) caster sugar
125 g (4 oz) unsalted butter, chopped

1 Place the flour and butter in a bowl and cut
the butter into the flour with two knives until it
resembles large crumbs. Gradually add about
½ cup (125 ml/4 fl oz) chilled water, stirring
with a knife and pressing together, until a rough
dough forms. Turn onto a lightly floured board

and roll into a rectangle. The dough will be
crumbly and hard to manage at this point. Fold
the pastry into thirds; turn it so the hinge is on
your left and roll into a large rectangle. Always
turn the pastry the same way so the hinge is
on the left. Refrigerate in plastic wrap for
30 minutes.
2 Complete two more turns and folds before
refrigerating the pastry for another 30 minutes.
Repeat the process so that you have completed
6 folds and turns. Wrap the pastry in plastic wrap
and refrigerate before use. The pastry can be
stored in the refrigerator for 2 days or in the
freezer for up to 3 months.
3 Preheat the oven to moderately hot 190°C
(375°F/Gas 5). Roll the pastry out on a lightly
floured surface until 3 mm (⅛ inch) thick. Cut
into eight 10 cm (4 inch) rounds. Peel and core
the apples and slice thinly. Arrange the apples in
a spiral on the pastry. Sprinkle well with sugar
and dot with unsalted butter. Bake on greased
baking trays for 20–30 minutes, until the pastry is
crisp and golden. Serve warm.

ABOVE: Apple galettes

129

MAKING FLAKY PASTRY

Knead the pastry until it is just smooth.

Roll the dough into a rectangle and dot the top two-thirds with cubes of chilled butter.

Fold the bottom third of the pastry up over the butter and then the top third down.

Turn the pastry so the hinge is to the right. Press the edges down to seal, then roll and fold as before.

OPPOSITE PAGE: Banana tart (top); Feuilleté with cherries jubilee

---

BANANA TART

Preparation time: 40 minutes + chilling
Total cooking time: 35 minutes
Serves 6

✲ ✲

Flaky pastry

1³/₄ cups (215 g/7 oz) plain flour
160 g (5¹/₂ oz) unsalted butter
  (chill 100 g/3¹/₂ oz of it)

rind and juice of 2 oranges
4 tablespoons soft brown sugar
¹/₄ teaspoon cardamom seeds
1 tablespoon rum
3–4 ripe bananas

1 For the pastry, sift the flour into a bowl with a pinch of salt and rub in the unchilled butter. Add enough water (about 155 ml/5 fl oz), mixing with a flat-bladed knife to make a dough-like consistency. Turn onto a floured surface and knead until just smooth. Roll into a rectangle 10 x 30 cm (4 x 12 inches), cut a third of the chilled butter into cubes and dot all over the top two-thirds of the pastry, leaving a little room around the edge. Fold the bottom third of the pastry up and the top third down and press the edges down to seal. Now turn the pastry to your left, so the hinge is on your right, and roll and fold as before. Chill for 20 minutes, then with the hinge to your right, roll it out again, cover the top two-thirds of the pastry with another third of the butter and roll and fold. Repeat, using the rest of the butter and then roll and fold once more without adding any butter.
2 Roll the pastry out on a floured surface into a rectangle 25 x 30 cm (10 x 12 inches), cut a 2 cm (³/₄ inch) strip off each side and use this to make a frame on the pastry by brushing the edges of the pastry with water and sticking the strips onto it. Trim off any excess and put the tart base on a baking tray lined with baking paper, cover with plastic wrap and refrigerate until required.
3 Combine the orange rind, juice, brown sugar and cardamom seeds in a small pan, bring to the boil, simmer for 5 minutes, then remove from the heat and add the rum. Set aside to cool. Preheat the oven to hot 220°C (425°F/Gas 7).
4 Slice the bananas in half lengthways, arrange on the tart in an even layer, cut-side-up and brush with a little syrup. Bake on the top shelf for 20–30 minutes, making sure the pastry does not overbrown. Brush with syrup and serve.

FEUILLETE WITH CHERRIES JUBILEE

Preparation time: 15 minutes + chilling
Total cooking time: 25 minutes
Serves 4

✲ ✲

375 g (12 oz) puff pastry
1 egg, lightly beaten
20 g (³/₄ oz) unsalted butter
20 g (³/₄ oz) sugar
500 g (1 lb) cherries, pitted
300 ml (9 fl oz) thick (double) cream
¹/₂ cup (125 ml/4 fl oz) brandy or Kirsch
icing sugar, to dust

1 Roll the pastry out on a floured work surface and cut out four rectangles of 10 x 12 cm (4 x 5 inches) each. Put them on a baking tray and brush with the egg glaze, being careful not to let any drip down the sides of the pastry. Refrigerate for 30 minutes. Preheat the oven to hot 220°C (425°F/Gas 7).
2 Melt the butter and sugar together in a saucepan and add the pitted cherries. Cook over high heat for about 1 minute, then reduce the heat and simmer for about 3 minutes, or until the cherries are tender. Reduce the heat to low and keep the cherries warm.
3 Bake the feuilleté on the top shelf of the oven for 15 minutes until golden and puffed, then cut them in half horizontally and gently pull any doughy bits out of the centre. Turn the oven off and and put the feuilleté back in the oven and allow to dry out for a couple of minutes.
4 When you are ready to serve, whisk the cream until it reaches stiff peaks. Place a warm feuilleté base on each serving plate. Heat the brandy or Kirsch in a small saucepan and set it alight, then pour it over the cherries (keep a saucepan lid nearby in case the flames get too high). Spoon some cherries into each feuilleté and top with a little cream. Put the lids on and dust with icing sugar before serving.

HELP WITH YOUR PASTRY

To make sure you get a well-cooked base on pastry, put a baking tray on the shelf of the oven when you preheat the oven and put the baking tray with the pastry on it straight on top of this.

SHORTCRUST TIPS The

secret of good pastry is to work quickly and lightly, with cool ingredients, in a cool

room and, preferably, not on a hot day. A cold marble slab is the ideal work surface.

If you don't have a marble slab, rest a tray of iced water on the work surface for a while before you start. Use *real* unsalted butter for pastry, not margarine or softened butter blends.

Unsweetened pastry works well with sweet fillings, giving a good contrast of flavours. Add two tablespoons of caster sugar to the flour for a sweet pastry. Some recipes contain egg yolks to enrich the pastry and give good colour.

SHORTCRUST PASTRY

To make enough to line a 23 cm (9 inch) tin, use 1½ cups (185 g/6 oz) plain flour, 100 g (3½ oz) chopped chilled unsalted butter, and 2–4 tablespoons chilled water.

1 Sift the flour into a large bowl and add the butter. Using just your fingertips, rub the butter into the flour until the mixture resembles fine breadcrumbs.
2 Make a well in the centre, then add

2–4 tablespoons water and mix with a flat-bladed knife. Use a cutting rather than a stirring action and turn the bowl with your free hand. The mixture will come together in small beads of dough. To test if you need more water, pinch a little dough between your fingers. If it doesn't hold together, add a little more water. If the pastry is too dry, it will fall apart when you roll it; if too wet it will be sticky and shrink when baked.

3 Gently gather the dough together with your hand and lift out onto a sheet of baking paper or a floured work surface.

4 Press, don't knead, the dough together into a ball. Handle gently, keeping your actions light and to a minimum.

5 Press the dough into a flat disc, wrap and refrigerate for 20 minutes. Roll out between 2 sheets of baking paper or plastic wrap, or on a lightly floured surface. Always roll from the centre outwards, rotating the dough, rather than rolling backwards and forwards.

6 If you used baking paper to roll out the pastry, remove the top sheet, carefully invert the pastry over the tin (make sure you centre the pastry, as it can't be moved once in place), and then peel away the paper. If you rolled out on a lightly floured surface, roll the pastry back over the rolling pin so it is hanging, and ease it into the tin.

7 Once the pastry is in the tin, quickly lift up the sides so they don't break over the edges of the tin, which can be sharp, particularly in metal flan tins. Use a small ball of excess dough to help ease and press the pastry shell into the side of the tin. Allow the excess to hang over the side and, if using a flan tin, roll the rolling pin over the top of the tin, to cut off the excess pastry. If you are using a glass or ceramic pie dish, use a small sharp knife to cut away the excess pastry.

8 However gently you handle dough, it is bound to shrink a little, so let it sit a little above the sides of the tin. If you rolled off the excess pastry with a rolling pin, you may find it has 'bunched' down the sides. Gently press the sides of the pastry with your thumbs to flatten and lift it a little. Refrigerate the pastry in the tin for 15 minutes to relax it and prevent or minimise shrinkage. Preheat the oven.

BLIND BAKING

If pastry is to have a moist filling, it will probably require partial blind baking to prevent the base becoming soggy. If it is not cooked again after filling, it will need to be fully blind baked. This means baking the pastry without the filling, but with some weight to prevent it rising. Line the shell with crumpled greaseproof or baking paper. Pour in some baking beads, dried beans or uncooked rice (these can be used again). Bake the pastry for the given time, then lift out the filled paper. Return the pastry to the oven. When cooked, it should look dry with no greasy patches. Small pastry shells can just be pricked with a fork to prevent them rising or bubbling, but only do this if specified, as the filling may run through.

Cool pastry completely before filling. Cooked filling should also be cooled before adding, to prevent soggy pastry.

133

GLAZING WITH JAM

Heat the jam for glazing until liquid, then sieve to remove any lumps. Gently brush over the fruit.

FRUIT TART

Preparation time: 40 minutes + chilling
Total cooking time: 40 minutes
Serves 6

★★

Shortcrust pastry

1¼ cups (155 g/5 oz) plain flour
2 tablespoons caster sugar
90 g (3 oz) chilled unsalted butter, chopped
1 egg yolk
1 tablespoon chilled water

Filling

1 cup (250 ml/8 fl oz) milk
3 egg yolks
¼ cup (60 g/2 oz) caster sugar
2 tablespoons plain flour
1 teaspoon vanilla essence
strawberries, kiwi fruit and blueberries
apricot jam, to glaze

BELOW: Fruit tart

1 Sift the flour into a bowl and stir in the sugar. Add the butter and using just your fingertips, rub into the flour until the mixture resembles breadcrumbs. Make a well in the centre, add the egg yolk and water. Using a knife, mix to a dough. Turn out onto a lightly floured surface and gather together into a ball. Press together gently until smooth, and then roll out to fit a 34 x 10 cm (13½ x 4 inch) loose-bottomed, fluted flan tin. Line the tin with pastry and trim away any excess. Refrigerate for 20 minutes. Preheat the oven to moderately hot 190°C (375°F/Gas 5).
2 Line the pastry-lined tin with a sheet of crumpled baking paper and spread a layer of baking beads or rice evenly over the paper. Bake for 15 minutes, remove the paper and beads and bake for another 20 minutes, until cooked on the base and golden brown around the edge. Set aside to cool completely.
3 To make the filling, put the milk into a small pan and bring to the boil. Set aside while quickly whisking the egg yolks and sugar together in a bowl, until light and creamy. Whisk in the flour. Pour the hot milk slowly onto the egg mixture,

whisking constantly. Wash out the pan, return the milk mixture and bring to the boil over medium heat, stirring with a wire whisk. Boil for 2 minutes, stirring occasionally. Transfer to a bowl, stir in the vanilla essence, and leave to cool, stirring frequently to avoid a skin forming. When cooled to room temperature, cover the surface with plastic wrap and refrigerate until cold.

4 Cut the strawberries in half and peel and slice the kiwi fruit. Spoon the cold custard into the cold pastry shell, then arrange the fruit over the custard, pressing in slightly. Heat the jam in the microwave or in a small pan until liquid, sieve to remove any lumps, then, using a pastry brush, glaze the fruit. Serve the tart on the same day, at room temperature. If it is to be left for a while on a hot day, refrigerate it.

NOTE: If you don't have a rectangular tin, this tart may be made in a 23 cm (9 inch) flan tin. You can use different fruits to top the tart, according to taste and season.

LEMON ALMOND TART

Preparation time: 40 minutes + chilling
Total cooking time: 1 hour
Serves 6–8

★★

Lemon pastry

2 cups (250 g/8 oz) plain flour, sifted

1/4 cup (60 g/2 oz) caster sugar

125 g (4 oz) chilled unsalted butter, softened

1 teaspoon finely grated lemon rind

2 egg yolks

Filling

350 g (11 oz) ricotta, sieved

1/3 cup (90 g/3 oz) caster sugar

3 eggs, well beaten

1 tablespoon finely grated lemon rind

80 g (2³/4 oz) blanched almonds, finely chopped

3 tablespoons flaked almonds

icing sugar, to dust

1 Combine the flour, sugar and a pinch of salt in a large bowl. Make a well in the centre and add the butter, rind and egg yolks. Work the flour into the centre with the fingertips of one hand until a smooth dough forms (add a little more flour if necessary). Wrap in plastic wrap, flatten slightly, then refrigerate for 20 minutes.

2 To make the filling, with electric beaters, beat the ricotta and sugar together. Add the eggs gradually, beating well after each addition. Add the rind, beating briefly to combine, and then stir in the chopped almonds.

3 Preheat the oven to moderate 180°C (350°F/Gas 4). Brush a 20 cm (8 inch) fluted flan tin with melted unsalted butter. Roll out the pastry on a lightly floured surface and line the tin, trimming away the excess pastry. Pour in the filling and smooth the top. Sprinkle with the flaked almonds and bake for 55 minutes to 1 hour, or until lightly golden and set.

4 Cool to room temperature, then carefully remove the sides from the tin. Lightly dust with icing sugar and serve at room temperature or chilled.

ABOVE: Lemon almond tart

PASTRY TIPS

To stop a pastry base becoming soggy when it has a wet filling, sprinkle a tablespoon of dried breadcrumbs or semolina into the base before adding the filling. Alternatively, brush the base with egg white and rebake it for a few minutes, or brush it with a glaze such as apricot jam.

If the pastry base splits when you cook it, plug any gaps with raw pastry and rebake it for 5 minutes, then brush it with egg white and rebake it for a couple of minutes.

Tart cases which are not going to hold runny fillings can be pricked all over with a fork to help them cook evenly and also to get rid of air bubbles.

Smaller tart cases which are fiddly to line with paper and rice or baking beads can be lined with another tart mould while baking. They will need to be dried out for a minute or two when the mould has been taken out.

Wet fillings in covered pies will steam so it is important to make holes in the pastry.

BUTTERSCOTCH TART

Preparation time: 30 minutes + chilling
Total cooking time: 1 hour
Makes one tart

★★

Shortcrust pastry

2 cups (250 g/8 oz) plain flour
125 g (4 oz) chilled unsalted butter, chopped
2 tablespoons caster sugar
1 egg yolk
1 tablespoon chilled water

Butterscotch filling

1 cup (185 g/6 oz) soft brown sugar
1/3 cup (40 g/1 1/4 oz) plain flour
1 cup (250 ml/8 fl oz) milk
45 g (1 1/2 oz) unsalted butter
1 teaspoon vanilla essence
1 egg yolk

Meringue

2 egg whites
2 tablespoons caster sugar

1 Preheat the oven to moderate 180°C (350°F/ Gas 4). Grease a deep, 22 cm (9 inch) flan tin. Sift the flour into a large bowl and rub in the butter with your fingertips until the mixture resembles breadcrumbs. Stir in the sugar, yolk and water. Mix to a soft dough, then gather into a ball. Wrap and chill for 20 minutes.

2 Roll the pastry between two sheets of baking paper, to cover the base and side of the tin. Trim the edge and prick the pastry evenly with a fork. Chill again for 20 minutes. Line the pastry with a sheet of crumpled baking paper and spread baking beads or rice over the paper. Bake for 35 minutes, then remove the paper and beads.

3 For the filling, place the sugar and flour in a small pan. Make a well and gradually whisk in the milk to form a smooth paste. Add the butter and stir with a whisk over low heat for 8 minutes, or until the mixture boils and thickens. Remove from the heat, add the essence and yolk and whisk until smooth. Spread into the pastry case and smooth the surface.

4 Beat the egg whites until firm peaks form. Add the sugar gradually, beating until thick and glossy and all the sugar has dissolved. Spoon over the filling and swirl into peaks with a fork or flat-bladed knife. Bake for 5–10 minutes, or until the meringue is golden. Serve warm or cold.

RIGHT: Butterscotch tart

DATE AND MASCARPONE TART

Preparation time: 50 minutes + chilling
Total cooking time: 40–45 minutes
Serves 6–8

★ ☆

Coconut pastry

¹/₂ cup (90 g/3 oz) rice flour

¹/₂ cup (60 g/2 oz) plain flour

100 g (3¹/₂ oz) chilled unsalted butter, chopped

2 tablespoons icing sugar

¹/₄ cup (25 g/³/₄ oz) desiccated coconut

100 g (3¹/₂ oz) marzipan, grated

Filling

8 fresh dates (about 200 g/6¹/₂ oz), pitted

2 eggs

2 teaspoons custard powder

125 g (4 oz) mascarpone

2 tablespoons caster sugar

¹/₃ cup (80 ml/2³/₄ fl oz) cream

2 tablespoons flaked almonds

1 Preheat the oven to moderate 180°C (350°F/ Gas 4). Grease a shallow, 10 x 34 cm (4 x 14 inch) fluted loose-bottomed flan tin. Sift the flours into a large bowl. Using just your fingertips, rub in the butter until the mixture resembles breadcrumbs, then press the mixture together gently. Stir in the icing sugar, coconut and marzipan. Turn out onto a lightly floured surface and gather together into a ball. Flatten slightly, cover with plastic wrap and refrigerate for 15 minutes.

2 Roll out the pastry between two sheets of baking paper until large enough to line the tin. Ease the pastry into the tin and trim the edge. Refrigerate for 5–10 minutes. Line the pastry-lined tin with a crumpled sheet of baking paper and spread a layer of baking beads or rice evenly over the paper. Place the tin on a baking tray and bake for 10 minutes. Remove the paper and beads, bake for another 5 minutes, or until just golden, then allow to cool.

3 Cut the dates into quarters lengthways and arrange over the pastry. Whisk together the eggs, custard powder, mascarpone, caster sugar and cream until smooth. Pour the mixture over the dates, then sprinkle with the flaked almonds. Bake for 25–30 minutes, or until golden and just set, then allow to cool slightly. Serve warm. The tart can be decorated if you wish.

ABOVE: Date and mascarpone tart

137

ABOVE: Banoffie pie

resembles breadcrumbs. Mix in 2–3 tablespoons chilled water with a flat-bladed knife to form a firm dough. Add more water if needed. Turn onto a floured surface and gather together into a ball. Wrap and chill for 15 minutes. Roll out to fit a 23 cm (9 inch) flan tin; chill for 20 minutes.
2 Preheat the oven to moderate 180°C (350°F/ Gas 4). Line the pastry base with crumpled baking paper and spread baking beads or rice over paper. Bake for 15 minutes, then remove the paper and beads. Bake the pastry for 10 minutes, or until lightly golden. Set aside to cool completely.
3 To make the filling, place the condensed milk, butter and golden syrup in a small pan. Stir over medium heat for 5 minutes, until it boils and thickens and turns a light caramel colour. Cool slightly, then arrange half the bananas over the pastry and pour the caramel over the top. Smooth the surface and chill for 30 minutes.
4 Drop spoonfuls of cream over the caramel and arrange the remaining banana on top. Drizzle with melted chocolate.

LATTICE MINCEMEAT TARTS

Preparation time: 40 minutes
Total cooking time: 1 hour + chilling
Serves 6

⋆⋆

1/2 cup (60 g/2 oz) self-raising flour
1 1/2 cups (185 g/6 oz) plain flour
125 g (4 oz) chilled unsalted butter, chopped
2 tablespoons caster sugar
egg, lightly beaten, to glaze
icing sugar, to dust

Mincemeat

1/4 cup (35 g/1 1/4 oz) currants
1/3 cup (40 g/1 1/4 oz) sultanas
2 tablespoons mixed peel
1/4 cup (30 g/1 oz) slivered almonds
1/4 cup (45 g/1 1/2 oz) soft brown sugar
1/4 teaspoon ground nutmeg
1/4 teaspoon ground cinnamon
1 apple, grated
1 teaspoon grated orange rind
1 teaspoon grated lemon rind
100 g (3 1/2 oz) pitted fresh cherries
100 g (3 1/2 oz) white grapes, halved
1 tablespoon whisky

BANOFFIE PIE
Originally, the filling for Banoffie pie was made by boiling the unopened tins of condensed milk until they had formed a sticky caramel inside. The recipe here is an easier and quicker method. A similar substance called *dulce de leche* is eaten in South America. Dulce is the Spanish word for sweet.

BANOFFIE PIE

Preparation time: 35 minutes + chilling
Total cooking time: 30 minutes
Serves 8

⋆⋆

Walnut pastry

1 1/4 cups (155 g/5 oz) plain flour
2 tablespoons icing sugar
85 g (3 oz) ground walnuts
80 g (2 3/4 oz) chilled unsalted butter, chopped

Filling

400 g (13 oz) can condensed milk
30 g (1 oz) unsalted butter
1 tablespoon golden syrup
4 bananas, sliced
1 1/2 cups (375 ml/12 fl oz) cream, whipped
50 g (1 3/4 oz) dark chocolate, melted

1 To make the walnut pastry, sift the flour and icing sugar into a large bowl. Add the walnuts and butter and rub the butter into the flour, using just your fingertips, until the mixture

1 Preheat the oven to moderately hot 200°C (400°F/Gas 6). Brush six 8 cm (3 inch) fluted loose-bottomed 3 cm (1¼ inch) deep tart tins with oil or melted butter.

2 To make the pastry, sift the flours into a bowl, then use just your fingertips to rub in the butter until the mixture resembles breadcrumbs. Stir in the sugar and mix in 2–3 tablespoons iced water, using a flat-bladed knife. Turn onto a floured surface and gather together. Wrap with plastic wrap and refrigerate for 15 minutes.

3 Set aside one-quarter of the dough. Divide the remaining dough into six. Roll each portion out and line the base and side of the tins. Chill for 10 minutes. Line the pastry cases with crumpled baking paper and fill with baking beads or rice. Bake for 10 minutes, remove the paper and beads and cook for another 10 minutes. Cool. Reduce the oven to moderate 180°C (350°F/Gas 4).

4 Mix together all the mincemeat ingredients. Spoon into the pastry cases.

5 Roll out the remaining pastry on a lightly floured surface to 3 mm (⅛ inch) thick. Using a lattice pastry cutter, run it along the length of the pastry. Gently pull the lattice open. Using a 10 cm (4 inch) cutter, cut out 6 rounds. Brush the tart edges with beaten egg, place the pastry lattice rounds on top and press gently to seal. Brush with beaten egg and bake for 45 minutes, or until golden brown. Leave in the tin for 5 minutes, then carefully remove and cool on a rack. Dust with icing sugar before serving.

CUSTARD TART

Preparation time: 20 minutes + chilling
Total cooking time: 1 hour
Serves 8

★ ★

1½ cups (185 g/6 oz) plain flour

¼ cup (30 g/1 oz) custard powder

125 g (4 oz) chilled unsalted butter, chopped

1½ tablespoons caster sugar

1 egg yolk

Custard

4 eggs, lightly beaten

2 teaspoons vanilla essence

½ cup (125 g/4 oz) caster sugar

1½ cups (375 ml/12 fl oz) milk

¼ teaspoon ground nutmeg

1 Sift the flour and custard powder into a bowl. Using just your fingertips, rub in the butter until the mixture resembles breadcrumbs. Stir in the sugar, then use a flat-bladed knife to mix in the yolk and 1–2 tablespoons water, to form a soft dough. Wrap in plastic and chill for 30 minutes.

2 Preheat the oven to moderately hot 190°C (375°F/Gas 5). Lightly grease a pie plate, about 20 cm (8 inch) diameter. Roll the pastry out between two sheets of baking paper and line the base and side of the plate. Trim the edge with a sharp knife. Make a decorative edge if you wish. Line with crumpled baking paper, fill with baking beads or rice and bake for 10 minutes. Remove the paper and beads and bake for 5 minutes, or until the base is dry (cover the edges with foil if overbrowning). Cool. Reduce the oven to moderate 180°C (350°F/Gas 4).

3 To make the custard, mix together the eggs, vanilla essence and sugar. Bring the milk to the boil, remove from the heat and gradually pour onto the egg mixture. Place the pie plate on a baking tray, strain the egg mixture into the pastry case and sprinkle with ground nutmeg. Bake for 40 minutes, or until just set in the centre. Allow to cool and serve cut into wedges.

BELOW: Custard tart

PUMPKIN PIE

Preparation time: 30 minutes + chilling
Total cooking time: 55 minutes
Serves 8

★ ☆

Shortcrust pastry

1¼ cups (155 g/5 oz) plain flour
100 g (3½ oz) chilled unsalted butter, chopped
2 teaspoons caster sugar
4 tablespoons chilled water
1 egg yolk, lightly beaten
1 tablespoon milk

Filling

2 eggs, lightly beaten
1 cup (185 g/6 oz) soft brown sugar
500 g (1 lb) pumpkin, cooked, mashed
    and cooled
⅓ cup (80 ml/2¾ fl oz) cream
1 teaspoon ground cinnamon
½ teaspoon ground nutmeg
½ teaspoon ground ginger

1 Preheat the oven to moderate 180°C (350°F/ Gas 4). Sift the flour into a large bowl. Rub in the butter using just your fingertips, until the mixture resembles breadcrumbs. Stir in the sugar and add almost all the liquid. Mix to a firm dough, adding more liquid if necessary. Turn onto a lightly floured surface and gather together into a ball. Flatten slightly, cover in plastic wrap and refrigerate for at least 30 minutes.
2 Roll out the pastry between two sheets of baking paper to cover the base and side of a 23 cm (9 inch) pie dish. Roll out the trimmings to 2 mm (⅛ inch) thick and cut into leaf shapes. Score vein markings on the leaves. Beat the egg yolk with the milk and brush onto the pastry edge. Arrange the leaves around the edge, pressing on gently and brush them lightly with egg mixture.
3 Line the pastry base with crumpled baking paper and spread baking beads or rice evenly over the paper. Bake for 10 minutes, remove the paper and beads, then bake for 5 minutes, or until lightly golden. Set aside to cool.
4 To make the filling, whisk the eggs and brown sugar in a large bowl. Add the pumpkin, cream and spices, then combine thoroughly. Pour into the pastry shell and bake for 40 minutes, or until set. If the pastry edge begins to brown too much during cooking, cover with foil. Serve at room temperature.

ANZAC APPLE TART

Preparation time: 25 minutes + chilling
Total cooking time: 50 minutes
Serves 6

★ ☆

Shortcrust pastry

1 cup (125 g/4 oz) plain flour
75 g (2½ oz) chilled unsalted butter, chopped
1 egg yolk, lightly beaten
1 tablespoon chilled water

Filling

1¼ cups (125 g/4 oz) rolled oats
¼ cup (60 g/2 oz) caster sugar
½ cup (60 g/2 oz) plain flour
100 g (3½ oz) unsalted butter
2 tablespoons golden syrup
410 g (13 oz) can pie apple

1 Preheat the oven to moderate 180°C (350°F/ Gas 4). Sift the flour into a large bowl and add the butter. Using just your fingertips, rub the butter into the flour until the mixture resembles breadcrumbs. Add the egg yolk and almost all the water and mix to a firm dough, adding more water if necessary. Turn onto a lightly floured surface and gather together into a ball. Flatten slightly, cover in plastic wrap and refrigerate for at least 30 minutes.
2 Roll out the pastry between two sheets of baking paper until it is large enough to fit the base and side of a 20 cm (8 inch) round flan tin. Line the pastry-lined tin with a sheet of crumpled baking paper and spread a layer of baking beads or rice evenly over the paper. Bake for 10 minutes, then remove the paper and beads. Bake the pastry for another 5 minutes, or until lightly golden. Set aside to cool.
3 To make the filling, combine the oats, caster sugar and sifted flour in a large bowl and make a well in the centre. Combine the butter and golden syrup in a small pan. Stir over low heat until the butter has melted, then add to the dry ingredients. Stir until well combined.
4 Spread the pie apple into the pastry shell. Spoon the oat mixture on top and smooth out with the back of a spoon. Bake for 30 minutes, or until golden brown. Leave in the tin for 15 minutes before cutting for serving.

PUMPKIN PIE
The pumpkin probably originated in Europe. Recipes date back to the Renaissance and the cuisine of Northern Italy uses pumpkin with almonds and orange in *Crosta di Zucca*. English recipes for pumpkin pie appear in the 17th and 18th centuries, but seemed to go out of fashion after that. To get the best flavour from pumpkin, cut it into halves or quarters and bake it. The flesh will be much firmer and will not become watery.

OPPOSITE PAGE:
Pumpkin pie (top);
Anzac apple tart

LEMONS

Historians seem unable to agree on where the lemon originated. However, it has been documented by the Greeks and Romans, in China and in the Indus Valley. Lemons have had all kinds of properties attributed to them—the Romans believed they were an antidote to poisons, and French ladies in the time of Louis XIV used to suck on them to keep their lips looking red. Lemons remained expensive for a long time, but luckily the prices dropped by the time the British Admiralty began to issue sailors with lemon juice to prevent scurvy in 1795—the connection between scurvy and the lack of vitamin C had been made in the late 16th century.

Lemons are used in sweet and savoury dishes. They are usually juiced and/or zested and used for flavouring in lemon pies, tarts, puddings, ice creams and sorbets.

ABOVE: Lemon meringue pie

LEMON MERINGUE PIE

Preparation time: 1 hour + chilling
Total cooking time: 45 minutes
Serves 6

★ ★

1¹/₂ cups (185 g/6 oz) plain flour

2 tablespoons icing sugar

125 g (4 oz) chilled unsalted butter, chopped

3 tablespoons iced water

Filling and topping

¹/₄ cup (30 g/1 oz) cornflour

¹/₄ cup (30 g/1 oz) plain flour

1 cup (250 g/8 oz) caster sugar

³/₄ cup (185 ml/6 fl oz) lemon juice

3 teaspoons grated lemon rind

40 g (1¹/₄ oz) unsalted butter, chopped

6 eggs, separated

1¹/₂ cups (375 g/12 oz) caster sugar, extra

¹/₂ teaspoon cornflour, extra

1 Sift the flour and icing sugar into a large bowl. Rub the butter into the flour with your fingertips until the mixture resembles breadcrumbs. Add almost all the water and mix to a firm dough, adding more liquid if necessary. Turn onto a lightly floured surface and gather together into a ball. Roll between two sheets of baking paper until large enough to fit a 23 cm (9 inch) pie plate. Line the pie plate with the pastry, trim the edge and chill for 20 minutes. Preheat the oven to moderate 180°C (350°F/Gas 4).

2 Line the pastry with a sheet of crumpled baking paper and spread a layer of baking beads or rice evenly over the paper. Bake for 10 minutes, then remove the paper and beads. Bake for another 10 minutes, or until the pastry is lightly golden. Leave to cool.

3 To make the filling, place the flours and sugar in a medium pan. Whisk in the lemon juice, rind and 1¹/₂ cups (375 ml/12 oz) water. Whisk continually over medium heat until the mixture boils and thickens. Reduce the heat and cook for another minute, then whisk in the butter and egg yolks, one at a time. Transfer to a bowl, cover the surface with plastic wrap and allow to cool completely.

4 To make the topping, preheat the oven to hot 220°C (425°F/Gas 7). Beat the egg whites in a small, dry bowl with electric beaters, until soft peaks form. Add the extra sugar gradually, beating constantly until the meringue is thick and glossy. Beat in the extra cornflour. Pour the cold filling into the cold pastry shell. Spread with meringue to cover, forming peaks. Bake for 5–10 minutes, or until lightly browned. Serve hot or cold.

LIME CHIFFON PIE

Preparation time: 30 minutes + chilling
Total cooking time: 1 hour
Serves 12

✲ ✲

Almond pastry

1¼ cups (155 g/5 oz) plain flour
90 g (3 oz) ground almonds
90 g (3 oz) chilled unsalted butter, chopped
1–2 tablespoons chilled water

Filling

6 egg yolks
½ cup (125 g/4 oz) caster sugar
100 g (3½ oz) unsalted butter, melted
⅓ cup (80 ml/2¾ fl oz) lime juice
2 teaspoons finely grated lime rind
2 teaspoons gelatine
½ cup (125 ml/4 fl oz) cream, whipped
½ cup (125 g/4 oz) sugar
rind of 4 limes, finely shredded

1 Sift the flour into a large bowl and add the almonds and butter. Using just your fingertips, rub in the butter until the mixture resembles breadcrumbs. Add almost all the water and mix to a firm dough, adding more liquid if necessary. Turn onto a lightly floured surface and gather together into a ball. Roll the pastry out to fit a 23 cm (9 inch) fluted flan tin. Line the tin, trim the edges and refrigerate for 20 minutes.
2 Preheat the oven to moderate 180°C (350°F/ Gas 4). Line the pastry-lined tin with a sheet of crumpled baking paper and spread a layer of baking beads or rice evenly over the paper. Bake for 20 minutes, remove the paper and beads and bake the pastry for another 20 minutes, or until lightly golden. Allow to cool completely.
3 To make the filling, place the egg yolks, sugar,

butter, lime juice and rind in a heatproof bowl. Whisk to combine thoroughly and dissolve the sugar. Stand the bowl over a pan of simmering water and stir constantly for 15 minutes, or until the mixture thickens. Remove from the heat and cool slightly. Put 1 tablespoon water in a small heatproof bowl, sprinkle the gelatine in an even layer over the surface and leave to go spongy. Do not stir. Bring a small pan filled with about 4 cm (1½ inches) water to the boil, remove from the heat and place the bowl into the pan. The water should come halfway up the side of the bowl. Stir the gelatine until clear and dissolved. Cool slightly, add to the lime curd and stir to combine. Cool to room temperature, stirring occasionally.
4 Fold the cream through the lime curd and pour into the pastry case. Refrigerate for 2–3 hours, until set. Leave the pie for 15 minutes at room temperature before serving.
5 To prepare the lime rind, combine the sugar with 1 tablespoon water in a small pan. Stir over low heat until the sugar has dissolved. Bring to the boil, add the rind and simmer for 3 minutes. Drain the rind on a wire rack, then decorate the lime chiffon pie to serve.

ABOVE: Lime chiffon pie

TART TATIN

Cook the butter and sugar until brown. Stir and cook until golden brown.

Arrange the prepared apples upright in concentric circles in the pan, packing them in tightly.

Lay the circle of pastry over the apples and quickly tuck the edges into the side of the pan.

TART TATIN

Preparation time: 35 minutes + chilling
Total cooking time: 1 hour 15 minutes
Serves 6

★★★

85 g (3 oz) unsalted butter, softened
1 egg yolk
1 1/3 cups (165 g/5 1/2 oz) plain flour
100 g (3 1/2 oz) unsalted butter, extra
3/4 cup (185 g/6 oz) sugar
10 apples

1 Cream the butter, egg yolk and 1/4 teaspoon salt together in a bowl with 30 ml (1 fl oz) cold water. Sift the flour over the top and mix it in with a flat-bladed knife. If the pastry appears to be dry, add water, teaspoon by teaspoon until it comes together in a ball. Wrap in plastic wrap, flatten slightly and chill for 30 minutes.

2 Melt the extra butter in a 25 cm (10 inch) frying pan with an ovenproof handle. Add the sugar and cook until the sugar starts to caramelize and turn brown. Stir and continue cooking until the caramel turns golden brown. Cool. Do not worry if the butter separates from the sugar.

3 Peel, halve and core the apples and arrange upright in concentric circles in the pan. Pack them in tightly as they will shrink as they cook. Put the pan back on a gentle heat and cook the apples for 15 minutes, or until they start to turn golden brown. Carefully turn them over and cook the other side until evenly coloured. Cook off any liquid that comes out of the apples over a higher heat. The caramel should be sticky rather than runny when you come to put the pastry on. Remove from the heat and leave to cool. Preheat the oven to hot 220°C (425°F/Gas 7).

4 Roll the pastry out on a floured surface to make a disc slightly bigger than the top of the pan, then lay it over the apples and quickly tuck the edges into the side of the pan. Bake for 20–25 minutes, or until the pastry is golden. Turn out to serve. Warm the tart on the top of the stove if you are not turning it out straight away, just to make sure the caramel is melted. If any apples stick to the bottom of the pan, just poke them back into the gap they came out of.

NOTE: As the moisture content of apples varies, so may the cooking time. Golden delicious, pink lady or fuji are good to use as they don't break down during cooking.

RIGHT: Tart tatin

ORANGE MACADAMIA TARTS

Preparation time: 40 minutes + chilling
Total cooking time: 45 minutes
Serves 6

★★

Shortcrust pastry

1 1/2 cups (185 g/6 oz) plain flour
100 g (3 1/2 oz) chilled unsalted butter, chopped
3–4 tablespoons chilled water

Filling

1 1/2 cups (240 g/7 1/2 oz) macadamia nuts
1/4 cup (45 g/1 1/2 oz) soft brown sugar
2 tablespoons light corn syrup
20 g (3/4 oz) unsalted butter, melted
1 egg, lightly beaten
2 teaspoons finely grated orange rind
icing sugar, to dust

1 Preheat the oven to moderate 180°C (350°F/ Gas 4). Sift the flour into a bowl, add the butter and, using just your fingertips, rub it in until the mixture resembles breadcrumbs. Add almost all the water and mix in with a flat-bladed knife until the mixture comes together, adding more water if necessary. Turn onto a lightly floured surface and gather together into a ball. Divide into six equal portions, roll out and line six 8 cm (3 inch) fluted flan tins, then refrigerate for 15 minutes. Cut sheets of baking paper to fit the pastry-lined tins, crumple the paper, put in the tins, then spread baking beads or rice evenly over the paper. Put the tins on a baking tray and bake for 15 minutes. Remove the beads and paper. Bake for another 10 minutes, or until the pastry is lightly golden. Cool completely.
2 Spread the macadamia nuts in a single layer on a flat baking tray. Bake for about 8 minutes, until lightly golden. Set aside to cool.
3 Divide the macadamia nuts evenly among the pastry shells. With a wire whisk, beat together the brown sugar, light corn syrup, butter, egg, orange rind and a pinch of salt. Pour the mixture over the nuts and bake for 20 minutes, or until set and lightly browned. Dust with icing sugar.

ABOVE: Orange macadamia tarts

PRUNE AND ALMOND TART

Preparation time: 1 hour + soaking + chilling
Total cooking time: 50 minutes
Serves 6–8

★ ★

375 g (12 oz) pitted prunes
2/3 cup (170 ml/5 1/2 fl oz) brandy
1/3 cup (105 g/3 1/2 oz) redcurrant jelly

Almond pastry

1 1/2 cups (185 g/6 oz) plain flour
125 g (4 oz) chilled unsalted butter, chopped
1/3 cup (60 g/2 oz) ground almonds
1/4 cup (60 g/2 oz) caster sugar
1 egg yolk
2–3 tablespoons chilled water
50 g (1 3/4 oz) marzipan, grated

Custard cream

1/4 cup (30 g/1 oz) custard powder
1 2/3 cups (410 ml/13 fl oz) milk
1 tablespoon caster sugar
1/2 cup (125 g/4 oz) sour cream
2 teaspoons vanilla essence

ABOVE: Prune and almond tart

1 Put the prunes in a pan with the brandy, leave to soak for 1 hour, then simmer over very low heat for 10 minutes, or until the prunes are tender but not mushy. Remove the prunes with a slotted spoon and leave to cool. Add the redcurrant jelly to the pan and stir over low heat until dissolved. Cover and set aside.

2 To make the almond pastry, sift the flour into a large bowl. Rub in the butter with just your fingertips, until the mixture resembles breadcrumbs. Stir in the almonds and sugar using a flat-bladed knife. Add the egg yolk and water, until the dough just comes together. Turn out onto a lightly floured surface and gather together into a ball. Flatten slightly, cover with plastic wrap and refrigerate for 15 minutes. Preheat the oven to moderate 180°C (350°F/Gas 4) and heat a baking tray.

3 Roll out the chilled pastry between 2 sheets of baking paper until large enough to line the base and side of a lightly greased 23 cm (9 inch) loose-bottomed flan tin. Ease the pastry into the tin and trim the edge. Refrigerate for 15 minutes. Line the pastry with a sheet of crumpled baking paper and spread a layer of baking beads or rice evenly over the paper, then bake on the heated baking tray for 15 minutes.

4 Remove the paper and beads and bake the pastry for another 5 minutes. Reduce the heat to warm 160°C (315°F/Gas 2–3). Sprinkle marzipan over the pastry base, then bake for another 5–10 minutes, or until golden. Leave in the tin to cool.

5 To make the custard cream, in a small bowl, mix the custard powder with a little milk until smooth. Transfer to a pan and add the remaining milk and sugar. Stir over medium heat for 5 minutes, or until the mixture boils and thickens. Stir in the sour cream and vanilla essence, remove from the heat and cover the surface with plastic wrap to prevent a skin forming. Allow to cool slightly.

6 Spread the custard cream, while it is still warm, evenly over the pastry case. Cut the prunes in half lengthways and arrange over the custard. Warm the redcurrant mixture and carefully spoon over the tart to cover it completely. Refrigerate for at least 2 hours to allow the custard to firm before serving.

RASPBERRY SHORTCAKE

Preparation time: 30 minutes + chilling
Total cooking time: 20 minutes
Serves 6–8

☆ ☆

1 cup (125 g/4 oz) plain flour
1/3 cup (40 g/1 1/4 oz) icing sugar
90 g (3 oz) chilled unsalted butter, chopped
1 egg yolk
1/2 teaspoon vanilla essence
cream, for serving

Topping

750 g (1 1/2 lb) fresh raspberries
1/4 cup (30 g/1 oz) icing sugar
1/3 cup (105 g/3 1/2 oz) redcurrant jelly

1 Sift the flour and icing sugar into a large bowl. Rub in the butter, using just your fingertips, until the mixture resembles breadcrumbs. Add the egg yolk, vanilla essence and 1/2–1 tablespoon water, enough to make the ingredients come together, then mix to a dough with a flat-bladed knife. Turn out onto a lightly floured surface and gather together into a ball. Flatten slightly, wrap in plastic wrap and refrigerate for 30 minutes.

2 Preheat the oven to moderate 180°C (350°F/ Gas 4). Roll out the pastry to fit a fluted 34 x 10 cm (13 x 4 inch) loose-bottomed flan tin and trim the edges. Prick all over with a fork and chill for 20 minutes. Line the pastry with a sheet of crumpled baking paper and spread a layer of baking beads or rice evenly over the paper. Bake for 15–20 minutes, or until golden. Remove the paper and beads and bake for another 15 minutes. Cool on a wire rack.

3 To make the topping, set aside 500 g (1 lb) of the best raspberries and mash the rest with the icing sugar. Spread the mashed raspberries over the shortcake just before serving.

4 Cover with the whole raspberries. Heat the redcurrant jelly in a small pan until melted and smooth. Use a soft pastry brush to coat the raspberries heavily with warm glaze. Cut into slices and serve with cream.

NOTE: Strawberry shortcake is a classic American dish. It is usually made as a round of shortcake which is split, then filled or topped with fresh strawberries.

ABOVE: Raspberry shortcake

LIME PIES WITH BLUEBERRY MARMALADE

Preparation time: 1 hour + standing
Total cooking time: 35–40 minutes
Serves 8

★★

Almond pastry

1/4 cup (45 g/1 1/2 oz) rice flour
1/2 cup (60 g/2 oz) plain flour
100 g (3 1/2 oz) chilled unsalted butter, chopped
45 g (1 1/2 oz) ground almonds
2 tablespoons icing sugar

Lime filling

1 tablespoon custard powder
1 tablespoon sugar
1/4 cup (60 ml/2 fl oz) lime juice
3/4 cup (185 ml/6 fl oz) cream
1/3 cup (90 g/3 oz) sour cream

Blueberry marmalade

1 cup (250 g/8 oz) caster sugar
2 tablespoons lemon juice
125 g (4 oz) blueberries
1 cinnamon stick

BELOW: Lime pies with blueberry marmalade

1 Preheat the oven to moderate 180°C (350°F/ Gas 4). Grease eight 60 ml (2 fl oz) fluted tart tins.

2 Sift the flours into a large bowl, then add the butter. Use just your fingertips to rub the butter in until the mixture resembles breadcrumbs. Stir in the almonds and sugar, add 1 teaspoon water and mix with a flat-bladed knife until the mixture comes together into a ball. Chill for 20 minutes.

3 Divide the dough into eight, roll out between two sheets of baking paper and press into the tins. Trim the edges. Place crumpled baking paper over the pastry and spread baking beads or rice over the paper. Bake for 15 minutes, remove the paper and beads and bake for 3 minutes, or until golden. Leave for 5 minutes, then cool on a rack.

4 Combine the custard powder, sugar, juice and cream in a heavy-based pan. Stir constantly over low heat until the mixture boils and thickens. Remove from the heat and cool slightly. Fold in the sour cream. Divide the custard evenly among the pastry shells and refrigerate until firm.

5 For the marmalade, combine the sugar and juice with 2/3 cup (170 ml/5 1/2 fl oz) water in a heavy-based pan. Stir over low heat, without boiling, until the sugar has dissolved. Add the blueberries and cinnamon stick. Bring to the boil, reduce the heat and simmer for 5 minutes, stirring occasionally. Remove and allow to cool, before serving with the lime pies.

DEEP DISH APPLE PIE

Preparation time: 1 hour + chilling
Total cooking time: 1 hour
Serves 6–8

★ ★

Shortcrust pastry

1 cup (125 g/4 oz) self-raising flour
1 cup (125 g/4 oz) plain flour
125 g (4 oz) chilled unsalted butter, chopped
2 tablespoons caster sugar
2 eggs
1–2 tablespoons milk

8 large apples, peeled, cored and thickly sliced
2 thick strips lemon rind
6 whole cloves
1 cinnamon stick
1/2 cup (125 g/4 oz) sugar

1 Grease a deep, 20 cm (8 inch) round springform tin. Line the base with baking paper, grease the paper, dust lightly with flour and shake off the excess.

2 Sift the flours, then rub in the butter using just your fingertips until the mixture resembles breadcrumbs. Mix in the sugar, add 1 egg and almost all the milk and mix with a flat-bladed knife until the mixture comes together, adding more liquid if necessary. Turn onto a lightly floured surface and gather together. Roll two-thirds of the pastry between two sheets of baking paper to cover the base and side of the tin. Ease into the tin. Roll out the remaining pastry large enough to fit the top of tin. Chill for 20 minutes.

3 Put the apples, rind, cloves, cinnamon, sugar and 2 cups (500 ml/16 fl oz) water in a large pan. Cover and simmer for 10 minutes, or until tender. Remove from the heat, drain and cool. Discard the rind, cloves and cinnamon.

4 Preheat the oven to moderate 180°C (350°F/ Gas 4). Spoon the filling into the pie shell. Cover with the pie top, lightly beat the remaining egg and brush over the pastry edges to seal. Prick the top with a fork. Trim the edges and crimp to seal. Brush with beaten egg and bake for 50 minutes. Leave in the tin for 10 minutes before removing.

ABOVE: Deep dish apple pie

149

BEAUTY TIPS
Traditionally, only savoury pies were decorated, to distinguish them at a glance from sweet pies. Today we are unlikely to bake more than one pie in a day, so confusion shouldn't be a problem.

Pies are usually double crusted (with a pastry base and top) or just crusted on the top, whereas tarts are generally open with no pastry on top. Pies or tarts which are made in pie dishes with a lip can all be decorated around the edge.

As well as making pies look attractive, decorating can be practical—it seals the edges of a double crusted pie, uses up pastry trimmings and helps identify the filling of your pie.

DECORATIVE CRUST EDGES
1 Fork pressed—press a lightly floured fork around the edge of the pie crust.
2 Fluted— press the pastry edge between your thumbs at a slight angle, to create a ripple effect.
3 Crimped—press the pastry between thumb and forefinger, while indenting with the other forefinger.
4 Scalloped—mark or cut out semi-circles with a spoon.

5 Checkerboard—make cuts in the pastry edge. Turn every other square inward.
6 Leaves—cut out leaf shapes with a cutter or template and place over the lip of the pie, fixing with water or egg glaze.
7 Plait—cut three long strips and plait them to the length of the circumference of the tart. Brush the pastry edge with a little water and press gently into place.
8 Rope—twist two long sausages of pastry together and attach to the edge with water.

9 Feathering—lift the pastry off the lip so it stands upright and snip diagonally into the edge of the pie. Push one point inwards and one outwards.

DECORATIVE TOPS

When decorating with pastry trimmings, don't make the shapes too thick or they won't cook through. Re-roll the leftover pastry to an even thickness and cut out shapes with small cutters. If you want to make a shape you don't have a cutter for, draw it on a piece of stiff card and cut out to make a template. The shapes can indicate the pie filling, such as cherries or apples, or be purely whimsical, such as hearts or stars. Attach the shapes to the pastry top with the glaze (often egg white, though for a rich colour, you might use a lightly beaten egg), then glaze them as well.

You can place pastry shapes onto an open tart or around the edge. If the filling is quite liquid, cook the shapes separately and arrange on the middle of the tart after it is baked and the filling has set.

If your tart cooks for a long time, check that the edges are not over-browning and cover with pieces of foil if necessary.

LATTICE TOP

A lattice makes a very impressive top for a pie, and is actually quite easy to make. On a sheet of baking paper, roll the pastry out to a square or rectangle a little larger than the pie (just as you would to cover normally). Using a fluted pastry wheel, or a small, sharp knife, cut strips of pastry about 1.5 cm (5/8 inch) wide. Use a ruler to make perfect straight lines. Lay half the strips on another sheet of baking paper, all in the same direction, and about 1 cm (1/2 inch) apart. Fold alternate strips of pastry back away from you (all the way back to start with). Lay a strip of pastry horizontally across the unfolded strips, then fold them back into place. Fold the lower strips back this time, and lay another strip of pastry across. Repeat with all the strips, alternating the vertical strips. If the pastry is very soft, refrigerate it until firm. Invert the lattice onto the pie and peel the paper away. Press the edges to seal, and trim off the excess pastry. Alternatively, make life easy for yourself and buy a special lattice-cutter, then simply roll out your pastry and roll over it once with your cutter, gently open the lattice out and lift it onto your pie and then trim the edges.

CLOCKWISE, FROM TOP LEFT: Crimped; Checkerboard; Scalloped; Rope; Lattice; Fork pressed; Plait; Leaves; Fluted

151

APPLES

Apples were possibly the first fruit to be cultivated by humans. The original apple was probably a wild type of crab apple. Apples have long been significant in mythology and are related to the acquisition of knowledge. There are many metaphors using apples, the 'apple of someone's eye' dates back to King Alfred, and in cockney rhyming slang 'apples and pears' means stairs. There are thousands of varieties of apple but those available tend to be the types that travel and keep well. Apples should feel heavy and be firm with no wrinkles, bruises or broken flesh. Store in plastic bags in the refrigerator to keep the flesh crisp.

OPPOSITE PAGE: Tart au citron (top); Apple tart

TART AU CITRON

Preparation time: I hour + chilling
Total cooking time: I hour 40 minutes
Serves 6–8

★ ★

Pastry

I cup (125 g/4 oz) plain flour
75 g (2½ oz) unsalted butter, softened
I egg yolk
2 tablespoons icing sugar, sifted

3 eggs
2 egg yolks
¾ cup (185 g/6 oz) caster sugar
½ cup (125 ml/4 fl oz) cream
¾ cup (185 ml/6 fl oz) lemon juice
I½ tablespoons finely grated lemon rind
2 small lemons
⅔ cup (160 g/5½ oz) sugar

1 To make the pastry, sift the flour and a pinch of salt into a large bowl. Make a well and add the butter, egg yolk and icing sugar. Work together the butter, yolk and sugar with your fingertips, then slowly incorporate the flour. Bring together into a ball—you may need to add a few drops of cold water. Flatten the ball slightly, cover with plastic wrap and refrigerate for 20 minutes.
2 Preheat the oven to moderately hot 200°C (400°F/Gas 6). Lightly grease a shallow loose-bottomed flan tin, about 2 cm (¾ inch) deep and 21 cm (8½ inches) across the base.
3 Roll out the pastry between two sheets of baking paper until it is 3 mm (⅛ inch) thick, to fit the base and side of the tin. Trim the edge. Chill for 10 minutes. Line the pastry with crumpled baking paper, fill with baking beads or rice and bake for 10 minutes, or until cooked. Remove the paper and beads and bake for another 6–8 minutes, or until the pastry looks dry all over. Cool the pastry and reduce the oven temperature to slow 150°C (300°F/Gas 2).
4 Whisk the eggs, yolks and sugar together, add the cream and juice and mix well. Strain into a jug and then add the rind. Place the flan tin on a baking sheet on the middle shelf of the oven and carefully pour in the filling right up to the top. Bake for 40 minutes or until it is just set—it should wobble in the middle when the tin is firmly tapped. Cool the tart before removing from its tin.
5 Wash and scrub the lemons well. Slice very thinly (about 2 mm/⅛ inch thick). Combine the sugar and 200 ml (6½ fl oz) water in a small frying pan and stir over low heat until the sugar has dissolved. Add the lemon slices and simmer over low heat for 40 minutes, or until the peel is very tender and the pith looks transparent. Lift out of the syrup and drain on baking paper. If serving the tart immediately, cover the surface with the lemon slices. If not, keep the slices covered and decorate the tart when ready to serve. Serve warm or chilled, with a little cream.

APPLE TART

Preparation time: 30 minutes + chilling
Total cooking time: I hour I5 minutes
Serves 6–8

★ ★

Pastry

I½ cups (185 g/6 oz) plain flour
100 g (3½ oz) chilled unsalted butter, chopped
2–3 tablespoons chilled water

2 cooking apples
3 tablespoons sugar
I egg
⅓ cup (80 ml/2¾ fl oz) cream
I tablespoon Calvados or Kirsch

1 Sift the flour into a bowl, then, using just your fingertips, rub the butter into the flour until the mixture resembles breadcrumbs. Make a well in the centre and add almost all the water. Using a knife, mix to a dough, adding more water if necessary. Gather together and turn out onto a sheet of baking paper. Press together gently until smooth, wrap and chill for 15 minutes. Roll out to fit a 23 cm (9 inch) loose-bottomed, fluted flan tin. Line the tin with the pastry, trimming any excess. Chill for 20 minutes. Preheat the oven to moderately hot 190°C (375°F/Gas 5).
2 Line the pastry with a sheet of crumpled baking paper and fill with baking beads or rice. Bake for 10 minutes, remove the paper and beads and bake for 15 minutes, until cooked on the base and golden around the edge; cool.
3 Peel, core and thinly slice the apples. Arrange in the pastry shell with the slices overlapping, sprinkle with 2 tablespoons sugar and bake for 15 minutes. Meanwhile, whisk together the egg, remaining sugar and the cream. Stir in the liqueur, then pour carefully over the apples. Bake for 35 minutes, or until the cream mixture has set and is puffed and golden (it will sink down as it cools). Serve hot or at room temperature.

Native to North America, pecans are grown across America, as well as in Australia and South Africa. Pecans look like long versions of walnuts but have a smooth, very hard, brown-red shell. The trees can grow to 50 metres and the nuts have to be harvested by shaking the trees, sometimes with mechanical tree shakers. The nuts are usually sold shelled—the hard shells have to be cracked carefully to extract the nuts intact. Pecan pie is a popular dessert that appears on tables around the world but always seems American.

ABOVE: Pecan pie

PECAN PIE

Preparation time: 30 minutes + chilling
Total cooking time: 1 hour 15 minutes
Serves 6

★ ★

Shortcrust pastry

1^{1}/$_{2}$ cups (185 g/6 oz) plain flour
125 g (4 oz) chilled unsalted butter, chopped
2–3 tablespoons chilled water

Filling

200 g (6^{1}/$_{2}$ oz) pecans
3 eggs, lightly beaten
50 g (1^{3}/$_{4}$ oz) unsalted butter, melted and cooled
^{3}/$_{4}$ cup (140 g/4^{1}/$_{2}$ oz) soft brown sugar
^{2}/$_{3}$ cup (170 ml/5^{1}/$_{2}$ fl oz) light corn syrup
1 teaspoon vanilla essence

1 Preheat the oven to moderate 180°C (350°F/ Gas 4). Sift the flour into a large bowl, then rub in the butter, using just your fingertips, until the mixture resembles breadcrumbs. Add almost all the water and mix until the mixture comes together, adding more water if necessary. Turn out onto a lightly floured surface and gather together into a ball.

2 Roll out the pastry to a 35 cm (14 inch) round. Line a 23 cm (9 inch) flan tin with pastry, trim the edges and refrigerate for 20 minutes. Pile the pastry trimmings together, roll out on baking paper to a rectangle about 2 mm (^{1}/$_{8}$ inch) thick, then refrigerate.

3 Line the pastry-lined tin with a sheet of crumpled baking paper and spread a layer of baking beads or rice evenly over the paper. Bake for 15 minutes, remove the paper and beads and bake for another 15 minutes, or until lightly golden. Cool completely.

4 To make the filling, spread the pecans over the pastry base. In a large jug, whisk together the eggs, butter, sugar, corn syrup, vanilla essence and a pinch of salt until well combined, then pour over the nuts.

5 Using a fluted pastry wheel or small sharp knife, cut narrow strips from half the pastry. Cut out small stars with a biscuit cutter from the remaining pastry. Arrange decoratively over the filling. Bake the pie for 45 minutes, or until firm. Allow to cool completely and serve at room temperature.

CHERRY PIE

Preparation time: 25 minutes
  + chilling
Total cooking time: 40 minutes
Serves 6–8

★ ★

Almond pastry

1 1/4 cups (155 g/5 oz) plain flour
1/4 cup (30 g/1 oz) icing sugar
100 g (3 1/2 oz) chilled unsalted butter,
  chopped
60 g (2 oz) ground almonds
3 tablespoons chilled water

2 x 700 g (1 lb 7 oz) jars pitted
  morello cherries, drained
1 egg, lightly beaten
caster sugar, to decorate
cream or ice cream, optional,
  for serving

1 Sift the flour and icing sugar into a bowl. Add the butter and rub in with just your fingertips until the mixture is fine and crumbly. Stir in the ground almonds, then add almost all the water and stir into the flour mixture with a flat-bladed knife until the mixture forms a dough, adding the remaining water if necessary.
2 Turn the dough onto a lightly floured surface and gather together into a ball. Roll out on a sheet of baking paper into a circle about 26 cm (10 1/2 inches) in diameter. Flatten slightly, cover with plastic wrap and refrigerate for 20 minutes. Spread the cherries into a 23 cm (9 inch) round pie dish.
3 Preheat the oven to moderately hot 200°C (400°F/Gas 6). Cover the pie dish with the pastry and trim the overhanging edge. Roll out the remaining scraps of pastry and use a small sharp knife to cut out decorations. Brush the pastry top all over with beaten egg and arrange the decorations on top. Brush these with beaten egg as well, and then sprinkle lightly with caster sugar. Place the pie dish on a baking tray (the cherry juice may overflow a little) and cook for 35–40 minutes, or until golden brown. Serve warm or at room temperature, with cream or ice cream, if you like.

ALMONDS

Almonds are the seeds of a tree related to the apricot and peach trees. Almonds are native to the Middle East and have a tough, oval, pale brown outer shell which is pointed at one end. In Europe, almonds are also picked when the shell is still covered by a velvety green outer coating. The inner shell has a dark brown skin which can be removed by blanching. Almonds are available whole in shells, shelled with their skins on, blanched, flaked, chopped and ground. Ground almonds are the basis of many biscuits and cakes, as well as being used in pastries and desserts.

ABOVE: Cherry pie

155

RHUBARB

Originating in northern Asia, rhubarb was first documented in China in about 2700 BC. It was used as a medicine for the next few centuries and was believed to be a purgative. It was grown in monastery gardens and by herbalists but was not eaten as a food until around 1800. Rhubarb became common in the British diet as it was easily grown in gardens. It is used in pies, crumbles, fools and, of course, rhubarb and custard. Only the stalks are eaten as the leaves contain oxalic acid and are poisonous in quantity. Forced rhubarb, grown in hothouses in the off season, has a redder, more tender stem than that available in season which has a greener, thicker stem sometimes requiring peeling. Buy stalks which are still crisp and have not wilted. Redder stems give a sweeter flavour.

ABOVE: Farmhouse rhubarb pie

FARMHOUSE RHUBARB PIE

Preparation time: 40 minutes + chilling
Total cooking time: 50 minutes
Serves 6

★ ★

Shortcrust pastry

1 1/2 cups (185 g/6 oz) plain flour, sifted
2 tablespoons icing sugar
125 g (4 oz) chilled unsalted butter, chopped
1 egg yolk

1 cup (250 g/8 oz) sugar
750 g (1 1/2 lb) rhubarb, chopped
2 large apples, peeled, cored and chopped
2 teaspoons grated lemon rind
3 pieces preserved ginger, sliced
2 teaspoons sugar
sprinkle of ground cinnamon

1 Sift the flour into a large bowl, add the icing sugar, then use just your fingertips to rub in the butter until the mixture resembles breadcrumbs. Add the egg yolk and 1 tablespoon water and mix with a knife until the dough comes together. Turn onto a floured surface, gather into a ball, flatten slightly and refrigerate in plastic wrap for 15 minutes. Preheat the oven to moderately hot 190°C (375°F/Gas 5). Roll the pastry out to a rough 35 cm (14 inch) circle and line a greased 20 cm (8 inch) pie plate, leaving the extra pastry to hang over the edge. Refrigerate while you prepare the filling.
2 Heat the sugar and 1/2 cup (125 ml/4 fl oz) water in a pan for 4–5 minutes, or until syrupy. Add the rhubarb, apple, lemon rind and ginger, then cover and simmer for 5 minutes, until the rhubarb is cooked but still holds its shape.
3 Drain off the liquid and cool the rhubarb. Spoon into the pastry base and sprinkle with the sugar and cinnamon. Fold the overhanging pastry roughly over the fruit and bake for 40 minutes, or until golden. Dust with icing sugar. Delicious with ice cream or custard.

REAL LEMON PIE

Preparation time: 30 minutes + standing
Total cooking time: 50–55 minutes
Serves 8–10

★★

Lemon filling

4 thin-skinned lemons

2 cups (500 g/1 lb) caster sugar

4 eggs

Shortcrust pastry

1³/₄ cups (220 g/7 oz) plain flour

150 g (5 oz) chilled unsalted butter, chopped

2 tablespoons caster sugar

milk, for glazing

1 Wash the lemons. Slice 2 unpeeled lemons very thinly and remove the seeds. Peel the other lemons, removing all the pith, and slice the flesh very thinly. Remove the seeds. Put all the lemons in a bowl with the sugar and stir until all the slices are coated. Cover and leave overnight.

2 Preheat the oven to moderate 180°C (350°F/ Gas 4). Sift the flour and a pinch of salt into a bowl. Use your fingertips to rub in the butter until crumbly. Stir in the sugar. Gradually add 1–2 tablespoons water, mixing with a knife. Gather the dough together, divide in half and roll each portion into a 25 cm (10 inch) circle. Lightly grease a 23 cm (9 inch) pie dish and line with pastry. Cover and chill the other circle.

3 Beat the eggs and add to the lemon slices, mixing gently but thoroughly. Spoon into the pastry shell and cover with the pastry circle, crimping the edges to seal. Decorate the top with pastry scraps, brush with milk and bake for 50–55 minutes, or until golden brown.

NOTE: To use this pastry for a delicious apple pie, peel, core and slice 5 apples into thin slices, toss the apple slices in 3 tablespoons caster sugar and a large pinch of cinnamon and fill the pie. Cover with the pastry lid and press the edges together to seal. Trim the edges and make two or three slashes in the top of the the pie. Dust with 1 tablespoon caster sugar and bake in a preheated moderate 180°C (350°F/Gas 4) oven for 50 minutes.

BELOW: Real lemon pie

BERRY PIE

Preparation time: 30 minutes + chilling
Total cooking time: 40 minutes
Serves 4–6

★ ★

1 cup (125 g/4 oz) self-raising flour
1 cup (125 g/4 oz) plain flour
125 g (4 oz) chilled unsalted butter, chopped
2 tablespoons caster sugar
1 egg, lightly beaten
3–4 tablespoons milk
1 egg yolk, extra, mixed with 1 teaspoon water,
    to glaze
icing sugar, to dust

BELOW: Berry pie

Berry filling

2 tablespoons cornflour
2–4 tablespoons caster sugar, to taste
1 teaspoon grated orange rind
1 tablespoon orange juice
600 g (1 1/4 lb) fresh berries such as
    boysenberries, blackberries, loganberries,
    mulberries, raspberries or youngberries

1 Sift the flours into a large bowl. Rub in the butter using just your fingertips until the mixture resembles breadcrumbs. Stir in the sugar, then add the egg and almost all the milk and mix with a flat-bladed knife until the mixture comes together, adding more milk if necessary. Turn out onto a lightly floured surface and gather together into a ball. Divide into 2 portions and roll each portion out on a sheet of baking paper, making sure one is the right size to fit the top of a 750 ml (24 fl oz) pie dish. Cover with plastic wrap and refrigerate for 30 minutes.

2 To make the berry filling, mix the cornflour, caster sugar, orange rind and juice in a medium pan. Add half the berries to the pan and stir over low heat for 5 minutes, or until the mixture boils and thickens. Remove from the heat and set aside to cool. Add the remaining berries to the pan, pour into the pie dish and smooth the surface with the back of a spoon.

3 Preheat the oven to moderate 180°C (350°F/Gas 4). Place the pie top over the fruit and trim the edges. Make sure you do not stretch the pastry or it may shrink during baking and fall back into the dish. Using heart-shaped pastry cutters of various sizes, cut out enough hearts to cover the pie top. Arrange them on top of the pie, moistening each one with a little water to make it stick.

4 Brush all over the surface with the egg glaze. Bake for 35–40 minutes or until the pastry is crisp and golden brown. Sprinkle the top with icing sugar just before serving. Serve the pie warm or cold.

NOTE: Use just one variety of berry or a combination if you prefer. If you want to make the pie when the berries are out of season, use frozen berries. Defrost the berries thoroughly, reserving the juice. Add the berries and juice to the filling and omit the orange juice. You can use canned berries if you drain them well first.

TREACLE TART

Preparation time: 30 minutes + chilling
Total cooking time: 30 minutes
Serves 4–6

☆ ☆

Shortcrust pastry

1¼ cups (155 g/5 oz) plain flour

90 g (3 oz) chilled unsalted butter, chopped

2–3 tablespoons chilled water

1 egg, beaten, to glaze

Filling

1 cup (350 g/11 oz) golden syrup

25 g (¾ oz) unsalted butter

½ teaspoon ground ginger

1¾ cups (140 g/4½ oz) fresh white
   breadcrumbs

1 Sift the flour into a large bowl. Rub in the
butter using just your fingertips until the mixture
resembles breadcrumbs. Add almost all the water
and mix to a firm dough, adding more water if

necessary. Turn onto a lightly floured surface
and gather together into a ball. Cover with
plastic wrap and refrigerate for 20 minutes.
2 Brush a 20 cm (8 inch) diameter flan tin with
melted butter or oil. Roll out the pastry large
enough to fit the base and side of the tin
(allowing a 4 cm/1½ inch overhang). Ease the
pastry into the tin and trim by running a rolling
pin firmly across the top of the tin. Re-roll the
trimmed pastry to a rectangle 20 x 10 cm
(8 x 4 inches). Using a sharp knife or fluted
pastry wheel, cut into long 1 cm (½ inch) strips.
Cover the pastry-lined tin and strips with plastic
wrap and refrigerate for 20 minutes.
3 Preheat the oven to moderate 180°C (350°F/
Gas 4). Combine the golden syrup, butter and
ginger in a small pan and stir over low heat until
the butter melts. Stir in the breadcrumbs until
combined. Pour the mixture into the pastry case.
Weave the pastry strips in a lattice pattern over
the tart, starting at the centre and working
outwards (see page 151). Brush the lattice with
beaten egg. Bake for 30 minutes, or until the
pastry is lightly golden. Serve warm or at room
temperature. You can dust the top with icing
sugar and serve with ice cream or cream.

ABOVE: Treacle tart

CHOUX PASTRY

Remove the heated butter from the stove and quickly beat in the flour.

Return the pan to the heat and continue beating until the mixture comes together and leaves the side of the pan.

Gradually add the beaten egg, about 3 teaspoons at a time, beating well until all the egg is used and the mixture is thick and glossy.

The mixture is ready when a wooden spoon will stand upright in it.

ABOVE: Profiteroles

PROFITEROLES

Preparation time: 20 minutes
Total cooking time: 50 minutes
Makes 32

★ ★

Choux pastry

50 g (1³/4 oz) unsalted butter
³/4 cup (90 g/3 oz) plain flour, sifted twice
3 eggs, lightly beaten

Filling

1¹/2 cups (375 ml/12 fl oz) milk
4 egg yolks
¹/3 cup (90 g/3 oz) caster sugar
3 tablespoons plain flour
1 teaspoon vanilla essence

110 g (3¹/2 oz) good-quality dark chocolate
2 teaspoons vegetable oil

1 Preheat the oven to hot 210°C (415°F/Gas 6–7). Put the butter in a large heavy-based pan with ³/4 cup (185 ml/6 fl oz) water and stir over medium heat until coming to the boil. Remove from the heat and quickly beat in the flour. Return to the heat and continue beating until the mixture comes together and leaves the side of the pan. Allow to cool slightly.

2 Transfer to a bowl and beat to release any more heat. Gradually add the beaten egg about 3 teaspoons at a time, beating well until all the egg has been added and the mixture is thick and glossy—a wooden spoon should stand upright in it. (If it is too runny, the egg has been added too quickly. Beat for several more minutes, or until thickened.) Spoon the mixture onto two baking trays, leaving room for spreading. A heaped teaspoonful of mixture will make 1 small puff. Sprinkle the baking trays with water—this creates steam, helping the puffs to rise. Bake for 20–30 minutes, or until browned and hollow sounding, then remove and make a small hole in the base of each one. Return to the oven for 5 minutes to dry out. Cool on a wire rack.
3 To make the filling, put the milk into a small pan and bring to the boil. Set aside while quickly whisking the yolks and sugar in a bowl, until light and creamy. Whisk in the flour. Pour the hot milk slowly onto the egg mixture, whisking constantly. Wash out the pan, return the milk mixture and bring to the boil, stirring with a wire whisk. Boil for 2 minutes, stirring often. Transfer to a bowl, stir in the vanilla, cover the surface of the custard with plastic wrap to prevent a skin forming, then refrigerate until cold.
4 Pipe the filling into the profiteroles through the hole in the base, using a piping bag and nozzle. Melt the chocolate and oil gently, stir until smooth and dip the profiterole tops in the chocolate.

PARIS BREST

Preparation time: 50 minutes
Total cooking time: 1 hour 15 minutes
Serves 6–8

★★

Choux pastry

50 g (1¾ oz) unsalted butter
¾ cup (90 g/3 oz) plain flour, sifted
3 eggs, lightly beaten

Filling

3 egg yolks
¼ cup (60 g/2 oz) caster sugar
2 tablespoons plain flour
1 cup (250 ml/8 fl oz) milk
1 teaspoon vanilla essence
1 cup (250 ml/8 fl oz) cream,
   whipped
200 g (6½ oz) raspberries or
   250 g (8 oz) strawberries, or a mixture

Topping

125 g (4 oz) dark chocolate, chopped
30 g (1 oz) unsalted butter
1 tablespoon cream

1 Preheat the oven to hot 210°C (415°F/ Gas 6–7). Brush a large tray with melted butter or oil and line the tray with baking paper and mark a 23 cm (9 inch) circle on the paper.
2 Stir the butter with ¾ cup (185 ml/6 fl oz) water in a medium pan over low heat until the butter has melted and the mixture boils. Remove from the heat, add the flour all at once and, using a wooden spoon, beat until smooth. Return to the heat and beat until the mixture thickens and comes away from the side of the pan. Remove from the heat and cool slightly.
3 Transfer to a large bowl. Using electric beaters, add the eggs gradually, beating until stiff and glossy. Place heaped tablespoons of mixture touching each other, using the marked circle as a guide. Bake for 25–30 minutes, or until browned and hollow sounding when the base is tapped. Turn off the oven and leave the pastry to dry in the oven.
4 To make the filling, whisk the yolks, sugar and flour in a bowl until pale. Heat the milk in a pan until almost boiling. Gradually add to the egg mixture, stirring constantly. Return to the pan and stir constantly over medium heat until

the mixture boils and thickens. Cook for another 2 minutes, stirring constantly. Remove from the heat and stir in the vanilla essence. Transfer to a bowl, cover the surface with plastic wrap to prevent a skin forming and set aside to cool.
5 To make the topping, combine the chocolate, butter and cream in a heatproof bowl. Stand the bowl over a pan of simmering water and stir until the chocolate has melted and the mixture is smooth. Cool slightly.
6 To assemble, cut the pastry ring in half horizontally using a serrated knife. Remove any excess dough that remains in the centre. Fold the whipped cream through the custard and spoon into the base of the pastry. Top with raspberries or halved strawberries. Replace the remaining pastry half on top. Using a flat-bladed knife, spread the chocolate mixture over the top of the pastry. Leave to set.
NOTE: The pastry ring may be made up to 4 hours in advance. Store in an airtight container. Custard may be made up to 4 hours in advance; refrigerate until required. Assemble close to serving time.

ABOVE: Paris brest

CROQUEMBOUCHE

Literally *crunch in the mouth*, croquembouche is a traditional French dessert made of profiteroles filled with cream or crème patisserie, stacked into a cone shape and decorated with spun sugar. The cone is formed around a stainless steel mould and the profiteroles are attached to each other with caramel. The finished dessert is lifted off the mould. Some versions are placed on a nougatine base and decoration varies. Croquembouche is usually served at celebrations such as weddings and first communions.

ABOVE: Croquembouche

CROQUEMBOUCHE

Preparation time: 1 hour 30 minutes
Total cooking time: 1 hour 30 minutes
Serves 10–12

✩ ✩ ✩

Choux pastry

100 g (3¹/₂ oz) unsalted butter
1¹/₂ cups (185 g/6 oz) plain flour, sifted
6 eggs, beaten
4 cups (1 kg/2 lb) sugar

Filling

1¹/₂ cups (375 ml/12 fl oz) milk
1 vanilla bean
3 egg yolks
¹/₄ cup (60 g/2 oz) caster sugar
2 tablespoons plain flour
¹/₄ cup (60 ml/2 fl oz) Grand Marnier
1¹/₂ cups (375 ml/12 fl oz) cream

1 Preheat the oven to hot 210°C (415°F/Gas 6–7). Put the butter in a large heavy-based pan with 1¹/₂ cups (375 ml/12 fl oz) water and stir over medium heat until the mixture comes to the boil. Remove from the heat and quickly beat in the flour. Return to the heat and continue beating until the mixture comes together and leaves the side of the pan. Allow to cool slightly.

2 Beat the mixture to release any more heat. Gradually add the beaten egg, about 3 teaspoons at a time. Beat well between each addition until all the egg has been added and the mixture is thick and glossy—a wooden spoon should stand upright in it. (If it is too runny, the egg has been added too quickly. Beat for several more minutes, or until thickened.) Sprinkle 3 baking trays with water—this creates steam, helping the puffs to rise. Spoon the mixture onto the trays, leaving plenty of room for spreading. You will need about eight large puffs (use 1 tablespoon mixture for each). Vary the remainder, gradually reducing the size. One small puff is equal to about 1 heaped teaspoonful of mixture. Bake for 20–30 minutes,

or until browned and hollow sounding when the base is tapped. Turn the oven off and leave the puffs inside to dry out. (You may need to prepare and cook them in two batches.)

3 To make the filling, put the milk and vanilla bean in a pan. Heat gently until the milk almost boils. Remove from the heat and cool slightly. Beat the yolks, sugar and flour until thick and pale. Gradually whisk in the warm milk. Stir over medium heat until the custard boils and thickens. Remove from the heat and stir in the liqueur. Discard the vanilla bean. Cover the surface of the custard with plastic wrap to prevent a skin forming and cool completely.

4 Whip the cream into stiff peaks and fold into the custard. Put into a piping bag with a nozzle less than 1 cm (1/2 inch). Poke a small hole in the base of each puff and fill with custard.

5 Put 2 cups of the sugar in a pan with 1 cup (250 ml/8 fl oz) of water. Stir over low heat, without boiling, until dissolved. Bring to the boil and cook until lightly golden. Remove from the heat and plunge the base of the pan in cold water.

6 To assemble, begin with the large puffs. Dip the bases in enough toffee to coat and arrange in a large circle, with the sides touching—you don't need to have any in the centre. Build up into a cone shape, using smaller puffs nearer the top.

7 Make the rest of the toffee and then dip two forks in it. Rub the backs of the forks together until tacky, then gently pull them apart (see page 248). Spin toffee around the Croquembouche.

CHERRY CHEESE STRUDEL

Preparation time: 25 minutes
Total cooking time: 35–40 minutes
Serves 8–10

✷ ✷

500 g (1 lb) ricotta

2 teaspoons lemon or orange rind

1/4 cup (60 g/2 oz) sugar

1/2 cup (40 g/1 1/4 oz) fresh breadcrumbs

2 tablespoons ground almonds

2 eggs

425 g (14 oz) can pitted black cherries

2 teaspoons cornflour

8 sheets filo pastry

60 g (2 oz) unsalted butter, melted

2 tablespoons dry breadcrumbs

icing sugar, to dust

1 Preheat the oven to moderate 180°C (350°F/ Gas 4). Lightly grease a baking tray with melted butter. Combine the ricotta, rind, sugar, breadcrumbs and almonds in a bowl. Add the eggs and mix well. Drain the cherries, reserving half the juice. Blend the cornflour with the reserved cherry juice in a small pan. Stir over heat until the mixture boils and thickens, then cool slightly.

2 Layer the pastry sheets, brushing between each sheet with melted butter and sprinkling with a few breadcrumbs. Form a large square by placing the second sheet halfway down the first sheet. Alternate layers, brushing with melted butter and sprinkling with breadcrumbs.

3 Place the ricotta mixture along one long edge of the pastry. Shape into a log and top with cherries and cooled syrup. Roll the pastry around the ricotta filling, folding in the edges as you roll. Finish with a pastry edge underneath. Place on the prepared tray and bake for 35–40 minutes, or until the pastry is golden. Serve in slices, warm or cold, heavily dusted with icing sugar. Can be served with cream.
NOTE: To make an apple strudel, fill the strudel with a mixture of cooked apples with some sultanas or raisins, roll and bake.

STRUDEL PASTRY
Traditional strudel dough uses flour with a high gluten content which makes the pastry strong and less tearable. It is rolled as thinly as possible before being layered with breadcrumbs and wrapped around the filling. Filo is an easier option which gives a similar result. Strudel is an Austrian speciality although it appears in the cuisine of many countries and the name means literally *whirlpool*.

BELOW: Cherry cheese strudel

2 Roll the pastry between two layers of baking paper to 5 mm (¼ inch) thick. Using a 7 cm (2¾ inch) fluted round cutter, cut 18 rounds from the pastry. Place on the prepared trays and bake for 8 minutes, or until cooked through. Transfer to a wire rack to cool.

3 Place a biscuit on a serving plate, top with a little cream and some strawberries. Top with a second biscuit, cream and strawberries, then a third biscuit. Repeat to make another five stacks. Dust each with a little sifted cocoa and icing sugar. For the sauce, process the strawberries and sugar until smooth and stir in 1–2 tablespoons water, until pourable. Serve with the shortbreads.

CUSTARD ROLLS

Preparation time: 35 minutes
Total cooking time: 20 minutes
Makes 18 rolls

★ ★

1½ cups (375 ml/12 fl oz) milk
½ cup (125 g/4 oz) caster sugar
½ cup (60 g/2 oz) semolina
1 teaspoon grated lemon rind
1 egg, lightly beaten
12 sheets filo pastry
125 g (4 oz) unsalted butter, melted
2 tablespoons icing sugar
½ teaspoon ground cinnamon

1 Put the milk, caster sugar, semolina and lemon rind in a pan and stir until coming to the boil. Reduce the heat and simmer for 3 minutes.
2 Remove from the heat and gradually whisk in the egg. Pour into a bowl, cover the surface with plastic wrap and set aside to cool. Preheat the oven to moderate 180°C (350°F/Gas 4). Lightly brush two baking trays with melted butter.
3 Work with 2 sheets of filo at a time. Cover the rest with a tea towel. Brush one with butter, then top with another. Cut lengthways into three strips. Brush the edges with melted butter.
4 Spoon about a tablespoon of custard 5 cm (2 inches) in from the short edge of each pastry strip. Roll the pastry over the filling, fold the ends in, then roll up. Repeat with the remaining pastry and custard. Arrange on the trays 2 cm (¾ inch) apart. Brush with the remaining butter. Bake for 12–15 minutes, or until crisp and golden. Cool on a wire rack. Dust with a little combined icing sugar and cinnamon.

CHOCOLATE SHORTBREADS

Preparation time: 25 minutes
Total cooking time: 10 minutes
Serves 6

★ ★

1½ cups (185 g/6 oz) plain flour
⅓ cup (40 g/1¼ oz) cocoa powder
¾ cup (90 g/3 oz) icing sugar
225 g (7¼ oz) chilled unsalted butter, chopped
2 egg yolks
1 teaspoon vanilla essence
1 cup (250 ml/8 fl oz) cream, whipped
250 g (8 oz) strawberries, quartered

Berry sauce

250 g (8 oz) fresh strawberries, or frozen, thawed
1 tablespoon caster sugar

1 Preheat the oven to hot 210°C (415°F/Gas 6–7). Line two baking trays with baking paper. Sift the flour, cocoa and icing sugar into a large bowl. Rub in the butter, using just your fingertips, until the mixture resembles breadcrumbs. Add the yolks and vanilla and mix with a knife until the mixture comes together. Turn onto a lightly floured surface and gather together into a ball.

ABOVE: Chocolate shortbreads

SABLES WITH BERRIES AND CREAM

Preparation time: 50 minutes
Total cooking time: 50 minutes
Serves 6

★ ★

1 cup (185 g/6 oz) plain flour
1/3 cup (40 g/1 1/4 oz) icing sugar
125 g (4 oz) chilled unsalted butter,
  chopped
1 egg yolk
1 tablespoon lemon juice
1 1/2 cups (375 ml/12 fl oz) cream
1 teaspoon vanilla essence
1 tablespoon icing sugar
400 g (13 oz) mixed berries
icing sugar, to dust

1 Preheat the oven to warm 160°C (315°F/ Gas 2–3). Grease two baking trays and line with baking paper. Sift the flour and sugar together into a bowl. Using just your fingertips, rub the butter into the flour until fine and crumbly. Make a well, add the egg yolk and juice and mix to a dough with a knife. Gather together into a ball, cover and refrigerate for 15 minutes.

2 Divide the dough in half. Roll out one half between well-floured sheets of baking paper (be careful as this dough is very rich and delicate), to 3 mm (1/8 inch) thick. Slide the pastry onto a tray and refrigerate for 5–10 minutes. Using a 7.5 cm (3 inch) round or heart-shaped biscuit cutter dipped in flour, cut out nine shapes. Place on the prepared trays, prick with a fork and refrigerate for 10 minutes. Bake for 20–25 minutes, or until the biscuits are firm but not coloured. Allow to cool slightly on the tray before transferring to a wire rack to cool completely. Repeat with the remaining dough.

3 Whisk the cream, vanilla essence and icing sugar together until firm. Spoon or pipe in the middle of a third of the biscuits. Arrange some fruit around the cream and top with another biscuit. Repeat with the remaining biscuits, cream and berries, assembling 3-tier biscuits. Lightly dust with icing sugar.

BELOW: Sables with berries and cream

1 To make the syrup, combine the sugar and lemon juice with ⅔ cup (170 ml/5½ fl oz) water in a small pan. Stir constantly over low heat until the sugar has dissolved. Bring to the boil, reduce the heat and simmer, without stirring, for 10 minutes. Cool completely.

2 Preheat the oven to moderate 180°C (350°F/ Gas 4). Brush the sides and base of a shallow 18 x 28 cm (7 x 11 inch) ovenproof dish with melted butter or oil. Combine the walnuts, almonds, spices and sugar in a bowl, then divide into 3 portions. Place 1 sheet of pastry on a work surface. Brush half the sheet with the combined butter and oil mixture, then fold in half widthways. Trim the edges to fit the dish. Place into the base of the prepared dish. Repeat the process with another three sheets of pastry.

3 Sprinkle one portion of walnut mixture over the pastry. Repeat the pastry process with 4 more sheets. Sprinkle with the second portion of walnut mixture. Continue with another 4 sheets of pastry, the remaining walnut mixture and the final 4 sheets of pastry. Carefully trim the edges.

4 Brush the top of the pastry with the remaining butter and oil mixture. Cut the slice evenly into four, lengthways. (Do not cut through to the base.) Bake for 30 minutes, or until the pastry is golden and crisp. Pour the cooled syrup over the hot baklava. When completely cold, cut the baklava into squares or diamonds.

BAKLAVA

Preparation time: 25 minutes
Total cooking time: 45 minutes
Serves 4–6

★★ ☆

Syrup

1 cup (250 g/4 oz) sugar

3 teaspoons lemon juice

3½ cups (435 g/14 oz) walnuts, finely chopped, not ground

1 cup (155 g/5 oz) almonds, finely chopped

½ teaspoon ground cinnamon

½ teaspoon ground mixed spice

1 tablespoon caster sugar

60 g (2 oz) unsalted butter, melted

1 tablespoon olive oil

16 sheets filo pastry

ABOVE: Baklava

SICILIAN CANNOLI

Preparation time: 30 minutes
Total cooking time: 10 minutes
Makes 18

★★ ☆

2 cups (250 g/8 oz) plain flour

2 teaspoons instant coffee

2 teaspoons cocoa

2 tablespoons caster sugar

60 g (2 oz) chilled unsalted butter, chopped

oil, for deep-frying

Filling

250 g (8 oz) ricotta

1½ cups (185 g/6 oz) icing sugar

4 teaspoons orange flower water

30 g (1 oz) dark chocolate, grated

60 g (2 oz) candied peel

icing sugar, to dust

1 To make the pastry, stir together the flour, coffee, cocoa, sugar and a pinch of salt. Rub the butter into the flour until you have fine breadcrumbs, then work in up to ½ cup (125 ml/4 fl oz) water to make a soft dough. Knead lightly and divide into two. Roll each half out between two sheets of baking paper into sheets about 3 mm (⅛ inch) thick. Cut into 18 squares (7.5 cm/2¾ inches). Place metal cannoli moulds or cannelloni pasta tubes diagonally across the squares and fold the corners across to overlap in the middle. Moisten the overlapping dough, then press firmly to seal. (If you use cannelloni pasta tubes, discard them after use.)

2 Deep-fry the tubes, a few at a time, in hot oil deep enough to cover them. When golden and crisp, remove with a slotted spoon and leave to cool, still on their moulds.

3 To prepare the filling, beat the ricotta, icing sugar and orange flower water until smooth. Fold in the chocolate and peel. Set in the fridge.

4 Slide the pastry tubes off the moulds. Using a piping bag or a spoon, stuff the tubes with filling, leaving some exposed at each end. Dust with icing sugar before serving. Cannoli don't keep beyond a couple of hours once filled.

PEAR DUMPLINGS

Preparation time: 40 minutes + cooling
Total cooking time: 40 minutes
Serves 4

★ ★

1 cup (250 g/8 oz) caster sugar
2 cinnamon sticks
2 cloves
4 pears
2 cups (250 g/8 oz) plain flour
150 g (5 oz) chilled unsalted butter, chopped
⅔ cup (85 g/3 oz) icing sugar
⅓ cup (80 ml/2¾ fl oz) lemon juice
1 egg, lightly beaten

1 Stir the sugar with 1.5 litres water in a large pan over low heat until the sugar has completely dissolved. Add the cinnamon sticks and cloves and bring to the boil.

2 Peel the pears, leaving the stems intact. Add to the pan, cover and simmer for about 10 minutes, until just tender when tested with the point of a sharp knife. Remove the pears, drain thoroughly and cool completely. Remove the pear cores

using a melon baller—leave the stem attached.

3 Sift the flour into a large bowl and rub in the butter until it resembles fine breadcrumbs. Stir in the icing sugar. Add almost all the juice and mix with a flat-bladed knife until the mixture comes together, adding more juice if necessary. Turn onto a lightly floured work surface and gather together into a ball. Chill for 20 minutes.

4 Preheat the oven to moderate 180°C (350°F/ Gas 4). Line a flat baking tray with baking paper. Divide the dough into 4 equal portions and roll one portion out to a 23 cm (9 inches) diameter circle. Place a pear in the centre of the pastry, cut the pastry into a wide cross and set cut-out sections aside. Carefully fold one section of pastry at a time up the side of the pear, trimming and pressing the edges together to neatly cover. Repeat with the remaining pears.

5 Cut leaf shapes from the leftover pastry. Brush the pears all over with egg and attach the leaves, then brush the leaves with egg. Put the pears on the tray and bake for 30 minutes, or until golden brown. Serve warm with custard or cream.

PEAR DUMPLINGS

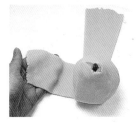

Fold one section at a time up the side of the pear.

Brush the pear with beaten egg and attach the leaves.

ABOVE: Pear dumplings

BAKED DESSERTS

Baked desserts are the stuff of childhood dreams... reminiscences of chilly afternoons and the hot rush of spicy-sweet air when the oven door is opened. The majority of the recipes in this chapter are real old-fashioned favourites—crumbles and cobblers, betties and puddings. Comfort food to warm and nurture; often an irresistible combination of autumn fruits and buttery doughs. But that's not to say this is strictly a cold-weather chapter... the truly dedicated can enjoy their baked desserts all year round.

COBBLERS, CRUMBLES AND CRISPS

These are simple fruit desserts, with a topping, that are served straight from the oven. The fruit base should be juicy, not overthickened, so it soaks into the topping.

Cobblers are topped with a scone-type dough, in shapes like cobbles.

Crisps and crumbles are topped with a rubbed in mixture of flour, butter and sugar. Additions such as nuts and oats vary the flavour and texture. They can also be topped with biscuit crumbs, muesli and breadcrumbs.

A pandowdy is made with sliced fruit, topped with a pastry crust, which is broken into squares and pushed back into the fruit for the end of the cooking time. Dowdying means breaking up the dough.

Slumps and grunts are like cobblers, but are often cooked on top of the stove rather than baked. The fruit supposedly 'grunts' as it cooks.

ABOVE: Apple cobbler

APPLE COBBLER

Preparation time: 30 minutes
Total cooking time: 1 hour 15 minutes
Serves 6

★★

1 kg (2 lb) cooking apples, peeled and cored
1/4 cup (60 g/2 oz) caster sugar
25 g (3/4 oz) unsalted butter, melted
1 teaspoon grated orange rind
2 tablespoons fresh orange juice

Topping

2/3 cup (85 g/3 oz) self-raising flour
1/3 cup (40 g/1 1/4 oz) plain flour
50 g (1 3/4 oz) unsalted butter, chopped
2 tablespoons caster sugar
1 egg, lightly beaten
2–3 tablespoons milk
1 teaspoon raw sugar

1 Preheat the oven to moderate 180°C (350°F/ Gas 4). Cut the apples into 8–12 wedges and combine them with the caster sugar, butter and orange rind and juice in a large bowl. Mix well until all the apple pieces are thoroughly coated. Transfer to a 1.5 litre ovenproof dish about 5 cm (2 inches) deep, cover with foil and bake for 40 minutes, or until the apples are tender, stirring once during cooking.

2 When the apples have been cooking for about 30 minutes, start to prepare the topping. Sift the flours into a bowl and rub the butter into the mixture until it resembles fine breadcrumbs. Stir in the sugar and make a well in the centre of the mixture. Using a flat-bladed knife, stir in the egg and enough milk to make a mixture of thick dropping consistency.

3 Remove the foil and drop spoonfuls of the mixture onto the surface of the cooked apples, covering the surface. Sprinkle with the raw sugar and return to the oven. Bake for 35 minutes or until a skewer inserted into the topping comes out clean. Serve hot. Cobbler can be served with cream or custard.

SLUMP

Preparation time: 30 minutes
Total cooking time: 30 minutes
Serves 6

★ ☆

500 g (1 lb) fresh or canned cherries,
  pitted
caster sugar, to taste
1½ cups (185 g/6 oz) self-raising flour
1 teaspoon baking powder
50 g (1¾ oz) unsalted butter, chilled
  and cubed
¼ cup (55 g/2 oz) demerara sugar
150 ml (5 fl oz) cream

1 Cook the cherries in ¼ cup (60 ml/2 fl oz) water in a large pan over moderate heat for 5 minutes, or until they have begun to soften. Add the sugar and transfer to a 1 litre ovenproof dish to cool. Preheat the oven to moderately hot 200°C (400°F/Gas 6).

2 Sift the flour, baking powder and a little salt into a large bowl, add the butter and demerara sugar and rub in, using just your fingertips, to form fine crumbs. Pour in the cream and stir well to mix everything together—you should have a spreadable mixture.

3 Cover the cooled cherries with blobs of the scone topping, leaving small gaps between the blobs. Bake for 25 minutes, or until the topping is puffed and golden. Slump can be served with cream or lightly whipped cream.

PLUM COBBLER

Preparation time: 15 minutes
Total cooking time: 45 minutes
Serves 6–8

★ ☆

750 g (1½ lb) blood plums, or other plums
¼ cup (60 g/2 oz) caster sugar

Topping

1 cup (125 g/4 oz) self-raising flour
½ cup (60 g/2 oz) plain flour
¼ cup (60 g/2 oz) caster sugar
125 g (4 oz) unsalted butter, chopped
1 egg
½ cup (125 ml/4 fl oz) milk
icing sugar, to dust

1 Preheat the oven to moderate 180°C (350°F/Gas 4). Lightly grease a 2 litre ovenproof dish. Cut the blood plums into quarters, discarding the stones.

2 Put the plums in a pan with the sugar and 1 tablespoon water. Stir over low heat for 5 minutes, or until the sugar dissolves and the fruit softens slightly. Spread the plum mixture in the prepared dish.

3 Sift the flours into a bowl, add the sugar and stir. Rub in the butter, using just your fingertips, until the mixture is fine and crumbly. Combine the egg and milk and whisk until smooth. Stir into the flour mixture.

4 Place large spoonfuls of mixture on top of the plums. Bake for 30–40 minutes, or until the top is golden and cooked through. Dust with icing sugar before serving.

BELOW: Plum cobbler

the flour and 2 tablespoons of the cocoa into a large bowl. Stir in ½ cup (125 g/4 oz) of the sugar and make a well in the centre.

2 Pour in the combined milk, egg, butter and vanilla. Stir until smooth, but do not overbeat. Pour into the dish and dissolve the remaining cocoa and sugar in 2½ cups (600 ml/20 fl oz) boiling water. Pour gently over the back of a spoon over the pudding mixture.

3 Bake the pudding for 40 minutes, or until a skewer comes out clean when inserted into the centre.

4 To make the orange cream, beat the cream, orange rind, icing sugar and Grand Marnier with electric beaters until soft peaks form.

5 Dust the pudding with sifted icing sugar and serve immediately with the orange cream.

EVE'S PUDDING

Preparation time: 25 minutes
Total cooking time: 55 minutes
Serves 4–6

✷✷

500 g (1 lb) cooking apples
2 tablespoons sugar
125 g (4 oz) unsalted butter
½ cup (125 g/4 oz) caster sugar
2 eggs
1 teaspoon vanilla essence
½ cup (125 ml/4 fl oz) milk
1½ cups (185 g/6 oz) self-raising flour

1 Preheat the oven to moderate 180°C (350°F/Gas 4). Grease a deep, 1.5 litre ovenproof dish with oil or melted butter. Line the base with baking paper.

2 Peel, core and thickly slice the apples. Place the apple slices, sugar and 1 tablespoon water into a pan. Cover and cook over medium heat for 12 minutes, or until the apples are soft but still hold together. Using a slotted spoon, spoon the apples into the base of the prepared dish. Allow to cool.

3 Using electric beaters, beat the butter and sugar until light and creamy. Add the eggs, one at a time, beating well after each addition. Using a large metal spoon, fold in the combined essence and milk alternately with the sifted flour.

4 Spoon the mixture over the apples and smooth the surface. Bake for 40–45 minutes, or until the pudding is cooked when tested with a skewer.

SELF-SAUCING CHOCOLATE PUDDING

Preparation time: 25 minutes
Total cooking time: 40 minutes
Serves 4–6

✷✷

1 cup (125 g/4 oz) self-raising flour
⅓ cup (40 g/1¼ oz) cocoa powder
1¼ cups (310 g/10 oz) caster sugar
½ cup (125 ml/4 fl oz) milk
1 egg
60 g (2 oz) unsalted butter, melted
1 teaspoon vanilla essence
icing sugar, to dust

Orange cream

1¼ cups (315 ml/10 fl oz) cream
1 teaspoon grated orange rind
1 tablespoon icing sugar
1 tablespoon Grand Marnier

ABOVE: Self-saucing chocolate pudding

1 Preheat the oven to moderate 180°C (350°F/Gas 4) and grease a 2 litre ovenproof dish. Sift

LEMON DELICIOUS

Preparation time: 20 minutes
Total cooking time: 40 minutes
Serves 4

★ ★

60 g (2 oz) unsalted butter

3/4 cup (185 g/6 oz) caster sugar

3 eggs, separated

1 teaspoon grated lemon rind

1/3 cup (40 g/1 1/4 oz) self-raising flour,
    sifted

1/4 cup (60 ml/2 fl oz) lemon juice

3/4 cup (185 ml/6 fl oz) milk

icing sugar, to dust

1 Preheat the oven to moderate 180°C (350°F/
Gas 4). Brush a 1 litre ovenproof dish with oil.
Using electric beaters, beat the butter, sugar, egg
yolks and rind in a small bowl until the mixture
is light and creamy. Transfer to a medium bowl.
2 Add the flour and stir with a wooden spoon
until just combined. Add the juice and milk and
stir to combine.
3 Place the egg whites in a small, dry bowl.
Using electric beaters, beat until firm peaks
form. Fold in the pudding mixture with a metal
spoon until just combined.
4 Spoon into the ovenproof dish and place the
dish in a deep baking dish. Pour in boiling water
to come one-third of the way up the side of the
pudding dish. Bake for 40 minutes. Dust with
icing sugar. Spoon some sauce on each serving.

LEMON TIPS

When buying lemons,
select fruit that are heavy
for their size and feel firm.
Thinner-skinned lemons
such as *Lisbon* and *Meyer*
are juicier than thick-
skinned ones such as
Eureka. *Lisbon* and *Eureka*
have more acidity and are
tarter than *Meyer* lemons.

The juice of one lemon
is usually about three
tablespoons. Lemons at
room temperature, or
those warmed in the
microwave for a few
seconds, juice more easily
than cold ones.

To grate rind easily,
cover the fine side of a
grater with a piece of
baking paper and grate
through the paper. Pull the
paper off the grater and
scrape off the rind.

The essential oils
contained in lemon rind
(zest) give a perfume
rather than flavour. The
flavour comes mainly from
the juice.

Discard any lemons
which have soft patches or
look as if they are about to
go mouldy. Lemons will go
mouldy more quickly if
stored with other fruit, so
store separately.

ABOVE: Lemon delicious

APPLE BETTY

Preparation time: 15 minutes
Total cooking time: 50 minutes
Serves 4–6

⭐

5 cooking apples, peeled, cored and chopped
100 g (3¹/₂ oz) unsalted butter
¹/₂ cup (95 g/3 oz) soft brown sugar,
 plus 1 tablespoon
grated rind of 1 lemon
¹/₄ teaspoon ground cinnamon
pinch of ground nutmeg
3 cups (240 g/7¹/₂ oz) fresh breadcrumbs

1 Cook the apples with 1 tablespoon of the butter, 1 tablespoon brown sugar and the rind, cinnamon and nutmeg, for 10–15 minutes, until the apples are soft enough to beat to a purée.
2 Preheat the oven to moderate 180°C (350°F/Gas 4). Melt the remaining butter in a frying pan over low heat and add the breadcrumbs and the remaining brown sugar. Toss everything together until all the crumbs are coated, and continue tossing while you fry the crumbs until golden brown.
3 Spread one-third of the crumbs in a 1 litre ovenproof dish and add half the apple purée in an even layer. Repeat with another one-third of the crumbs and the remaining apple, then finish with a layer of crumbs. Bake for 20 minutes, or until crisp and golden brown on top.

APPLE CRUMBLE

Preparation time: 20 minutes
Total cooking time: 45 minutes
Serves 4–6

⭐

8 cooking apples (about 1.4 kg)
2 tablespoons caster sugar
1 cup (125 g/4 oz) plain flour
¹/₂ cup (95 g/3 oz) soft brown sugar
³/₄ teaspoon ground cinnamon
100 g (3¹/₂ oz) butter, chopped

1 Preheat the oven to moderate 180°C (350°F/Gas 4). Peel and core the apples and cut each one into 8 wedges. Place in a saucepan with ¹/₄ cup (60 ml/2 fl oz) water, bring to the boil, then reduce the heat to low and cover. Cook for about 15 minutes, or until the apples are just

OPPOSITE PAGE: Rhubarb crumble (top); Apple betty

soft. Remove from the heat, drain and then stir in the sugar. Spoon the apple into a 1.5 litre ovenproof dish.
2 Place the flour in a bowl and stir in the brown sugar and cinnamon. Add the butter and rub with just your fingertips until the mixture resembles coarse breadcrumbs. Sprinkle evenly over the top of the apple mixture to cover completely. Bake for 25–30 minutes, or until crisp and golden brown. Serve immediately with cream or ice cream.

RHUBARB CRUMBLE

Preparation time: 15 minutes
Total cooking time: 25 minutes
Serves 4–6

⭐

1 kg (2 lb) rhubarb
²/₃ cup (160 g/5¹/₂ oz) sugar
100 g (3¹/₂ oz) unsalted butter
³/₄ cup (90 g/3 oz) plain flour
¹/₃ cup (75 g/2¹/₂ oz) demerara sugar
10 Amaretti biscuits, crushed

Crunchy maple cream

200 ml (6¹/₂ fl oz) thick (double) cream
2 tablespoons golden syrup or pure
 maple syrup
3 Amaretti biscuits, crushed

1 Preheat the oven to moderately hot 200°C (400°F/Gas 6). Trim the rhubarb, cut into short lengths and put in a pan with the sugar. Stir over low heat until the sugar has dissolved, then cover and simmer for 8–10 minutes, or until the rhubarb is soft but still chunky. Spoon into a deep 1.5 litre ovenproof dish.
2 Rub the butter into the flour until the mixture resembles fine breadcrumbs, then stir in the demerara sugar and biscuits.
3 Sprinkle the crumble over the stewed rhubarb and bake for 15 minutes, or until the topping is golden brown. Serve with the crunchy maple cream.
4 To make the crunchy maple cream, place the cream in a bowl, carefully swirl the golden syrup through, then the crushed biscuits. Do not overmix—there should be rich veins of the crunchy syrup through the cream.
NOTE: Taste the rhubarb, as you may need to add a little more sugar.

CUSTARD PUDDING WITH STEWED APPLE

Preparation time: 25 minutes
Total cooking time: 1 hour 5 minutes
Serves 6

★ ★

Custard

1¹/₂ tablespoons custard powder
¹/₂ cup (125 ml/4 fl oz) milk
1 tablespoon sugar
¹/₃ cup (90 g/3 oz) sour cream

180 g (5³/₄ oz) unsalted butter
¹/₂ cup (125 g/4 oz) caster sugar
2 eggs
1¹/₄ cups (155 g/5 oz) self-raising flour
¹/₄ cup (30 g/1 oz) custard powder
¹/₄ cup (45 g/1¹/₂ oz) ground almonds
1 cup (250 ml/8 fl oz) cream
4 cooking apples
2 tablespoons sugar
icing sugar, to dust

BELOW: Custard pudding with stewed apple

1 To make the custard, combine the custard powder and a little of the milk in a bowl and mix until smooth. Add the remaining milk and mix together. Pour into a pan, add the sugar and sour cream and stir over medium heat until the custard thickens and boils. Remove from the heat and cover the surface with plastic wrap to prevent a skin forming.

2 Preheat the oven to moderate 180°C (350°F/Gas 4). Beat the butter and sugar together until light and creamy. Add the eggs one at a time, beating well after each addition. Fold in the sifted flour, custard powder and ground almonds alternately with the cream.

3 Place half the pudding mixture in a 2 litre ovenproof dish and spoon the custard over it. Top with the remaining pudding mixture. The mixture will be a little stiff, pile it on top of the custard and smooth it out gently with the back of a spoon. Bake for 45–50 minutes, or until the pudding is firm to the touch. Dust with icing sugar.

4 Meanwhile, peel, core and thinly slice the apples and place in a pan with the sugar and 2 tablespoons water. Bring to the boil, reduce the heat and simmer, covered, for 10 minutes, until the apples are tender. Serve the pudding from the dish, accompanied by the warm apples.

RICE PUDDING

Preparation time: 10 minutes
Total cooking time: 3 hours
Serves 4

★

¹/₄ cup (55 g/2 oz) short-grain rice
1²/₃ cups (410 ml/13 fl oz) milk
1¹/₂ tablespoons caster sugar
³/₄ cup (185 ml/6 fl oz) cream
¹/₄ teaspoon vanilla essence
¹/₄ teaspoon freshly grated nutmeg
1 bay leaf

1 Preheat the oven to slow 150°C (300°F/Gas 2). Butter a 1 litre ovenproof dish. Mix together the rice, milk, caster sugar, cream and vanilla essence and pour into the dish. Dust the surface with the nutmeg and float the bay leaf on top.

2 Bake the rice pudding for 3 hours, by which time the rice should have absorbed most of the milk and be creamy in texture with a brown skin on top.

RICE PUDDING

Short-grain rice is traditionally used for rice pudding, as the starch in the grains breaks down to thicken the pudding and give it a creamy quality. Short-grain rice is also much more absorbent. Long-grain rice can also be used but, as it does not contain the same amount of starch or have the same kind of absorbency, it needs a creamy mixture added to it to give the same effect. As a rule, rice grains absorb up to four or five times their own volume in liquid when cooked slowly in the oven or on the stovetop. Baked rice puddings do not require quite as much work as they do not need to be stirred as they cook. Asian rice puddings use glutinous black or white rice to give either creamy, silky puddings, or sticky puddings which can be cut into pieces.

RICE PUDDING WITH LEMON THYME AND STRAWBERRIES

Preparation time: 20 minutes + standing
Total cooking time: 1 hour 15 minutes
Serves 6–8

✫✫

500 g (1 lb) strawberries

2 tablespoons balsamic vinegar

1/3 cup (90 g/3 oz) caster sugar

3/4 cup (150 g/5 oz) long-grain rice

3 cups (750 ml/24 fl oz) milk

6 x 3 cm (1 1/4 inch) sprigs lemon thyme

1/3 cup (90 g/3 oz) sugar

3 egg yolks

1 egg

1 Trim the stalks from the strawberries and cut the strawberries in half. Put in a bowl with the vinegar. Sprinkle the caster sugar over the top and stir to combine. Leave to absorb the flavours, turning occasionally.

2 Preheat the oven to warm 160°C (315°F/ Gas 2–3). Brush a 1.5 litre ovenproof dish with oil or melted butter.

3 Rinse the rice well and put in a medium pan with 1 1/2 cups (375 ml/12 fl oz) water. Bring to the boil, cover and cook over low heat for 8–10 minutes. Remove from the heat and leave the pan with the lid on for 5 minutes, until the liquid is absorbed and the rice is soft.

4 Heat the milk with the lemon thyme and sugar in a small pan. When bubbles form at the edge, remove from the heat and set aside for 10 minutes so that it absorbs flavour from the lemon thyme. Strain. Beat the egg yolks and egg in a large bowl, add the rice and gradually stir in the warm milk. Pour into the prepared dish. Place the dish in a baking dish and carefully pour in enough warm water to come halfway up the side of the pudding dish. Bake for 50–60 minutes, or until the pudding is just set (timing may vary according to the dish used). Remove from the oven and allow to stand for 10 minutes. Serve warm or cold with the strawberries.

ABOVE: Rice pudding with lemon thyme and strawberries

BREAD AND BUTTER PUDDING

Preparation time: 20 minutes + soaking + chilling
Total cooking time: 40 minutes
Serves 4

☆

60 g (2 oz) mixed raisins and sultanas

2 tablespoons brandy or rum

30 g (1 oz) unsalted butter

4 slices good-quality white bread or
    brioche loaf

3 eggs

3 tablespoons caster sugar

3 cups (750 ml/24 fl oz) milk

1/4 cup (60 ml/2 fl oz) cream

1/4 teaspoon vanilla essence

1/4 teaspoon ground cinnamon

1 tablespoon demerara sugar

ABOVE: Bread and butter pudding

1 Soak the raisins and sultanas in the brandy or rum for about 30 minutes. Butter the slices of bread or brioche and cut each piece into 8 triangles. Arrange the bread in a 1 litre ovenproof dish.
2 Mix the eggs with the sugar, add the milk, cream, vanilla and cinnamon and mix well. Drain the raisins and sultanas and add any liquid to the custard.
3 Scatter the soaked raisins and sultanas over the bread and pour the custard over the top. Cover with plastic wrap and refrigerate for 1 hour.
4 Preheat the oven to moderate 180°C (350°F/ Gas 4). Remove the pudding from the refrigerator and sprinkle with the demerara sugar. Bake for 35–40 minutes, or until the custard is set and the top crunchy and golden.
NOTE: It is very important that you use good-quality bread for this recipe. Ordinary sliced white bread will tend to go a bit claggy when it soaks up the milk.

CARAMEL BREAD PUDDING

Preparation time: 40 minutes + standing
  + chilling
Total cooking time: 1 hour
Serves 6–8

✷ ✷

2/3 cup (160 g/5 1/2 oz) caster sugar

500 g (1 lb) panettone or brioche

1/2 cup (125 g/4 oz) caster sugar, extra

2 cups (500 ml/16 fl oz) milk

2 wide strips lemon rind, white pith
  removed

3 eggs, lightly beaten

fresh fruit and cream, optional, for serving

1 Preheat the oven to moderate 180°C (350°F/
Gas 4). Lightly brush a 23 x 13 x 7 cm
(9 x 5 x 2 3/4 inch), 1.25 litre loaf tin with
oil or melted butter.
2 Place the caster sugar with 2 tablespoons water
in a small pan over medium heat and stir,
without boiling, until the sugar has completely
dissolved. Bring to the boil, reduce the heat
slightly and simmer, without stirring, for about
10 minutes, until the syrup becomes a rich
golden colour. Watch carefully towards the end
of cooking to prevent burning. As soon as it
reaches the colour you desire, pour into the loaf
tin and leave to cool.
3 Using a large serrated knife, cut the panettone
or brioche into 2 cm (3/4 inch) thick slices and
remove the crusts. Trim into large pieces to fit
the tin in three layers, filling any gaps with
panettone cut to size.
4 Stir the extra caster sugar, milk and lemon
rind in a pan over low heat until the sugar has
dissolved. Bring just to the boil, remove from
the heat and transfer to a jug to allow the lemon
flavour to be absorbed and the mixture to cool.
Remove the lemon rind and whisk in the beaten
eggs. Pour the mixture gradually into the tin,
allowing it to soak into the panettone after each
addition. Set aside for 20 minutes to let the
panettone soak up the liquid.
5 Place the loaf tin into a large baking dish and
pour in enough hot water to come halfway up
the sides of the tin. Bake the pudding for
50 minutes, until just set. Carefully remove
the tin from the baking dish and set aside to
cool. Refrigerate the pudding overnight.
6 When ready to serve, turn out onto a plate
and cut into slices. Serve with fresh fruit and
cream, if desired.

BREAD AND BUTTER PUDDING

Bread and butter pudding can be made with
all sorts of bread or cake leftovers.
Croissants, Danish pastries, panettone,
brioche and any kind of fruit loaf and buns
make luscious bread and butter puddings. A
sprinkling of demerara sugar or crushed
sugar cubes will give a lovely crunchy
topping. For a shiny top, glaze the hot
pudding with apricot jam.

*ABOVE: Caramel
bread pudding*

1 Soak the muscatels or sultanas in Cointreau for 2 hours, or overnight. Drain, reserving the liquid. Preheat the oven to moderate 180°C (350°F/ Gas 4). Beat together the eggs, honey, milk, cream and reserved Cointreau. Grease four 250 ml (8 fl oz) ramekins and divide half the muscatels among the ramekins.

2 Slice the bread thickly. Remove the crusts. Put a slice in each ramekin, trimming to fit. Sprinkle the remaining muscatels over the bread, then top with another slice of bread. Pour the egg mixture over the top, giving it time to soak in. Put the ramekins in a baking dish and pour water into the dish to come halfway up the sides of the ramekins. Bake for 25–30 minutes, or until set. Leave for 5 minutes before turning out.

3 To make the orange cream, whip together the cream and icing sugar until peaks form. Fold in the Cointreau, rind and nutmeg. Serve with the puddings.

CABINET PUDDING

Preparation time: 25 minutes + soaking
Total cooking time: 50 minutes
Serves 6

★★

4 tablespoons sugar
100 g (3¹/2 oz) mixed dried fruit
2 tablespoons rum or boiling water
150 g (5 oz) sponge cake
2 cups (500 ml/16 fl oz) milk
4 eggs
1 teaspoon vanilla essence
cream, for serving

1 Preheat the oven to moderate 180°C (350°F/ Gas 4). Grease six 185 ml (6 fl oz) dariole moulds. Sprinkle the base and side with 1 tablespoon sugar. Soak the fruit in the rum for 15–20 minutes.

2 Cut the sponge into 5 mm (¹/4 inch) cubes and combine with the fruit and rum mixture. Spoon evenly into the moulds. Warm the milk in a small pan, until bubbles appear around the edge. Whisk the eggs and remaining sugar together until well combined. Whisk in the warm milk and vanilla essence. Pour evenly into the moulds over the sponge mixture.

3 Place the moulds in a large baking dish, half filled with boiling water. Bake for 40–45 minutes, or until the custard is set. Remove from the water and leave for 2–3 minutes before turning out onto a warm plate. Serve with cream.

COINTREAU BREAD PUDDINGS WITH ORANGE CREAM

Preparation time: 40 minutes + soaking
Total cooking time: 30 minutes
Serves 4

★★

60 g (2 oz) muscatels or sultanas
¹/3 cup (80 ml/2³/4 fl oz) Cointreau
5 eggs
¹/3 cup (115 g/4 oz) honey
1 cup (250 ml/8 fl oz) milk
1 cup (250 ml/8 fl oz) cream
1 loaf crusty white bread

Orange cream

1 cup (250 ml/8 fl oz) cream
2 teaspoons icing sugar
2 teaspoons Cointreau
grated rind of 1 orange
sprinkle of ground nutmeg

ABOVE: Cointreau bread puddings with orange cream

CHERRY CLAFOUTIS

Preparation time: 15 minutes
Total cooking time: 35 minutes
Serves 6–8

★

500 g (1 lb) fresh cherries, or 800 g
   (1 lb 10 oz) can pitted cherries,
   well drained
1/2 cup (60 g/2 oz) plain flour
1/3 cup (90 g/3 oz) sugar
4 eggs, lightly beaten
1 cup (250 ml/8 fl oz) milk
25 g (3/4 oz) unsalted butter, melted
icing sugar, to dust

1 Preheat the oven to moderate 180°C (350°F/
Gas 4). Brush a 23 cm (9 inch) glass or ceramic
shallow pie plate with melted butter.
2 Pit the cherries and spread onto the pie plate
in a single layer. If using canned cherries, drain
them thoroughly in a sieve before spreading in
the plate. If they are still wet, they will leak into
the batter.
3 Sift the flour into a bowl, add the sugar and
make a well in the centre. Gradually add the
combined eggs, milk and butter, whisking until
smooth and free of lumps.
4 Pour the batter over the cherries and bake for
30–35 minutes. The batter should be risen and
golden. Remove from the oven and dust
generously with icing sugar. Serve immediately.
NOTE: A clafoutis (pronounced 'clafootee') is a
classic French batter pudding, a speciality of the
Limousin region. Clafoutis comes from Clafir,
a dialect verb meaning 'to fill'. It is traditionally
made with cherries. Other berries such as
blueberries, blackberries, raspberries, or small
well-flavoured strawberries may be used. Use
a shallow pie plate or the top will not turn
golden brown.

ABOVE: Cherry clafoutis

3 In a large bowl, whisk the eggs, sugar and vanilla together. Whisk in the chocolate mixture, then stir in the sifted flour, cocoa and coffee powder. Do not overbeat. Pour into the tin and bake for 40 minutes. Cool in the tin until warm.
4 Lift the brownie from the tin, using the baking paper. Using an 8 cm (3 inch) round biscuit cutter, cut out 6 rounds while the brownie is still warm. Place each round on a serving plate, top with 3 small scoops of ice cream and dust lightly with drinking chocolate. Serve immediately.

ICE CREAM BROWNIE SANDWICH

Preparation time: 20 minutes
Total cooking time: 40 minutes
Serves 6

✲✲

1 litre vanilla ice cream, slightly softened
125 g (4 oz) unsalted butter, chopped
185 g (6 oz) good-quality dark chocolate, chopped
1 cup (250 g/8 oz) caster sugar
2 eggs, lightly beaten
1 cup (125 g/4 oz) plain flour, sifted
1/2 cup (60 g/2 oz) chopped walnuts
cocoa, for dusting

1 Preheat the oven to moderate 180°C (350°F/ Gas 4). Line a baking tray with baking paper and spread out the ice cream to form a 15 x 20 cm (6 x 8 inch) rectangle, cover the surface with baking paper and re-freeze it. Lightly grease a 20 x 30 cm (8 x 12 inch) tin and line the base with baking paper, leaving a little hanging over the two longer sides.
2 Put the butter and chocolate in a heatproof bowl, bring a large pan filled with 5 cm (2 inches) water to the boil, then remove from the heat. Stand the bowl over the pan, making sure the bowl does not touch the water, and stir the chocolate until melted. Remove the bowl and cool slightly. Whisk in the sugar and eggs, then sift on the flour and add the walnuts. Stir until just combined, then spoon into the tin, smoothing the surface. Bake for 30 minutes, or until firm. Cool completely in the tin, then lift out, using the baking paper.
3 Cut the brownie into 12 portions and the ice cream into six. Sandwich the ice cream between two pieces of brownie and dust with cocoa.

BROWNIE SANDWICH

When the brownie is cooked, cool completely in the tin, lift out using the paper, then cut into squares.

Sandwich each square of ice cream between two squares of brownie, then dust with cocoa.

ABOVE: Cappuccino brownies

CAPPUCCINO BROWNIES

Preparation time: 20 minutes
Total cooking time: 40 minutes
Serves 6

✲

150 g (5 oz) unsalted butter
125 g (4 oz) good-quality dark chocolate
3 eggs
1 1/2 cups (375 g/12 oz) caster sugar
1 teaspoon vanilla essence
1 cup (125 g/4 oz) plain flour
1/4 cup (30 g/1 oz) cocoa powder
2 tablespoons instant coffee powder
1 litre vanilla ice cream
1 teaspoon drinking chocolate

1 Preheat the oven to moderate 180°C (350°F/ Gas 4). Grease a 28 x 18 cm (11 x 7 inch) shallow baking tin and line the base with baking paper, extending over two sides.
2 Place the butter and chocolate in a small heatproof bowl. Stand the bowl over a pan of steaming water, off the heat, and stir until melted and smooth. Remove from the pan and allow to cool slightly.

HAZELNUT PUDDINGS

Preparation time: 40 minutes
Total cooking time: 30 minutes
Serves 8

★★

30 g (1 oz) unsalted butter, melted
60 g (2 oz) ground hazelnuts
125 g (4 oz) unsalted butter
1/2 cup (125 g/4 oz) caster sugar
3 eggs, lightly beaten
2 cups (250 g/8 oz) self-raising flour, sifted
60 g (2 oz) sultanas
1/3 cup (80 ml/2 3/4 fl oz) brandy
1/3 cup (80 ml/2 3/4 fl oz) buttermilk

Chocolate cream sauce

1 cup (250 ml/8 fl oz) cream
30 g (1 oz) unsalted butter
200 g (6 1/2 oz) good-quality dark chocolate, chopped

1 Preheat the oven to moderate 180°C (350°F/ Gas 4). Brush eight 125 ml (4 fl oz) ovenproof pudding moulds or ramekins with the melted butter and coat with the ground hazelnuts, shaking off the excess. Beat together the butter and sugar with electric beaters, until light and creamy. Add the eggs gradually, beating well after each addition. Fold in the flour, sultanas, brandy and buttermilk. Divide among the ramekins, cover each with a piece of greased foil with a pleat in it, and secure with string.
2 Place the puddings in a large baking dish and pour in enough water to come three-quarters of the way up the sides of the ramekins. Bake for 25 minutes, topping up with more water if necessary. A skewer inserted into the centre of the pudding will come out clean when cooked.
3 To make the sauce, put the cream, butter and chocolate in a small pan and stir over low heat until melted and smooth. Unmould the warm puddings onto plates. If they are reluctant to come out, run a knife around the edges of the mould. Serve with chocolate cream sauce. Can also be served with crème anglaise and decorated with chocolate curls (see page 238).

BELOW: Hazelnut puddings

BRIOCHE DOUGH

Brioche dough, as used here, is a rich dough containing up to half its weight in butter, plus other enriching ingredients such as sugar and eggs. These ingredients all contribute to a softer, more crumbly texture which makes the dough a little harder to handle. Lots of kneading and slow rising help this dough take on a smoothness. Yeast needs a little sugar to help it rise, but too much sugar will inhibit it and have the reverse effect. The sugar syrups for the savarin and babas are what give them their sweetness.

ABOVE: Pineapple savarin

PINEAPPLE SAVARIN

Preparation time: 40 minutes + rising
Total cooking time: 40 minutes
Serves 6–8

✯ ✯ ✯

7 g (¹/₄ oz) dried yeast
²/₃ cup (170 ml/5¹/₂ fl oz) unsweetened pineapple juice, warmed
2 teaspoons caster sugar
2 cups (250 g/8 oz) plain flour
3 eggs, lightly beaten
90 g (3 oz) unsalted butter, softened

Rum syrup

1 cup (250 g/8 oz) caster sugar
1¹/₂ cups (375 ml/12 fl oz) unsweetened pineapple juice
5 cm (2 inch) piece lemon rind
¹/₂ cup (125 ml/4 fl oz) dark rum

1 Grease a 25 cm (10 inch) deep savarin ring. Dissolve the yeast in the pineapple juice, then stir in the sugar. Set aside for 5 minutes, or until frothy. Sift the flour and ¹/₄ teaspoon salt into a large bowl. Add the yeast and eggs and beat with a cupped hand for 5 minutes. Add the butter and beat by hand for 5 minutes. Cover and set aside in a warm place for 45 minutes, or until bubbly and well-risen. Press down on the dough to push the air out, and beat by hand for 1–2 minutes.
2 Ladle into the ring and cover loosely with plastic wrap. Set aside in a warm place for 10 minutes. Preheat the oven to moderately hot 190°C (375°F/Gas 5). Bake on a baking tray for 25 minutes, or until firm and golden (it may overflow a little in the centre).
3 Meanwhile, to make the rum syrup, stir the sugar, juice and rind in a small pan over low heat until the sugar has dissolved. Bring to the boil and boil, without stirring, for 10–15 minutes, or until slightly thickened. Remove the rind. Add the rum.
4 When the savarin is cooked, trim to a flat base with a knife. Turn out of the tin and stand on a rack over a tray. Prick all over with a toothpick. While the savarin is still hot, drizzle with rum syrup, pouring the excess back from where it is caught in the tray, until all the syrup is absorbed.

RUM BABA WITH FIGS

Preparation time: 40 minutes + standing
Total cooking time: 30 minutes
Makes 10

☆ ☆ ☆

1¹/2 cups (185 g/6 oz) plain flour

7 g (¹/4 oz) dried yeast

2 teaspoons sugar

¹/3 cup (80 ml/2³/4 fl oz) lukewarm milk

80 g (2³/4 oz) unsalted butter, chopped

3 eggs, lightly beaten

1¹/2 cups (375 g/12 oz) caster sugar

¹/3 cup (80 ml/2³/4 fl oz) dark rum, plus
    2 tablespoons, extra

³/4 cup (240 g/7¹/2 oz) apricot jam

4–6 fresh figs

1 Brush ten 125 ml (4 fl oz) dariole or baba moulds lightly with oil. Place 1 tablespoon of the flour with the yeast, sugar, milk and ¹/4 teaspoon salt in a small bowl. Leave, covered with plastic wrap, in a warm place for about 10 minutes, or until foamy. Using just your fingertips, rub the butter into the remaining flour in a large bowl, until the mixture has a fine crumbly texture.
2 Add the yeast mixture and the eggs to the flour mixture. Beat with a cupped hand for 2 minutes, until smooth and glossy. Scrape the mixture down the side of the bowl. Leave, covered with plastic wrap, in a warm place for 45 minutes, until well risen.
3 Preheat the oven to hot 210°C (415°F/ Gas 6–7). Using a wooden spoon or your hand, beat the mixture again for 2 minutes. Divide among the prepared tins. Set aside, covered with plastic wrap, for another 10 minutes, until well risen.
4 Bake for 20 minutes, until golden brown. Meanwhile, combine the sugar with 2 cups (500 ml/16 fl oz) water in a pan. Stir over low heat, without boiling, until the sugar has completely dissolved. Bring to the boil, reduce the heat slightly and simmer, without stirring, for 15 minutes. Remove from the heat, cool slightly and add the rum.
5 Turn the babas out onto a wire rack placed over a shallow baking tray. Prick all over with a toothpick. Brush the warm babas liberally with warm rum syrup until well soaked, then allow to drain. Pour the excess syrup from the baking tray into a jug, straining if necessary to remove any crumbs.

6 Heat the apricot jam in a small pan or in the microwave, then strain through a fine sieve. Add the extra rum, stir to combine and brush warm jam all over the babas, to glaze. To serve, place one or two babas on each plate, drizzle a pool of reserved syrup around them. Cut the figs in half and serve beside the babas.
NOTE: Rum babas are best served on the day they are made. If you do not have dariole or baba moulds, use empty baked bean tins. The 130 g (4¹/2 oz) size is best. Wash and dry the tins thoroughly and prepare as directed.

A baba is a yeasted, open-textured cake which is soaked in rum and sugar syrup. It originated in Poland, baba meaning 'old woman'. Babas sometimes include raisins in their dough.

RUM BABA

Use your cupped hand to beat the mixture vigorously.

ABOVE: Rum baba with figs

QUEEN OF PUDDINGS

Preparation time: 15 minutes + soaking
Total cooking time: 55 minutes
Serves 6

★★

1 cup (80 g/2¾ oz) fresh white breadcrumbs
2 cups (500 ml/16 fl oz) milk, scalded
2 eggs, separated
⅓ cup (90 g/3 oz) sugar
3 tablespoons strawberry jam
150 g (5 oz) strawberries, sliced

1 Preheat the oven to moderate 180°C (350°F/ Gas 4). Place the breadcrumbs in a bowl with the hot milk and leave for 10 minutes. Beat the egg yolks with half the sugar and stir into the crumb mixture.
2 Spoon the custard into a greased ovenproof dish and bake for 45 minutes, or until firm. Reduce the oven to warm 160°C (315°F/Gas 2–3).
3 Combine the jam and sliced strawberries and spread over the custard. Whisk the egg whites until stiff, then beat in the remaining sugar to form a meringue. Swirl over the top. Bake for 8–10 minutes, or until the meringue is set and lightly browned. Serve hot or warm.

BELOW: Apple charlotte

APPLE CHARLOTTE

Preparation time: 50 minutes
Total cooking time: 40 minutes
Serves 8

★★

1.25 kg (2 lb 8 oz) cooking apples, peeled, cored and sliced
½ cup (125 g/4 oz) caster sugar
rind of 1 lemon
1 cinnamon stick
30 g (1 oz) unsalted butter
1 loaf sliced white bread, crusts removed
a little softened unsalted butter

Garnish

20 g (¾ oz) unsalted butter
3 tablespoons sugar
1 large apple, peeled, cored and sliced
200 ml (6½ fl oz) orange juice

1 Cook the apples in a large pan with the sugar, lemon rind, cinnamon stick and butter, over low heat, stirring occasionally, until the apples are tender and the mixture is thick.
2 Preheat the oven to moderately hot 200°C (400°F/Gas 6). Brush eight 125 ml (4 fl oz) ramekins with melted butter, or a 1.25 litre capacity charlotte tin or pudding basin. To make the mini charlottes, cut 16 rounds of bread, spread with softened butter and put a round in each ramekin, buttered-side-down. Cut the remaining bread into wide strips, butter and use to line the sides of the ramekins, either cutting to fit, or overlapping a little, with the buttered side against the ramekin. Spoon the apple into the ramekins, pressing down firmly. Put the remaining buttered rounds of bread on top, buttered-side-up. Press down firmly and bake for 15 minutes, or until golden.
3 For the large charlotte, cut a round of bread to fit the base and wide strips to line the sides. Leave enough bread to cover the top. Butter the bread and line the mould, butter-side-out. Fill with the apple, cover with the remaining bread and bake for 30–40 minutes. Cover if it starts to overbrown. Cool a little before turning out.
4 For the garnish, melt the butter, add the sugar and stir to dissolve. Add the apple and brown lightly. Add the juice, bring to the boil, reduce the heat and simmer until cooked. Remove the apple and reduce the syrup by two-thirds. Put apple on the charlotte, pour syrup over and serve.

ORANGES
There are two main types of orange, the *Valencia* and the *navel*. Valencia oranges, available in summer, have a thin, light orange peel and a virtually seedless juicy flesh. Navel oranges, a winter fruit, have a characteristic depression or navel at one end and a dark, thick peel which comes off easily. They also segment well and are very good eating oranges. Blood oranges have a sweet but sharp taste and their dark red flesh and juice give deep colour to desserts.

ALMOND ORANGE SYRUP PUDDING

Preparation time: 45 minutes
Total cooking time: 50 minutes
Serves 6–8

★ ★

125 g (4 oz) unsalted butter
3/4 cup (185 g/6 oz) caster sugar
2 eggs, lightly beaten
3 teaspoons finely grated orange rind
1 1/2 cups (280 g/9 oz) ground almonds
1 cup (125 g/4 oz) semolina
1/4 cup (60 ml/2 fl oz) orange juice
250 g (8 oz) blueberries, to decorate
icing sugar, to dust
thick (double) cream, optional, for serving

Syrup

1 cup (250 ml/8 fl oz) orange juice, strained
1/2 cup (125 g/4 oz) caster sugar

1 Preheat the oven to moderate 180°C (350°F/ Gas 4). Lightly brush a 20 cm (8 inch) ring tin with oil or melted butter and line the base with baking paper.
2 Using electric beaters, beat the butter and sugar in a small bowl until light and creamy. Add the eggs gradually, beating well after each addition. Add the rind and beat to combine.
3 Transfer to a large bowl. Using a metal spoon, fold in the almonds and semolina alternately with the juice. Stir until just combined and the mixture is smooth. Spoon into the tin and smooth the surface. Bake for 40 minutes, or until a skewer comes out clean.
4 To make the syrup, stir the juice and sugar in a small pan over low heat, until the sugar completely dissolves. Bring to the boil, reduce the heat slightly and simmer for 10 minutes. Remove from the heat and cool slightly.
5 Pour half the warm syrup over the warm cake while still in the tin. Leave for 3 minutes, then place the cake onto a serving plate. Brush the remaining syrup over the cake, then allow to cool. Fill the centre with blueberries dusted with icing sugar. Serve with cream if you wish.

ABOVE: Almond orange syrup pudding

SEMOLINA, SAGO and TAPIOCA

Semolina is a kind of wheat flour. The names derives from *simila*, a fine wheat flour in Latin, and *semola*, Italian for bran. Semolina is the coarse particles left when wheat is milled, then sifted. Semolina sprinkled in the base of a fruit tart soaks up any excess juice.

Sago is made from the powdered starch made from the pith of various palm trees, including the sago palm. The name is from the Malay, *sagu*. It is a flavourless, easily digested starch, sometimes sold as 'seed tapioca'.

Tapioca is starch from the cassava or manioc root. The moist starch is shaken in drops onto a hot plate which makes it form 'pearls'. Tapioca and sago are interchangeable.

ABOVE: Semolina

SEMOLINA

Preparation time: 10 minutes
Total cooking time: 30 minutes
Serves 6

★★

3/4 cup (90 g/3 oz) semolina

2 cups (500 ml/16 fl oz) milk

4 tablespoons sugar

40 g (1 1/4 oz) unsalted butter

2 tablespoons ground almonds

1/4 teaspoon vanilla essence

2 eggs

50 g (1 3/4 oz) blanched almonds, optional, for serving

1 Preheat the oven to moderate 180°C (350°F/ Gas 4). Combine the semolina, milk and 3 tablespoons of the sugar in a saucepan and bring to the boil. Reduce the heat and simmer for about 10 minutes, stirring continuously, until thick. When cooked, add the butter, ground almonds, vanilla essence and eggs. Mix until well combined.

2 Pour into six 125 ml (4 fl oz) ramekins or moulds, sprinkle with the remaining sugar and bake for 15 minutes, or until golden brown. When baked, score the top with a hot metal skewer. (Heat the skewer over a gas flame or on an electric ring. When it is very hot, lay it across the top of the pudding until it leaves a mark. Repeat to form a pattern.)

3 To serve, roast the blanched almonds, if using, until golden brown, chop finely and sprinkle over the top.

COCONUT TAPIOCA

Combine 2/3 cup (150 g/5 oz) small pearl tapioca and 3 1/2 cups (875 ml/28 fl oz) coconut milk in a large heavy-based pan with a vanilla bean. Stir over low heat until the tapioca pearls turn translucent, about 15 minutes. Keep stirring so the tapioca doesn't stick and burn. Add 1/2 cup (125 g/ 4 oz) caster sugar and stir until dissolved. Transfer the tapioca to a bowl, leave to cool, then refrigerate until cold. Serve in small dishes with a little coconut milk poured over, and sprinkled with chopped pistachio nuts.

RICOTTA POTS WITH RASPBERRIES

Preparation time: 20 minutes
Total cooking time: 25 minutes
Serves 4

★

4 eggs, separated
$^{1}/_{2}$ cup (125 g/4 oz) caster sugar
350 g (11$^{1}/_{4}$ oz) ricotta
35 g (1$^{1}/_{4}$ oz) finely chopped pistachio nuts
1 teaspoon grated lemon rind
2 tablespoons lemon juice
1 tablespoon vanilla sugar (see note)
200 g (6$^{1}/_{2}$ oz) raspberries
icing sugar, to dust

1 Preheat the oven to moderate 180°C (350°F/ Gas 4). Beat the egg yolks and sugar in a small bowl until thick and pale. Transfer to a large bowl and add the ricotta, pistachio nuts, lemon rind and juice and mix well.

2 In a separate bowl, whisk the egg whites to stiff peaks. Beat in the vanilla sugar, then gently fold into the ricotta mixture, until just combined.

3 Lightly grease four 250 ml (8 fl oz) ramekins. Divide the raspberries among the dishes and spoon the ricotta filling over the top. Place on a baking tray and bake for 20–25 minutes, or until puffed and lightly browned. Serve immediately, dusted with a little icing sugar.

NOTE: You can buy vanilla sugar or make your own. Split a whole vanilla bean in half lengthways and place in a jar of caster sugar (about 1 kg/2 lb). Leave for at least 4 days before using.

JAM ROLY POLY

Preheat the oven to moderately hot 180°C (350°F/Gas 4). Sift 2 cups (250 g/8 oz) self-raising flour into a bowl and add 125 g (4 oz) roughly chopped butter. Using your fingertips, rub the butter into the flour until fine and crumbly. Stir in 2 tablespoons caster sugar. Mix in 50 ml (1$^{3}/_{4}$ fl oz) each of milk and water with a knife, to form a dough, adding more water if necessary. Turn out onto a lightly floured surface and gather together to form a smooth dough. Roll out into a rectangle, about 5 mm ($^{1}/_{4}$ inch) thick, 30 cm (12 inches) long and 23 cm (9 inches) wide. Spread with $^{1}/_{3}$ cup (105 g/3$^{1}/_{2}$ oz) jam, leaving a 5 mm ($^{1}/_{4}$ inch) border around the edge. Roll up lengthways like a swiss roll and place on a lined baking tray. Brush with 1 tablespoon milk and bake for 35 minutes, or until golden and cooked through. Serve warm slices with custard. Serves 4–6.

PISTACHIO NUTS

Pistachio nuts have a green kernel covered by a husk which is pink, green and purple. This, in turn, is covered by a thin shell which splits when mature. More brightly coloured pistachios are fresher than darker ones. Although native to the Middle East, where they are used extensively in both sweet and savoury cooking, pistachios have become absorbed into the cuisine of many countries. In France and Germany they appear in terrines, sausages and nougat, and in Greece and Turkey they are used in baklava and Turkish delight.

LEFT: Ricotta pots with raspberries

STICKY AND STEAMED

'What's for pudding?' The steamed pudding has become such a national institution in Britain that the word is now taken to refer to any dessert, from apple pie to lemon sorbet. Even the French call steamed puds *'le pouding'* in acknowledgement of their country of origin. So what is it that has made the steamed pudding one of the most beloved dishes since recipes were first written down? So adored that a special pudding is made every year and ritually eaten on Christmas Day? Just one sticky mouthful, with a pouring of hot sauce, and it's not too difficult to understand.

FULL STEAM AHEAD

Steamed puddings are one of the oldest, most traditional desserts. Whether dense

and rich or light and cakey, they're usually served hot with a sauce.

Originally, pudding mixture was tied in a floured and buttered cloth and suspended from a wooden spoon in a pan of boiling water to cook. Now, it is more common to use pudding basins, available in ceramic, glass, steel and aluminium. Ceramic ones don't have a lid but are the best insulators and let the pudding cook through without overcooking the edges—the outside should still be soft when the centre is cooked.

TO STEAM A PUDDING...
First you will need a pudding basin with the right capacity. Measure this carefully by filling it with water from a measuring jug or cup. If your basin is too small, you might find your pudding expanding right out of it.

Next, you need a large pan with a tight-fitting lid. The pan should comfortably hold a trivet or upturned saucer with the basin on top, with space for the lid to fit properly. You can, of course, use a steamer to cook puddings, and collapsible metal vegetable steamers can have their handles unscrewed so that you can stand a basin on them. Mini puddings can be cooked in a bamboo steamer or *bain marie* in the oven.

Prepare the pudding basin by greasing it and placing a circle of baking paper in

the bottom (the base may be very small but, if you don't do it, turning out your pudding can be a messy business). Next, make the foil and paper covering to go over the pudding while it cooks. Place a sheet of foil on the work surface, then a sheet of baking paper on top of it (a few dabs of oil on the foil will hold the paper in place). Grease the paper. Make a large pleat across the width of the foil and paper to allow for expansion as the pudding rises and pushes against it. Place the empty basin in the pan on top of its trivet and pour in cold water to come halfway up the side of the basin. Remove the empty pudding basin from the pan and put the water on to boil.

Prepare the pudding mixture and spoon it into the basin, levelling off the top. Place the foil and paper across the top of the basin, foil-side-up, and smooth it down the side—do not press it onto the top of the pudding. If you are using a metal basin, just clip on the lid. If not, tie a double piece of string around the rim of the basin—ceramic basins have a rim under which the string will sit tightly. Tie the string tightly in a knot and then, using another double piece of string, tie a handle onto the string around the basin— this will enable you to lift the pudding in and out of the water easily. If you make steamed puddings often, you may want to buy a pudding cloth for this purpose.

Whatever you use, the covering should be reasonably watertight as you need to keep the mixture dry.

Lower the pudding carefully into the boiling water and lower the heat to a fast simmer. Cover with the lid and cook as directed. If your lid fits well, you should not have to replenish the water too often, but you will need to keep an eye on the water level and top it up with boiling water (to keep the cooking temperature constant) when necessary.

When the cooking time is up, remove the basin from the pan and take off the foil and paper cover. If the pudding is a solid one, test it with a skewer (a fruit pudding, however, may leave the skewer sticky if you hit a piece of fruit) or press the top gently—it should be firm in the centre and well risen. Do not overcook the pudding—it should be moist with a light, even texture. If the pudding is not cooked, simply re-cover it and continue cooking until done. Leave to stand for 5 minutes, then invert carefully onto a plate.

If the pudding is reluctant to come out of the basin, carefully run a palette or flat-bladed knife around the edge.

put a sheet of baking paper on top. Grease the paper. Make a large pleat in the centre.

2 Sift the flour into a large bowl. Add the suet, fruit, sugar, spices and bicarbonate of soda. Stir with a wooden spoon, make a well and add the egg and buttermilk. Mix well, but don't overbeat. Spoon into the basin and smooth the surface. Place the foil and paper over the basin, foil-side-up, and smooth it down the sides. Cover if your basin has a lid. If not, tie a double piece of string around the rim, knot tightly and, using another double piece of string, tie a handle onto the string.

3 Lower the basin into the water, cover and steam at a fast simmer for 2 hours 30 minutes, topping up the water, if necessary. Turn onto a plate. Serve warm. Can be served with custard or cream.

GOLDEN SYRUP PUDDING

Preparation time: 30 minutes
Total cooking time: 1 hour 30 minutes
Serves 6

★ ★

4 tablespoons golden syrup
185 g (6 oz) butter, softened
3/4 cup (185 g/6 oz) caster sugar
1 teaspoon vanilla essence
3 eggs
1/2 cup (60 g/2 oz) plain flour
1 cup (125 g/4 oz) self-raising flour
90 g (3 oz) golden syrup, warmed, for serving

1 Grease a 1.5 litre pudding basin and line the base with baking paper. Place a sheet of foil on a work surface and put a sheet of baking paper on top. Grease the paper. Make a large pleat in the centre. Put the empty basin in a saucepan, on a trivet, and pour in enough water to come halfway up the side of the basin. Remove the basin and put the water on to boil.

2 Pour the golden syrup into the basin. Cream the butter and sugar with electric beaters. Add the vanilla, eggs and combined sifted flours and beat on low to mix. Spoon into the basin; level the top. Place the foil and paper over the basin, foil-side-up, and smooth it down the sides—do not press it onto the pudding. Cover if your basin has a lid. If not, tie a double piece of string around the rim, knot tightly and, using another double piece of string, tie a handle onto the string.

3 Lower carefully into the boiling water and turn down to a fast simmer. Cover and steam for 1 hour 30 minutes, topping up the water when

CLOOTIE DUMPLING
Traditionally eaten at Hogmanay, the clootie dumpling is a Scottish suet pudding which is named after the clout or cloth it is traditionally boiled in. It can also be made in a pudding basin.

CLOOTIE DUMPLING

Preparation time: 25 minutes
Total cooking time: 2 hours 30 minutes
Serves 6–8

★ ★

3 cups (375 g/12 oz) self-raising flour
125 g (4 oz) grated suet
150 g (5 oz) currants
60 g (2 oz) sultanas
60 g (2 oz) raisins, chopped
3/4 cup (185 g/6 oz) caster sugar
1 1/2 teaspoons ground cinnamon
1 1/2 teaspoons mixed spice
1/2 teaspoon bicarbonate of soda
1 egg, lightly beaten
2 cups (500 ml/16 fl oz) buttermilk

1 Grease a 2 litre pudding basin and line the base with a circle of baking paper. Place the empty basin in a saucepan, on a trivet, and pour in enough water to come halfway up the side of the basin. Remove the basin and put the water on to boil. Place a sheet of foil on a work surface and

ABOVE: Clootie dumpling

necessary. Remove from the pan, test with a skewer or by pressing the top gently—it should be firm in the centre and well risen. If not cooked, re-cover and cook until done. Set aside for 5 minutes, then invert onto a plate. Serve with the golden syrup. Can be served with custard.

CHOCOLATE PUDDING

Preparation time: 20 minutes
Total cooking time: 1 hour 20 minutes
Serves 6

★★

90 g (3 oz) unsalted butter
1/2 cup (95 g/3 oz) soft brown sugar
3 eggs, separated
125 g (4 oz) dark chocolate, melted and cooled
1 teaspoon vanilla essence
1 cup (125 g/4 oz) self-raising flour
1 tablespoon cocoa powder
1/2 teaspoon bicarbonate of soda
1/4 cup (60 ml/2 fl oz) milk
2 tablespoons brandy

Chocolate sauce

125 g (4 oz) dark chocolate, broken
1/4 cup (60 ml/2 fl oz) cream
1 tablespoon brandy

1 Grease a 1.25 litre pudding basin and line the base with a circle of baking paper. Preheat the oven to moderate 180°C (350°F/Gas 4). Cream the butter and half the sugar until light and creamy. Beat in the egg yolks, chocolate and vanilla. Sift together the flour, cocoa and bicarbonate of soda. Fold into the mixture, alternating with spoonfuls of the combined milk and brandy. Beat the egg whites until soft peaks form. Gradually beat in the remaining sugar, until stiff and glossy. Fold into the chocolate mix.
2 Pour into the pudding basin. Cover tightly with foil. Secure with string, put in a deep ovenproof tray and pour in enough hot water to come halfway up the side of the basin. Bake for 1 1/4 hours, or until a skewer comes out clean. Unmould onto a serving plate.
3 To make the chocolate sauce, combine the ingredients in a heatproof bowl set over a pan of steaming water and stir until smooth. Serve the pudding with the sauce and cream.

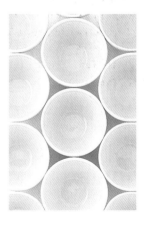

ABOVE: Chocolate pudding

BOILED METHOD

Cut a square from a piece of calico or a tea towel and boil it in a pan of boiling water for 20 minutes.

Spread the cloth out and dust with a thick, even layer of sifted flour, leaving a margin around the edge.

Bring the points of the cloth together, gathering in all the excess. Try to make the folds neat and even.

Tie the top as tightly as possible with a piece of unwaxed string, so that no water can get in.

OPPOSITE PAGE:
Christmas puddings:
Steamed (top); Boiled

CHRISTMAS PUDDING

Preparation time: 40 minutes + standing
Total cooking time: 7– 8 hours
Makes 2 x 570 ml (1 lb 3 oz) or 1 x 1.2 litre

★★★

500 g (1 lb) mixed sultanas, currants and raisins

300 g (10 oz) mixed dried fruit, chopped

50 g (1³/4 oz) mixed peel

¹/2 cup (125 ml/4 fl oz) brown ale

2 tablespoons rum or brandy

juice and rind of 1 orange

juice and rind of 1 lemon

225 g (7 oz) suet, grated

1¹/3 cups (245 g/8 oz) soft brown sugar

3 eggs, lightly beaten

2¹/2 cups (200 g/6¹/2 oz) fresh white breadcrumbs

³/4 cup (90 g/3 oz) self-raising flour

1 teaspoon mixed spice

¹/4 teaspoon freshly grated nutmeg

60 g (2 oz) blanched almonds, roughly chopped

STEAMED METHOD

1 The day before you want to make the pudding, put the dried fruit, mixed peel, ale, rum, orange and lemon juice and rind into a large bowl, cover and leave overnight.

2 Mix the fruit mixture, suet, sugar, eggs, breadcrumbs, flour, spices, almonds and ¹/4 teaspoon salt in a large bowl—the mixture should fall from the spoon—if it is too stiff, add a little more ale. Place the pudding basin on a trivet in a large pan, with a lid, which will comfortably hold it, and pour in enough water to reach halfway up the side of the basin. Remove the basin and put the water on to boil.

3 Grease the pudding basin and line the base with a circle of baking paper. Fill with the mixture. Cut a sheet of greaseproof paper and a sheet of foil big enough to fit comfortably over the top of the basin and come halfway down the sides. Lay the greaseproof on top of the foil, grease the paper, then make a pleat in the centre of the whole lot. Put the cover, greased-side-down on top of the pudding and fold everything down over the edge. Cover with a lid if your basin has one, or tie a double piece of string securely around the rim of the basin, just under the lip, and make a handle which runs across the top with another piece of string.

4 Place the basin carefully on the trivet in the pan and turn the water down to a fast simmer. Cover the pan and steam for 8 hours,

replenishing the water when necessary. If you want to keep your pudding and reheat it later, then steam it for 6 hours and steam it for another 2 hours on the day you would like to eat it.

BOILED METHOD

1 Make up the pudding mixture as before but do not add any extra ale if the mixture is too stiff. Leave the mixture to stand for 10 minutes so the breadcrumbs absorb any extra liquid and the mixture thickens.

2 Cut an 80 cm (32 inch) square from a clean piece of calico or an old tea towel and boil it in a pan of boiling water for 20 minutes. Remove, wring out (wearing rubber gloves will stop you burning yourself) and spread on a clean work surface. Dust the calico with a thick, even layer of sifted plain flour, leaving a border around the edge. Spread the flour out using your hands—it is important that you get an even covering as the flour will form a seal between the pudding and the water and stop the pudding absorbing any water. Place the pudding mixture in the centre of the calico and bring the points of the material together. (Drape the calico over a bowl if you find it easier.) Gather in all the excess, trying to make the folds neat and even (they will leave an imprint on the finished pudding). Tie the top as tightly as possible with a piece of unwaxed string—it is important the top is tight and there is no gap between the calico and the pudding so that no water can get in. Tie a loop into the end of one of the pieces of string—this will act as a handle for getting the pudding in and out of the water. Hook a wooden spoon handle through the loop of string and lower the pudding into a large pan of boiling water with a trivet at the bottom—the pan should be large enough for the pudding to move around. Cover the pan and boil for 5 hours. If the water level drops, add a little more boiling water around the edges of the pudding. The pudding should not rest on the base of the pan. Remove the pudding from the water and hang it in a well ventilated, dry area where it will not touch anything else. Make sure the calico ends all hang to one side so they do not drip all over the pudding. Leave overnight.

3 Untie the cloth and if there are still damp patches, spread it out to make sure the calico dries out thoroughly all over. When completely dry, re-wrap and tie with a new piece of unwaxed string and store hanging in a cool, dry place for up to 4 months. When you wish to serve, boil for 2 hours, hang it for 15 minutes, then remove it from its cloth. The floured crust will get darker as it stands. Serve wrinkled side down!

FIG PUDDING WITH BRANDY SAUCE

Preparation time: 40 minutes + standing
Total cooking time: 4 hours
Serves 8–10

★ ★

240 g (7½ oz) soft dessert figs, chopped
225g (7¼ oz) pitted dates, chopped
90 g (3 oz) raisins
80 g (2¾ oz) glacé ginger, chopped
2 tablespoons brandy or orange juice
⅓ cup (60 g/2 oz) soft brown sugar
3 cups (240 g/7½ oz) fresh white breadcrumbs
2 cups (250 g/8 oz) self-raising flour, sifted
160 g (5¼ oz) unsalted butter, melted
3 eggs, lightly beaten
½ cup (125 ml/4 fl oz) milk
2 teaspoons grated lemon rind
3 tablespoons lemon juice
figs, to decorate, optional

BELOW: Fig pudding with brandy sauce

Brandy sauce
¼ cup (30 g/1 oz) cornflour
¼ cup (60 g/2 oz) caster sugar
2 cups (500 ml/16 fl oz) milk
30 g (1 oz) unsalted butter
⅓ cup (80 ml/2¾ fl oz) brandy

1 Combine the figs, dates, raisins and ginger in a bowl. Stir in the brandy or orange juice and set aside for at least 2 hours. Grease a 2 litre pudding basin and line the base with baking paper. Place the empty basin in a saucepan, on a trivet, and pour in enough water to come halfway up the side of the basin. Remove the basin and put the water on to boil. Place a sheet of foil on a work surface and put a sheet of baking paper on top. Grease the paper. Make a large pleat in the centre of the foil and paper.

2 Combine the brown sugar, breadcrumbs and sifted flour. Stir in the soaked fruit, then add the butter, eggs, milk, lemon rind and juice and stir until evenly mixed. Spoon into the basin and press firmly to eliminate any air bubbles. Smooth the surface, cover with the foil and paper, foil-side-up, and smooth it down the sides. Do not press onto the top of the pudding. Cover if your basin has a lid. If not, tie a double piece of string around the rim, knot tightly and, using another double piece of string, tie a handle onto the string so you can lift the pudding in and out.

3 Gently lower the basin into the pan of boiling water, reduce to a fast simmer, cover the pan and cook for 4 hours, or until a skewer comes out clean. Remove the basin from the water, remove the coverings and leave for 5 minutes before turning out onto a serving plate.

4 To make the sauce, combine the cornflour and sugar in a pan and mix to a smooth paste with a little milk. Add the remaining milk and whisk over medium heat for 3–4 minutes, until the sauce boils and thickens. Stir in the butter and brandy. Serve with the hot fig pudding. Decorate with sliced figs if you wish.

BRANDY BUTTER

Using electric beaters, beat 250 g (8 oz) soft butter and 1½ cups (185 g/6 oz) sifted icing sugar until smooth and creamy. Gradually add ¼ cup (60 ml/2 fl oz) brandy, beating thoroughly between each addition. Refrigerate or fill a piping bag fitted with a star-shaped nozzle, pipe rosettes onto a baking tray lined with baking paper and refrigerate until required. Serves 8–10.

JAM PUDDING

Preparation time: 30 minutes
Total cooking time: 50 minutes
Serves 6

✷ ✷

185 g (6 oz) unsalted butter, softened
³/4 cup (185 g/6 oz) caster sugar
1 teaspoon vanilla essence
3 eggs, lightly beaten
¹/2 cup (60 g/ 2 oz) plain flour
1 cup (125 g/4 oz) self-raising flour
¹/2 cup (160 g/5¹/2 oz) berry jam

1 Preheat the oven to moderate 180°C (350°F/ Gas 4). Lightly grease six 250 ml (8 fl oz) fluted or plain heatproof moulds.
2 Beat the butter, sugar and vanilla essence with electric beaters for 1–2 minutes, or until light and creamy. Add the eggs gradually, beating well after each addition. Using a metal spoon, fold in the combined sifted flour, a quarter at a time.
3 Spoon the mixture evenly into the moulds and smooth the surface. Cover each with a piece of greased foil, pleated in the middle. Secure with string. Place in a large deep baking dish filled with enough boiling water to come halfway up the sides of the moulds. Bake for 45 minutes, or until a skewer comes out clean. Put the jam in a small pan and warm over low heat for 3–4 minutes, or until liquid. Leave the puddings for 5 minutes before loosening the sides with a knife and turning out. Top with the jam. Can be served with custard, cream or ice cream.

SUSSEX POND PUDDING

Preparation time: 20 minutes
Total cooking time: 3–4 hours
Serves 4–6

✷ ✷ ✷

2³/4 cups (340 g/11 oz) self-raising flour
170 g (5¹/2 oz) suet or unsalted butter, frozen
150 ml (5 fl oz) milk
250 g (8 oz) unsalted butter, cubed
250 g (8 oz) demerara sugar
1 thin-skinned lemon

1 Grease a 1.5 litre pudding basin and place in a saucepan on a trivet. Pour in enough water to come halfway up the side of the basin. Remove the basin and put the water on to boil. Place a sheet of foil on a work surface and put a sheet of baking paper on top. Grease the paper. Make a large pleat in the centre of the foil and paper.
2 Sift the flour into a large bowl, wrap one end of the frozen suet or butter in foil and grate into the flour. Mix into the flour, then mix in the milk and 150 ml (5 fl oz) water, using a flat-bladed knife. Bring together with your hand.
3 Keep one-quarter of the pastry aside for the lid and roll the rest into a 25 cm (10 inch) circle, leaving the middle thicker than the edges. Lift this into the basin and press upwards against the sides until it fits, leaving a little bit above the rim.
4 Put half the butter and sugar in the basin, prick the lemon all over with a skewer and add to the basin with the rest of the butter and sugar. Fold the edge of the pastry into the basin and brush with water. Roll out the remaining pastry to form a lid and press firmly onto the rim of the pastry. Place the foil and paper over the basin, foil-side-up. Cover if your basin has a lid. If not, tie a double piece of string around the rim, knot tightly and, using another double piece of string, tie a handle onto the string to make it easier to remove when ready. Lower the basin into the water. Cover the pan with a lid and steam for 3–4 hours, topping up the water when necessary.
5 Invert the pudding onto a plate with a rim. When cut, juices will flow out to form the 'pond'.

SUSSEX POND

Press the pastry upwards against the sides of the basin until it fits, leaving a little bit above the rim.

Add half the butter and sugar, then the lemon which has been pricked all over, followed by the remaining butter and sugar.

ABOVE: Jam pudding

199

1 Combine the sugar and 3 tablespoons of water in a clean, heavy-based pan and stir over low heat, tipping the pan from side to side, until the sugar dissolves. Bring to the boil, reduce the heat and simmer, without stirring, until the mixture turns a golden caramel. (This should take about 6 minutes but watch carefully, as it can burn quickly.) As soon as the mixture has turned golden, pour it quickly into the pudding basin. Set aside.

2 Grease a 1.5 litre heatproof glass or ceramic pudding basin with melted butter or oil. Don't use a metal basin or the pudding will stick. Place the empty basin in a saucepan, on a trivet, and pour in enough water to come halfway up the side of the basin. Remove the basin and put the water on to boil. Line the base with baking paper and grease the paper. Place a sheet of foil on a work surface and put a sheet of baking paper on top. Grease the paper. Make a large pleat in the centre of the foil and paper.

3 Drain the mangoes and reserve the juice. Cut 5 long strips of mango, set aside and roughly chop the rest. Beat the butter, sugar and lime rind in a small bowl until light and creamy. Add the eggs one at a time, beating well after each addition. Transfer to a large bowl. Fold in half the flour and the chopped mango. Add the remaining flour, ground almonds and cardamom and mix well.

4 Arrange the reserved strips of mango in a single layer on the caramel in the base of the basin. Spoon the pudding mixture into the basin. Place the foil and paper over the basin, foil-side-up, and smooth it down the sides. Cover if your basin has a lid. If not, tie a double piece of string around the rim, knot tightly and, using another double piece of string, tie a handle onto the string so you can lift the pudding in and out.

5 Carefully lower the basin into the boiling water, reduce to a fast simmer, cover the pan and simmer for 1 hour 15 minutes, topping up the water if necessary during cooking. When cooked, the pudding should appear well risen and feel firm to the touch.

6 While the pudding is cooking, make the sauce. Combine the reserved mango juice in a pan with the lime juice. Whisk in the arrowroot and cook over gentle heat, stirring constantly, until the sauce boils, thickens and becomes clear. Loosen the pudding from the basin by running a knife around the edges before turning out. If any pieces of mango stick to the basin, put them back onto the pudding. Serve with the warm mango sauce.

STEAMED UPSIDE-DOWN MANGO PUDDING

Preparation time: 35 minutes
Total cooking time: 1 hour 30 minutes
Serves 4–6

★ ★ ★

3 tablespoons sugar
425 g (14 oz) can mangoes in natural juices
100 g (3 1/2 oz) soft unsalted butter
1/2 cup (125 g/4 oz) caster sugar
1/2 teaspoon grated lime rind
2 eggs
1 cup (125g/4 oz) self-raising flour
3 tablespoons ground almonds
pinch of crushed cardamom seeds
1 tablespoon lime juice
2 teaspoons arrowroot

ABOVE: Steamed upside-down mango pudding

HOT LIME
SHORTCAKE PUDDING

Preparation time: 45 minutes + chilling
Total cooking time: 1 hour 20 minutes
Serves 6

★ ★

3 cups (375 g/12 oz) plain flour, sifted
1 1/2 teaspoons baking powder
200 g (6 1/2 oz) chilled unsalted butter, chopped
1/2 cup (45 g/1 1/2 oz) desiccated coconut
250–300 ml (8–10 fl oz) cream
1/2 cup (160 g/5 1/2 oz) lime marmalade

Hot lime syrup

3/4 cup (185 g/6 oz) caster sugar
juice and finely grated rind of 3 limes
60 g (2 oz) unsalted butter

1 Combine the sifted flour, baking powder and a pinch of salt in a large bowl. Rub in the chopped butter until the mixture resembles fine breadcrumbs, then stir in the coconut. Use a knife to mix in almost all the cream. Add the rest, if necessary, to form a soft dough. Bring the dough together with your hands. Roll the dough out between 2 sheets of baking paper into a 25 x 40 cm (10 x 16 inch) rectangle. Spread with marmalade, roll up lengthways and chill for 20 minutes.

2 Preheat the oven to moderate 180°C (350°F/ Gas 4). Grease a 1.5 litre pudding basin. Cut the roll into 2 cm (3/4 inch) slices and arrange to cover the base and side of the basin. Fill the centre with the remaining slices.

3 To make the hot lime syrup, combine all the syrup ingredients in a small pan with 3/4 cup (185 ml/6 fl oz) water and stir over low heat until the sugar dissolves. Bring to the boil and pour over the pudding. Put the basin on a tray, to catch drips, and bake for 1 hour 15 minutes, or until a skewer comes out clean when inserted into the centre. Leave for 15 minutes before turning out.

SHORTCAKE PUDDING

Arrange the shortcake rolls around the base and side, then fill the centre.

ABOVE: Hot lime shortcake pudding

SPOTTED DICK

Preparation time: 15 minutes + standing
Total cooking time: 1 hour 30 minutes
Serves 4

★★

1½ cups (185 g/6 oz) plain flour
1½ teaspoons baking powder
½ cup (125 g/4 oz) sugar
1½ teaspoons ground ginger
2 cups (160 g/5½ oz) fresh
　breadcrumbs
60 g (2 oz) sultanas
110 g (3½ oz) currants
125 g (4 oz) suet, grated
2 teaspoons finely grated lemon rind
2 eggs, lightly beaten
⅔ cup (170 ml/5½ fl oz) milk

SPOTTED DICK

This traditional suet pudding is usually made in the shape of a cylinder. It was also once known as Spotted Dog and Plum Bolster.

BELOW: Spotted dick

1 Sift the flour, baking powder, sugar and ginger into a large bowl. Add the breadcrumbs, sultanas, currants, suet and lemon rind. Mix thoroughly with a wooden spoon.
2 Combine the egg and milk, add to the dry ingredients and mix well. Add a little more milk if necessary, then set aside for 5 minutes.
3 Lay a sheet of baking paper on a work surface and form the mixture into a roll shape about 20 cm (8 inches) long. Roll the pudding in the paper and fold up the ends—do not wrap it too tight as it has to expand as it cooks. Wrap the roll in a tea towel, put it in the top of a bamboo or metal steamer, cover and steam for 1 hour 30 minutes. Do not let the pudding boil dry— replenish with boiling water as the pudding cooks. Unmould the pudding onto a plate and slice. Can be served with custard or cream.

UPSIDE-DOWN BANANA CAKE

Preparation time: 20 minutes
Total cooking time: 45 minutes
Serves 8

★

50 g (1¾ oz) butter, melted
⅓ cup (60 g/2 oz) soft brown sugar
6 ripe large bananas, halved lengthways
125 g (4 oz) butter, softened
1¼ cups (230 g/7½ oz) soft brown
　sugar, extra
2 eggs, lightly beaten
1½ cups (185 g/6 oz) self-raising flour
1 teaspoon baking powder
2 large bananas, extra, mashed

1 Preheat the oven to moderate 180°C (350°/ Gas 4). Grease and line a 20 cm (8 inch) square cake tin, pour the melted butter over the base of the tin and sprinkle with the sugar. Arrange the bananas cut-side-down over the brown sugar.
2 Cream the butter and extra brown sugar until light and fluffy. Add the eggs gradually, beating well after each addition.
3 Sift the flour and baking powder into a bowl, then fold into the cake mixture with the mashed banana. Carefully spread into the tin. Bake for 45 minutes, or until a skewer comes out clean when inserted in the centre of the cake. Turn out while still warm.
NOTE: The bananas must be very ripe or they will not be tender and squashy when cooked.

BANANA PUDDING WITH BUTTERSCOTCH SAUCE

Preparation time: 30 minutes
Total cooking time: 1 hour 40 minutes
Serves 6–8

★★

150 g (5 oz) unsalted butter

3/4 cup (140 g/4 1/2 oz) soft brown sugar

1 1/2 cups (185 g/6 oz) self-raising flour

1/2 cup (60 g/2 oz) plain flour

1/2 teaspoon bicarbonate of soda

1/2 teaspoon ground nutmeg

1 teaspoon vanilla essence

2 eggs, lightly beaten

3/4 cup (185 ml/6 fl oz) buttermilk

2 small ripe bananas, mashed

Butterscotch sauce

125 g (4 oz) unsalted butter

2/3 cup (125 g/4 oz) soft brown sugar

1 cup (315 g/10 oz) condensed milk

1 1/3 cups (350 ml/11 fl oz) cream

1 Grease a 2 litre pudding basin and line the base with baking paper. Place the empty basin in a saucepan, on a trivet, and pour in enough water to come halfway up the side of the basin. Remove the basin and put the water on to boil. Place a sheet of foil on a work surface and put a sheet of baking paper on top. Grease the paper. Make a large pleat in the centre.

2 Stir the butter and sugar over low heat until dissolved. Remove from the heat. Sift the combined flours, soda and nutmeg into a bowl and make a well. Add the butter mixture, vanilla, egg and buttermilk. Stir with a wooden spoon until smooth. Stir in the banana. Spoon into the basin. Place the foil and paper over the basin, foil-side-up. Cover if your basin has a lid. If not, tie a double piece of string around the rim, knot tightly and, using another double piece of string, tie a handle onto the string. Lower the basin into the boiling water, reduce to a fast simmer, cover the pan and boil for 1 hour 30 minutes, or until a skewer comes out clean. Top up the water if necessary. Leave for 5 minutes then turn out.

3 To make the sauce, combine the ingredients in a pan and stir over low heat until the sugar is dissolved. Bring to the boil, reduce the heat and simmer for 3–5 minutes. Serve hot.

ABOVE: Banana pudding with butterscotch sauce

203

SWEET SAUCES What a marriage

made in heaven... deliciously sweet sauces poured over sponge puddings that soak

up their syrup and soften into irresistible gooeyness.

BUTTERSCOTCH SAUCE

Stir 75 g (2½ oz) butter, 1 cup (185 g/
6 oz) soft brown sugar and ¾ cup
(185 ml/6 fl oz) cream in a small pan
over low heat until the butter has melted
and the sugar dissolved. Bring to the boil,
reduce the heat and simmer for 2 minutes.
Makes 1⅔ cups (410 ml/13 fl oz).

CARAMEL BAR SAUCE

Chop four Snickers® bars. Put in a pan
with ¼ cup (60 ml/2 fl oz) milk and
¾ cup (185 ml/6 fl oz) cream and stir
over low heat until melted. Add 100 g
(3½ oz) chopped milk chocolate and stir
until melted. Cool to room temperature.
Makes 2¼ cups (560 ml/18 fl oz).

DARK CHOCOLATE SAUCE

Put 150 g (5 oz) chopped dark chocolate
in a bowl. Bring 300 ml (10 fl oz) cream
to the boil in a pan. Stir in 2 tablespoons
caster sugar, then pour over the chocolate.
Leave for 2 minutes, then stir until smooth.
Add a spoonful of any liqueur. Serve
warm. Makes 2 cups (500 ml/16 fl oz).

CHOCOLATE FUDGE SAUCE

Put 1 cup (250 ml/8 fl oz) cream, 30 g (1 oz) butter, 1 tablespoon golden syrup and 200 g (6½ oz) chopped dark chocolate in a pan. Stir over low heat until melted and smooth. Serve hot or warm. Makes 2 cups (500 ml/16 fl oz).

LIQUEUR TOKAY SYRUP

Put 250 g (8 oz) sugar and 250 ml (8 fl oz) water in a medium pan. Slowly bring to the boil, stirring to dissolve the sugar. Add half a vanilla bean and boil, without stirring for 5 minutes. Add 250 ml (8 fl oz) liqueur tokay, liqueur muscat or sauterne and stir. Bring back to the boil and cook for 15 minutes, depending on the thickness desired. Makes 2 cups (500 ml/16 fl oz).

VANILLA HAZELNUT SAUCE

Pour 300 ml (10 fl oz) cream into a small pan. Split 1 vanilla bean and scrape the seeds into the cream. Add the pod and bring to the boil. Remove from the heat, cover and leave for 10 minutes, then strain. Put 200 g (6½ oz) chopped white chocolate in a bowl, reheat the cream and pour over the chocolate. Leave for 2 minutes, then stir until melted. Stir in 30 g (1 oz) chopped roasted hazelnuts. Makes 2 cups (500 ml/16 fl oz).

RICH BRANDY SAUCE

Bring 2 cups (500 ml/16 fl oz) cream to the boil in a heavy-based pan. Whisk 4 egg yolks with ½ cup (125 g/4 oz) caster sugar until creamy. Slowly pour the hot cream in, stirring. Return to the pan and stir over low heat for 5–6 minutes, until slightly thickened; do not boil. Stir in 3 tablespoons brandy before serving. Makes 3¼ cups (810 ml/26 fl oz).

CITRUS SYRUP

Cut the rind from an orange, a lemon and a lime. Remove the pith. Cut the rind into fine strips. Put in a pan with the juice from the lime and half the juice from the lemon and orange. Add 125 g (4 oz) sugar and 125 ml (4 fl oz) water. Stir over low heat to dissolve. Add half a vanilla bean. Simmer for 10 minutes; do not stir. Makes 1 cup (250 ml/8 fl oz).

FROM LEFT: Butterscotch; Caramel bar; Dark chocolate; Liqueur Tokay; Chocolate fudge; Vanilla hazelnut; Rich brandy; Citrus syrup

PECAN AND MAPLE SYRUP PUDDING

Preparation time: 20 minutes
Total cooking time: 2 hours
Serves 8–10

★

200 g (6¹/₂ oz) unsalted butter
1 cup (250 g/8 oz) caster sugar
4 eggs, lightly beaten
1 teaspoon vanilla essence
3 cups (375 g/12 oz) self-raising flour, sifted
200 g (6¹/₂ oz) pecans, chopped
¹/₂ teaspoon ground cinnamon
grated rind of 1 lemon
³/₄ cup (185 ml/6 fl oz) milk
1 cup (250 ml/8 fl oz) maple syrup

1 Preheat the oven to moderate 180°C (350°F/Gas 4). Beat the butter and sugar with electric beaters until creamy. Gradually beat in the eggs, then the vanilla. Combine the flour, three-quarters of the pecans, cinnamon and rind and fold in, alternating with spoonfuls of milk, until smooth.
2 Grease a 2.25 litre pudding basin and line the base with a circle of baking paper. Pour three-quarters of the maple syrup into the basin and add the remaining pecans. Fill with mixture and pour the rest of the syrup over.
3 Cover with foil and put in a large baking dish. Pour enough water into the dish to come halfway up the side of the bowl, then bake for 2 hours. Test with a skewer—it should come out clean. Turn out onto a large serving plate. Serve with ice cream or cream, if desired.

STEAMED ORANGE PUDDING

Preparation time: 30 minutes
Total cooking time: 1 hour 30 minutes
Serves 4

★

1 thin-skinned orange
90 g (3 oz) butter, softened
1 tablespoon sugar
2 eggs
4 tablespoons chunky marmalade
rind of 1 orange
2 cups (250 g/8 oz) self-raising flour
pinch of salt
4 tablespoons milk

ABOVE: Pecan and maple syrup pudding

1 Grease a 1.25 litre pudding basin and line the base with a circle of baking paper. Place the empty basin in a saucepan on a trivet and pour in enough cold water to come halfway up the side of the basin. Remove the basin and put the water on to boil. Place a sheet of foil on a work surface and put a sheet of baking paper on top. Grease the paper. Make a pleat in the centre of the whole lot to allow for expansion.

2 Remove the skin and pith from the orange by cutting off the top and bottom and cutting downwards all the way round. Slice the orange thinly, place one slice in the bottom of the basin and arrange the others around the sides.

3 Beat the butter and sugar until light and creamy. Add the eggs, one at a time, and beat well. Add the marmalade and rind, mix in, then add the sifted flour and salt and mix thoroughly. Add the milk and spoon the mixture into the basin without disturbing the orange slices. Place the foil and paper over the basin, foil-side-up, and smooth it down the sides. Cover if your basin has a lid. If not, tie a double piece of string around the rim, knot tightly and, using another double piece of string, tie a handle onto the string so you can lift the pudding in and out. Cover the pan and steam for 1 hour 30 minutes, replenishing the water when necessary. Turn out to serve.

STICKY DATE PUDDING WITH CARAMEL SAUCE

Preparation time: 30 minutes + standing
Total cooking time: 1 hour 10 minutes
Serves 6–8

★

370 g (12 oz) pitted dates
1½ teaspoons bicarbonate of soda
1 teaspoon grated fresh ginger
90 g (3 oz) unsalted butter
1 cup (250 g/8 oz) caster sugar
3 eggs
1½ cups (185 g/6 oz) self-raising flour
½ teaspoon mixed spice
crème fraîche, for serving

Caramel sauce

150 g (5 oz) unsalted butter
1¼ cups (230 g/7½ oz) soft brown sugar
⅓ cup (80 ml/2¾ fl oz) golden syrup
¾ cup (185 ml/6 fl oz) cream

1 Preheat the oven to moderate 180°C (350°/Gas 4). Grease and line the base of a deep 23 cm (9 inch) diameter cake tin. Chop the dates and put them in a pan with 1¾ cups (440 ml/14 fl oz) water. Bring to the boil, then remove from the heat, add the bicarbonate of soda and ginger and leave to stand for 5 minutes.

2 Cream together the butter, sugar and 1 egg. Beat in the remaining eggs one at a time. Fold in the sifted flour and spice, add the date mixture and stir until well combined. Pour into the tin and bake for 55–60 minutes, or until a skewer comes out clean when inserted into the middle. Cover with foil if overbrowning during cooking. Leave to stand for 5 minutes before turning out onto a serving plate.

3 To make the caramel sauce, stir all the ingredients in a pan over low heat until the sugar has dissolved. Simmer, uncovered, for about 3 minutes, or until thickened slightly. Brush some sauce over the top and sides of the pudding until well-glazed. Serve immediately with the sauce and a dollop of crème fraîche.

ABOVE: Sticky date pudding with caramel sauce

PASSIONFRUIT
Native to Brazil, passionfruit were named for their flowers which the Jesuit missionaries thought were a pictorial representation of the crucifix. There are 350 members of the Passiflora species, three of which are the ones most commonly available. Banana passionfruit have a long yellow fruit with a less acidic flesh and juice. Common passionfruit have a deep-purple, wrinkled skin, a red pith and a much more orangy fruit with small black seeds. Yellow passionfruit have a smoother skin and yellower colour, but less intense flavour. To use the pulp without the seeds, push it through a sieve.

ABOVE: Sticky orange and passionfruit pudding

STICKY ORANGE AND PASSIONFRUIT PUDDING

Preparation time: 35 minutes + chilling
Total cooking time: 55 minutes
Serves 6

★

3 cups (375 g/12 oz) plain flour
1 1/2 teaspoons baking powder
200 g (6 1/2 oz) chilled unsalted butter, chopped
1/2 cup (45g/1 1/2 oz) desiccated coconut
300 ml (9 1/2 fl oz) cream
1/2 cup (160 g/5 1/4 oz) orange marmalade
2 tablespoons passionfruit pulp

Passionfruit syrup

1/2 cup (125 ml/4 fl oz) orange juice
3/4 cup (185 g/6 oz) caster sugar
1/4 cup (60 g/2 oz) passionfruit pulp

1 Sift the flour, baking powder and a pinch of salt into a bowl. Rub in the butter with just your fingertips until fine and crumbly. Stir in the coconut. With a flat-bladed knife, mix in most of the cream. Add the rest, if needed, to bring the mixture together. Press together into a soft dough and roll between 2 sheets of baking paper to make a 25 x 40 cm (10 x 16 inch) rectangle.

2 Spread marmalade over the dough and drizzle with passionfruit pulp. Roll up lengthways like a swiss roll. Chill for 20 minutes, or until firm.

3 Preheat the oven to 180°C (350°F/Gas 4). Brush a deep 20 cm (8 inch) round cake tin with melted butter or oil; line the base with baking paper. Cut the rolled dough into 2 cm (3/4 inch) slices; arrange half over the base of the tin. Place a second layer over the gaps where the bottom slices join. Place the tin on a baking tray.

4 To make the passionfruit syrup, put all the ingredients with 1/4 cup (60 ml/2 fl oz) water in a pan. Stir over low heat, without boiling, until the sugar has dissolved. Bring to the boil, then pour over the pudding. Bake for 50 minutes, or until a skewer comes out clean. Leave for 15 minutes before turning out.

SAGO PLUM PUDDING WITH RUM BUTTER

Preparation time: 30–35 minutes + soaking
Total cooking time: 3¹/₂–4 hours
Serves 6–8

★ ★

¹/₃ cup (65 g/2¹/₄ oz) sago
1 cup (250 ml/8 fl oz) milk
1 teaspoon bicarbonate of soda
³/₄ cup (140 g/4¹/₂ oz) dark brown sugar
2 cups (160 g/5¹/₄ oz) fresh white breadcrumbs
60 g (2 oz) sultanas
75 g (2¹/₂ oz) currants
90 g (3 oz) dates, chopped
2 eggs, lightly beaten
60 g (2 oz) unsalted butter, melted
raspberries, blueberries and icing sugar,
   to decorate

Rum butter

125 g (4 oz) unsalted butter, softened
³/₄ cup (140 g/4¹/₂ oz) dark brown sugar
4 tablespoons rum

1 Combine the sago and milk in a small bowl, cover and refrigerate overnight. Lightly brush a 1.5 litre pudding basin with melted butter or oil and line the base with a circle of baking paper. Place the empty basin in a saucepan, on a trivet, and pour in enough water to come halfway up the side of the basin. Remove the basin and put the water on to boil. Place a sheet of foil on a work surface and put a sheet of baking paper on top. Grease the paper. Make a large pleat in the centre of the whole lot.
2 Place the soaked sago and milk in a large bowl and stir in the bicarbonate of soda until dissolved. Stir in the sugar, breadcrumbs, dried fruit, beaten eggs and melted butter and mix together well.
3 Spoon the mixture into the basin and smooth the surface. Cover with the foil and paper, foil-side-up. Cover if your basin has a lid. If not, tie a double piece of string around the rim, knot tightly and, using another double piece of string, tie a handle onto the string so you can lift the pudding in and out.
4 Carefully lower the basin into the boiling water. Reduce to a rapid simmer, cover and cook for 3¹/₂–4 hours, or until a skewer inserted into the centre comes out clean. Add more boiling water to the pan as necessary—don't let it boil dry. Remove the basin from the pan, remove the coverings and leave for 5 minutes before turning the pudding out onto a large serving plate. Decorate with raspberries and blueberries, dust with icing sugar and serve hot with cold rum butter.
5 To make the rum butter, beat together the butter and brown sugar with electric beaters for about 3–4 minutes, or until light and creamy. Gradually beat in the rum, one tablespoon at a time. Add more rum to taste, if you like. Transfer to a serving dish, cover and refrigerate until required.

BELOW: Sago plum pudding with rum butter

GOLDEN SYRUP DUMPLINGS

Preparation time: 15 minutes
Total cooking time: 30 minutes
Serves 4

★

1 cup (125 g/4 oz) self-raising flour
40 g (1¼ oz) unsalted butter, chopped
1 egg
1 tablespoon milk

Syrup

1 cup (250 g/8 oz) sugar
40 g (1¼ oz) unsalted butter
2 tablespoons golden syrup
¼ cup (60 ml/2 fl oz) lemon juice

1 Sift the flour and a pinch of salt into a bowl. Rub in the butter until fine and crumbly, and make a well. Using a flat-bladed knife, stir in the combined egg and milk to form a soft dough.
2 Put the syrup ingredients in a pan with 2 cups (500 ml/16 fl oz) water and stir over medium heat until the sugar has dissolved. Bring to the boil, then gently drop dessertspoons of dough into the syrup. Cover and reduce the heat to simmer for 20 minutes, or until a knife inserted into a dumpling comes out clean. Spoon onto plates; drizzle with syrup. Can be served with cream.

ABOVE: Golden syrup dumplings

BLACK RICE PUDDING

Preparation time: 10 minutes + soaking
Total cooking time: 40 minutes
Serves 6–8

★

2 cups (400 g/13 oz) black glutinous rice
3 fresh pandan leaves
2 cups (500 ml/16 fl oz) coconut milk
80 g (2¾ oz) palm sugar, grated
3 tablespoons caster sugar
coconut cream, for serving

1 Put the rice in a large glass or ceramic bowl and cover with water. Soak for 8 hours. Drain and put in a pan with 1 litre water. Bring slowly to the boil, stirring frequently, and cook at a low boil for 20 minutes, or until tender. Drain.
2 Pull your fingers through the pandan leaves to shred, then knot them. In a large heavy-based pan, heat the coconut milk until almost boiling. Add the sugars and pandan leaves and stir until the sugars have dissolved.
3 Add the rice to the pan and cook, stirring, for 3–4 minutes without boiling. Turn off the heat, cover and leave for 15 minutes. Remove the leaves. Serve warm with coconut cream.
NOTE: If you can't find pandan leaves at an Asian grocer, substitute 1 teaspoon vanilla essence.

CARAMEL STICKY RICE

Preparation time: 40 minutes + soaking
Total cooking time: 1 hour 15 minutes
Serves 4

★

2 cups (400 g/13 oz) white glutinous rice
250 ml (8 fl oz) coconut milk
85 g (3 oz) palm sugar, grated

1 Put the rice in a sieve and wash until the water runs clear. Put in a glass or ceramic bowl, cover with water and soak for 8 hours. Drain.
2 Line a bamboo steamer with baking paper or a damp tea towel and place over a water-filled wok. Don't let the base of the steamer touch the water. Spread the rice over the paper, fold the paper or tea towel over the rice and cover with another sheet of paper or tea towel—tuck it in so the rice is completely encased. Cover with the bamboo lid and steam on medium for 50 minutes, checking the water regularly, until just cooked.

3 Stir the coconut milk, palm sugar and a pinch of salt in a small pan until boiling. Reduce the heat and simmer for 15 minutes, or until thick.
4 Pour a quarter of the caramel over the rice, fork it through, cover with the paper and lid and steam for 5 minutes. Repeat with the remaining caramel, cooking until the rice is plump and sticky. Transfer the rice to a metal tray or lamington tin, pressing in lightly, then set aside until firm. Cut into diamonds and serve warm.

COCONUT SAGO PUDDINGS

Preparation time: 10 minutes + chilling
Total cooking time: 1 hour
Serves 8

☆

220 ml (7 fl oz) coconut milk
1/4 cup (90 g/3 oz) grated palm sugar
1 stem lemon grass, bruised
250 g (8 oz) sago
1 teaspoon grated lime rind
1 egg white, lightly beaten
4 guavas, thinly sliced

Lime syrup

2 cups (500 g/1 lb) caster sugar
1 tablespoon finely shredded fresh ginger
rind of 2 limes

1 Lightly grease eight 125 ml (4 fl oz) dariole moulds. Put the coconut milk, palm sugar and lemon grass in a pan with 3 cups (750 ml/24 fl oz) water. Bring just to the boil. Add the sago and lime rind and cook over low heat, stirring, for 35–40 minutes, until the sago is thick and clear.
2 Remove from the heat and cool slightly. Remove the lemon grass. Whisk the egg white into stiff peaks and gently fold into the sago. Spoon the mixture in the moulds, cover with plastic wrap and chill for 3 hours, or until firm. Stand the moulds in hot water for 20 seconds before turning out.
3 To make the lime syrup, put the sugar and 1 cup (250 ml/8 fl oz) water in a pan and stir over low heat until the sugar is dissolved. Bring to the boil and cook for 10 minutes, without stirring, until the syrup thickens. Add the ginger and lime rind and cook for another 5 minutes. Arrange the sliced guava on a plate, pour over the lime syrup and serve with the puddings.

SAGO PUDDINGS

Cook the sago over low heat, stirring, until the mixture is thick and clear.

Spoon the mixture into the lightly greased dariole moulds, cover with plastic wrap, then chill for 3 hours.

ABOVE: Coconut sago puddings

GATEAUX AND TRIFLES

A gateau is simply a cake with its best frock on. More often than not, layered and drenched with liqueur, then lavishly assembled with peaks of cream, fruit, custard or chocolate, the gateau has taken the simple cake from its humble afternoon tea setting to the dizzy heights of spectacular dessert stardom. How ironic that the trifle, like the fool and the flummery, takes its silly name from a 'thing of little importance', a trifling matter in a world of bullying rumbustious main courses. Had it been created in today's more enlightened times, the trifle might perhaps have been named the 'importance'.

HAZELNUT TORTE

Preparation time: 40 minutes + chilling
Total cooking time: 35 minutes
Serves 6–8

★★

185 g (6 oz) hazelnuts
6 egg whites
3/4 cup (185 g/6 oz) caster sugar
1 teaspoon white wine vinegar
1/2 teaspoon vanilla essence
1/2 teaspoon ground cardamom
cocoa powder and melted chocolate, for serving

Cardamom cream

1 cup (250 ml/8 fl oz) cream
1/2 teaspoon ground cardamom
2 tablespoons caster sugar

1 Preheat the oven to moderate 180°C (350°F/ Gas 4). Brush the bases of two shallow 20 cm (8 inch) round cake tins with oil or melted butter. Line the bases with baking paper.

2 Bake the nuts on a baking tray for 8 minutes, or until roasted. Remove and rub in a tea towel to remove the skins. When cool, grind finely in a blender or food processor.

3 Beat the egg whites until stiff peaks form. Add the sugar gradually, beating until the sugar has dissolved and the mixture is thick and glossy. Using a metal spoon, gently fold in the nuts, vinegar, vanilla and cardamom.

4 Divide the mixture evenly between the cake tins. Bake for 25 minutes, or until the cakes are firm on top and set through (they will not rise at all and will be moist, but not wet, in the centre when tested with a skewer). Run a knife around the edges so that when the cakes sink slightly they will do so evenly. Leave for 5 minutes, then turn out onto a wire rack. Remove the paper.

5 To make the cardamom cream, beat the cream until soft peaks form. Add the cardamom and sugar and beat until stiff peaks form.

6 Place a cake layer on a plate and spread with a third of the cream. Place the other cake on top, spread with more cream and pipe the remainder around the edge. Chill for at least 5 hours before cutting. Dust with cocoa powder and drizzle with melted chocolate to serve.

ABOVE: Hazelnut torte

SPONGE FINGERS
Sponge finger biscuits are
available in different sizes
and under different names.
Sometimes called savoiardi
biscuits, lady-fingers or
boudoir biscuits, they
are served with chilled
desserts, ice cream and
fruit purées, and are used
as a border for various
desserts. They are made
from a light sponge batter
which is baked to form a
firm biscuit.

CHARLOTTE MALAKOFF

Preparation time: 1 hour + chilling
Total cooking time: Nil
Serves 8–12

★★

250 g (8 oz) sponge finger biscuits
1/2 cup (125 ml/4 fl oz) Grand Marnier
500 g (1 lb) strawberries, hulled and halved
whipped cream and strawberries, for serving

Almond cream

125 g (4 oz) unsalted butter
1/3 cup (90 g/3 oz) caster sugar
1/4 cup (60 ml/2 fl oz) Grand Marnier
1/4 teaspoon almond essence
3/4 cup (185 ml/6 fl oz) cream, whipped
140 g (4 1/2 oz) ground almonds

1 Brush a deep 1–1.5 litre soufflé dish with
melted butter or oil. Line the base with
greaseproof paper and grease the paper. Trim
the sponge finger biscuits to fit the sides of the
dish. Quickly dip the sponge fingers into the
liqueur that has been mixed with 1/2 cup
(125 ml/4 fl oz) water. Arrange upright
around the side of the dish, rounded-side-down.
2 To make the almond cream, using electric
beaters, beat the butter and sugar until light and
creamy. Add the liqueur and almond essence.
Continue beating until the mixture is smooth
and the sugar has dissolved. Using a metal
spoon, fold in the cream and almonds.
3 Spoon one-third of the almond cream into
the base of the dish and cover with strawberry
halves. Top with a layer of dipped sponge
fingers. Continue layering, finishing with
a layer of sponge fingers, then press down.
4 Cover with foil and place a small plate and
weight on top. Refrigerate for 8 hours, or
overnight. Remove the plate and foil and turn
onto a chilled serving plate. Remove the
greaseproof paper. Decorate with whipped
cream and strawberries.
NOTE: This dessert is very rich and should be
served after a light main course. It is also
splendid to serve when you have guests for
coffee and cake, rather than a meal, and is
lovely for a party.

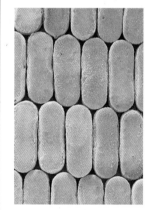

ABOVE: Charlotte malakoff

215

TRIFLES and ZUPPA INGLESE

Trifles were originally flavoured creams eaten by the Elizabethans. They changed gradually: the cream was thickened, biscuits and other ingredients were added and decorations were used. In 1755, Hannah Glasse had a recipe for a 'Grand Trifle', described as 'fit to go on a King's table'. It contained biscuits and ratafias soaked in alcohol, a layer of custard, then syllabub on top. Trifle means 'a thing of little importance' and this is where the dish got its name.

Zuppa inglese means 'English soup' in Italian, presumably because the dish resembles the English trifle. Originally it was baked but modern versions are not cooked.

OPPOSITE PAGE: English trifle (top); Zuppa inglese

ENGLISH TRIFLE

Preparation time: 25 minutes + chilling
Total cooking time: 10 minutes
Serves 6

✫

4 slices Madeira cake or trifle sponges
1/4 cup (60 ml/2 fl oz) sweet sherry or Madeira
250 g (8 oz) raspberries
4 eggs
2 tablespoons caster sugar
2 tablespoons plain flour
2 cups (500 ml/16 fl oz) milk
1/4 teaspoon vanilla extract
1/2 cup (125 ml/4 fl oz) cream
1/4 cup (25 g/3/4 oz) flaked almonds, to decorate
raspberries, to decorate

1 Put the cake in a decorative bowl and sprinkle with the sherry. Scatter the raspberries over the top and crush them gently into the sponge with the back of a spoon, leaving some of them whole.
2 Mix the eggs, sugar and plain flour together in a bowl. Heat the milk in a pan, pour it over the egg mixture, stir well and pour back into a clean pan. Cook over medium heat until the custard boils and thickens and coats the back of a spoon. Stir in the vanilla, cover the surface with plastic wrap and leave to cool.
3 Pour the cooled custard over the raspberries and leave to set in the fridge, it will firm up but not become solid. Whip the cream and spoon it over the custard. Decorate with almonds and raspberries and refrigerate until needed.

TIPSY TRIFLE

Preparation time: 25 minutes + chilling
Total cooking time: Nil
Serves 6

✫

20 cm (8 inch) sponge cake
1/2 cup (160 g/5 1/2 oz) apricot jam
1/2 cup (125 ml/4 fl oz) brandy
85 g (3 oz) packet apricot jelly crystals
2 sliced bananas, sprinkled with a little lemon juice
2 cups (500 ml/16 fl oz) prepared custard
1 cup (250 ml/8 fl oz) cream, whipped
60 g (2 oz) toasted almonds, chopped
pulp of 2 passionfruit

1 Cut the sponge into small cubes and put in a large serving bowl, or layer the trifle in individual parfait glasses. Combine the jam, brandy and 1/2 cup (60 ml/2 fl oz) water and sprinkle over the sponge.
2 Add the jelly crystals to 2 cups (500 ml/16 fl oz) boiling water and stir until dissolved. Pour into a 27 x 18 cm (11 x 7 inch) rectangular tin. Refrigerate until set, then cut into cubes with a rubber spatula.
3 Put the jelly cubes over the sponge and top with the bananas and custard. Decorate with whipped cream, almonds and passionfruit. Refrigerate until required.

ZUPPA INGLESE

Preparation time: 35 minutes + chilling
Total cooking time: 10 minutes
Serves 6

✫

2 cups (500 ml/16 fl oz) milk
1 vanilla bean, split lengthways
4 egg yolks
1/2 cup (125 g/4 oz) caster sugar
2 tablespoons plain flour
300 g (10 oz) Madeira cake, cut into 1 cm (1/2 inch) slices
1/3 cup (80 ml/2 3/4 fl oz) rum
30 g (1 oz) chocolate, grated or shaved
50 g (1 3/4 oz) flaked almonds, toasted

1 Grease a 1.5 litre serving dish with flavourless oil or melted butter. Place the milk and vanilla bean in a pan and slowly heat until bubbles appear around the edge of the pan. Whisk the egg yolks, sugar and flour together in a bowl, until thick and pale.
2 Discard the vanilla bean, whisk the warm milk slowly into the egg mixture and blend well. Return the custard mixture to a clean pan and stir over medium heat until the custard boils and thickens.
3 Line the base of the prepared dish with one-third of the cake slices and brush well with the rum combined with 1 tablespoon of water. Spread one-third of the custard over the cake, top with cake slices and brush with rum mixture. Repeat this process, finishing with a layer of custard. Cover and refrigerate for at least 3 hours. Sprinkle with grated or shaved chocolate and toasted flaked almonds just before serving.

TIRAMISU

Fold the beaten egg whites into the cream mixture with a metal spoon.

Dip the biscuits into the coffee mixture and arrange in the serving dish.

ABOVE: Tiramisu

TIRAMISU

Preparation time: 30 minutes + chilling
Total cooking time: Nil
Serves 6–8

★

3 cups (750 ml/24 fl oz) strong black coffee,
    cooled

3 tablespoons brandy or Kahlua

2 eggs, separated

3 tablespoons caster sugar

250 g (8 oz) mascarpone

1 cup (250 ml/8 fl oz) cream, whipped

16 large sponge finger biscuits

2 teaspoons dark cocoa powder

1 Put the coffee and liqueur in a bowl. Using electric beaters, beat the egg yolks and sugar in a small bowl for 3 minutes, or until thick and pale. Add the mascarpone and beat until just combined. Fold in the cream with a metal spoon.

2 Beat the egg whites until soft peaks form. Fold quickly and lightly into the cream mixture with a metal spoon, trying not to lose the volume.

3 Quickly dip half the biscuits, one at a time, into the coffee mixture. Drain off any excess and arrange the biscuits in the base of a deep serving dish. Spread half the cream mixture over the biscuits.

4 Dip the remaining biscuits and repeat the layers. Smooth the surface and dust liberally with cocoa powder. Refrigerate for 2 hours, or until firm, to allow the flavours to develop.

STRAWBERRY SWISS ROLL

Preparation time: 25 minutes + standing
Total cooking time: 10 minutes
Serves 6–8

★ ★

3 eggs, separated
1/2 cup (125 g/4 oz) caster sugar, plus
  1 tablespoon, extra
3/4 cup (90 g/3 oz) self-raising flour, sifted
1/2 cup (160 g/5 1/2 oz) strawberry jam
3/4 cup (185 ml/6 fl oz) cream
250 g (8 oz) strawberries, quartered

1 Preheat the oven to moderately hot 200°C
(400°F/Gas 6). Sprinkle a tablespoon of sugar
over a piece of baking paper 30 x 35 cm
(12 x 14 inch), resting on a tea towel. Brush a
25 x 30 cm (10 x 12 inch) swiss roll tin with oil
or melted butter and line with baking paper.
2 Beat the egg whites until soft peaks form.
Gradually add the sugar and beat until dissolved.
Beat in the lightly beaten egg yolks until thick.
3 Fold in the flour and 2 tablespoons hot water.
Spread into the tin and bake for 8–10 minutes, or
until firm and golden. Turn out onto the
sugared paper and peel the paper from the base.
Using the tea towel as a guide, roll up loosely
from the narrow end. Leave for 20 minutes, or
until cooled, then unroll. (This prevents the
sponge cracking when rolled with filling.)
4 Beat the cream and extra sugar until soft peaks
form. Spread the roll with jam and top with
cream and strawberries. Re-roll and chill.

FLOURLESS CHOCOLATE ROLL

Preparation time: 20 minutes
Total cooking time: 25 minutes
Serves 6

★ ★

5 eggs, separated
140 g (4 1/2 oz) caster sugar
225 g (7 oz) good-quality cooking chocolate,
  chopped
1 cup (250 ml/8 fl oz) cream
icing sugar, to dust

1 Line a baking tray 20 x 30 cm (8 x 12 inch)
with baking paper and sprinkle with a little
caster sugar. Preheat the oven to moderately hot
200°C (400°F/Gas 6).

2 Place the egg yolks and sugar in a bowl and
whisk with electric beaters until light, fluffy and
mousse-like. Put the chocolate in a small
saucepan with 75 ml (2 1/2 fl oz) water, place
over low heat and melt slowly. When melted,
stir into the egg yolk mixture.
3 Put the egg whites in a large clean glass bowl
and whisk until stiff peaks form. Stir one
tablespoon into the chocolate mixture to loosen
it, then fold in the remainder. Spread into the
tin and bake for 12–15 minutes, or until cooked.
4 Lift the paper and roll onto a cooling rack,
cover with a tea towel to stop it drying out and
leave to cool. Whip the cream to stiff peaks.
Place the roll on a work surface and spread the
bottom two-thirds with the cream, leaving a
small margin around the edge. Roll up, using
the paper to help, and pulling it off as you roll.
Don't worry if the roll cracks—stick it together
and dust the whole thing with icing sugar.

*ABOVE: Strawberry
swiss roll*

SPECIAL CHRISTMAS TRIFLE

Preparation time: 20 minutes + chilling
Total cooking time: 10 minutes
Serves 6–8

★

Custard

3 egg yolks
2 tablespoons sugar
1 tablespoon cornflour
1½ cups (375 ml/12 fl oz) milk
½ teaspoon vanilla essence

¾ cup (185 ml/6 fl oz) brandy or sherry
200 g (6½ oz) dried fruit salad, chopped
500 g (1 lb) Christmas cake, crumbled
60 g (2 oz) glacé ginger, finely chopped
1 cup (250 ml/8 fl oz) cream
glacé fruit, to decorate

1 To make the custard, whisk the egg yolks, sugar and cornflour together in a small bowl. Pour the milk into a small pan, bring it almost to the boil, then pour the milk over the egg mixture. Stir well, then pour back into a clean pan and bring to the boil, stirring constantly. Add the vanilla essence and pour the custard into a bowl. Cover the surface with a layer of plastic wrap and leave to cool.
2 Put ½ cup (125 ml/4 fl oz) brandy or sherry with the fruit in a small pan and stir over medium heat for 5 minutes, or until the fruit is plump. Remove from the heat.
3 Put the cake in a large serving bowl and sprinkle with the remaining brandy or sherry. Add the fruit and ginger and stir well. Cover and refrigerate until cold.
4 Pour the custard over the cake and fruit, cover and chill until ready to serve. Lightly whip the cream and spoon onto the custard layer. Serve the trifle decorated with glacé fruit.
NOTE: Serve trifles in cut glass decorative bowls for maximum effect. The curved bowl and glass facets show off the trifle layers very well.

APPLE TRIFLE

Preparation time: 35 minutes + chilling
Total cooking time: 20 minutes
Serves 6

★

Custard

3 egg yolks
2 tablespoons sugar
1 tablespoon cornflour
1½ cups (375 ml/12 fl oz) milk
½ teaspoon vanilla essence

1 kg (2 lb) apples
¾ cup (185 g/6 oz) sugar
½ teaspoon nutmeg
1 teaspoon grated lime or lemon rind
6 sponge finger biscuits
½ cup (125 ml/4 fl oz) cream, whipped
1 tablespoon icing sugar
1 teaspoon ground mixed spice

1 To make the custard, whisk the egg yolks, sugar and cornflour together in a small bowl. Pour the milk into a small pan, bring it almost to the boil, then pour the milk over the egg mixture. Stir well, then pour back into a clean pan and bring to the boil, stirring constantly. Add the vanilla essence and pour the custard into a bowl. Cover the surface with a layer of plastic wrap and leave to cool.
2 Peel and slice the apples and cook in 2 tablespoons water in a large heavy-based pan over low heat for 10–15 minutes, or until the apples are tender. Remove from the heat and mash with a fork. Stir in the sugar, nutmeg and lime or lemon rind.
3 Break the sponge finger biscuits into even-sized pieces and use them to line the base of six glass dessert dishes. Top with a layer of apple and then a layer of custard. Cover and refrigerate for 3–4 hours.
4 Decorate with piped whipped cream. Dust lightly with the combined icing sugar and spice.

OPPOSITE PAGE: Special Christmas trifle (top); Apple trifle

SPICES & HERBS While herbs are

the leaves of plants, spices can be the root, bark, bud, seed, fruit or stem. Spices are

best bought in small quantities and stored in airtight containers in a cool, dark place.

ALLSPICE
Also known as Jamaican pepper and myrtle pepper, allspice is a berry, the size of a baby pea, which can be used whole or ground. Used in Christmas pudding.

BAY LEAF
A dark, glossy green when fresh, bay leaves respond well to drying which intensifies their flavour. They go well

with desserts—baked custards are often flavoured with bay leaves. Fresh bay leaves keep for a few days in a plastic bag in the refrigerator (wash before use).

CARDAMOM
Cardamom pods are pale green. The brown variety are not true cardamoms and taste different. Each pod contains black and brown seeds, sometimes sold

separately. Seeds and ground cardamom lose flavour quickly so it is best to buy pods and bruise them slightly before use, or extract the seeds. Use cardamom sparingly or it can taste medicinal. It goes well with coffee and chocolate.

CINNAMON AND CASSIA
These come from the bark of different types of laurel trees. Cassia is coarser and

redder than cinnamon, with a stronger flavour. Cinnamon is more supple and rolled up into quills. Much of what is sold as cinnamon is actually cassia. Ground cinnamon and cassia do not retain their flavour as well and should not be stored too long. Quills should be stored in an airtight container away from light. Cinnamon mixed with sugar is delicious on baked apples and fruit puddings.

GINGER

Ginger is available fresh, dried, ground, pickled, preserved in sugar syrup, glacé or crystallized. Ground ginger is best used in baking as it has a slightly harsh flavour. Crystallized, glacé and preserved ginger need to be kept in a cool, dark place or refrigerated—they are good in desserts and ice creams. Ginger complements rhubarb, apples and melon.

CLOVES

Cloves have a highly aromatic perfume and flavour which can be bitter in large doses. They are used whole or ground in sweet dishes, especially festive food such as Christmas puddings and mincemeat. Don't store cloves longer than 6 months.

NUTMEG AND MACE

Two of the strangest looking spices, these are the fruit of a tree, indigenous to the Spice Island, that contains a hard, dark brown kernel (nutmeg) surrounded by a lacy red covering which dries to a hard yellowy brown (mace). Mace has a milder flavour and is used in cakes and desserts. Nutmeg has a warm flavour which marries well with stewed fruit, custard, rice puddings and eggnog. Ground nutmeg loses its flavour quickly so grate your own on the fine side of a grater.

STAR ANISE

This brown star-shaped pod has eight segments, each containing a seed. The pod contains most of the flavour and aroma and can be used whole or ground. It is an ingredient of 5-spice powder, and is used in custards, shortbreads and syrups.

VANILLA BEAN (POD)

These beans should be dark and supple. Keep in airtight containers in a dark, cool place for months. To re-use, rinse and dry out. When buying extract or essence, look for those marked 'natural' or 'pure extract'.

CLOCKWISE, FROM TOP LEFT: Allspice, cinnamon sticks, cassia, cloves, fresh ginger, star anise, vanilla beans, nutmeg, mace, crystallized ginger, glacé ginger, dried ginger, ground ginger, cassia, cinnamon sticks, cardamom pods, bay leaves

WHIPPING CREAM

Whipping cream is easier and safer to whip if it is cold—when cream is overwhipped, it turns to butter, which happens much faster if the cream is too warm. Cream for whipping needs to have at least 35% butterfat. Cream whipped to soft peaks can be easily folded into other mixtures. Cream whipped until stiff can be piped and used for decoration, but be very careful not to overwhip it before piping it, or it will split when it is handled in the bag.

BLACK FOREST GATEAU

Preparation time: 1 hour + standing
Total cooking time: 50–60 minutes
Serves 8–10

★

125 g (4 oz) unsalted butter
1 cup (250 g/8 oz) caster sugar
2 eggs, lightly beaten
1 teaspoon vanilla essence
1/3 cup (40 g/1 1/4 oz) self-raising flour
1 cup (125 g/4 oz) plain flour
1 teaspoon bicarbonate of soda
1/2 cup (60 g/2 oz) cocoa powder
3/4 cup (185 ml/6 fl oz) buttermilk

Filling

1/4 cup (60 ml/2 fl oz) Kirsch
3 cups (750 ml/24 fl oz) cream, whipped
425 g (14 oz) can pitted morello or black
    cherries, drained

Topping

100 g (3 1/2 oz) good-quality dark chocolate
100 g (3 1/2 oz) milk chocolate
cherries with stalks, to decorate

1 Preheat the oven to moderate 180°C (350°F/ Gas 4). Brush a deep, 20 cm (8 inch) round cake tin with oil or melted butter. Line the base and side with baking paper.

2 Using electric beaters, beat the butter and sugar until light and creamy. Add the eggs gradually, beating well after each addition. Add the vanilla essence and beat until well combined. Transfer to a large bowl. Using a metal spoon, fold in the sifted flours, bicarbonate of soda and cocoa alternately with the buttermilk. Mix until combined and the mixture is smooth.

3 Pour the mixture into the tin and smooth the surface. Bake for 50–60 minutes, or until a skewer comes out clean when inserted into the centre. Leave the cake in the tin for 30 minutes before turning it onto a wire rack to cool. When cold, cut horizontally into 3 layers, using a long serrated knife. The easiest way to do this is to rest the palm of one hand lightly on top of the cake while cutting into it. Turn the cake every few strokes so the knife cuts in evenly all the way around the edge. When you have gone the whole way round, cut through the middle. Remove the first layer so it will be easier to see what you are doing while cutting the next one.

4 To make chocolate shavings, leave the chocolate in a warm place for 10–15 minutes, or until soft but still firm. With a vegetable peeler, and using long strokes, shave curls of chocolate

*RIGHT: Black
Forest gateau*

from the side of the block. If the block is too soft, chill it to firm it up. Making curls takes a little practice to perfect (see page 238).

5 To assemble, place one cake layer on a serving plate and brush liberally with Kirsch. Spread evenly with one-fifth of the whipped cream. Top with half the cherries. Continue layering with the remaining cake, cream and liqueur cherries, finishing with the cream on top. Spread the cream evenly on the outside of the cake. Coat the side with chocolate shavings by laying the shavings on a small piece of greaseproof and then gently pressing them into the cream. If you use your hands, they will melt, so the paper acts as a barrier. Pipe rosettes of cream around the top edge of the cake and decorate with fresh or maraschino cherries on stalks and more chocolate shavings.

NOTE: Black Forest gateau is probably one of the most famous cakes in the world. It originated in Swabia in the Black Forest region and is always flavoured with Kirsch, a colourless cherry liqueur. In its native Germany, it is known as 'Black Forest Torte'.

PEACHES AND CREAM TRIFLE

Preparation time: 20 minutes + chilling
Total cooking time: Nil
Serves 6–8

★

1 day-old sponge cake, cut into cubes
825 g (1 lb 11 oz) can sliced peaches
1/4 cup (60 ml/2 fl oz) Marsala, peach schnapps liqueur or Grand Marnier
1 cup (250 ml/8 fl oz) cream
200 g (6 1/2 oz) mascarpone
25 g (3/4 oz) flaked almonds, toasted

1 Put the cake cubes in a 2 litre dish and press down firmly. Drain the peaches, reserving 1/2 cup (125 ml/4 fl oz) of juice. Mix the Marsala with the juice and drizzle over the cake.
2 Arrange the peach slices over the cake. Beat the cream until soft peaks form. Add the mascarpone and beat briefly, to just mix. Spread over the peaches. Refrigerate for 1 hour to allow the flavours to develop. Sprinkle with almonds just before serving.

ABOVE: Peaches and cream trifle

4 Begin layering the raspberries and cream evenly into six tall dessert glasses, ending with the cream. Refrigerate for 2 hours and serve sprinkled with toasted oats.

NOTE: In Scotland, charms are placed into cranachan at Halloween, somewhat like the customary coins in English Christmas puddings. This dessert is also known as cream crowdie.

CHOCOLATE CHERRY TRIFLE

Preparation time: 30 minutes + chilling
Total cooking time: 10 minutes
Serves 6

★

350 g (11 oz) chocolate cake
30 g (1 oz) toasted slivered almonds
  and whipped cream, for serving

Filling

2 x 450 g (14 oz) cans pitted dark cherries
1/4 cup (60 ml/2 fl oz) Kirsch
2 egg yolks
2 tablespoons sugar
1 tablespoon cornflour
1 cup (250 ml/8 fl oz) milk
1 teaspoon vanilla essence
3/4 cup (185 ml/6 fl oz) cream,
  lightly whipped

1 Cut the cake into thin strips. Line the base of a 1.75 litre serving bowl with one third of the cake.

2 Drain the cherries, reserving the juice. Combine one cup of the juice with the Kirsch and sprinkle some liberally over the cake. Spoon some cherries over the cake.

3 To make the custard, whisk the egg yolks, sugar and cornflour in a heatproof bowl until thick and pale. Heat the milk in a pan until almost boiling. Remove from the heat and add gradually to the egg mixture, beating constantly. Return to a clean pan and stir over medium heat for 5 minutes, or until the custard boils and thickens. Remove from the heat and add the vanilla. Cover the surface with plastic wrap and allow to cool, then fold in the whipped cream.

4 To assemble, spoon a third of the custard over the cherries and cake in the bowl. Top with more cake, syrup, cherries and custard. Repeat the layering process, ending with custard on top. Cover and refrigerate for 3–4 hours. Decorate with almonds and whipped cream.

CRANACHAN

Preparation time: 30 minutes + chilling
Total cooking time: 10 minutes
Serves 6

★

2 tablespoons medium oatmeal
1 cup (250 ml/8 fl oz) cream
2 tablespoons honey
1 tablespoon whisky
500 g (1 lb) raspberries or strawberries
2 tablespoons rolled oats, toasted

1 Put the oatmeal in a small pan. Stir over low heat for 5 minutes, or until lightly toasted. Remove from the heat and cool completely.

2 Using electric beaters, beat the cream in a small bowl until soft peaks form. Add the honey and whisky and beat until just combined.

3 Fold the cooled, toasted oatmeal into the cream mixture with a metal spoon.

ABOVE: Cranachan

ORANGE, LEMON AND WHITE CHOCOLATE GATEAU

Preparation time: I hour
Total cooking time: 30 minutes
Serves 8–10

★★

1 cup (125 g/4 oz) plain flour
4 eggs
2/3 cup (160 g/5 1/2 oz) caster sugar
60 g (2 oz) unsalted butter, melted and cooled

Filling

2 tablespoons cornflour
1/3 cup (80 ml/2 3/4 fl oz) lemon juice
1/3 cup (80 ml/2 3/4 fl oz) orange juice
1 teaspoon finely grated lemon rind
1 teaspoon finely grated orange rind
1/3 cup (90 g/3 oz) caster sugar
2 egg yolks
20 g (3/4 oz) unsalted butter

Topping

200 g (6 1/2 oz) white chocolate, chopped
1/2 cup (125 ml/4 fl oz) cream
60 g (2 oz) unsalted butter
white chocolate curls and candied rind

1 Preheat the oven to 180°C (350°F/Gas 4). Grease two shallow 20 cm (8 inch) cake tins and line the base and sides with baking paper.
2 Sift the flour three times onto a sheet of greaseproof paper. Beat the eggs and sugar until thick, pale and increased in volume.
3 Using a metal spoon, fold in the flour in two batches, quickly and lightly until just combined. Add the melted butter with the second batch, discarding any white sediment in the butter. Spread into the tins and bake for 20 minutes, until lightly golden. Leave for 2 minutes before turning out onto a wire rack to cool.
4 To make the filling, blend the cornflour with a tablespoon of water. Place 3 tablespoons water, the juice, rind and sugar in a small pan and stir over medium heat, without boiling, until the sugar has dissolved. Add the cornflour and stir until the mixture boils and thickens. Cook, stirring, for another minute. Remove from the heat, add the egg yolks and butter and stir well. Transfer to a bowl, cover the surface with plastic wrap and cool completely.
5 To make the topping, place the chocolate, cream and butter in a small pan and stir over low heat until melted. Transfer to a bowl, cover with plastic wrap and allow to cool completely. Do not refrigerate. Using electric beaters, beat until fluffy.
6 Using a serrated knife, cut the cakes in half horizontally. Place one cake layer on a serving plate and spread evenly with the filling. Continue layering cake and filling, ending with a cake layer on top. Spread the top and sides of the cake with topping. Decorate with white chocolate curls and candied lemon rind.
NOTE: To make your own candied lemon rind, cut each lemon into quarters and pull out the flesh. Put the lemon rind in a pan of cold water and bring to the boil. Reduce the heat, simmer for 2 minutes, then discard the water and repeat. This will remove the bitterness from the pith. Drain. Combine 220 g (7 oz) sugar and 1 cup (250 ml/8 fl oz) water in a pan and dissolve the sugar over low heat, stirring constantly. When the sugar has dissolved, bring to the boil, reduce the heat and simmer. Add a few drops of lemon juice and the pieces of lemon peel and cook over very low heat until the pith and peel look translucent. Leave to cool in the syrup, then remove and drain. Cut out star shapes, using a cutter or sharp knife. Roll the shapes in caster sugar.

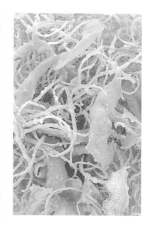

BELOW: Orange, lemon and white chocolate gateau

HAZELNUT ROLL WITH RASPBERRY CREAM

Preparation time: 40 minutes
+ chilling
Total cooking time: 15 minutes
Serves 8

★ ★

100 g (3¹/₂ oz) roasted hazelnuts
5 eggs, separated
³/₄ cup (185 g/6 oz) sugar
1 teaspoon vanilla essence
¹/₃ cup (40 g/1¹/₄ oz) self-raising flour
1 tablespoon plain flour
cream, raspberries and chocolate curls,
to decorate

Raspberry cream

²/₃ cup (170 ml/5¹/₂ fl oz) cream
200 g (6¹/₂ oz) raspberries, lightly
mashed
1 tablespoon caster sugar
1 tablespoon brandy

*ABOVE: Hazelnut roll
with raspberry cream*

1 Preheat the oven to moderate 180°C (350°F/ Gas 4). Brush a 30 x 25 (12 x 10 inch) swiss roll tin with oil. Line the base and sides with paper and grease the paper. Sprinkle with a little caster sugar. Chop the hazelnuts in a food processor for 15 seconds, or until finely crushed.
2 Beat the egg yolks and sugar with electric beaters until thick and pale, then add the vanilla.
3 In a clean, dry bowl, beat the egg whites until stiff peaks form. Using a metal spoon, fold the whites and sifted flours into the yolks, one-third at a time. Fold in the nuts with the last third. Spoon the mixture into the tin and smooth the surface. Bake for 15 minutes, or until lightly golden and springy to touch. Turn onto a dry tea towel covered with greaseproof paper and sprinkled with sugar and leave to stand for 1 minute. Using the tea towel as a guide, carefully roll the cake up with paper, then leave for 5 minutes, or until cool. Unroll and discard the paper.
4 To make the raspberry cream, beat the cream until stiff peaks form. Fold in the raspberries, sugar and brandy (cream should have a marbled look). Spread the cream over the cake, leaving a 1.5 cm (⁵/₈ inch) border. Gently re-roll and refrigerate for 2 hours before serving. Decorate with cream, raspberries and chocolate curls.

MASCARPONE TRIFLE

Preparation time: 40 minutes + chilling
Total cooking time: 10 minutes
Serves 4–6

☆

175 g (6 oz) plain sponge cake
1/2 cup (125 ml/4 fl oz) Tia Maria or Kahlua
70 g (21/4 oz) dark chocolate, grated
500 g (1 lb) strawberries, hulled
cocoa powder and icing sugar, to dust

Custard

4 egg yolks
2 tablespoons sugar
2 teaspoons cornflour
1/2 cup (125 ml/4 fl oz) cream
1/2 cup (125 ml/4 fl oz) milk
2 teaspoons vanilla essence
11/3 cups (350 ml/11 fl oz) cream, extra
250 g (4 oz) mascarpone

1 Cut the cake into chunks and put in the base of a 1.75 litre dish. Spoon the liqueur over the cake and sprinkle with half the grated chocolate. Slice a third of the strawberries and sprinkle over the top. Cover and refrigerate.

2 To make the custard, whisk together the yolks, sugar and cornflour until thick and pale. Heat the cream and milk in a pan until almost boiling, then gradually whisk into the yolk mixture. Pour into a clean pan and return to low heat, until the custard thickens and coats the back of a spoon. Remove from the heat and stir in the vanilla essence and remaining grated chocolate until smooth. Cover the surface with plastic wrap, to stop a skin forming, and allow to cool.

3 Whip a third of the extra cream until soft peaks form and gently fold this and the mascarpone into the cooled custard. Spoon over the cake and strawberries, cover with plastic wrap and then refrigerate until needed. When you are ready to serve, whip the remaining cream until stiff peaks form and spoon over the trifle. Cut the remaining strawberries in half and arrange on top. Dust with a mixture of cocoa powder and icing sugar to serve.

NOTE: Mascarpone is made with cream and looks more like cream than cheese. Slightly sweet with an acidic edge, it is softer than cream cheese.

ABOVE: Mascarpone trifle

SHOW STOPPERS

It's time to show off, amaze and thrill. There are moments in life when a simple bowl of ice cream just isn't enough... you need something spectacular, awe-inspiring and attention-grabbing. You need a SHOW STOPPER. The wonderful thing about this selection of recipes is that they make you look like a master chef when actually, with a little time, patience and enthusiasm, most of our fabulous creations are rather easy to make. Just don't let anyone in on the secret.

CHOCOLATE CHESTNUT BLISS

After brushing the largest rounds of cake with syrup, spread a layer of chestnut cream over them.

Spread the reserved chestnut cream as thinly and smoothly as possible all over the outside of each cake to form smooth sides.

With the cakes on a wire rack over a baking tray, spoon the topping over the cakes to cover completely, then refrigerate until set.

Snip off a corner of the bag and drizzle the melted chocolate into concentric circles onto a baking tray.

OPPOSITE PAGE:
Chocolate chestnut bliss

CHOCOLATE CHESTNUT BLISS

Preparation time: 50 minutes + chilling
Total cooking time: 30 minutes
Serves 6

★ ★ ★

100 g (3½ oz) unsalted butter, chopped
80 g (2¾ oz) dark chocolate, chopped
½ cup (125 ml/4 fl oz) milk
½ cup (125 g/4 oz) caster sugar
¼ cup (25 g/¾ oz) desiccated coconut
¼ cup (30 g/1 oz) cocoa powder
½ cup (60 g/2 oz) self-raising flour
2 eggs, lightly beaten

Amaretto syrup

2 tablespoons caster sugar
¼ cup (60 ml/2 fl oz) Amaretto

Chestnut filling

30 g (1 oz) unsalted butter, softened
1 cup (260 g/8 oz) unsweetened
    chestnut purée
¼ cup (30 g/1 oz) icing sugar

Chocolate topping

75 g (2½ oz) unsalted butter
150 g (5 oz) dark chocolate, chopped
2 tablespoons light corn syrup

Raspberry sauce

150 g (5 oz) frozen raspberries, thawed
2 tablespoons caster sugar

Chocolate swirls

60 g (2 oz) dark chocolate

1 Preheat the oven to moderate 180°C (350°F/ Gas 4). Lightly grease a 30 x 25 cm (12 x 10 inch) swiss roll tin and cover the base and side with baking paper. Combine the butter, chocolate, milk and sugar in a small pan and stir over low heat until the sugar and chocolate have dissolved. Remove from the heat and allow to cool slightly. Combine the coconut, cocoa and flour in a bowl, pour in the chocolate mixture and the beaten eggs and mix well. Pour into the tin and bake for 15 minutes, or until just firm to touch. Leave for 5 minutes before turning onto a rack to cool.
2 To make the Amaretto syrup, combine the sugar and ¼ cup (60 ml/2 fl oz) water in a small pan and stir over low heat until the sugar has dissolved. Remove from the heat, stir in the Amaretto and allow to cool.
3 To make the chestnut filling, beat the butter, chestnut purée and icing sugar in a bowl until smooth. Cut rounds from the chocolate cake using 3 cm (1¼ inch), 5 cm (2 inch), 7 cm (2¾ inch) cutters, making six of each size. (Any leftover chocolate cake can be frozen and made into rum balls if it doesn't get eaten first.)
4 Reserve ½ cup (125 ml/4 fl oz) of the chestnut cream. Place large rounds of cake on a baking paper covered baking tray, brush well with some of the syrup and spread with a layer of the chestnut cream. Top with another round of cake, slightly smaller than the first, brush well with syrup and top with some chestnut cream. Top with the remaining round of cake and brush with remaining syrup. Spread the reserved chestnut cream as thinly and smoothly as possible over the outside of each cake, to form smooth sides. Refrigerate for 1 hour, or until the chestnut cream has firmed slightly.
5 To make the chocolate topping, combine the butter, chocolate and corn syrup in a bowl, place over a pan of simmering water and stir until melted. Lift the cakes onto a wire rack over a baking tray, spoon topping over each cake to completely cover, then refrigerate until just set.
6 Meanwhile, to make the raspberry sauce, combine the raspberries and sugar in a small saucepan, then simmer for 5 minutes. Strain through a plastic sieve and allow to cool.
7 To make the chocolate swirls, melt the dark chocolate and spoon into a paper piping bag or small plastic bag. Snip off a corner and drizzle chocolate into concentric circles, about 7 cm in diameter, on a baking paper covered baking tray, then refrigerate until firm. Place the chocolate bliss onto a serving plate, decorate with the chocolate swirls, dust the top lightly with icing sugar and spoon raspberry sauce onto the side of the plate.

LICORICE ALL-SORT ICE CREAM

Preparation time: 1 hour + freezing
Total cooking time: 30 minutes
Serves 6–8

☆ ☆ ☆

Coconut meringue

2 egg whites
1/2 cup (125 g/4 oz) caster sugar
1 cup (90 g/3 oz) desiccated coconut
1 tablespoon cornflour

Raspberry ice cream

200 g (6 1/2 oz) fresh or frozen raspberries
2/3 cup (170 ml/5 1/2 fl oz) milk
1/3 cup (90 g/3 oz) caster sugar
1/2 cup (125 ml/4 fl oz) cream

Licorice ice cream

60 g (2 oz) soft eating licorice, chopped
1 cup (250 ml/8 fl oz) milk
3/4 cup (185 ml/6 fl oz) cream
1/4 cup (60 g/2 oz) caster sugar
black food colouring

Mango ice cream

1 large mango
2/3 cup (170 ml/5 1/2 fl oz) milk
1/3 cup (90 g/3 oz) caster sugar
1/2 cup (125 ml/4 fl oz) cream

1 Preheat the oven to slow 150°C (300°F/ Gas 2). Cover two baking trays with baking paper and draw six 25 x 7 cm (10 x 2 3/4 inch) rectangles. For the coconut meringues, beat the egg whites in a small bowl, with electric beaters, until stiff peaks form. Gradually add the sugar, beating well after each addition until the sugar has dissolved. Stir in the combined coconut and cornflour. Spread evenly over the rectangles. Bake for about 20 minutes, or until just firm to touch. Turn the oven off and leave to cool in the oven with the door slightly ajar.

2 Lightly grease two 25 x 7.5 cm (10 x 3 inch), 4 cm (1 1/2 inches) deep bar tins and line completely with plastic wrap. Trim the edges of all the meringues to fit neatly into the bar tins.

3 To make the raspberry ice cream, purée the raspberries and press through a plastic strainer to remove the seeds (do not use a metal strainer or the raspberries will discolour). You will need 2/3 cup (170 ml/5 1/2 fl oz) of purée. Combine the milk and sugar in a small pan, stir over heat without boiling, until the sugar has dissolved, remove from heat, stir in the cream and allow to cool. When cool, stir in the purée, pour into a shallow metal container and freeze until semi-frozen. Chop the mixture and beat in a large bowl with electric beaters until thick and creamy, then divide between the prepared tins. Top each with a trimmed coconut meringue and freeze.

4 To make the licorice ice cream, stir the licorice, milk and cream together in a small pan over low heat, stirring gently until the licorice is soft and melting. Press through a strainer to remove any remaining lumps. Add the sugar, stir until dissolved, then allow to cool. Tint a deeper colour with food colouring if desired. Pour the mixture into a shallow metal container and freeze until firm. Chop the mixture, beat in a large bowl with electric beaters until thick and creamy, then spread over the meringues and top each with another meringue. Freeze.

5 To make the mango ice cream, purée the mango until smooth. You will need 2/3 cup (180 ml/5 1/2 fl oz) purée. Follow the same method as for the raspberry ice cream. Spread over the meringues, top the mango ice cream with the remaining meringues, cover and freeze until firm. When ready to serve, invert the ice cream onto a cutting board, remove the plastic and cut into slices.

NOTE: The ice creams can also be made in an ice cream machine. You can freeze the three ice creams at once, to save on preparation time.

LICORICE

Licorice, or liquorice, is the root of a small plant. Licorice reached Europe via the Arab spice routes and in the 17th century, ground licorice was used to flavour cakes, desserts and drinks. Now, the most common usage is to extract the juice of the root to flavour a variety of sweets and the Italian liqueur, Sambucca. Licorice is available as a root or as a powder.

OPPOSITE PAGE: Licorice all-sort ice cream

CHOCOLATE

It was the Aztecs who discovered the delights of the cocoa bean and indulged themselves with chocolate drinks, and sixteenth century Spanish explorers who introduced the bean to Europe.

Chocolate comes from cocoa beans which grow in pods on the cacao tree. It is made up of several different components which are extracted from the bean and then reformed. The beans are roasted and their shells removed to leave the nibs, which are then ground to produce chocolate liquor (a bitter chocolate). It is this liquor that forms the base for all chocolate products. It is pressed to extract the cocoa butter, leaving a dry substance which is ground into cocoa powder. Cocoa liquor then has varying amounts of cocoa butter and flavouring added to produce different types of chocolate. Next, the chocolate is 'conched' or stirred and rolled until smooth. Good quality chocolate is glossy and smooth with a slightly reddish colour. It breaks cleanly, melts easily (cocoa butter melts at body temperature) and has a high percentage of cocoa solids and real vanilla extract as a flavouring. The golden rule for cooking with chocolate is to always use the best-quality that you can afford. The white powdery bloom that sometimes appears on

chocolate is caused either by sugar forming crystals on the surface when it is humid or the cocoa butter forming crystals on the surface when it gets too hot. If chocolate is not wrapped tightly in the fridge, it will appear to sweat and as the water evaporates, it will leave behind the sugar crystals. Bloom does not affect the taste.

TO MELT CHOCOLATE...

Chocolate needs to be handled carefully. Water will make it seize and go clumpy, as will overheating. Always make sure you use a clean dry heatproof bowl and don't try to hurry the process—only melt as much chocolate as you need at any one time. Chop the chocolate finely, place it in the bowl and set the bowl over a pan with about 4 cm (1¹/₂ inches) water that

has been boiled and taken off the heat. The bottom of the bowl should not touch the water and should fit the pan tightly so that no moisture can get into the bowl and seize the chocolate. Leave the chocolate to soften, then stir until smooth. Either remove the bowl from the pan to cool the chocolate slightly or leave in place if you want to keep it liquid. Do not overheat chocolate or it will scorch, seize and taste bitter.

Chocolate can also be melted in a microwave: place in a microwave safe bowl and cook in 15-second bursts on Medium (50%), stirring after every burst until smooth. The chocolate may keep its shape but it will become shiny and sag slightly around the edges as it melts. If it seizes, try adding a few drops of vegetable oil or shortening and stir until smooth.

TEMPERING CHOCOLATE

Cocoa butter is made up of several different fats which melt and set at different temperatures. We temper chocolate to stabilise the fats—this gives moulded or dipped chocolate a lovely shiny surface, as well as ensuring that it sets properly. Tempering is a process that involves heating and cooling the chocolate to exact temperatures—a process usually too complicated to do at home, although there is a quick method which helps stabilise the chocolate before use. Grate the chocolate and melt two-thirds of it as above. Then stir in the remaining chocolate in batches until it has all melted. The chocolate should now be tempered and its temperature should be about 88–90°F for dark chocolate and 85–88°F for milk chocolate.

CHOCOLATE DECORATIONS

THINGS TO MAKE

CHOCOLATE COLLAR Collars are beautiful decorations for cheesecakes or cakes. Remove the cheesecake or cake from the tin and put it on a board. Measure the height and add 1 cm (½ inch). Cut a strip of baking paper or mat contact this wide and long enough to easily go round the dessert. Spread a thin even layer of melted chocolate over the paper or shiny side of the contact, allow to set a little (but the chocolate must still be pliable) and wrap round the cake, paper-side-out. Fix in place and chill until set, then peel off the paper. Make spotted or patterned collars by piping white, dark or milk

chocolate spots or lines on the paper first, allowing them to set a little, then spreading all over with a different coloured chocolate.

CHOCOLATE CURLS Pour melted chocolate onto a marble work surface or a heavy chopping board. When it has cooled and just set, scrape off curls by pulling a knife set at a 45° angle across the chocolate. If the chocolate hardens too much it will splinter and crack, so work quickly once it has reached the right temperature. Make striped curls by pouring melted chocolate onto the surface and making ridges through it with a fork or comb scraper. Leave this layer to set, then pour

a layer of different coloured melted chocolate over the top. Scrape off curls as above. Or pour lines of different coloured chocolate side by side and make curls as above. Small chocolate curls or shavings can be made by pulling a potato peeler over a block of chocolate.

CHOCOLATE CUPS Spread a circle of chocolate onto a piece of freezer wrap or plastic wrap and drape it over a mould. Allow it to harden completely before removing the chocolate cup and pulling out the plastic wrap. Cups can also be made by lining a mould with plastic wrap, filling it with water, then freezing

it until you have a solid block of ice. Remove the ice-filled plastic wrap from the mould and dip it in the melted chocolate. It should set immediately. The insides of moulds can also be brushed with oil and then with chocolate. The chocolate shrinks as it cools—a few minutes in the refrigerator helps and the chocolate cup should pull away from the inside of the mould. This gives a smooth shiny surface.

CHOCOLATE BOXES Melt chocolate and spread it in a thin, even layer on a piece of baking paper. When it has begun to set, cut it into equal squares with a sharp knife (heat the knife if the chocolate has set too much). Use more melted chocolate to glue the squares together to make into a box.

PIPED SHAPES Put melted chocolate into a piping bag and pipe shapes onto a piece of baking paper. Peel the shapes off the baking paper and stick them together with a little more melted chocolate to give three-dimensional effects, or use them flat to pattern surfaces.

CHOCOLATE LEAVES Wash the underside of non-toxic, unsprayed leaves such as rose or camellia, and dry well. Brush each leaf with a thin layer of melted chocolate, leave until set, then carefully peel the leaf away from the chocolate shape.

TYPES OF CHOCOLATE

SEMI-SWEET and **BITTER-SWEET** chocolate have vanilla, sugar and cocoa butter added. They are interchangeable.

MILK chocolate was developed on a large scale by the Swiss (who had little chocolate and sugar but lots of milk) in the 1870s.

WHITE chocolate is not strictly chocolate as it does not contain cocoa liquor. It is a mixture of cocoa butter, sugar and milk.

COMPOUND or baking chocolate is used for cooking and decorations. It contains vegetable fat instead of cocoa butter. It does not need to be tempered. Also available as 'melts', 'buttons' and 'drops'. Known as 'summer coating' in America.

COUVERTURE has a higher percentage of cocoa butter and is not as stable as ordinary chocolate. It needs to be tempered before use. It is used mainly by the catering industry as it melts and coats easily.

CHARLOTTE

A charlotte was originally a hot apple pudding baked in a bread- or cake-lined deep mould. It appears in British cookbooks in the 18th century and is possibly named after Queen Charlotte who was apparently an apple enthusiast. The charlotte then transformed to the Charlotte Russe in which the centre was filled with a cold custard or Bavarian type mixture and chilled. This was supposedly invented by the French chef Antonin Carême in 1802 and originally called *charlotte à la parisienne* before he renamed it in honour of Czar Alexander.

ABOVE: Charlotte russe

CHARLOTTE RUSSE

Preparation time: 40 minutes + chilling
Total cooking time: 10 minutes
Serves 8–10

★ ★ ★

250 g (8 oz) sponge finger biscuits
  (30–35 fingers)
9 egg yolks
³/₄ cup (185 g/6 oz) caster sugar
2 cups (500 ml/16 fl oz) milk
1 teaspoon vanilla essence
5 teaspoons gelatine
¹/₂ cup (125 g/4 oz) sour cream
¹/₂ cup (125 ml/4 fl oz) cream
berries and cream, optional, for serving

1 Choose a charlotte mould or round cake tin of 2 litre capacity. Cover the base with baking paper to prevent sticking. If necessary, cut the biscuits so they are wider at one end than the other, then arrange the biscuits to fit snugly, side by side, round the inside of the mould so that there are no gaps.
2 Beat the egg yolks until thick, add the sugar and continue beating vigorously until the mixture is thick but still runny. Heat the milk with the vanilla until the first small bubbles appear on the side of the pan. Immediately but slowly, pour the milk into the egg mixture, continually beating. Return the mixture to a clean pan. Heat again, stirring constantly, until it thickens, but do not boil. Remove from the heat. Sprinkle the gelatine in an even layer over 3 tablespoons water in a small heatproof bowl and leave until spongy. Stand the bowl in a pan of hot water (off the heat) and stir until the gelatine has completely dissolved. Add to the custard and stir well. Cover the surface of the custard with cling wrap and leave to cool. Whip the creams until thick and stir into the custard.
3 Cover the surface of the custard again and refrigerate for about 1 hour, stirring a few times until the custard is thick but not set (if it is too runny the biscuits may float to the surface). Pour into the biscuit mould and refrigerate overnight.
4 To serve, invert the serving plate on top of the mould and carefully flip both over. The mould should come off easily unless there were cracks in the biscuit mould and custard has stuck to the side. In that case, use a wet knife to ease off any difficult areas. Decorate with a few berries and serve with cream or maybe a fruit purée.

ZUCCOTTO

Preparation time: 1 hour + chilling
Total cooking time: Nil
Serves 6–8

★ ★ ★

1 slab sponge cake
1/3 cup (80 ml/2¾ fl oz) Kirsch
1/4 cup (60 ml/2 fl oz) Cointreau
1/3 cup (80 ml/2¾ fl oz) rum, Cognac,
    Grand Marnier or maraschino
2 cups (500 ml/16 fl oz) cream
90 g (3 oz) dark roasted almond
    chocolate, chopped
175 g (6 oz) finely chopped mixed glacé fruit
100 g (3½ oz) good-quality dark
    chocolate, melted
70 g (2¼ oz) hazelnuts, roasted and chopped
cocoa powder and icing sugar, to decorate

1 Line a 1.5 litre pudding basin with damp muslin. Cut the cake into curved pieces with a sharp knife (you will need about 12 pieces). Work with one strip of cake at a time, lightly brushing it with the combined liqueurs and arranging the pieces closely in the basin. Put the thin ends in the centre so the slices cover the base and side of the basin. Brush with the remaining liqueur to soak the cake. Chill.
2 Beat the cream until stiff peaks form, then divide in half. Fold the almond chocolate and glacé fruit into one half and spread evenly over the cake in the basin, leaving a space in the centre.
3 Fold the cooled melted chocolate and hazelnuts into the remaining cream and spoon into the centre cavity, packing it in firmly. Smooth the surface, cover and chill for 8 hours to allow the cream to firm slightly.
4 Turn out onto a serving plate and decorate by dusting generously with cocoa powder and icing sugar. You can make a cardboard template to help you dust separate wedges neatly—you may need help holding it in place.
NOTE: The sponge cake needs to be about 30 x 25 x 2 cm (12 x 10 x ¾ inch). This recipe is best made one or two days in advance to give the flavours time to develop during chilling.

ZUCCOTTO

Cut the cake into curved pieces with a sharp knife (or use a template).

If you make a template to dust the cake you may need help holding it in place.

LEFT: Zuccotto

WHITE CHOCOLATE
White chocolate is a blend of cocoa butter, sugar, milk solids, vanilla and a stabiliser. It contains no cocoa liquor and therefore is not a true chocolate. In America, it cannot be called chocolate and instead is often labelled 'confectionery coating'. White chocolate is softer than other types of chocolate and is not as easy to handle. It seizes more easily on melting and cannot be easily substituted for other chocolates in recipes.

RASPBERRY MIROIRE

Preparation time: 1 hour + chilling
Total cooking time: 30 minutes
Serves 8–10

★★★

Sponge base

1 egg
2 tablespoons caster sugar
2 tablespoons self-raising flour
1 tablespoon plain flour

Raspberry mousse

500 g (1 lb) fresh or frozen raspberries
4 egg yolks
1/2 cup (125 g/4 oz) caster sugar
1 cup (250 ml/8 fl oz) milk
1 1/2 tablespoons gelatine
1/4 cup (60 ml/2 fl oz) crème de cassis liqueur
1 cup (250 ml/8 fl oz) cream

Raspberry topping

2 teaspoons gelatine
1 tablespoon crème de cassis liqueur

Chocolate bark

100 g (3 1/2 oz) white choc melts, melted

raspberries, to decorate
icing sugar, to dust
cream, for serving, optional

1 Preheat the oven to moderate 180°C (350°F/ Gas 4). Lightly grease a 22 cm (8¾ inch) springform tin and line the base with baking paper. Beat the egg and sugar in a small bowl with electric beaters, for 5 minutes, or until thick and fluffy. Sift the flours together three times, then fold into the egg mixture with a metal spoon. Spread evenly into the prepared tin and bake for 10–15 minutes, or until lightly browned and shrunk slightly away from the edge. Remove from the tin and leave to cool on a wire rack. Clean the springform tin, fit the base into the tin upside down and lightly oil the pan and line the base and side with plastic wrap.

2 To make the raspberry mousse, blend or process the raspberries in batches until smooth and press through a plastic strainer (not a metallic one or the raspberries may discolour) to remove the seeds. Reserve 1/2 cup (125 ml/ 4 fl oz) raspberry purée for the topping. Beat the egg yolks and sugar in a heatproof bowl for 5 minutes, or until thick and pale. Bring the milk to the boil and gradually pour onto the egg mixture, beating continually. Place the bowl over a pan of simmering water and stir for about 10 minutes, or until the mixture thickens slightly and coats the back of a spoon. Allow to cool.
3 Sprinkle the gelatine in an even layer over 1/4 cup (60 ml/2 fl oz) water in a small heatproof bowl and leave to go spongy. Put a large pan with about 4 cm (1 1/2 inches) water on to boil. When it boils, remove from the heat and carefully lower the gelatine bowl into the water (it should come halfway up the side of the bowl), then stir until dissolved. Cool slightly. Stir the gelatine mixture, raspberry purée and liqueur into the custard mixture, then refrigerate until thick but not set. Beat the cream until soft peaks form and fold into the raspberry mixture with a metal spoon. Place the sponge into the base of the prepared pan and pour the raspberry mixture evenly over the top. Refrigerate for several hours, or until firm.
4 For the topping, sprinkle the gelatine in an even layer over 1/3 cup (80 ml/3 fl oz) water in a heatproof bowl and leave to go spongy. Put a large pan filled with about 4 cm (1 1/2 inches) water on to boil. When it boils, remove from the heat and lower the gelatine bowl into the water (it should come halfway up the side of the bowl), then stir until completely dissolved. Cool slightly. Stir in the reserved raspberry purée and the liqueur, pour evenly over the set mousse, then refrigerate until set.
5 To make the chocolate bark, cover a baking tray firmly with plastic wrap, spread the chocolate thinly over the plastic and allow to set. When set, break into large angular pieces.
6 To serve, cut the miroire into wedges, place pieces of chocolate on the back of each slice and keep in place with a dob of cream. Decorate with extra raspberries, dust lightly with icing sugar and serve with cream if desired.
NOTE: Miroire denotes the shiny jelly topping, meaning 'mirror' in French.

OPPOSITE PAGE:
Raspberry miroire

PASHKA

Preparation time: 30 minutes + draining
  + soaking + chilling
Total cooking time: Nil
Serves 8–10

★ ★

750 g (1 1/2 lb) ricotta
100 g (3 1/2 oz) glacé pineapple, chopped
100 g (3 1/2 oz) glacé ginger, chopped
60 g (2 oz) mixed peel
60 g (2 oz) sultanas
2 tablespoons white or dark rum
100 g (3 1/2 oz) unsalted butter, softened
1/2 cup (125 g/4 oz) caster sugar
2 egg yolks
60 g (2 oz) slivered almonds, toasted
2 teaspoons finely grated lemon rind
2 teaspoons finely grated orange rind
2 tablespoons lemon juice
1/2 cup (125 g/4 oz) sour cream
slivered almonds and glacé fruits, to decorate

1 Drain the ricotta overnight in a sieve. In a bowl, soak the pineapple, ginger, mixed peel and sultanas in the rum for 2 hours. Thoroughly wet a piece of muslin in boiling water, wring out the excess water and use to line a 2 litre pudding basin or charlotte mould.

2 Beat the butter and sugar in a bowl until light and creamy, then beat in the egg yolks one at a time. Add the almonds, rinds and lemon juice and mix well. Transfer to a large bowl and fold in the ricotta, sour cream and fruit mixture.

3 Press into the basin and fold the edges of the cloth over the top. Cover the top with plastic wrap, place a saucer on top and weigh down with a can placed on top of the saucer. Place the bowl on a plate and refrigerate overnight. Turn out of the basin and peel away the muslin. Transfer to a serving plate with the smaller end facing up. Decorate with almonds and glacé fruits and serve in small wedges.

NOTE: This will keep for up to two days in the refrigerator. If muslin is unavailable, use a new 'Chux' type cloth. Pashka is a Russian Easter dish, traditionally made in a cone or 4-sided pyramid shaped mould.

BELOW: Pashka

CHOCOLATE TART WITH ESPRESSO CONES

Preparation time: I hour + chilling + freezing
Total cooking time: 5–10 minutes
Serves 8

★ ★ ★

¹/4 cup (20 g/³/4 oz) instant coffee powder
I litre good-quality vanilla ice cream, softened

Tart base

100 g (3¹/2 oz) pecans
100 g (3¹/2 oz) dark chocolate-flavoured biscuits
I tablespoon cocoa powder
3 teaspoons soft brown sugar
I tablespoon overproof rum
30 g (I oz) unsalted butter, melted
40 g (1¹/4 oz) good-quality dark chocolate, melted

Filling

200 g (6¹/2 oz) good-quality dark chocolate
30 g (I oz) unsalted butter
¹/2 cup (125 ml/4 fl oz) cream
3 egg yolks, lightly beaten
I cup (250 ml/8 fl oz) cream, whipped

I To mould the ice cream into shape for the espresso cones, first prepare the moulds. Cover 8 large cream horn moulds with baking paper and secure with sticky tape. Pull the paper off the moulds and transfer the paper cones to the inside of the moulds. Stand the lined cream horn moulds, points down, in mugs to make it easier to spoon in the ice cream.
2 Using a metal spoon, mix the coffee powder with 1 tablespoon hot water and fold through the ice cream in a bowl. Stir until smooth, then spoon into the paper inside the moulds, before freezing overnight.
3 To make the tart base, grease a shallow, 23 cm (9 inch) round fluted flan tin. Process all the ingredients in short bursts in a food processor for 30 seconds, or until even and crumbly. Press into the base and side of the tin. Refrigerate until firm.
4 To make the filling, stir the chocolate, butter and cream together in a heavy-based pan over low heat until melted and smooth. Remove from the heat, whisk in the egg yolks and transfer to a bowl. Cool slightly. Using a metal spoon, fold in the cream. Stir until smooth, pour into the tart base, then refrigerate until set.
5 Serve a wedge of chocolate tart with each espresso cone.

ABOVE: Chocolate tart with espresso cones

CARAMEL

For creating real show stopping desserts caramel is an invaluable and delicious accessory. Glaze, dip, or spin it into golden threads, set nuts in caramel to make praline, or let it harden into a toffee topping.

There are two different ways to make caramel. The wet method involves dissolving the sugar in water and then boiling the sugar syrup; the dry method means melting the sugar on its own. The wet method is more complicated as the syrup can crystallize, but it is easier to keep an eye on as it starts to darken. The dry method needs a bit more practice to

avoid burning the sugar as it melts. For either method, use a heavy-based pan which gives an even heat all over the base. Non-stick pans and those with dark linings are harder to use as you cannot easily see the colour of the caramel. Use a coarser grade of sugar so you get less scum—granulated sugar is good as it dissolves easily and is not too refined.

WET METHOD

Put the water and sugar in a pan and stir over low heat until all the sugar has dissolved, then bring to the boil. If you boil before the sugar has completely dissolved, it will crystallize. Do not stir the syrup as it boils or crystals will form on the spoon. Do not allow any crystals to form on the side of the pan from

splashes—if they do, dip a clean dry pastry brush in cold water and brush down the side of the pan.

As the water evaporates off the syrup, the temperature will start to rise. Be very careful as the hot syrup can cause serious burns. Once the syrup reaches 160°C–175°C (315°F–335°F), all the water will have evaporated and the molten sugar which is left will start to caramelize. The syrup will be thicker and the bubbles will be bigger and break more slowly. At this point, the sugar will start to colour quite quickly, so keep an eye on it and remove from the heat the moment it reaches the colour you want. Swirl the pan to keep the colour of the caramel even, otherwise patches may darken and burn before the rest has coloured. To stop the caramel continuing to cook in

the pan after you've removed it from the heat, plunge the base of the pan into a sink of cold water. You can then remelt the caramel over low heat as you need it.

DRY METHOD
Sprinkle the sugar in an even layer over the base of the pan and place over low heat. Melt the sugar slowly, tipping the pan from side to side so that it melts evenly—keep the sugar moving or it might start to colour on one side before the other side has melted. When the caramel starts to colour, keep swirling until you have an even colour and then remove the pan from the heat. Stop the cooking by plunging the base of the pan into a sink of cold water.

If you find your caramel isn't dark enough, simply remelt it and cook until it

reaches the colour you want— if it gets too dark, there is no magic remedy and you will have to start again, so be careful. The darkest stage of caramel is known as black jack—this has a strong flavour and is used in very small amounts as a colouring for desserts, but is inedible on its own.

If the sugar syrup starts to crystallize, rescue it by adding a tablespoon of honey, a squeeze of lemon juice or a pinch of cream of tartar—these all slow down the crystallization by breaking down the sucrose into fructose and glucose. If you only have a few crystals, take your pan off the stove to allow it to cool a little, then add some more water and redissolve the crystals. If you are worried about crystallization, you can add a few drops of lemon juice to the sugar at the beginning.

CARAMEL DECORATIONS

THINGS TO MAKE

Caramel decorations must be made and used quickly—they do not store well and will soften in humidity. They will also soften and become sticky if refrigerated. The sugar in caramel will liquefy when it comes into contact with cream, ice creams, custard etc., so don't make your decorations sit too long before being served. If possible, add them just before serving. Make your caramel as described on the previous page. When the caramel reaches the colour you want, stop it cooking and colouring further and keep liquid by reheating gently when necessary.

CARAMEL SHEETS If you are making sheets of caramel, pour the caramel onto an oiled baking sheet and leave to cool (be careful as the baking sheet will become extremely hot). The sheets of caramel can then be broken into different shapes and sizes for decoration. It is easiest to break the caramel by hand, but don't stab yourself with a sharp piece. You can also pour the caramel into freeform threads or shapes, or pour it into a template cut from plasticine brushed with a little oil. The caramel can be coloured with food colouring and you can create whole pictures using different colours.

SPUN SUGAR Caramel can be spun into fine threads using two forks or a balloon whisk with the ends cut off. Keep the caramel liquid by standing the pan in a pan of hot water while you work. It will need to be thick enough to run in continuous streams from the ends of the forks. Oil the handle of a broom or long handled wooden spoon and place it between two chairs. Lay some newspaper on the floor under the handle. Hold two forks back to back and dip them in the caramel. Flick them backwards and forwards across the broom handle—sugar threads will form across the broom handle and hang

down on each side. Re-dip the forks as necessary until you have enough threads draped over the handle. Form the threads into decorative shapes by gently moulding them with your hands. Use immediately.

CARAMEL BASKETS Make caramel baskets by drizzling the caramel backwards and forwards across the bowl of a well oiled ladle or mould and leave to harden before carefully sliding the basket off the ladle. Lengths of caramel or crisscross patterns for decoration can be made by drizzling the caramel in patterns on a well oiled baking tray or any metal mould. Remember, the thicker the threads, the less likely they are to break, although with practice you should be able to make thinner more delicate decorations.

PRALINE Add toasted whole, flaked or slivered blanched almonds to a golden caramel made with an equal quantity of sugar to the weight of the nuts. Mix well, quickly tip out onto a marble surface or oiled baking sheet, then spread out into a single layer and cool. The praline can then either be broken into pieces or crushed in a plastic bag with a rolling pin or in a food processor. Store in an airtight container. Sheets of praline made with chopped almonds can be moulded into cup shapes by reheating the praline gently, then pressing it down onto an upturned mould.

LINING A MOULD Pour the liquid caramel into the bases of moulds used for desserts such as crème caramel and swirl them to coat the mould evenly. Be careful as the mould will get hot.

DIPPING FRUIT Whole fruit or nuts can be dipped in pale caramel to give a glossy sheen. Use a fork or skewer or hold the fruit by its stalk. Place on a piece of baking paper until completely cool.

CARAMEL BARK Sprinkle a foil-lined baking tray with a thin layer of sugar and place under a preheated grill. Watch carefully until the sugar melts and turns to caramel. Leave to set and then carefully lift the caramel off the foil and break into pieces.

TOFFEE GLAZES Pour liquid caramel onto crème brulées and other similar desserts to make a hard toffee topping. Pour the caramel over the surface and carefully tip from side to side to coat evenly. The caramel will harden quickly so work fast.

249

TUILE CONES WITH NOUGAT MOUSSE AND BLACKBERRY SAUCE

Preparation time: 1 hour 45 minutes + chilling
Total cooking time: 1 hour 15 minutes
Serves 6

✳ ✳ ✳

Nougat mousse

200 g (6¹/₂ oz) soft nougat
¹/₂ cup (125 ml/4 fl oz) milk
1 teaspoon finely grated orange rind
1¹/₄ cups (315 ml/10 fl oz) thick (double) cream

Blackberry sauce

150 g (5 oz) fresh or frozen blackberries
¹/₃ cup (80 ml/2³/₄ fl oz) good-quality red wine
2 tablespoons caster sugar
1 teaspoon cornflour

Tuile cones

40 g (1¹/₄ oz) unsalted butter
1 tablespoon honey
¹/₄ cup (30 g/1 oz) plain flour
1 egg white
¹/₄ cup (60 g/2 oz) caster sugar

Spun toffee

1 cup (250 g/8 oz) caster sugar

blackberries, extra, to decorate

1 Chop the nougat into small pieces, combine with the milk in a saucepan and stir constantly over low heat until the nougat has melted. Remove from the heat, stir in the rind and refrigerate until cold. Beat the cream until just thick, stir in the cold nougat mixture, then beat until thickened. Refrigerate until required.

2 For the sauce, combine the blackberries, wine and sugar in a small pan. Stir over heat until the sugar has dissolved, pressing the berries with the back of a spoon, then simmer for 2 minutes. Blend the cornflour with 2 teaspoons water, add to the pan and stir until the mixture boils and thickens. Strain to remove the seeds and allow to cool.

3 To make the tuile cones, preheat the oven to moderate 180°C (350°F/Gas 4). Draw a 17 cm (6¹/₂ inch) circle on baking paper, turn the paper over and place on a baking tray. Combine all the ingredients in a blender for 2 minutes, then spread 3 teaspoons of the mixture thinly and evenly over the circle to the edge.

4 Bake each tuile for 5–6 minutes, or until lightly golden. Working quickly, trim a piece the shape of a new moon off one side, then wrap firmly around a large metal horn mould, placing the point of the mould at the rounded edge of the tuile, opposite the trimmed edge (this will enable the tuile to stand up straight when filled). Repeat with the remaining tuile mixture. Store the tuiles in an airtight container as they will soften if left out.

5 To make the spun toffee, prepare the area you will be working in by first spreading a couple of sheets of newspaper on the floor underneath where you will be spinning the toffee. Then, place a wooden spoon on a work bench with the handle extending over the edge, above the newspaper. Place a chopping board or similar heavy object on top to weigh it down. Lightly oil the handle and remember to oil it each time. Place a heavy-based frying pan over medium heat, gradually sprinkle with sugar and as it melts, sprinkle with the remaining sugar. Stir to melt any lumps and prevent the sugar from burning. When the toffee is golden brown, remove from the heat and place the base of the pan in a large dish of cold water, to quickly cool the toffee and prevent it burning. This also will make the toffee thicken.

6 Dip two forks in the hot toffee and, using a flicking motion, carefully flick the toffee backwards and forwards over the handle of the wooden spoon, dipping the forks in the toffee again as often as necessary. If the toffee gets too thick, warm again slightly over low heat. You will need to do this three or four times. Before the toffee sets, quickly lift the toffee off the spoon handle and form into a nest shape. Store in an airtight container. Repeat with the remaining toffee to form 6 nest shapes. This may take some practice to master, but the results look fabulous.

7 To assemble, spoon the nougat mousse into a piping bag fitted with a large plain nozzle. Pipe the mousse into the cones and invert onto a serving plate. Spoon the blackberry sauce around the cone, serve with the reserved blackberries and top with a nest of spun toffee.

NOTE: The cones, sauce and mousse can be made a day ahead. The mousse may need to be beaten to thicken. The toffee should be made on the day of serving and stored in an airtight container. Humid days cause the toffee to become sticky and melt.

TUILE CONES

Spread 3 teaspoons of the tuile cone mixture thinly and evenly over the circle, to reach the edge.

Remove the tuile from the oven when golden and immediately trim off a piece shaped like a new moon.

Wrap the tuile firmly around a large metal horn mould, placing the point of the mould at the rounded edge of tuile.

Dip two forks in the hot toffee and carefully flick backwards and forwards over the handle of the wooden spoon.

OPPOSITE PAGE: Tuile cones with nougat mousse and blackberry sauce

PAPER PIPING BAGS

To make a paper piping bag to use with melted chocolate, cut a 25 cm (10 inch) square of baking paper. Fold it in half diagonally to form a triangle. Working with the longest side closest to you, curl the left point in to meet the top point. Hold in place while wrapping the other side around tightly to form a cone shape. Secure with tape or a staple. Tuck the upstanding ends into the cone. Fill with the melted chocolate and fold the top edges to seal. Snip off the tip and gently apply pressure from the top of the bag.

OPPOSITE PAGE:
Chocolate roulade (top);
Chocolate mud cake

CHOCOLATE ROULADE

Preparation time: 35 minutes
  + chilling
Total cooking time: 12 minutes
Serves 6–8

✷ ✷

3 eggs
1/2 cup (125 g/4 oz) caster sugar
1/4 cup (30 g/1 oz) plain flour
2 tablespoons cocoa powder
1 cup (250 ml/8 fl oz) cream
1 tablespoon icing sugar
1/2 teaspoon vanilla essence
icing sugar, extra, to dust

1 Preheat the oven to moderately hot 200°F (400°F/Gas 6). Lightly grease the base and sides of a 25 x 30 cm (10 x 12 inch) swiss roll tin. Line the base with paper and grease the paper. Place the eggs in a small bowl with 1/3 cup (90 g/3 oz) of the caster sugar. Beat with electric beaters for about 8 minutes, or until the mixture is thick and pale.
2 Sift the flour and cocoa together and gently fold into the egg mixture with a metal spoon. Spread the mixture evenly into the prepared tin. Bake for about 12 minutes, or until the cake is just set.
3 Meanwhile, place a clean tea towel on a work surface, top with a sheet of baking paper and sprinkle with the remaining caster sugar. When the cake is cooked, turn it out immediately onto the prepared paper and sugar. Trim off any crispy edges. Roll the cake up from the long side, rolling the paper inside the roll and using the tea towel as a guide. Stand the rolled cake on a wire cake rack for 5 minutes, then carefully unroll the cake and allow it to cool to room temperature.
4 Beat the cream, icing sugar and vanilla essence until stiff peaks form. Spread the cream over the cooled cake, leaving a 1 cm (1/2 inch) border around each edge. Roll the cake again, using the paper as a guide. Place the roll, seam-side-down, on a tray and refrigerate, covered, for about 30 minutes. Dust the top of the chocolate roulade with icing sugar before carefully cutting into slices to serve.

CHOCOLATE MUD CAKE

Preparation time: 30 minutes + chilling
Total cooking time: 1 hour 55 minutes
Serves 8–10

✷ ✷

250 g (8 oz) unsalted butter
250 g (8 oz) dark chocolate, broken
2 tablespoons instant espresso coffee powder
  or granules
150 g (5 oz) self-raising flour
150 g (5 oz) plain flour
1/2 cup (60 g/2 oz) cocoa powder
1/2 teaspoon bicarbonate of soda
550 g (1 lb 2 oz) sugar
4 eggs
2 tablespoons oil
1/2 cup (125 ml/4 fl oz) buttermilk

Glaze

250 g (8 oz) good-quality dark cooking chocolate, chopped
1/2 cup (125 ml/4 fl oz) cream
2/3 cup (160 g/5 1/2 oz) caster sugar

1 Preheat the oven to moderately slow 160°C (315°F/Gas 2–3). Brush a deep 22 cm (8 3/4 inch) round cake tin with melted butter or oil. Line the base and side with baking paper, extending at least 2 cm (1 inch) above the rim.
2 Stir the butter, chocolate and coffee in a pan with 185 ml (6 oz) hot water, over low heat, until the butter and chocolate have melted and the mixture is smooth. Remove from the heat.
3 Sift the flours, cocoa and bicarbonate of soda into a large bowl. Stir in the sugar and make a well. Add the combined eggs, oil and buttermilk and, using a large metal spoon, slowly stir in the dry ingredients, then the melted chocolate mix until combined.
4 Spoon the mixture into the tin and bake for 1 hour 40 minutes. Test with a skewer and, if it does not come out clean, cook for another 5–10 minutes. Cool in the tin. When completely cold, remove from the tin.
5 To make the glaze, stir all the ingredients in a pan over low heat until melted. Bring to the boil, reduce the heat and simmer for 4–5 minutes. Remove from the heat and cool slightly. Put a cooling rack on a baking tray and transfer the cake to the rack. Pour the glaze over the cake, making sure the sides are evenly covered. Decorate with chocolate (see page 238–239).

POACHED PEARS WITH CHOCOLATE SHORTBREAD FLOWERS

Preparation time: 50 minutes + chilling
Total cooking time: 1 hour 10 minutes
Serves 6

★★★

6 medium pears
1 1/2 cups (375 ml/12 fl oz) sweet
    dessert wine
1 vanilla bean, split lengthways

Cardamom custard

1 cup (250 ml/8 fl oz) milk
1/2 cup (125 ml/4 fl oz) cream
6 cardamom pods, crushed
3 egg yolks
2 tablespoons caster sugar

Chocolate shortbread flowers

60 g (2 oz) unsalted butter,
    chopped
2 tablespoons soft brown sugar
1 egg yolk
1 tablespoon cocoa powder
1/2 cup (60 g/2 oz) plain flour
1/4 cup (30 g/1 oz) cornflour

Toffee fingers

1 cup (250 g/8 oz) caster sugar

1 Peel the pears and remove the cores with a melon baller. Place in a saucepan large enough to hold all the pears. Add the wine and vanilla bean, cover and simmer for 20–25 minutes, or until soft (cooking time will depend on the ripeness of the pears). Remove the pan from the heat and allow the pears to cool in the syrup.

2 To make the cardamom custard, combine the milk, cream and cardamom pods in a small pan, bring to the boil and remove from the heat. Beat the egg yolks and sugar in a heatproof bowl for about 5 minutes, or until light and fluffy, then gradually pour in the hot milk mixture. Place the bowl over a pan of simmering water and stir with a wooden spoon for 10–15 minutes, or until the mixture coats the back of a wooden spoon. Strain and cool.

3 To make the chocolate shortbread flowers, preheat the oven to moderate 180°C (350°F/Gas 4). Beat the butter and sugar in a small bowl with electric beaters until light and creamy. Add the egg yolk, then the sifted cocoa and flours. Press together to form a soft dough. Wrap in plastic wrap and refrigerate for 30 minutes. Roll the dough out between two sheets of baking paper to 4 mm (1/4 inch) thick. Cut 42 rounds from the pastry, using a 3 cm (1 1/4 inch) round cutter. Cut the remaining pastry into 12 small leaves. For each flower, use 7 rounds, slightly overlapping, to form a flower on a baking tray lined with baking paper. Decorate with the leaves. Bake for 10–15 minutes, or until the pastry is firm to touch. Remove from the tray and cool on a wire rack.

4 To make the toffee fingers, line two or three baking trays with baking paper. Sprinkle the sugar over the base of a heavy-based frying pan, then stir gently until the sugar has dissolved and is light golden brown. Remove from the heat (the toffee will continue to darken away from the heat). Use a spoon to drizzle 12 cm (5 inch) lengths of toffee onto the prepared trays, about 5 mm (1/4 inch) wide, and allow to set until cold.

5 To assemble for serving, dust the shortbread flowers very lightly with icing sugar, place in the centre of a serving plate and position a well-drained pear on top. Spoon cardamom custard around the outside of the shortbread. Stand the toffee strips up around the outside of the pear like a tepee.

NOTE: The cardamom custard can be made three days ahead. Pears and shortbread rounds can be made a day ahead and the shortbread can be frozen for a month. Toffee fingers are best made on the day of serving and stored in an airtight container.

PEARS WITH SHORTBREAD

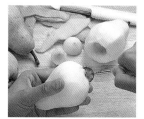

Peel the pears and remove the cores through the base with a melon baller.

Use 7 rounds for each flower, slightly overlapping them to form circles on a lined baking tray. Decorate with the leaves.

As soon as the sugar is light golden brown, remove it from the heat. It will continue to darken.

Drizzle lengths of toffee onto lined baking trays and leave to go cold and set.

OPPOSITE PAGE: Poached pears with chocolate shortbread flowers

ICE CREAM

Ice cream, as one of our most modern desserts, has enjoyed a spectacularly meteoric rise to become one of the most popular. It is not until relatively recent times, of course, that we learnt to make ice and freeze at will. So, while fire and hot food has been familiar to us since the days when we lived in caves, cold food has been treated with suspicion and even fear. Rumour has it that when custards, served at an American society ball in 1831, were found to be still frozen, the cry of 'poison' went up. The hostess herself, with no little bravado, polished one off and declared it 'delicious'. A somewhat inauspicious episode in the history of one of our modern favourites.

VANILLA ICE CREAM

To test the custard, run a finger through the mixture, across the back of a wooden spoon. It should leave a clear line.

Cover the surface of the custard with plastic wrap and freeze for 2 hours.

Beat the semi-frozen ice cream with electric beaters to break up any large ice crystals. Each time you beat the mixture, the ice crystals will get smaller and the mixture smoother.

OPPOSITE PAGE: Vanilla ice cream (top); Premium chocolate and cinnamon ice cream

VANILLA ICE CREAM

Preparation time: 30 minutes + chilling + freezing
Total cooking time: 15 minutes
Serves 4

★ ★

1 cup (250 ml/8 fl oz) milk
1 cup (250 ml/8 fl oz) cream
1 vanilla bean, split lengthways
6 egg yolks
1/2 cup (125 g/4 oz) caster sugar

1 Combine the milk and cream in a pan and add the vanilla bean. Bring to the boil, then remove from the heat and set aside for 10 minutes.
2 Using a wire whisk, beat the yolks and sugar together in a bowl for 2–3 minutes, until thick and pale, then whisk in the warm milk mixture. Scrape the seeds from the vanilla bean into the mixture. Discard the bean.
3 Wash the pan, and pour the mixture into it. Stir over very low heat until thickened. This will take about 5–10 minutes. To test, run a finger through the mixture across the back of the wooden spoon—if it leaves a clear line, the custard is ready.
4 Pour the custard into a bowl and cool to room temperature, stirring frequently to hasten cooling.
5 Pour into a shallow metal container, cover the surface of the custard with plastic wrap or baking paper and freeze for about 2 hours, until almost frozen. Scoop into a chilled bowl and beat with electric beaters until smooth, then return to the tray and freeze again. Repeat this step twice more before transferring to a storage container. Cover the surface with baking paper or plastic wrap to stop ice crystals forming on the surface, then a lid.
6 To serve, transfer the ice cream to the refrigerator for about 30 minutes, to soften slightly. Ice cream will keep, well sealed, in the freezer for up to 1 month.
NOTE: This recipe can also be made using an ice cream machine.
VARIATIONS: To make strawberry ice cream, chop 250 g (8 oz) strawberries in a food processor just until smooth. Stir into the custard mixture when it is well chilled (end of step 4). Freeze the ice cream as directed.
  To make banana ice cream, thoroughly mash 3 ripe bananas (or for a finer texture, purée in a food processor). Stir into the custard mixture when it is well chilled, along with 1 tablespoon lemon juice. Freeze as directed. Makes 1.5 litres.

PREMIUM CHOCOLATE AND CINNAMON ICE CREAM

Preparation time: 20 minutes + chilling + freezing
Total cooking time: 30 minutes
Serves 6–8

★ ★

2 cups (500 ml/16 fl oz) milk
200 g (6 1/2 oz) good-quality dark chocolate, chopped
4 cinnamon sticks
3/4 cup (185 g/6 oz) caster sugar
1 1/2 teaspoons ground cinnamon
4 egg yolks
2 cups (500 ml/16 fl oz) cream

1 Heat the milk, chocolate and cinnamon sticks in a heavy-based pan, stirring occasionally, over low heat for 15 minutes, or until the chocolate has melted and the mixture is well mixed. Do not allow to boil. Remove the cinnamon sticks.
2 Mix the sugar and cinnamon in a large heatproof bowl. Add the egg yolks and place the bowl over a pan of simmering water. Whisk until the mixture is thick and pale.
3 Gradually whisk the chocolate mixture into the eggs and sugar. Cook, whisking all the time, for 5 minutes or until the mixture coats the back of a spoon.
4 Chill for 30 minutes in the refrigerator, strain and slowly stir in the cream. Pour into a shallow metal container. Freeze for 2 hours (the edges will be frozen and the centre soft). Transfer to a large bowl and beat with electric beaters until smooth. Repeat this step twice more. Freeze in a 2 litre plastic container, covered with a piece of baking paper or plastic wrap, then a lid, for 7–8 hours, or until solid.
NOTE: This recipe can also be made using an ice cream machine.

ICE CREAM TIPS

The temperature of your freezer should be -18°C/0°F to ensure proper freezing. The freezer should also be free from ice build-up and not too full. Cover the surface of your ice cream with baking paper or plastic wrap to stop ice crystals forming on the surface.

  For full flavour, ice cream should not be eaten while rock hard, but slightly softened.

in the milk. Gradually add the coffee mixture with the beans and whisk until smooth. Strain the mixture and discard the beans.

3 Return the mixture to the pan and stir over low heat until the mixture thickens and will coat the back of a spoon. Do not boil. Remove from the heat and set aside to cool.

4 Put the mixture into the prepared tin and freeze until just firm. Transfer to a large chilled bowl and beat with electric beaters until thick. Return to the tin and cover with plastic wrap and freeze again until firm. Repeat, beating once more before transferring to a container for storage in the freezer. Cover the surface with plastic wrap or baking paper. Serve in scoops with frosted rose petals (see Note) or store in the freezer for up to 7 days.

NOTE: To frost rose petals, lightly whisk 1 egg white, dip clean dry petals in egg white (or brush lightly with a paintbrush), then sprinkle with sugar. Shake off the excess sugar and place on a paper-lined tray to dry.

NOTE: This recipe can also be made using an ice cream machine.

LEMON ICE CREAM

Preparation time: 20 minutes + freezing
Total cooking time: 15 minutes
Serves 4–6

★★

6 egg yolks
1 cup (250 g/8 oz) caster sugar
2 teaspoons grated lemon rind
1/3 cup (80 ml/2³/4 fl oz) lemon juice
2 cups (500 ml/16 fl oz) cream, lightly
   whipped
lemon rind strips, for serving

1 Whisk or beat the egg yolks in a heatproof bowl. Stand the bowl over a pan of steaming water, off the heat, and whisk until light and fluffy and increased in volume. Add the sugar, lemon rind and juice, and continue whisking until thick and pale. Allow to cool.

2 Using a metal spoon, fold the cream into the lemon mixture. Pour into a 1.25 litre capacity shallow metal container and freeze for 2 hours, or until firm. When half frozen around the edges, beat well, then freeze again. Repeat the beating and freezing twice more. Garnish with lemon rind strips.

NOTE: This recipe can also be made using an ice cream machine.

MOCHA ICE CREAM

Preparation time: 20 minutes + freezing
Total cooking time: 10–15 minutes
Serves 4–6

★★

1/2 cup (40 g/1¼ oz) espresso coffee beans
3 cups (750 ml/24 fl oz) cream
250 g (8 oz) good-quality dark cooking
   chocolate, chopped
3/4 cup (185 g/6 oz) caster sugar
6 egg yolks
1 cup (250 ml/8 fl oz) milk

1 Line a rectangular tin with plastic wrap and freeze. Combine the coffee beans and cream in a pan. Stir over medium heat until the mixture just starts to boil. Add the chocolate, remove from the heat and set aside for 1 minute before stirring.

2 Combine the sugar and egg yolks in a large bowl, whisk until slightly thickened, then whisk

ABOVE: Mocha ice cream

ICE CREAM and
ALCOHOL
The addition of alcohol to
ice creams lowers the
freezing point, sometimes
to a stage where it will not
freeze at all. Spirits lower
the freezing point of ice
cream by approximately
1°C per tablespoon and
sorbets by 6°C.

CHOCOLATE WHISKY LOAF

Preparation time: 10 minutes + freezing
Total cooking time: 10 minutes
Serves 6

★ ★

250 g (8 oz) good-quality dark chocolate,
  roughly chopped
60 g (2 oz) unsalted butter, softened
4 egg yolks
1¼ cups (315 ml/10 fl oz) cream
2 teaspoons vanilla essence
2 tablespoons whisky
3 tablespoons cocoa, to dust

1 Line a 21 x 14 x 7 cm (8½ x 5½ x 2¾ inch)
loaf tin with plastic wrap. Put the chocolate in a
heatproof bowl. Bring a small pan of water to a
simmer, remove from the heat and place the
bowl over the pan, being careful not to let the
bottom of the bowl touch the water. Stir the
chocolate over the hot water until melted.

Alternatively, melt the chocolate in the
microwave for 1 minute on High (100%),
stirring after 30 seconds. Allow to cool.
2 Beat the butter and egg yolks in a small bowl
until thick and creamy, then beat in the cooled
chocolate mixture. In a medium bowl, using
clean beaters, beat the cream and vanilla essence
until soft peaks form. Fold in the whisky. Using
a metal spoon, fold the cream and chocolate
mixtures together until just combined.
3 Pour the mixture into the prepared loaf tin,
cover the surface with plastic wrap and freeze
for 2–3 hours or overnight, or until firm.
Remove from the freezer, unmould and
carefully peel away the plastic wrap. Smooth
the wrinkles on the surface of the loaf using
a flat-bladed knife. Place on a serving plate
and dust with cocoa. If not serving immediately,
return to the freezer for up to 1 week. Cut into
slices to serve. Can be served with extra cream
and dessert wafers.
NOTE: This dessert is eaten firm but it will
not freeze as hard as ice cream because it
contains alcohol.

*ABOVE: Chocolate
whisky loaf*

CASSATA

Originating in Naples, cassata is traditionally composed of flavoured ice cream layered around a filling of ricotta and candied fruit in an oblong mould. Cassata means 'little case'. Cassata Siciliana is a traditional Sicilian dessert set in a dome-shaped mould and made with cake, green marzipan, crystallized fruit, ricotta and chocolate. Cassata Gelata alla Siciliana is an ice cream based on this. Vanilla and pistachio ice creams are layered with cake, then whipped egg whites, cream, chocolate and candied fruit and finally the two ice cream layers are repeated.

ABOVE: Ice cream cassata

ICE CREAM CASSATA

Preparation time: 50 minutes + freezing
Total cooking time: Nil
Serves 10

★ ★

First layer

2 eggs, separated
1/3 cup (40 g/1 1/4 oz) icing sugar
3/4 cup (185 ml/6 fl oz) cream
50 g (1 3/4 oz) flaked almonds, toasted

Second layer

130 g (4 1/2 oz) good-quality dark
   chocolate, chopped
1 tablespoon dark cocoa powder
2 eggs, separated
1/3 cup (40 g/1 1/4 oz) icing sugar
3/4 cup (185 ml/6 fl oz) cream

Third layer

2 eggs, separated
1/4 cup (30 g/1 oz) icing sugar
1/4 cup (60 ml/2 fl oz) cream
1/2 cup (125 g/4 oz) ricotta
250 g (8 oz) glacé fruit (pineapple, apricot,
   cherries, fig and peach), finely chopped
1 teaspoon vanilla essence

1 Line the base and sides of a deep 20 cm (8 inch) square tin with foil.

2 To make the first layer, beat the egg whites with electric beaters until soft peaks form. Add the icing sugar gradually, beating well after each addition. In a separate bowl, beat the cream until firm peaks form. Using a metal spoon, fold the yolks and beaten egg whites into the cream. Stir in the almonds. Spoon into the tin and smooth the surface. Tap the tin gently on the bench to level the surface, then freeze for 30–60 minutes, or until firm.

3 To make the second layer, melt the chocolate by stirring in a heatproof bowl over a pan of steaming water, off the heat. Make sure the base of the bowl does not touch the water. Stir in the cocoa until smooth. Cool slightly, then proceed as for step 1, beating the egg whites, icing sugar and then cream. Using a metal spoon, fold the chocolate into the cream. Fold in the yolks and beaten egg whites and stir until smooth. Spoon over the frozen first layer. Tap the tin on the bench to smooth the surface. Freeze for 30–60 minutes, or until firm.

4 To make the third layer, proceed as for step 1, beating the egg whites, icing sugar and then cream. Stir the ricotta into the cream. With a metal spoon, fold the yolks and egg white into the cream, then stir in the fruit and vanilla essence. Spoon over the chocolate layer, cover the surface with greaseproof paper, then freeze overnight. Slice to serve. Can be served with extra fuit.

CHRISTMAS ICE CREAM PUDDING

Preparation time: 1 hour + standing + freezing
Total cooking time: Nil
Serves 10

★ ★

50 g (1¾ oz) toasted almonds, chopped

45 g (1½ oz) mixed chopped candied citrus peel

60 g (2 oz) raisins, chopped

60 g (2 oz) sultanas

60 g (2 oz) currants

⅓ cup (80 ml/2¾ fl oz) rum

1 litre good-quality vanilla ice cream

100 g (3½ oz) red and green glacé cherries, quartered

1 teaspoon mixed spice

1 teaspoon ground cinnamon

½ teaspoon ground nutmeg

1 litre good-quality chocolate ice cream

1 Mix the almonds, peel, raisins, sultanas, currants and rum in a bowl, cover with plastic wrap and leave overnight. Chill a 2 litre metal or plastic pudding basin in the freezer.

2 Soften the vanilla ice cream slightly and mix in all the quartered cherries. Press this ice cream around the inside of the chilled pudding basin, spreading it evenly to cover the base and side of the basin. Return the basin to the freezer and leave overnight. It might be necessary to check the ice cream a couple of times and spread it again evenly to the top.

3 Next day, mix the spices and chocolate ice cream with the fruit mixture. Spoon it into the centre of the pudding bowl and smooth the top. Freeze overnight, or until very firm. Turn the pudding out onto a plate and decorate. Serve cut into wedges.

NOTE: You can put coins and charms into the pudding as with a traditional Christmas pudding. Wrap each one in baking paper and poke into the base of the pudding before turning it out. Warn people if you do, to avoid broken teeth.

ICE CREAM MOULDS

Traditionally, ice cream moulds are made of metal and have a lid. The lid helps inhibit the formation of ice crystals on the surface of the ice cream and metal is the best conductor of heat, so the heat escapes quickly on freezing and the mould is easy to turn out when warmed briefly. Moulds are usually made of aluminium, but expensive copper ones lined with tin are available. Antique moulds should be used with care as tinning on copper moulds does wear thin. Do not use moulds which may be made more for decoration and are lined with lead-based pewter. Ceramic and glass moulds meant for jellies and desserts may not stand up to freezer temperatures and thus crack. However, plastic works well. Decorated moulds are harder to fill and turn out than plain ones, as air pockets form when they are being filled. Expensive hinged moulds are available to help alleviate this problem.

LEFT: Christmas ice cream pudding

PRALINE ICE CREAM WITH CARAMEL BARK

Preparation time: 25 minutes + freezing
Total cooking time: 7 minutes
Serves 4

★ ★ ★

70 g (2¼ oz) blanched almonds, toasted
¼ cup (60 g/2 oz) caster sugar
¾ cup (185 ml/6 fl oz) cream
250 g (8 oz) mascarpone
125 g (4 oz) white chocolate, melted and cooled
2 tablespoons sugar
fresh figs and dessert wafers, for serving, optional

1 Line a flat baking tray with foil, brush the foil lightly with oil and put the almonds on the foil. Place the caster sugar in a small pan over low heat. Tilt the pan slightly (do not stir) and watch until the sugar melts and turns golden—this should take about 3–5 minutes.

BELOW: Praline ice cream with caramel bark

2 Pour the caramel over the almonds and leave until set and cold. Break into chunks, put in a plastic bag and crush with a rolling pin, or process briefly in a food processor until crumbly.
3 Whip the cream until stiff peaks form. Stir the mascarpone and chocolate in a large bowl to combine. Using a metal spoon, fold in the whipped cream and crushed praline. Transfer to a 1 litre metal tray, cover the surface with a piece of greaseproof paper and freeze for 6 hours, or overnight. Remove from the freezer 15 minutes before serving, to soften slightly.
4 To make the caramel bark, line a baking tray with foil and brush lightly with oil. Sprinkle the sugar evenly onto the tray and place under a hot grill for 2 minutes, until the sugar is melted and golden. Check frequently towards the end of cooking time, as the sugar may burn quickly. Remove from the heat, leave until set and completely cold, then break into shards. Serve with the ice cream, perhaps with fresh figs and dessert wafers.

BROWN BREAD ICE CREAM

Preparation time: 25 minutes + freezing
Total cooking time: 15–20 minutes
Serves 6

★

2 egg yolks
¼ cup (60 g/2 oz) caster sugar
½ cup (125 ml/4 fl oz) milk
1½ cups (125 g/4 oz) fine fresh
   brown breadcrumbs
55 g (2 oz) butter, melted
2 tablespoons soft brown sugar
1¼ cups (315 ml/10 fl oz) cream
1 tablespoon rum
strips of orange rind, to garnish

1 Preheat the oven to moderately hot 200°F (400°F/Gas 6). Whisk the egg yolks and sugar in a bowl until thick and pale. Heat the milk in a pan until simmering, but not boiling, and pour over the yolk mixture, whisking constantly.
2 Return the mixture to a clean pan and cook gently over low heat, stirring constantly until the mixture lightly coats the back of a wooden spoon. Remove from the heat. (Do not boil or it will curdle.) Transfer to a bowl. Cover the surface with plastic wrap and set aside to cool.
3 Mix the breadcrumbs with the butter and brown sugar. Spread on a tray and bake for

about 15 minutes. Stir and turn once or twice during cooking. Cool, then crumble.

4 Beat the cream until soft peaks form, then stir in the rum. Carefully fold the cream into the cold custard. Freeze for 1 hour in a metal or plastic container, stir in the breadcrumbs and freeze until firm. Garnish with orange rind.

TRIPLE CHOCOLATE TERRINE

Preparation time: I hour + freezing
Total cooking time: 15–20 minutes
Serves 8–10

★★

150 g (5 oz) milk chocolate, chopped

6 eggs

3/4 cup (90 g/3 oz) icing sugar

60 g (2 oz) unsalted butter

2 cups (500 ml/16 fl oz) cream

150 g (5 oz) white chocolate, chopped

2 teaspoons instant coffee

3–4 teaspoons dark rum

150 g (5 oz) good-quality dark chocolate, chopped

1 Line a 10 x 23 cm (4 x 9 inch) loaf tin with baking paper, extending above the top of the tin. Melt the milk chocolate in a small bowl, over a pan of steaming water, off the heat, making sure the bottom of the bowl does not touch the water, until smooth. Separate 2 of the eggs and beat the whites until soft peaks form. Gradually beat in 1/4 cup (30 g/1 oz) of the icing sugar, until thick and glossy. Beat in the 2 egg yolks and the cooled melted chocolate. Melt 20 g (1 oz) of the butter and beat in. Whip 2/3 cup (170 ml/5 1/2 fl oz) of the cream into soft peaks. Fold into the egg white mixture and then spoon into the tin, with the tin tilted on one side lengthways. Put in the freezer on this angle and leave for 1–2 hours, until just firm.

2 Repeat the same method with the white chocolate. Spoon this mixture into the other side of the tin so that the terrine becomes level. Put the tin flat in the freezer to set.

3 Repeat the same method with the remaining ingredients, folding in the coffee dissolved in 1 tablespoon of water, and rum, with the dark chocolate. Spoon into the tin and smooth the surface. Freeze for several hours. Turn out onto a plate, then cut into thin slices to serve. Can be garnished with chocolate leaves (see page 239).

ABOVE: Triple chocolate terrine

265

FRUIT SAUCES Fresh fruits, herbs

and spices can be used to make sublime sauces that transform a bowl of ice cream

or simple dessert into something quite out of the ordinary.

RHUBARB SAUCE

Chop 350 g (11 oz) rhubarb and place in a pan with ½ cup (95 g/3 oz) soft brown sugar, 1 cup (250 ml/8 fl oz) water and ¼ teaspoon ground mixed spice. Slowly bring to the boil, stirring to dissolve the sugar. Simmer for 10 minutes, stirring often. Push through a sieve and serve hot or cold. Makes 1½ cups (375 ml/12 fl oz).

LEMON GRASS, LIME AND CORIANDER SYRUP

Finely grate 250 g (8 oz) palm sugar and place in a small pan with 1 cup (250 ml/ 8 fl oz) water. Stir over low heat until the sugar has dissolved. Add 2 finely sliced stems lemon grass (white part only), 1 teaspoon lightly crushed coriander seeds, 1 teaspoon lime rind and 2 teaspoons lime juice. Bring to the boil and simmer for 15–20 minutes, or until syrupy. Strain, if you like, and serve with tropical fruits, ice cream or pancakes. Makes 1 cup (250 ml/8 fl oz).

MANGO COULIS

Chop 2 small mangoes. Blend in a food processor with 3 tablespoons orange juice and 2 teaspoons Cointreau (optional), until smooth. Makes 1⅓ cups (350 ml/11 fl oz).

PASSIONFRUIT COULIS

Put ½ cup (125 ml/4 fl oz) fresh passionfruit pulp (canned is not suitable for this recipe), ½ cup (125 ml/4 fl oz) water and 2 tablespoons caster sugar in a small pan. Slowly bring to the boil, stirring to dissolve the sugar. Simmer, without stirring, for 5 minutes.
Makes 1 cup (250 ml/8 fl oz).

HOT BLUEBERRY SAUCE

In a non-metallic bowl, combine 500 g (1 lb) blueberries, ¼ cup (60 g/2 oz) sugar and 1 tablespoon balsamic vinegar. Set aside for 30 minutes. Place in a pan with 2 tablespoons water and stir over low heat to dissolve the sugar. Bring to the boil and simmer for 5 minutes. Serve warm. Delicious on ice cream and good with fresh ricotta or warm chocolate cake. Makes 2 cups (500 ml/16 fl oz).

STRAWBERRY COULIS

Hull 250 g (8 oz) strawberries and place in a food processor with 2 tablespoons icing sugar, 2 teaspoons lemon juice and 1–2 teaspoons Grand Marnier (optional). Process until smooth and strain through a fine sieve, if desired.
Makes 1 cup (250 ml/8 fl oz).

BUMBLEBERRY COULIS

Place 300 g (10 oz) fresh or thawed frozen berries (use a combination of raspberry, strawberry, blueberry and blackberry) and 2 tablespoons icing sugar in a food processor. Blend in short bursts until smooth and glossy. Strain in a fine sieve to remove the seeds. Add 2 teaspoons lemon juice and 3 teaspoons Cassis liqueur (optional) and mix well. Makes 1 cup (250 ml/8 fl oz).

SPICY PEACH SAUCE

Place 500 g (1 lb) peaches in a bowl, cover with boiling water and leave for 20 seconds. Drain, peel and chop, then put in a pan with 1 cup (250 ml/8 fl oz) water, ½ vanilla bean, 2 cloves and a cinnamon stick. Bring to the boil, reduce the heat and simmer for 15–20 minutes, or until tender. Add 3 tablespoons sugar and stir over low heat until dissolved. Increase the heat and simmer for 5 minutes. Remove the vanilla and spices and cool slightly. Blend in a food processor or blender. Push through a fine sieve before serving. Makes 1¾ cups (440 ml/14 fl oz).

SAUCES CLOCKWISE, FROM TOP LEFT: Lemon grass, lime and coriander; Mango; Passionfruit; Bumbleberry; Spicy peach; Strawberry; Hot blueberry; Rhubarb

1 Put the egg yolks in a large heatproof bowl and gradually whisk in the sugar. Continue to whisk until the sugar has dissolved and the mixture is thick and pale. (Do not use an electric mixer as this will incorporate too much air into the mixture.) Stir in the sifted cocoa.

2 Combine the milk, cream and vanilla bean in a pan. Bring to the boil, scrape the seeds out of the vanilla bean into the milk, and discard the empty bean. Gently whisk the hot milk into the egg yolk mixture. Place the bowl over a pan of simmering water, and stir constantly over low heat until the custard coats the back of a wooden spoon. (This will take about 20 minutes.) Do not allow the mixture to boil, or the eggs will curdle. Remove from the heat, strain and pour into a clean bowl. Chill a deep 20 cm (8 inch) square cake tin in the freezer.

3 Put the chocolate in a heatproof bowl. Half fill a saucepan with water and bring to the boil. Remove from the heat and place the bowl over the pan, making sure it is not touching the water. Stir occasionally until the chocolate is melted. Add the warm chocolate to the warm custard and stir constantly until the chocolate has mixed through. Allow to cool. Pour the cooled mixture into the chilled container, cover and freeze until the ice cream has just set. Remove from the freezer and spoon into a large bowl. Beat with a wooden spoon or electric beaters until smooth and thick, then return to the container. Repeat the freezing and beating twice more, then cover with a layer of greaseproof paper and freeze overnight, or until completely set. Remove from the freezer and place in the refrigerator 15–20 minutes before serving, to allow the ice cream to soften slightly.

CHOCOLATE ICE CREAM

Preparation time: 1 hour + freezing
Total cooking time: 30 minutes
Serves 4

★ ★

8 egg yolks

1/2 cup (125 g/4 oz) caster sugar

2 tablespoons cocoa powder

2 cups (500 ml/16 fl oz) milk

1 cup (250 ml/8 fl oz) cream

1 vanilla bean, split lengthways

250 g (8 oz) good-quality dark
    chocolate, chopped

*ABOVE: Chocolate
ice cream*

ICE CREAM SAFETY

Ice creams, if wrongly handled, can be a perfect breeding ground for bacteria. Bacteria are normally killed when heated to a high enough temperature, and made inactive when cooled down enough or frozen. It is the temperatures between these points which are a problem, especially blood temperature. Custards should be cooled as quickly as possible and dairy products kept well chilled until used. Ice cream which is being thawed slightly and then re-frozen should be eaten quickly and not re-thawed again. Ice cream if thawed completely should be thrown away. All equipment should be thoroughly washed and the machine may benefit from being sterilised.

Divide the hot custard evenly between the bowls of dark and milk chocolate.

Pour the milk chocolate mixture over the frozen dark chocolate layer.

FROZEN CHOCOLATE PARFAIT

Preparation time: 40 minutes + freezing
Total cooking time: 25 minutes
Serves 8

★ ★

6 egg yolks
1/2 cup (125 g/4 oz) caster sugar
150 g (5 oz) dark chocolate, finely chopped
150 g (5 oz) milk chocolate, finely chopped
1 vanilla bean, split lengthways
1 cup (250 ml/8 fl oz) milk
1 1/3 cups (350 ml/11 fl oz) cream

1 Lightly grease a 1.25 litre terrine mould and line the entire mould with two layers of plastic wrap, allowing the plastic to extend over the sides. (This will help when removing the parfait once it has set.) Place the egg yolks in a bowl and gradually whisk in the sugar. Continue to whisk until the sugar has dissolved and the mixture is thick and pale. Place the chopped dark and milk chocolate in separate bowls and set aside.
2 Put the vanilla bean in a small pan with the milk. Slowly bring to the boil, then remove from the heat and scrape the seeds out of the vanilla bean and into the milk. Discard the empty bean. Gently pour the milk onto the egg yolks, whisking constantly. Return the mixture to a clean pan and cook over low heat, stirring constantly, until the custard coats the back of a wooden spoon. This will take about 20 minutes. Do not overcook or the egg will curdle.
3 Divide the hot custard evenly between the bowls of chocolate. Using a wooden spoon, quickly mix in the custard, stirring until the chocolate is completely melted. Allow to cool completely. Beat the cream with electric beaters until soft peaks form. Divide evenly between the cooled chocolate mixtures, and gently fold in. Carefully pour the dark chocolate mixture into the base of the terrine dish. Freeze for 30 minutes, or until firm. Pour the milk chocolate mixture over the back of a spoon to form an even layer, and smooth the top with the back of a spoon. Cover with a piece of greaseproof paper and freeze overnight, or until the terrine is completely frozen.
4 Just before serving, carefully remove the plastic wrap and parfait from the dish. Slice the parfait and immediately return the remaining portion to the freezer.

ABOVE: Frozen chocolate parfait

PEANUT BRITTLE PARFAIT

Preparation time: 40 minutes + freezing
Total cooking time: 15 minutes
Serves 8

★★

1½ cups (375 g/12 oz) caster sugar

2 cups (500 ml/16 fl oz) milk

6 egg yolks

1 tablespoon instant coffee powder

2½ cups (600 ml/20 fl oz) cream

120 g (4 oz) chocolate-coated peanut brittle,
    roughly chopped

1 Stir 1 cup (250 g/8 oz) sugar with ⅓ cup (80 ml/2¾ fl oz) water in a pan over low heat, without boiling, until the sugar dissolves. Brush down the sides of the pan with water to dissolve the sugar crystals. Bring to the boil, reduce the heat and simmer without stirring for 4 minutes, or until caramel. Remove from the heat and allow to cool slightly before stirring in the milk.

BELOW: Peanut brittle parfait

Be careful as the mixture will splutter. Return to the heat and stir until the toffee dissolves.
2 Line a 15 x 23 cm (6 x 9 inch) loaf tin with plastic wrap. Whisk the remaining sugar with the egg yolks in a metal or heatproof bowl. Beat in the milk mixture and the coffee blended with 1 teaspoon water. Stand the bowl over a pan of simmering water (or mix in the top of a double boiler). Whisk until the mixture thickens and coats the back of a spoon.
3 Cool the mixture, then add the cream. Pour into a large shallow tin and freeze until just firm. Transfer to a large bowl. Using electric beaters, beat until light and fluffy. Return to the tin and freeze until just firm. Repeat the beating process twice more. Fold the chopped peanut brittle through, spread the mixture into the loaf tin, cover the surface with a piece of greaseproof paper, then freeze until firm. Cut into slices to serve. Can be decorated with pieces of toffee.

ESPRESSO PARFAIT

Preparation time: 10 minutes + freezing
Total cooking time: 20 minutes
Serves 4–6

★★

½ cup (45 g/1½ oz) ground coffee

¾ cup (185 g/6 oz) sugar

4 egg yolks

1 cup (250 ml/8 fl oz) thick (double) cream

1 Put the coffee, sugar and ¾ cup (185 ml/ 6 fl oz) water in a pan, bring to the boil, remove from the heat and leave for 3 minutes. Strain through a filter paper or muslin-lined sieve. Pour back into the rinsed pan and keep warm.
2 Place the egg yolks in a heatproof bowl and whisk until pale and light. Whisk in the coffee syrup a little at a time. Place the bowl over a pan of simmering water and cook, stirring until the mixture thickens enough to coat the back of a spoon—do not boil or it will curdle. Remove from the heat and beat with electric beaters until doubled in volume. The mixture will hold a trail when it is allowed to run off the beaters. Chill until cold.
3 Whip the cream until soft peaks form, then fold into the egg mixture. Pour the mixture into a loaf tin lined with plastic wrap, cover the surface with greaseproof paper and freeze for at least 2 hours. Transfer the parfait to the fridge for 10 minutes before turning out and cutting into slices.

CAPPUCCINO ICE CREAM CAKES

Preparation time: 1 hour 45 minutes
Total cooking time: 30 minutes
Serves 10

★ ★

Chocolate cake

185 g (6 oz) unsalted butter
330 g (11 oz) caster sugar
2½ teaspoons vanilla essence
3 eggs
75 g (2½ oz) self-raising flour
225 g (7 oz) plain flour
1½ teaspoons bicarbonate of soda
¾ cup (90 g/3 oz) cocoa powder
280 ml (9 fl oz) buttermilk

1 tablespoon instant coffee powder
1 litre vanilla ice cream, softened
1 cup (250 ml/8 fl oz) thick (double) cream
1 tablespoon icing sugar
125 g (4 oz) dark chocolate melts, melted
cocoa powder, to dust

1 Lightly grease ten muffin holes (with 250 ml/8 fl oz capacity). Preheat the oven to moderate 180°C (350°F/Gas 4).
2 To make the cake, beat the butter and sugar with electric beaters until light and creamy. Beat in the vanilla essence. Add the eggs, one at a time, beating well after each addition.
3 Using a metal spoon, fold in the combined sifted flours, bicarbonate of soda and cocoa powder alternately with the buttermilk. Stir until the mixture is just combined.
4 Divide the mixture evenly among the muffin holes and bake for 25 minutes, or until a skewer comes out clean. Cool in the tins for 5 minutes before turning onto a wire cake rack to cool.
5 Dissolve the coffee powder in 2 tablespoons boiling water, then cool. Roughly break up the vanilla ice cream in a large bowl and stir until smooth. Stir in the coffee mixture and freeze until required.
6 Beat the cream and icing sugar together in a small bowl with an electric mixer until soft peaks form. Refrigerate until ready to use.
7 Draw the outline of a small spoon, ten times, on a piece of baking paper, then turn the paper over. Spoon the melted chocolate into a paper piping bag. Snip the end off the bag and draw a chocolate outline around the spoons, then

fill in with melted chocolate. Allow the chocolate to set.
8 Cut the top off each cake, leaving a 1 cm (½ inch) border around the top edge of each cake and reserving the tops. Use a spoon to scoop out some of the cake, leaving a 1 cm (½ inch) shell of cake. (Leftover cake can be frozen for another use.)
9 Soften the coffee ice cream with a spoon and pile into the cakes so it comes slightly above the top. Replace the tops and press gently. Spread cream mixture roughly over the top of each cake to represent the froth. Dust the tops with cocoa and serve with a chocolate spoon tucked into the cream.

ABOVE: Cappuccino ice cream cakes

GREEN TEA ICE CREAM

Preparation time: 15 minutes + freezing
Total cooking time: 30 minutes
Serves 4

✯ ✯

4 tablespoons Japanese green tea leaves
2 cups (500 ml/16 fl oz) milk
6 egg yolks
1/2 cup (125 g/4 oz) caster sugar
2 cups (500 ml/16 fl oz) cream

1 Combine the green tea leaves with the milk in a saucepan and slowly bring to simmering point. This step should not be rushed—the longer the milk takes to come to a simmer, the better the infusion of flavour. Set aside for 5 minutes before straining.
2 Whisk the egg yolks and sugar in a heatproof bowl until thick and pale, then add the infused milk. Place the bowl over a saucepan of simmering water, making sure that the base of the bowl is not touching the water.
3 Stir the custard until it is thick enough to coat the back of spoon, then remove from the heat and allow to cool slightly before adding the cream.
4 Pour the mixture into a metal tray and freeze for 3–4 hours, or until just frozen around the edges. Transfer the mixture to a bowl, beat with electric beaters until thick and creamy, then return to the metal tray. Repeat the freezing and beating twice more. Transfer to a storage container, cover the surface with greaseproof paper and freeze overnight.
NOTE: If you want your green tea ice cream green, add a few drops of food colouring.

RASPBERRY RIPPLE

Preparation time: 30 minutes + freezing
Total cooking time: Nil
Serves 8–10

✯

250 g (8 oz) raspberries
1 litre good-quality vanilla ice cream
1 cup (250 ml/8 fl oz) cream
raspberries, extra, for serving

1 Line the base and sides of a 1.75 litre loaf tin with plastic or foil.
2 Purée the raspberries in a food processor until smooth. Remove the ice cream from the freezer and allow to soften. Beat the cream until soft peaks form. Using a metal spoon, gently fold the cream into the raspberry purée. Pour the mixture into a metal freezer tray and put in the freezer until cool but not frozen solid. Stir occasionally until thick. When half frozen, remove from the freezer and beat well.
3 Spoon blobs of softened vanilla ice cream over the base of the prepared loaf tin. Spoon the raspberry mixture between the vanilla blobs. Using a sharp knife or skewer, swirl the two together, being careful not to dig into the foil.
4 Freeze for 2 hours, or until half frozen, then smooth the edges of the ice cream. Freeze overnight. When ready, it may be served in scoops or removed from the tin and cut in slices. Garnish with extra raspberries.

MANGO ICE CREAM

Preparation time: 20 minutes + freezing
Total cooking time: Nil
Makes about 900 ml (30 fl oz)

✯

3 mangoes (about 1.5 kg/3 lb)
1/2 cup (125 g/4 oz) caster sugar
300 ml (91/2 fl oz) cream

1 Cut the mango flesh into pieces and purée in a food processor until smooth. Transfer to a bowl, add the sugar and stir until the sugar has dissolved.
2 Beat the cream in a bowl until stiff peaks form, then fold it through the mango purée.
3 Spoon the mixture into a shallow rectangular tray, cover and freeze for 11/2 hours, or until partially frozen. Quickly spoon the mixture into a bowl and beat with electric beaters for 30 seconds, or until smooth. Return to the tray or a plastic container, cover and freeze. Repeat the freezing and beating twice more. Cover the surface with greaseproof paper and freeze for at least 8 hours. Remove from the freezer 15 minutes before serving, to allow the ice cream to soften a little. Serve in scoops with fresh mango if you wish.
NOTE: This recipe can also be made using an ice cream machine.

ICE CREAM MACHINE

Pour the prepared mixture into the ice cream machine.

Turn the machine on to start the churning.

When the ice cream is ready, it will be thickened and frozen, but not solid.

Transfer the frozen mixture to a metal container and freeze until firm.

OPPOSITE PAGE, FROM TOP: Green tea ice cream; Mango ice cream; Raspberry ripple

PARFAITS
These are American style parfaits with layers of ice cream, fruit and sauces made to classic 'soda fountain' formulae. The original French parfait was a type of ice cream made with eggs, sugar and cream.

VANILLA AND CARAMEL PARFAIT
Heat 90 g (3 oz) unsalted butter in a heavy-based pan. Add ¾ cup (140 g/ 4½ oz) soft brown sugar and stir over low heat, without boiling, until the sugar is dissolved. Increase the heat and simmer, without boiling, for 3 minutes, or until golden. Remove from the heat

and cool slightly. Stir in ⅔ cup (170 ml/ 5½ fl oz) cream, allow to cool, then whisk until smooth. Layer 500 g (1 lb) vanilla ice cream, halved chocolate-coated malt balls and the caramel sauce into four parfait glasses and top with some more halved malt balls. Serve immediately.
Serves 4.

STRAWBERRY AND RASPBERRY PARFAIT
Stir an 85 g (3 oz) packet strawberry-flavoured jelly crystals in 2 cups boiling water until the crystals have dissolved, then refrigerate until set. Process 125 g (4 oz) chopped strawberries in a food processor for 30 seconds. Layer 500 g (1 lb) vanilla ice cream, the jelly, 125 g

(4 oz) chopped strawberries, 100 g (3½ oz) raspberries and the strawberry purée in six parfait glasses. Serve immediately. Serves 6.

SPICED CHERRY BRANDY PARFAIT

Place 3 tablespoons sugar, 2 tablespoons soft brown sugar, 1 teaspoon mixed spice and 3 tablespoons brandy in a pan with 1 cup of water and stir without boiling until all the sugar has dissolved, then bring to the boil. Add 500 g (1 lb) pitted cherries and reduce the heat, simmer for 10 minutes, remove from the heat and cool. Layer the cherries with 1 litre vanilla ice cream in tall glasses and top with some of the cherry syrup. Serve with brandy snaps.
Serves 6.

CHOCOLATE KAHLUA PARFAIT

Combine 125 g (4 oz) chopped chocolate and vanilla cream biscuits with 2 tablespoons Kahlua in a bowl. Set aside for 5 minutes. Layer 500 g (1 lb) chocolate ice cream, the biscuit mixture, 1 cup (250 ml/8 fl oz) cream, whipped, and 60 g (2 oz) choc-bits, alternately, in four parfait glasses. Finish with whipped cream, sprinkle with choc-bits. Serves 4.

CARAMEL NUT PARFAIT

Put 100 g (3½ oz) butter, 2 tablespoons golden syrup, ½ cup (95 g/3 oz) soft brown sugar and 1 cup (250 ml/8 fl oz) cream in a pan and stir over low heat until dissolved. Do not boil. Cool slightly. Layer 1 litre of vanilla ice cream and the warm sauce in parfait glasses. Sprinkle with chopped nuts. Serves 4–6.

BANANA SPLIT

Put 200 g (6½ oz) good-quality dark chocolate, ¾ cup (185 ml/6 fl oz) cream and 30 g (1 oz) butter in a pan and stir over low heat until smooth. Cool slightly. Split 4 ripe bananas lengthways, and place one half on each side of a glass dish. Place 3 scoops of ice cream between the bananas and pour the chocolate sauce over the top. Sprinkle chopped nuts over the banana splits. Serves 4.

FROM LEFT: Vanilla and caramel parfait; Strawberry and raspberry parfait; Spiced cherry brandy parfait; Chocolate Kahlua parfait; Caramel nut parfait; Banana split

SORBETS, SHERBETS AND SPOOMS

Sorbets are water-based ices which traditionally do not contain dairy products or eggs, although it is now common for beaten egg whites to be added. Sorbets are served as palate cleansers between courses as well as refreshing desserts. Escoffier mentions that sorbets should be eaten when they are almost a drinkable consistency. Sorbets are called 'water ices' in America and *sorbetto* in Italy. They can be churned or still frozen.

Sherbets are water ices which contain some milk or cream. The word is derived from the Arabic word *sharab/sharbah*, which means 'sweetened, cold drink'. In America, sorbets are often called sherbets. Sherbets can be churned or still frozen.

Spooms are sorbets which have an equal volume of Italian meringue mixed into them and are then refrozen without any further mixing or beating. Spooms can be churned or still frozen before having the meringue added.

ABOVE: Lemon lime sorbet

LEMON LIME SORBET

Preparation time: 25 minutes + freezing
Total cooking time: 10 minutes
Serves 4

★

1 cup (250 g/8 oz) sugar
3/4 cup (185 ml/6 fl oz) lemon juice
3/4 cup (185 ml/6 fl oz) lime juice
2 egg whites, lightly beaten

1 Stir 2 cups (500 ml/16 fl oz) water with the sugar in a pan, over low heat, until the sugar has dissolved. Bring to the boil, reduce the heat to low, simmer for 5 minutes, then cool.
2 Add the lemon and lime juice to the syrup and pour into a metal tray. Cover with a piece of greaseproof paper and freeze for 2 hours. Transfer the icy mixture to a food processor or bowl and process or beat with electric beaters to a slush, then return to the freezer. Repeat the beating and freezing twice more.
3 Transfer to a bowl or food processor. With the electric beaters or processor motor running, add the egg whites and blend. Return to the freezer container, cover with a piece of greaseproof paper and freeze until firm.
4 If you are using an ice cream machine, add the egg white when the sorbet is almost churned and the machine is still running.

PINEAPPLE SORBET

Preparation time: 25 minutes + freezing
Total cooking time: 15 minutes
Serves 4

★

850 ml (27 fl oz) can unsweetened pineapple juice
1 1/2 cups (375 g/12 fl oz) sugar
3 tablespoons lemon juice, strained
1 egg white, lightly beaten

1 Stir the juice and sugar in a large pan over low heat until the sugar has dissolved. Bring to the boil, reduce the heat and simmer for 5 minutes. Skim off any scum.
2 Stir in the lemon juice and pour into a metal tray. Cover with a sheet of greaseproof and freeze for 2 hours. Transfer the icy mixture to a bowl or food processor and beat with electric beaters, or process, to a slush, then return to the freezer. Repeat the beating and freezing twice more, then process or beat for a final time adding the egg white until it is all incorporated. Beat or process until smooth. Return to the freezer container, cover with a piece of greaseproof paper and freeze until firm.
3 If you are using an ice cream machine, add the egg white when the sorbet is almost churned and the machine is still running.

SPEARMINT CITRUS SORBET

Preparation time: 25 minutes + freezing
Total cooking time: 35 minutes
Serves 4

★

1 1/2 cups (375 g/12 oz) caster sugar
2 cups (50 g/1 3/4 oz) spearmint leaves
3/4 cup (185 ml/6 fl oz) lemon or grapefruit juice
1 1/4 cups (315 ml/10 fl oz) orange juice
1/2 cup (125 ml/4 fl oz) dry white wine
1/2 cup (15 g/1/2 oz) finely sliced spearmint leaves

1 Put the sugar, spearmint leaves and 3 cups (750 ml/24 fl oz) water in a pan. Stir over low heat until the sugar dissolves. Bring to the boil, reduce the heat and simmer for 30 minutes. Strain and discard the spearmint leaves.
2 Stir in the juices and wine. Pour into a metal container and, when cool, stir in the finely sliced spearmint leaves. Freeze until just firm.
3 Transfer to a bowl or food processor and beat with electric beaters, or process, until smooth. Return to the freezer. Repeat the beating and freezing twice more. Cover with greaseproof paper. Freeze overnight, or until firm. Allow to soften slightly before scooping out.

PASSIONFRUIT AND ORANGE SORBET

Preparation time: 15 minutes + freezing
Total cooking time: Nil
Serves 4

★

3 cups (750 ml/24 fl oz) orange juice
3/4 cup (185 ml/6 fl oz) passionfruit pulp
1/2 cup (125 g/4 oz) caster sugar
2 egg whites, lightly beaten

1 Mix the orange juice, passionfruit pulp and sugar in a large bowl. Pour into a metal tray and freeze until just firm around the edges. Do not allow to become too firm. Transfer to a bowl or food processor and beat with an electric whisk or process. Refreeze. Repeat this step twice more, adding the egg white the final time, with the beaters or motor running. Return to the tray, cover with greaseproof paper and freeze for 3 hours, or until firm.
2 Alternatively, pour the mixture into an ice cream machine and churn for about 30 minutes.

LAVENDER ICE CREAM

Preparation time: 15 minutes + freezing
Total cooking time: 15 minutes
Serves 6–8

★ ★

8 stems English lavender (or 4–6 if the lavender
  is in full flower, so has a stronger flavour)
2 1/2 cups (600 ml/20 fl oz) thick (double) cream
1 small piece lemon rind
2/3 cup (160 g/5 1/4 oz) sugar
4 egg yolks, lightly whisked

1 Wash and dry the English lavender. Put in a pan with the cream and lemon rind. Heat until almost boiling, then stir in the sugar until dissolved. Strain through a fine sieve, then pour onto the egg yolks, return to the pan and stir over low heat until the mixture is thick enough to coat the back of a spoon; do not boil. Pour into a chilled metal tray to cool.
2 Freeze the mixture until frozen around the edge (but not in the middle). In a food processor or bowl, beat until smooth. Freeze again and repeat this process twice more. Cover with greaseproof paper and freeze.

BELOW: Passionfruit and orange sorbet (left); Spearmint citrus sorbet

KULFI and SEMIFREDDO

Kulfi is a traditional Indian ice cream made by boiling milk until it reduces in volume. It is a time consuming procedure but one which gives a unique flavour. Kulfi has a dense icy texture and is traditionally set in cone shaped moulds. If you can't find any moulds, you can use cream horn moulds or any other shape. They are usually served with a cross cut in the top to make them easier to eat. Quick kulfis can be made using evaporated or condensed milk instead.

Semifreddo means 'half frozen' in Italian. It does not freeze as hard as other ice creams due to its alcohol and sugar content. It is also known as *perfetti* in Italy and is set in a mould without churning.

OPPOSITE PAGE: Kulfi (top); Semifreddo

KULFI

Preparation time: 20 minutes + freezing
Total cooking time: 50 minutes
Serves 6

✳ ✳

1 1/2 litres milk
8 cardamom pods
4 tablespoons caster sugar
20 g (3/4 oz) blanched almonds, finely chopped
20 g (3/4 oz) pistachios, finely chopped

1 Put the milk and cardamom pods in a large heavy-based pan, bring to the boil, reduce the heat and simmer, stirring often until it has reduced by about one-third, to 1 litre—this will take some time. Keep stirring or it will stick.
2 Add the sugar and cook for 2–3 minutes. Strain out the cardamom pods and add the nuts. Pour the kulfi into a shallow metal or plastic container, cover the surface with a sheet of baking paper and freeze for 1 hour. Remove from the freezer and beat to break up any ice crystals, freeze again and repeat twice more.
3 Line 6 cream horn moulds with baking paper or lightly brush six 250 ml (8 fl oz) pudding basins with flavourless oil and divide the kulfi among them, then freeze overnight. To serve, unmould each kulfi and cut a cross 1/2 cm (1/4 inch) deep in the top.

DEEP-FRIED ICE CREAM IN COCONUT

Preparation time: 20 minutes + several days freezing
Total cooking time: 1 minute
Serves 6

✳ ✳

2 litres vanilla ice cream
1 egg
1 cup (125 g/4 oz) flour
1 1/2 cups (150 g/5 oz) fine dry breadcrumbs
2 tablespoons desiccated coconut
oil, for deep-frying

1 Make 6 large scoops of ice cream and return them to the freezer.
2 Make a thick batter of egg, flour and 3/4 cup (185 ml/6 fl oz) water. Coat the ice cream balls with the batter, then roll in the breadcrumbs and coconut to coat thickly. Return to the freezer to freeze for several days.
3 Heat the oil to 180°C (350°F). A cube of bread will sizzle and turn golden brown in 15 seconds when the oil is ready. Slide in one ice cream ball at a time to cook for a few seconds until the surface is golden. Take care not to melt the ice cream. Remove and serve at once.

SEMIFREDDO

Preparation time: 20 minutes
Total cooking time: 30 minutes
Serves 8

✳ ✳

9 egg yolks
1 cup (250 g/4 oz) caster sugar
1/3 cup (80 ml/2 3/4 fl oz) Marsala
1 1/2 cups (375 ml/12 fl oz) thick (double) cream, whipped
grated rind of 2 oranges

Caramel oranges

2 oranges
1/2 cup (125 g/4 oz) sugar

1 Combine the egg yolks, sugar and Marsala in a heatproof bowl. Set the bowl over a pan of steaming water, off the heat (make sure the bottom of the bowl does not touch the water). Beat with a balloon whisk or electric beaters until very thick and pale and doubled in volume (make sure the sugar is fully dissolved). Remove from the heat and beat over ice until cooled. Fold in the cream and freeze until partially frozen, but still soft. Fold in the rind. Spoon into a 1.5 litre mould or loaf tin lined with plastic wrap. Freeze for 4 hours, or overnight.
2 To make the caramel oranges, cut the bases off the oranges and place, cut-side-down, on a board. Slicing downwards and following the curve of the oranges, trim off the skin and pith. Slice the oranges and place them in a glass bowl. Melt the sugar gradually in a small pan over low heat. When melted, turn the heat up a little until the sugar caramelizes. Tip the pan from side to side so the sugar caramelizes evenly. When it turns golden brown, carefully add 1/3 cup (80 ml/2 3/4 fl oz) water, being careful as it may splutter, re-melt the caramel and pour it over the oranges. Cover with plastic wrap and chill.
3 Cut the semifreddo into slices and serve with caramel oranges.

STRAWBERRY GRANITA

Chop the strawberries until smooth, then add the cooled sugar syrup and process to combine.

Pour the strained purée into a metal container, then cover and freeze until the granita around the edge of the tray is frozen.

Break up the ice crystals with a fork, then return to the freezer and repeat. Repeat this process until the mixture is smooth.

ABOVE: Coffee granita

COFFEE GRANITA

Preparation time: 20 minutes + freezing
Total cooking time: 5 minutes
Serves 6

✰

¾ cup (185 g/6 oz) caster sugar
1½ tablespoons cocoa powder
1.25 litres strong espresso coffee

1 Put the sugar and cocoa powder in a large pan, gradually add ½ cup (125 ml/4 fl oz) water and stir over low heat until the sugar dissolves. Bring to the boil, then reduce the heat and simmer for 3 minutes.
2 Remove from the heat and add the fresh coffee. Pour into a shallow metal container or tray and cool completely. Freeze until partially set, then stir with a fork to distribute the ice crystals evenly. Freeze again until firm.
3 Using a fork, work the granita into fine crystals and return to the freezer for 1 hour before serving. Spoon into glasses to serve.
NOTE: This is extremely hard when frozen, so should be put into a shallow tray and broken up when partially frozen. It is difficult to break up if frozen in a deep container.

STRAWBERRY GRANITA

Preparation time: 15 minutes + freezing
Total cooking time: 10 minutes
Serves 4

✰

½ cup (125 g/4 oz) sugar
500 g (1 lb) strawberries
2 tablespoons lemon juice

1 Stir the sugar and ½ cup (125 ml/4 fl oz) water together in a pan over low heat until the sugar has dissolved. Bring to the boil and simmer for 5 minutes. Leave to cool.
2 Hull the strawberries and chop in a food processor or blender with the lemon juice for 30 seconds, or until smooth. Add the cooled sugar syrup and process to combine.
3 Sieve the purée to remove the seeds. Pour into a shallow metal container, cover and freeze for 2 hours, or until the granita around the edge of the tray is frozen. Stir with a fork to break up the ice crystals. Return to the freezer for 1 hour and stir again with a fork. Repeat this until the mixture is a smooth consistency of ice crystals, then pour into a storage container, cover with

greaseproof paper and return to the freezer for 3–4 hours, or until set.

4 To serve, soften the frozen mixture in the refrigerator for 15–20 minutes and stir again with a fork to break up the ice crystals and freeze again.

NOTE: If you have stored the granita for a few days, you may need to fork and freeze it again more than once until you to get it to the correct consistency for serving. It is delicious with a dollop of cream.

ORANGE SORBET

Preparation time: 20 minutes + freezing
Total cooking time: Nil
Serves 6

☆

10–12 oranges
3/4 cup (90 g/3 oz) icing sugar
2 teaspoons lemon juice

1 Cut the oranges in half and carefully squeeze out the juice, taking care not to damage the skins. Dissolve the icing sugar in the orange juice, add the lemon juice and pour into a freezer container. Cover the surface with baking paper and freeze for 1 hour.

2 Scrape the remaining flesh and membrane out of six of the orange halves, cover the skins with plastic wrap and refrigerate.

3 After 1 hour, stir any frozen juice that has formed around the edge of the sorbet into the centre and return to the freezer. Repeat every hour, or until nearly frozen. Freeze overnight. Divide the sorbet among the orange skins and freeze until ready to serve. This sorbet may seem very hard when it has frozen overnight but it will melt quickly, so work fast.

BELLINI SORBET

Preparation time: 20 minutes + freezing
Total cooking time: 25 minutes
Serves 6

☆

2 cups (500 g/8 oz) caster sugar
5 large peaches
3/4 cup (185 ml/6 fl oz) Champagne
2 egg whites, lightly beaten

1 Combine the sugar with 1 litre water in a large pan and stir over low heat until the sugar has dissolved. Bring to the boil, add the peaches and simmer for 20 minutes. Remove the peaches with a slotted spoon and cool completely. Reserve 1 cup (250 ml/8 fl oz) of the poaching liquid.

2 Peel the peaches, remove the stones and cut the flesh into chunks. Chop in a food processor until smooth, add the reserved liquid and the Champagne and process briefly until combined. Pour into a shallow metal tray and freeze for about 6 hours, until just firm. Transfer to a large bowl and beat until smooth with electric beaters.

3 Refreeze and repeat this step twice more, adding the egg white on the final beating. Place in a storage container, cover the surface with greaseproof paper and freeze until firm. Serve the sorbet in scoops, with sliced fresh peaches and dessert wafers if desired.

NOTE: Bellini is a cocktail served at Harry's Bar in Venice. It is made of peach juice and a sparkling wine called prosecco.

ABOVE: Bellini sorbet

LOW-FAT

So, you're lusting after tiramisu but your waistline won't allow it? Fancy a reckless fling with a chocolate mousse, but can't risk the calories? Think again. If you're on a diet, this is exactly the time you need a little guilt-free cheering up. Desserts aren't just for the skinny people; we all need a sweet treat now and then, even when we're watching our weight. This selection of desserts (all with a fat content per serving at the start of the recipe) will help make any diet bearable... even enjoyable.

CREAMY RICE POTS

Fat per serve: 3.5 g
Preparation time: 15 minutes
Total cooking time: 1 hour 10 minutes
Serves 4

☆

1/2 cup (110 g/3 1/2 oz) short-grain rice
1 litre skim milk
1/4 cup (60 g/2 oz) caster sugar
1 teaspoon grated orange rind
1 teaspoon grated lemon rind
1 teaspoon vanilla essence
20 g (3/4 oz) hazelnuts
1 tablespoon soft brown sugar

1 Wash the rice in a sieve under cold water until the water runs clear, then drain thoroughly. Put the milk and sugar in a pan and stir over low heat until the sugar has dissolved. Add the rice and rind and stir briefly. Bring to the boil and reduce the heat to as low as possible. Cook for 1 hour, stirring occasionally, until thick and creamy and the rice is tender. Stir in the vanilla essence.
2 Spread the hazelnuts on a baking tray and toast in a moderate 180°C (350°F/Gas 4) oven for about 5 minutes. Rub the hot nuts in a tea towel to remove as much of the skin as possible. Cool

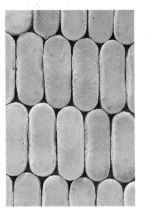

ABOVE: Creamy rice pots

and grind in a food processor to a coarse texture, not too fine. Preheat a grill to very hot.
3 Spoon the rice into four heatproof 185 ml (6 fl oz) ramekins. Combine the sugar and ground hazelnuts and sprinkle over the rice. Grill briefly until the sugar melts and the nuts are lightly browned. Serve immediately.

TIRAMISU

Fat per serve: 5.5 g
Preparation time: 15 minutes + chilling
Total cooking time: 5 minutes
Serves 6

☆ ☆

3 tablespoons custard powder
1 cup (250 ml/8 fl oz) skim milk
2 tablespoons caster sugar
2 teaspoons vanilla essence
2 x 130 g (4 1/2 oz) tubs light vanilla frûche or
    fromage frais
2 egg whites
1 2/3 cups (400 ml/13 fl oz) espresso coffee, cooled
2 tablespoons Amaretto
250 g (8 oz) sponge finger biscuits
2 tablespoons unsweetened dark cocoa powder

1 Stir the custard powder in a small pan with about 2 tablespoons of the skim milk until dissolved. Add the remaining skim milk with the sugar and vanilla essence and stir over medium heat until the mixture boils and thickens. Remove from the heat. This will be a thick custard. Transfer to a bowl, cover the surface with plastic wrap and cool at room temperature.

2 Beat together the custard and frûche for 2 minutes. In a small bowl, whip the egg whites until soft peaks form, then fold into the custard.

3 Pour the espresso into a dish and add the Amaretto. Using half the biscuits, quickly dip each biscuit in the coffee mixture, just enough to cover (don't leave them in the liquid or they will go soggy) and arrange in a single layer over the base of a serving dish.

4 Using half of the custard mixture, smooth it evenly over the biscuits. Dust half the dark cocoa over the cream and then repeat the layers with the remaining biscuits and custard mixture. Cover the tiramisu with plastic wrap and refrigerate overnight, or for at least 6 hours. Lightly dust with dark cocoa powder to serve.

PASSIONFRUIT TART

Fat per serve: 6.5 g
Preparation time: 30 minutes + chilling
Total cooking time: 1 hour
Serves 8

★★

3/4 cup (90 g/3 oz) plain flour
2 tablespoons icing sugar
2 tablespoons custard powder
30 g (1 oz) butter
3 tablespoons light evaporated milk

Filling

4 tablespoons passionfruit pulp
   (about 8 passionfruit)
1/2 cup (125 g/4 oz) ricotta
1 teaspoon vanilla essence
1/4 cup (30 g/1 oz) icing sugar
2 eggs, lightly beaten
3/4 cup (185 ml/6 fl oz) light evaporated milk

1 Preheat the oven to moderately hot 200°C (400°F/Gas 6). Lightly spray a 23 cm (9 inch) loose-based flan tin with oil spray. Sift the flour, icing sugar and custard powder into a bowl and rub in the butter until the mixture resembles

fine breadcrumbs. Add enough milk to form a soft dough. Bring together on a lightly floured surface until just smooth. Form into a ball, wrap in plastic and refrigerate for 15 minutes.

2 Roll the pastry out on a floured surface, to fit the tin, then refrigerate for 15 minutes. Cover with baking paper and fill with uncooked rice or beans. Bake for 10 minutes, remove the rice or beans and paper and bake for another 5–8 minutes, or until golden. Cool. Reduce the oven to warm 160°C (315°F/Gas 2–3).

3 Strain the passionfruit to remove the seeds, reserving 2 teaspoons of seeds. Beat the ricotta with the essence and icing sugar until smooth. Add the eggs and passionfruit pulp, reserved seeds and milk, then beat well. Put the pastry case on a baking tray and gently pour in the mixture. Bake for 40 minutes, or until set. Cool in the tin. Dust the edges with icing sugar just before serving.

ABOVE: Tiramisu

285

STRAWBERRY AND BANANA ICE

Fat per serve: 3 g
Preparation time: 10 minutes + freezing
Total cooking time: Nil
Serves 4

★

300 g (10 oz) silken tofu, chopped
250 g (4 oz) strawberries, chopped
2 ripe bananas, chopped
1/4 cup (60 g/2 oz) caster sugar

1 Blend the tofu, strawberries, bananas and caster sugar in a blender or processor until smooth.
2 Freeze in a shallow cake tin until almost frozen, then chop roughly using a fork. Transfer to a large bowl and beat until smooth. Pour into a 15 x 25 cm (6 x 10 inch) loaf tin, cover and freeze again, until firm. Alternatively, freeze in an ice cream machine until thick and creamy. Refrigerate for about 30 minutes before serving to allow the ice to soften slightly.

ICE CREAM BOMBS

Fat per serve: 6 g
Preparation time: 15 minutes + freezing
Total cooking time: 2–3 minutes
Serves 6

★ ★

440 g (14 oz) can sliced pineapple in natural juice
1/2 x 300 g (10 oz) jam roll
6 scoops low-fat ice cream
2 egg whites
1/3 cup (90 g/3 oz) caster sugar

1 Preheat the oven to very hot 230°C (450°F/ Gas 8). Drain the pineapple and reserve the juice. You will need 6 slices of pineapple. Cut the jam roll into 6 even slices. Place on a baking paper covered tray and brush lightly with some of the reserved pineapple juice.
2 Top the slices with a piece of pineapple, then a scoop of ice cream (choose your favourite). Return to the freezer until required.
3 Whisk the egg whites in a clean dry bowl until soft peaks form. Gradually add the sugar, beating well after each addition, until stiff and glossy peaks form. Spread the meringue roughly over the top of each ice cream scoop, then bake for 2–3 minutes, or until browned on the outside. Serve immediately.

PASSIONFRUIT BAVAROIS

Fat per serve: 2.5 g
Preparation time: 10 minutes + chilling
Total cooking time: Nil
Serves 8

★ ★

2 x 170 g (5 1/2 oz) cans passionfruit syrup
300 g (10 oz) silken tofu, drained and chopped
600 ml (20 fl oz) buttermilk
2 tablespoons caster sugar
1 teaspoon vanilla essence
6 teaspoons gelatine
8 strawberries, to garnish
3/4 cup (185 ml/6 fl oz) passionfruit pulp

1 Push the canned passionfruit syrup through a sieve, discard the seeds, then blend on high for 90 seconds, with the tofu, buttermilk, caster sugar and vanilla essence. Leave in the blender.
2 Sprinkle the gelatine in an even layer onto 1 tablespoon water in a small bowl and leave to go spongy. Bring a small pan of water to the boil, remove from the heat and place the bowl into the pan. The water should come halfway up the side of the bowl. Stir the gelatine until dissolved. Leave to cool.
3 Place eight 200 ml (6 1/2 fl oz) dariole moulds in a baking dish. Add the gelatine to the blender and mix on high for 1 minute. Pour into the moulds, cover the dish with plastic wrap and refrigerate overnight.
4 Cut the strawberries in half. When ready to serve, carefully run a spatula around the edge of each mould and dip the bases into hot water for 2 seconds to make removal easier. Place each on a plate and spoon the passionfruit pulp around the bases. Garnish and serve.

OPPOSITE PAGE:
Strawberry and banana ice (top); Passionfruit bavarois

Strawberry sauce
125 g (4 oz) strawberries, chopped
1 teaspoon caster sugar
2 tablespoons orange juice

1 Combine 2 cups (500 ml/16 fl oz) water with the wine, sugar, cinnamon stick and cloves in a pan just large enough to fit the pears. Split the vanilla bean in half and scrape the seeds into the pan. Add the vanilla bean and stir over low heat until the sugar has dissolved.

2 Add the pears and simmer, covered, for 20 minutes, or until just soft when tested with a skewer. Leave to cool in the syrup. Drain and stand the pears on paper towels. Remove the cores of the pears through the base using a melon baller, then peel. Fill the base of each with the combined dates and sultanas.

3 To make the crepes, sift the flour into a bowl, gradually beat in the combined egg and milk, beating until smooth. Strain into a jug and set aside for 10 minutes.

4 Preheat the oven to moderately hot 200°C (400°F/Gas 6). Lightly oil a 24 cm (9½ inch) non-stick pan with oil spray, heat the pan and pour in a quarter of the batter, swirling to cover the base of the pan. Cook until lightly browned, turn and brown the other side. Remove and repeat with the remaining mixture.

5 Place the crepes on a work bench, place a quarter of the combined ground almonds, brown sugar and cinnamon in the centre of each and top with a pear. Gather the crepes around the pears and tie with kitchen string. Sprinkle with the flaked almonds. Bake on a lightly oiled baking tray for 10 minutes, or until the almonds and the edges of the crepes are golden and the pears just warm. Dust with icing sugar and serve with strawberry sauce.

6 To make the sauce, blend the strawberries, sugar and orange juice until smooth, then strain.

PEAR POUCHES WITH STRAWBERRY SAUCE

Fat per serve: 7 g
Preparation time: 45 minutes + standing
Total cooking time: 40 minutes
Makes 4

★★★

¼ cup (60 ml/2 fl oz) white wine

¼ cup (60 g/2 oz) caster sugar

1 cinnamon stick

2 cloves

1 vanilla bean

4 beurre bosc pears

4 dates, roughly chopped

2 tablespoons sultanas

⅔ cup (85 g/3 oz) plain flour

1 egg, lightly beaten

1 cup (250 ml/8 fl oz) skim milk

2 tablespoons ground almonds

1 tablespoon soft brown sugar

½ teaspoon ground cinnamon

1 tablespoon flaked almonds

ABOVE: Pear pouches with strawberry sauce

APPLE SNOW

Simmer 3 or 4 peeled, chopped apples with a little sugar, cinnamon and water until tender. Mash until puréed. Sprinkle 2 teaspoons of gelatine over a little water in a heatproof bowl and leave to go spongy. Put the bowl in a pan of boiling water, off the heat, and stir to dissolve. Stir into the hot purée. Cool a little. Beat the white of 3 eggs until stiff peaks form and fold into the hot purée—the heat should slightly cook the whites. Chill before serving. Serves 4.

BANANA AND BLUEBERRY TART

Fat per serve: 6 g
Preparation time: 30 minutes
Total cooking time: 25 minutes
Serves 6

★★

cooking oil spray
1 cup (125 g/4 oz) plain flour
1/2 cup (60 g/2 oz) self-raising flour
1 teaspoon cinnamon
1 teaspoon ground ginger
40 g (1 1/4 oz) butter, chopped
1/2 cup (95 g/3 oz) soft brown sugar
1/2 cup (125 ml/4 fl oz) buttermilk
200 g (6 1/2 oz) blueberries
2 bananas
2 teaspoons lemon juice
1 tablespoon demerara sugar

1 Preheat the oven to moderately hot 200°C (400°F/Gas 6). Spray a baking tray or pizza tray lightly with oil. Sift both the flours and the spices into a bowl. Add the butter and brown sugar, and rub in with your fingertips until the butter is combined well with the flour. Make a well in the centre and add enough buttermilk to mix to a soft dough.

2 Roll the dough out on a lightly floured surface to a 23 cm (9 inch) diameter round. Place on the tray and roll the edge to form a lip to hold the fruit in.

3 Spread the blueberries over the dough, keeping them within the lip. Slice the bananas and toss the slices in the lemon juice. Arrange the banana evenly over the top of the blueberries, then sprinkle with the demerara sugar and bake for 25 minutes, or until the base is browned. Serve immediately.

NOTE: The dough for this tart can be made in a food processor if you wish. The fruit topping can be varied by using raspberries. Other soft or stoned fruit also work very well.

BELOW: Banana
and blueberry tart

RHUBARB AND PEAR CRUMBLE

Fat per serve: 8 g
Preparation time: 20 minutes
Total cooking time: 25 minutes
Serves 6

★

600 g (1¼ lb) rhubarb
2 strips lemon rind
1 tablespoon honey, or to taste
2 firm ripe pears
½ cup (50 g/1¾ oz) rolled oats
¼ cup (35 g/1¼ oz) wholemeal plain flour
⅓ cup (60 g/2 oz) soft brown sugar
50 g (1¾ oz) unsalted butter

BELOW: Rhubarb and pear crumble

1 Trim the rhubarb, then wash it and cut into 3 cm (1¼ inch) pieces. Place in a pan with the lemon rind and 1 tablespoon water. Cook, covered, over low heat for 10 minutes, or until tender. Cool a little, then stir in the honey. Remove the lemon rind and discard.

2 Preheat the oven to moderate 180°C (350°F/ Gas 4). Peel and core the pears, then cut them into 2 cm (¾ inch) cubes and combine with the rhubarb. Pour into a 1.25 litre ovenproof dish and smooth the surface.

3 To make the crumble topping, combine the rolled oats, wholemeal flour and brown sugar in a bowl. Rub in the butter using just your fingertips, until the mixture looks crumbly. Spread the crumble evenly over the fruit. Bake for about 15 minutes, or until cooked and golden.

RASPBERRY MOUSSE

Fat per serve: 2 g
Preparation time: 30 minutes + chilling
Total cooking time: Nil
Serves 4

☆

3 teaspoons gelatine
I cup (250 g/8 oz) low-fat vanilla yoghurt
2 × 200 g (6¹/₂ oz) tubs light vanilla frûche or
 fromage frais
4 egg whites
150 g (5 oz) fresh raspberries, mashed, or
 frozen, thawed
fresh raspberries and mint leaves, to serve

1 Put 1 tablespoon hot water in a small heatproof bowl, sprinkle the gelatine over the top and leave to go spongy. Bring a small pan of water to the boil, remove from the heat and place the bowl into the pan. The water should come halfway up the side of the bowl. Stir the gelatine until dissolved. In a large bowl, stir the vanilla yoghurt and frûche together to combine, then add the cooled gelatine and mix well.
2 Using electric beaters, beat the egg whites until stiff peaks form, then fold through the yoghurt mixture until just combined. Transfer half the mixture to a separate bowl and fold the mashed raspberries through.
3 Divide the raspberry mixture among four long glasses, then top with the vanilla mixture. Refrigerate for several hours, or until set. Decorate with fresh raspberries and mint leaves.

CHOCOLATE MOUSSE

Fat per serve: 3 g
Preparation time: 20 minutes + chilling
Total cooking time: Nil
Serves 6

☆

2 tablespoons cocoa
I teaspoon gelatine
300 g (10 oz) silken tofu
I tablespoon brandy
2 egg whites
¹/₄ cup (60 g/2 oz) caster sugar

1 Stir the cocoa with ¹/₄ cup (60 ml/2 fl oz) hot water until dissolved. Sprinkle the gelatine in an even layer onto 1 tablespoon water in a small bowl and leave to go spongy. Bring a small pan of water to the boil, remove from the heat and place the bowl into the pan. The water should come halfway up the side of the bowl. Stir the gelatine until dissolved.
2 Drain the tofu and place in a blender. Add the cocoa mixture and brandy and blend until smooth, scraping down the sides. Transfer to a bowl and stir in the gelatine mixture.
3 Whisk the egg whites in a clean dry bowl until soft peaks form. Gradually add the sugar, beating well between each addition, until stiff and glossy peaks form. Fold into the chocolate mixture and spoon into six ¹/₂ cup (125 ml/4 fl oz) dishes. Refrigerate for several hours or until set.

ABOVE: Raspberry mousse

CHEESECAKE

Combine the butter and biscuit crumbs, then press the mixture evenly over the base of the tin.

Gently fold the beaten egg white into the ricotta mixture.

ABOVE: Lemon berry cheesecake

LEMON BERRY CHEESECAKE

Fat per serve: 6 g
Preparation time: 25 minutes + chilling
Total cooking time: Nil
Serves 10

★

1/2 cup (60 g/2 oz) plain un-iced biscuit crumbs

30 g (1 oz) butter, melted

300 g (10 oz) ricotta

2 tablespoons caster sugar

2 x 130 g (4¹/2 oz) tubs light vanilla frûche or
    fromage frais

2 x 130 g (4¹/2 oz) tubs light lemon frûche or
    fromage frais

2 teaspoons finely grated lemon rind

2 tablespoons fresh lemon juice

1 tablespoon gelatine

2 egg whites

250 g (8 oz) strawberries, cut in halves

1 Lightly oil and then line the base and sides of a 20 cm (8 inch) round springform tin with plastic wrap. Combine the biscuit crumbs and butter in a small bowl and press evenly over the base of the prepared tin. Refrigerate while preparing the filling.

2 Combine the ricotta and sugar in a food processor until smooth. Add all the frûche, lemon rind and juice, and mix well. Sprinkle the gelatine over 1/4 cup (60 ml/2 fl oz) water in a small heatproof bowl. Bring a small pan of water to the boil and remove from the heat. Lower the bowl into the pan and stir until dissolved. Allow to cool. Stir the gelatine mixture into the ricotta mixture, then transfer to a large bowl. Beat the egg whites until soft peaks form, then gently fold into the ricotta mixture.

3 Pour the mixture into the prepared tin and refrigerate for several hours or overnight, until set. Carefully remove from the tin by removing the side of the tin and easing the plastic from underneath. Decorate the top with the halved fresh strawberries.

BANANA AND RASPBERRY YOGHURT PUDDING

Fat per serve: 1 g
Preparation time: 10 minutes + chilling
Total cooking time: Nil
Serves 4

☆

2 large ripe bananas
125 g (4 oz) fresh raspberries
1 teaspoon caster sugar
2 cups (500 g/1 lb) low-fat natural yoghurt
4 tablespoons soft brown sugar

1 Combine the bananas, raspberries and caster sugar in a large bowl and mash them well. Divide among four individual serving dishes.
2 Divide the yoghurt among the dishes, making a smooth layer over the fruit. Sprinkle each with a layer of soft brown sugar. Cover the dishes with plastic wrap and leave in the refrigerator for at least 1 hour. The sugar on top should form a fudgy layer.

PEARS POACHED IN DARK GRAPE JUICE

Fat per serve: Nil
Preparation time: 10–15 minutes + chilling
Total cooking time: 1 hour 20 minutes
Serves 6

☆

6 beurre bosc (or any very firm) pears
2 tablespoons lemon juice
2 cups (500 ml/8 fl oz) dark grape juice
2 cups (500 ml/8 fl oz) blackcurrant juice
2 tablespoons sweet sherry
4 cloves
1 kg (2 lb) black grapes
1 cup (250 g/8 oz) low-fat natural yoghurt
1/2 teaspoon ground cinnamon
1 tablespoon honey

1 Core and peel the pears, leaving the stalks on. Place the pears, as you peel, in a bowl filled with cold water and the lemon juice, to prevent the pears browning.
2 Put the grape and blackcurrant juices, sherry and cloves in a saucepan large enough to hold the pears. (The size of the saucepan will depend

on the size of the pears.) Add the pears. Bring the liquid to the boil, then reduce to a simmer. Cover and cook for 35–40 minutes, or until the pears are tender. Remove from the heat and leave the pears to cool in the syrup. Gently transfer the pears and syrup to a bowl and cover with plastic wrap. Refrigerate overnight.
3 Strain the syrup into a pan, bring to the boil, then reduce the heat and simmer for 40 minutes, or until reduced by about two-thirds. To serve, place a pear on each serving dish. Cool the syrup slightly and pour over the pears.
4 Arrange some of the grapes next to the pears. Just before serving, thoroughly mix together the yoghurt, ground cinnamon and honey and spoon over the pears.

ABOVE: Pears poached in dark grape juice

INDEX

Page numbers in *italics* refer to photographs. Page numbers in **bold** type refer to margin notes.

ACKNOWLEDGEMENTS

HOME ECONOMISTS: Miles Beaufort, Anna Beaumont, Anna Boyd, Wendy Brodhurst, Kerrie Carr, Rebecca Clancy, Bronwyn Clark, Michelle Earl, Maria Gargas, Wendy Goggin, Kathy Knudsen, Michelle Lawton, Melanie McDermott, Beth Mitchell, Kerrie Mullins, Justine Poole, Tracey Port, Kerrie Ray, Jo Richardson, Maria Sampsonis, Christine Sheppard, Dimitra Stais, Alison Turner, Jody Vassallo

RECIPE DEVELOPMENT: Roslyn Anderson, Anna Beaumont, Wendy Berecry, Janelle Bloom, Wendy Brodhurst, Amanda Cooper, Anne Creber, Michelle Earl, Jenny Grainger, Lulu Grimes, Coral Kingston, Kathy Knudsen, Barbara Lowery, Rachel Mackey, Voula Mantzouridis, Rosemary Mellish, Kerrie Mullins, Sally Parker, Jacki Passmore, Rosemary Penman, Tracey Port, Jennene Plummer, Justine Poole, Kerrie Ray, Jo Richardson, Tracy Rutherford, Stephanie Souvilis, Dimitra Stais, Beverly Sutherland Smith, Alison Turner, Jody Vassallo

PHOTOGRAPHY: Jon Bader, Paul Clarke, Joe Filshie, Andrew Furlong, Chris Jones, Andre Martin, Luis Martin, Andy Payne, Hans Sclupp, Peter Scott

STYLISTS: Marie-Helene Clauzon, Georgina Dolling, Kay Francis, Mary Harris, Donna Hay, Vicki Liley, Rosemary Mellish, Lucy Mortensen, Sylvia Seiff, Suzi Smith

The publisher wishes to thank the following for their assistance in the photography for this book: The Bay Tree Kitchen Shop, NSW; Limoges Australia, NSW; MEC-Kambrook Pty Ltd, NSW; Orson & Blake Collectables, NSW; Pavillion Christofle, NSW; Sunbeam Corporation Ltd; Waterford Wedgwood Australia Limited, NSW.